INTERNATIONAL NEGOTIATION AND POLITICAL NARRATIVES

This book shows that political narratives can promote or thwart the prospects for international cooperation and are major factors in international negotiation processes in the 21st century.

In a world that is experiencing waves of right-wing and left-wing populism, international cooperation has become increasingly difficult. This volume focuses on how the intersubjective identities of political parties and narratives shape their respective values, interests, and negotiating behaviors and strategies. Through a series of comparative case studies, the book explains how and why narratives contribute to negotiation failure or deadlock in some circumstances and why, in others, they do not because a new narrative that garners public and political support has emerged through the process of negotiation. The book also examines how narratives interact with negotiation principles, and alter the bargaining range of a negotiation, including the ability to make concessions.

This book will be of much interest to students of international negotiation, economics, security studies, and international relations.

Fen Osler Hampson is Chancellor's Professor at Carleton University, Canada, and President of the World Refugee and Migration Council. He is also a Fellow of the Royal Society of Canada.

Amrita Narlikar is President of the German Institute for Global and Area Studies (GIGA) and Professor at Hamburg University, Germany. She is also an Honorary Fellow of Darwin College, University of Cambridge, UK.

ROUTLEDGE STUDIES IN SECURITY AND CONFLICT MANAGEMENT

This series will publish the best work in the field of security studies and conflict management. In particular, it will promote leading-edge work that straddles the divides between conflict management and security studies, between academics and practitioners, and between disciplines.

Multiparty Mediation in Violent Conflict
Peacemaking Diplomacy in the Tajikistan Civil War
Testuro Iji

International Negotiation and Political Narratives
A Comparative Study
Edited by Fen Osler Hampson and Amrita Narlikar

For more information about this series, please visit: www.routledge.com/Routledge-Studies-in-Security-and-Conflict-Management/book-series/RSSCM

INTERNATIONAL NEGOTIATION AND POLITICAL NARRATIVES

A Comparative Study

Edited by Fen Osler Hampson
and Amrita Narlikar

LONDON AND NEW YORK

First published 2022
by Routledge
2 Park Square, Milton Park, Abingdon, Oxon OX14 4RN

and by Routledge
605 Third Avenue, New York, NY 10158

Routledge is an imprint of the Taylor & Francis Group, an informa business

British Library Cataloguing-in-Publication Data
A catalogue record for this book is available from the British Library

Library of Congress Cataloging-in-Publication Data
Names: Hampson, Fen Osler, editor. | Narlikar, Amrita, editor.
Title: International negotiation and political narratives: a comparative study / Edited by Fen Osler Hampson and Amrita Narlikar.
Description: Abingdon, Oxon; New York, NY: Routledge, 2022. |
Series: Routledge studies in security and conflict management |
Includes bibliographical references and index.
Identifiers: LCCN 2021041967 (print) | LCCN 2021041968 (ebook) |
ISBN 9781032066486 (hardback) | ISBN 9781032066462 (paperback) |
ISBN 9781003203209 (ebook)
Subjects: LCSH: Diplomatic negotiations in international disputes. |
International cooperation. | Conflict management–Political aspects. |
Political parties–Social aspects.
Classification: LCC JZ6045 .I62 2022 (print) |
LCC JZ6045 (ebook) | DDC 327.1/7–dc23/eng/20211026
LC record available at https://lccn.loc.gov/2021041967
LC ebook record available at https://lccn.loc.gov/2021041968

ISBN: 978-1-032-06648-6 (hbk)
ISBN: 978-1-032-06646-2 (pbk)
ISBN: 978-1-003-20320-9 (ebk)

DOI: 10.4324/9781003203209

Typeset in Bembo
by Newgen Publishing UK

CONTENTS

ILLUSTRATIONS

Table

Figures

ACKNOWLEDGEMENTS

This book forms a part of the Processes in International Negotiation (PIN) project. We are grateful to all members of the Steering Committee of PIN, who have been valuable sparring partners for us throughout this process. The "tribal elder" of PIN – I. William Zartman – deserves a special note of thanks for his indefatigable support.

We would also like to thank colleagues and staff at the German Institute for Global and Area Studies (GIGA), where PIN is based, and where first drafts of the papers were presented in a workshop in 2019. Guy Olivier Faure, Liana Fix, Paul Meertz, and Nora Müller provided helpful feedback as discussants. We thank them and all the participants at the workshop for the constructive and rich debate over two days, which helped us refine our concept for the book and also bring coherence to papers on such a diverse set of topics.

Julia Kramer, from the GIGA, adopted many different roles to help us as we progressed through the project – from overseeing the work of the conference management team, to coordinating with PIN colleagues and helping us communicate with our team of contributors – and she took on these tasks with cheer and commitment. Our student assistants, Chris Anthony, Indi-Carolina Kryg, and Johannes Pimpl worked closely with us, with singular dedication, as we brought the project to its completion.

Andrew Humphrys from Routledge was incredibly supportive of the project; it was his idea to convert this book from a research book reaching out to a limited audience, to a textbook that would speak to students of negotiation as well as scholars and practitioners. We benefited enormously from the feedback of three anonymous reviewers, and further conversations with Andrew to help improve the project further.

Finally, this book would not have been possible without the commitment and responsiveness of our contributors. Despite all the different demands and difficulties imposed by the pandemic, our team of contributors did not falter from the task, and met all our requests with patience and good humour.

We are grateful to have the opportunity to bring together this range and depth of expertise within the covers of this book, and have learnt much in the process. By showing how narratives shape bargaining outcomes in diverse issue-areas, we hope this volume will enrich both the study and the practice of international negotiation.

CONTRIBUTORS

Thomas Bagger is the Director-General for Foreign Affairs at the Office of the President of the Federal Republic of Germany. Previously, he worked with the German Diplomatic Service. Thomas holds a MA in Government and Politics from the University of Maryland and a doctorate from Ludwig-Maximilian-University.

Dan Ciuriak is a senior fellow at the Centre for International Governance Innovation (CIGI), and fellow in residence with the C.D. Howe Institute. Previously, he had a 31-year career with Canada's civil service, retiring as deputy chief economist at the Department of Foreign Affairs and International Trade (now Global Affairs Canada).

Akhil Deo is currently a Master of International Affairs candidate at the Hertie School in Berlin. Previously, he was a Junior Fellow with the Technology and Media Initiative at the Observer Research Foundation (ORF) in New Delhi.

Henner Fürtig is Associate of the German Institute for Global and Area Studies (GIGA) and Professor at the University of Hamburg. Previously he acted as GIGA's Director for Institute of Middle East Studies. His research areas include the history and politics of the Middle East – especially the Gulf region.

Fen Osler Hampson is a fellow of the Royal Society of Canada, Chancellor's Professor at Carleton University, and Executive Director of the World Refugee Council. He holds a PhD from Harvard University. He is the author of 15 books on international affairs and co-editor of 30 other volumes.

Sophie Haspeslagh is Assistant Professor at the American University in Cairo. Previously, she was Head of Policy at Conciliation Resources. Sophie holds a

PhD from the London School of Economics and Political Science. She wrote *Proscribing Peace: How Listing Armed Groups Hurts Negotiations* (2021).

Meredith Lilly is the Simon Reisman Chair in International Economic Policy and Associate Professor at Carleton University. She previously served as foreign affairs and international trade advisor to Prime Minister Stephen Harper. She holds a PhD from the University of Toronto.

Amrita Narlikar is President of the German Institute for Global and Area Studies (GIGA) and Honorary Fellow of Darwin College, University of Cambridge. Her most recent book is *Poverty Narratives and Power Paradoxes in International Trade Negotiations and Beyond* (2020).

Rodger A. Payne is Professor of Political Science at the University of Louisville. For 17 years, Payne directed the Grawemeyer Award for Ideas Improving World Order, and in 2018, he was a Fulbright Canada Research Chair at Carleton University. He is the author of dozens of journal articles and book chapters.

Maria Ptashkina is Economics PhD candidate at the University of Pompeu Fabra. She is a former fellow at the International Centre for Trade and Sustainable Development and former delegate from the Russian Federation to the Asia-Pacific Economic Cooperation Forum.

Vlada Rodionova is a machine learning and artificial intelligence consultant. She holds a degree in Applied Math and Computer Science from Moscow State University and has 12 years' experience in building machine learning applications for banking, finance, and retail.

Valérie Rosoux is a research director at the Belgian National Fund for Scientific Research (FNRS). She teaches International Negotiation and Transitional Justice at the University of Louvain (UCLouvain). She has a License in Philosophy and a PhD in International Relations.

Samir Saran is the President of Observer Research Foundation (ORF). His research focuses on global governance, technology and new media, and India's foreign policy. He curates the Raisina Dialogue and has authored four books, various academic papers, and is featured regularly in Indian and international print and broadcast media.

Julia Strasheim is Deputy Managing Director and Program Director for European and International Affairs at the Bundeskanzler-Helmut-Schmidt-Stiftung in Hamburg and Research Associate at the German Institute for Global and Area Studies (GIGA). She holds a PhD from the University of Heidelberg.

Oliver Stuenkel is Associate Professor of International Relations at the FGV in São Paulo. He is also a non-resident Fellow at the Global Public Policy Institute in Berlin, a non-resident scholar at the Carnegie Endowment for International Peace in Washington DC and a columnist for EL PAÍS and Americas Quarterly.

Haley J. Swedlund is Associate Professor of International Relations at Radboud University. Her research sits at the nexus of international political economy, development, and conflict studies. She is the author of *The Development Dance: How Donors and Recipients Negotiate the Delivery of Foreign Aid* (2017).

Mikhail Troitskiy is Dean and Associate Professor at the School of Government and International Affairs at MGIMO University in Moscow and IMARES Program Professor at European University at St. Petersburg. His research focuses on international security, conflicts in Eurasia, and US-Russia relations.

Paul Twomey is a distinguished fellow at the Centre for International Governance Innovation (CIGI). Previously, he was the CEO of ICANN, the technical coordination body for the Internet. Prior, he was CEO of the Australian government's National Office for the Information Economy. He holds a PhD from the University of Cambridge.

Brendan Vickers is Head of the International Trade Policy Section at the Commonwealth Secretariat in London. He previously worked as Head of Research and Policy in the South African Department of Trade and Industry and holds a PhD from the University of London.

I. William Zartman is the Jacob Blaustein Distinguished Professor Emeritus of International Organization and Conflict Resolution at Johns Hopkins University-SAIS, former president of the Middle East Studies Association and founding president of the American Institute for Maghrib Studies. He holds a PhD from Yale and doctorates honoris causa from Louvain and Uppsala.

PART I

Theories, concepts, approaches

1

NARRATIVES, POLITICAL IDENTITY, AND INTERNATIONAL NEGOTIATION

Fen Osler Hampson and Amrita Narlikar

Introduction

Underlying most of the established models of the negotiation process is the notion of rational expectations: parties are generally seen as utility maximizing actors subject to the important qualification that utility preferences will change as new information becomes available. The cost-benefit calculations of the negotiating parties shape, and are in turn shaped by, the negotiation process through exchanges of information, learning and the exchange of concessions (Bazerman and Malhotra, 2007; Hampson, 1995; Hampson and Zartman, 2012; Hopmann, 1998; Narlikar, 2010; Odell and Tingley, 2013; Raiffa, 2002; Zartman, 1989). Departures from the rational "mean" in negotiating behavior are typically explained by "biases of the mind" and/or "emotions." These include, for example, the "fixed-pie bias" (whatever is good for the other side is bad for us, especially when it comes to the making concessions), non-rational escalation of commitment or what is sometimes referred to as the "winner's curse," and various kinds of self-serving attributions such as egocentrism, overconfidence, and irrational optimism (also see, e.g., Bazerman and Malhotra, 2007, pp.103–139; Bazerman and Samuelson, 1983; Dingwall, 2016, pp.103–124; Fisher and Shapiro, 2005). Scholars have also identified the importance of culture to help explain why parties may misread the signals, tactics, and negotiating behaviors of their interlocutors and tend to ignore the impact their own cultural biases and negotiating style may have on the way their messages are received on the opposite side of the negotiating table (Brett et al., 1998; Cohen, 1997; Lee, et al., 2012).

The purpose of this project is to explore another important dimension to international negotiation processes that warrants closer scrutiny in a world that is experiencing waves of right-wing and left-wing populism that are fueled by a fragmentation of politics at the national level defined more by identity and who

DOI: 10.4324/9781003203209-2

people are in terms of race, ethnicity, and economic status than ideas of human equality, rule of law, and unified shared values (Fukuyama, 2018). It focuses on the intersubjective identities of the parties and the political narratives or "stories" they carry in their own minds, which shape their respective values, interests, and negotiating behaviors in ways that may not be utility maximizing in the conventional sense.[1] As we explore here, such narratives influence negotiating behavior and strategies in different negotiating settings and on different issues in a number of key ways. (1) They can influence key decisions about whether to negotiate, that is, key prenegotiation choices, especially when core political identities are threatened; (2) Identity narratives may be critical to the way parties view their best alternative to a negotiated agreement (BATNA) and reservation price (the maximum price a party is prepared to pay or the minimum sale price) in negotiation; (3) Identity narratives can play a key role in the two-level games that are typically associated with any international negotiation (a compelling narrative may enlarge the win-win set between different domestic constituencies and build support for a "resolving formula" whereas a less-than-compelling narrative will reduce the likelihood of convergence); and (4) Persuasive narratives that bridge or cross different group identities can help build supportive international coalitions and/or social movements, which are crucial to managing bargaining processes, especially in a multilateral setting, and arriving at a successful negotiated outcome though they may be increasingly difficult to develop because of the power of populist-based, identity politics in many countries throughout the world.

Identity and narrative theory explained

Concepts of identity and narratives are used by constructivist international relations scholars (Barnett, 2013; Miskimmon et al., 2017; Suganami, 1999; Wendt, 1999) to explain how stories and frames of reference help to build intersubjective understandings, build consensus, and justify appropriate action. Narratives thus help to explain a social relationship or phenomenon.

Economists, more recently, have turned to narratives and concepts of social identity to help explain deviations from so-called rational or "optimal" outcomes where social actors pursue courses of action that are clearly suboptimal (Akerlof, 2007; Akerlof and Shiller, 2009; Akerlof and Kranton, 2011; Akerlof, 2017a, 2017b, 2018; Bruner, 1998; Fisher, 1984; Lamberson, 2016; Mokyr, 2017; Morson and Schapiro, 2017; Schiller, 2017). In traditional economic theory, motivations are derived from *a priori* assumptions about utility maximization. In identity theory, people are motivated by the stories they tell themselves at the time of their decisions. Such stories, or narratives, convey beliefs about who we are, how we should behave, what is important, and how the world works. Their impact on policy depends on the salience of the stories that get told. Policies, in turn, can shape and change stories (Akerlof, 2018; Davidson, 2016; Hall, 1993).

Importantly, narratives are also collections of stories that contain an understanding—no matter how rudimentary, crude (or just plain wrong)—about putative cause and effect in the real world. In other words, narratives are ways of organizing complex information to help understand reality and what may need to be done to deal with difficult and challenging circumstances. There are the memes that help us to understand and explain the world in terms of why things are the way they are and how we should act. The most successful narratives (in a political sense) are those that are simple and easily grasped by the layperson. Narratives don't have to be true or do justice to the facts—they simply have to be rhetorically persuasive and attractive to a particular political constituency and/or mobilized social network. As Paul Collier (2014) points out, narratives influence "how actors understand *causal relationships* by which the consequences of particular actions are determined: narratives may trump the direct observation of experience as means of learning about the world." As Bruce Wydick (2015) of the World Bank further explains,

> Why so often is narrative used in place of good data in impact claims? There are at least two reasons. The first is well-known: a lack of understanding of causal effects, or in some cases, an unwillingness to submit a program to rigorous evaluation. The second is more interesting: a good narrative soundly beats even the best data ... In the battle for hearts and minds of human beings, narrative will consistently outperform data in its ability to influence human thinking and motivate human action.
>
> *Wydick, 2015*

This is because people are psychologically predisposed to tune out reams of data, what Slovic refers to as "psychic numbing."

But narratives are not simply epiphenomenal, heuristic devices to deal with complexity. They unite members of a group and help forge and sustain a unique sense of identity within a social grouping or network. The most powerful narratives define the key values, norms, and social identity of the group (as well as those who are considered members of the out-group) as in key narratives about "imagined communities" like nations (Anderson, 2016). Identity narratives have both causal and thematic coherence (Bruner, 1998). In an individual or personal context, they contribute to ego identity and psychological well-being. In a group context, they give meaning and existence to the identity of the group or social network (De Fina, 2006; Fleetwood, 2016; Hammack, 2008). In other words, the most powerful narratives are perceived to have existential validity and help delineate the group's core values, behavioral norms, needs, and deeds. Narratives sometimes have a single author, but they may also have different authors who contribute to the story and adapt it through the retelling of the story over a period of time to different audiences and constituencies. The most powerful narratives help form (and reinforce) a sense of group identity and, accordingly, become foundational elements of the emotional belief system of the group or community in question.

As psychologists point out, identity narratives generally tend to fall into three generic categories (Adler et al., 2015; Fisher, 1984; Lapsley, 2010; McAdams and

McLean, 2013). They may be stories of *redemption* or *hope* that explain how an individual (or, by extension, a group) can transition from a negative to a more positive state of affairs, involving recovery, growth, sustainability, prosperity, security, and learning. There are also narratives about *contamination* that explain the proverbial "fall from grace" as a result of group victimization, exploitation, marginalization, abuse, betrayal, failed hopes, and/or disillusionment (McAdams et al., 2001; McAdams and Bowman, 2001). Most religions, for example, are based on powerful narratives that contain elements of both redemption and contamination. In Christianity, for example, there are many stories in the Bible about individuals who have sought (and achieved) redemption after having sinned or strayed from the teachings of God. Similarly, the Bible also cautions against falling under the spell of ungodly cultures which can lead into temptation. In the Old Testament, for example, the Israelites were warned about falling prey to the ungodly practices of those around them (Leviticus 18:1–5 and Deuteronomy 18:9–14). There are also narratives about individual or collective *agency*, that is, stories about how to achieve the pathway to success and secure greater individual or group fulfillment, self-actualization, and/or resiliency as a result of adopting a particular course of action through the exercise of agency or personal will (Adler, 2012; Dissanayake, 1996; Ogunyemi, 2014; Smith, 2017; Suganami, 1999).

It may also be useful to draw a distinction between *deep* versus *shallow* narratives. Deep narratives have existential validity or import and tap into a deep-rooted need that individuals have for a sense of identity and belonging to a social group. As such, the most powerful narratives shape and give voice to the shared values and behavioral norms that define the core beliefs of the group or social network (Bearman and Stovel, 2000). They are stories that elicit profound emotions of fear, dread, isolation, seclusion, or their opposite—hope, joy, belonging, and community. They are narratives that bind the group or social network and reinforce both a sense of community and pathways to collective action (Benford and Snow, 2000).

Shallow narratives, like deep narratives, are also stories about cause and effect, but they lack existential depth or import and are not a strong source of group identification or a basis for concerted, collective action. They may have cognitive value as simplifiers of a complex reality, but they are deficient in emotional appeal or resonance and rarely serve as a powerful driving force for collective action in the way that deep narratives do. When narratives point to different courses of action and are in conflict, deep narratives will always trump shallow narratives. When there is more than one set of deep narratives, the possibilities for collection action may be thwarted by the presence of multiple (and conflicting) equilibria. Deep narratives are thus "sticky" and hard to change or rewrite, as discussed below, especially after they have gained widespread acceptance.

To obtain greater social acceptability and political reach, narratives also require vectors of transmission via social networks that deliver stories to a wider audience (Wahman, 2003). These networks are "structures of social interaction which channel information and ... also have enormous power because they are vehicles or instruments through which narratives or 'stories' are moderated and accessed" (Collier, 2014). Narratives also necessarily require different kinds of human agency to achieve saliency and flourish (Cristackis and Fowler, 2011). They have to be articulated and communicated by key "nodal" actors who are not only influential within their respective networks and are often viewed as leaders within the group (i.e., they have high levels of Eigenvector centrality) (Bonancich, 1987; Rodan, 2011), but they can also be transmitted by other actors who sit at strategic points at the boundary of the network and can act as "connectors" and "boundary spanners" to other social networks (Cross and Prusak, 2002). Social media "influencers," for example, often play this kind of connector role. Although they are not necessarily central nodal actors or the authors and gatekeepers of a particular narrative, they may nonetheless help propagate the narrative through their own social network of online "followers."

Depending on how they are framed, narratives can have profound political consequences. As Prateek Raj observes,

> Just like in 1980, the 2016 elections presented us with newer narratives. President Donald Trump's core narrative of "Make America Great Again" may have been lacking in details, but it was rhetorically persuasive … It also matched some of President Trump's other ideas, like protectionism and higher tariffs, and it appealed to those who were most angry about the opening of walls due to globalization. If economists had foreseen the popular backlash against globalization fueled by the forceful narrative of "Build the Wall," they probably would have developed different trade models, so that the bottled-up anger of Americans would not explode. Did slogans like "Make America Great Again" or "Build the Wall" matter? If Trump's own meticulous emphasis on the slogans is any indication, they did.
>
> *Raj, 2017*

Narratives also play an important role in international negotiation, especially in the formation of supportive social networks and coalition-building in both the domestic and international sphere (Sebenius, 2013). But, as we discuss below, their impact and influence extend well beyond the formation of supportive constituencies to the actual details of the negotiation process itself and the framing of key issues under consideration. The presence of deeply accepted, rival narratives that are immutable may help to explain why some negotiations become deadlocked as in the North-South "stalemate" over an issue like agriculture (Narlikar, 2015; Narlikar, 2020), Brexit, or the Minsk negotiations to end conflict between Russia and Ukraine (Hampson and Troitskiy, 2018). Conflicting deep narratives about the "causes" of extremism and violent conflict (and agent culpability), which are based on different interpretations of the historical record, also contribute to perceptions that a conflict is "intractable" and a refusal to make concessions because of ingrained narratives that say the other party cannot be trusted to hold up its side of the bargain. Under normal circumstances, conflicts should move beyond a mutually hurting stalemate to a negotiated resolution if there is a modicum of trust and willingness to make concession, but powerful political narratives typically blind parties to the possibilities of doing so (Crocker et al., 2004; Zartman, 1989).

Similarly, nationalist/populist narratives, which are prevalent in contemporary international relations, are playing a key role in thwarting the prospects for cooperation in international trade, security, and diplomatic relations (Crocker et al., 2021). As is discussed further below and in many of the case studies in this volume, this presents a major challenge to negotiating new agreements that are intended to foster greater levels of international cooperation.

Under the right conditions new narratives can also emerge through the process of negotiation that help to break such deadlocks by transforming political attitudes and mobilizing supportive political constituencies at the domestic and/or international levels as in the case of negotiations between Germany and France that led to creation of the European Coal and Steel Community (Petzina et al., 1981). These narratives are generally advanced by powerful political (nodal) actors (as in the case of French Foreign Minister Robert Schuman) who are in a position to mobilize different social networks in support of their position usually in the aftermath of a major crisis, such as a major war that nobody wants to repeat again. They do so by telling compelling "stories" that convey a new set of meanings or views about the world that have both cognitive and emotional appeal and which, importantly, promote a new understanding about identity relationships that is supportive of a negotiated agreement and guides future decision-making behavior.

Identity narratives are typically exogenous variables in negotiation processes, especially after they have already acquired or gained widespread political acceptance and are part of the mainstream of political discourse. However, "new" narratives that are constructed by political actors during the actual course of a negotiations and are related to their efforts to "sell" the agreement to their constituents and build social consensus should be viewed as "endogenous" variables because they are part and parcel of the negotiation process itself. However, the exogeneity-endogeneity categorization of political narratives in any given negotiation may be complicated by the fact that "old" and "new" narratives are being manipulated by the different parties to the negotiation in order to gain strategic advantage. This interplay (or competition) between different narratives means that there is no tidy boundary or demarcation line between exogenous and endogenous factors.

Narratives and prenegotiation

Prenegotiation is defined as the phase where parties (or at least one of the parties) decide that it is interesting to pursue the negotiation option. This period, as defined by Zartman, covers two functional needs—"defining the problem and developing a commitment to negotiation," which is followed by the arranging of negotiations (Zartman, 1989; Stein, 1989). The first two elements are transformative because they involve a recognition that the relationship with the other party has to be redefined if one is going to sit down at the negotiating table and engage in a process that will involve a mutual exchange of concessions and the search for a cooperative agreement.

Narratives are critical to prenegotiation and overcoming the psychological and political roadblocks that stand in the way of a commitment to negotiate. Because key domestic constituencies may be opposed to negotiations as a matter of principle since any kind of negotiated agreement is seen as threatening to the identity of the group (and will also legitimate the identity and interests of one's opponent if one agrees to sit with them at the table), a new narrative has to be developed to provide reassurance that group identities will not be compromised but actually transmuted by negotiations. Crafting a new narrative of redemption or hope can help overcome these barriers and build a supportive political constituency for the negotiation option while also setting clear parameters within which an exchange of concessions can take place. (The converse is also true. Contamination narratives will also be manipulated by those who oppose negotiated solutions on the grounds that any kind of negotiated outcome will threaten the group's identity. These narratives draw a direct, negative causal connection between the onset of negotiations and the erosion of such identities.)

For example, in the prenegotiation phase leading up to the onset of Canada–US free trade negotiations in the mid-1980s, Canadians were wary of any loosening of trade restrictions because there was a generalized fear about being assimilated by the United States (also see: Hart, 1994; Cameron and Tomlin, 2002). For many Canadians, including key political elites, a deeply held narrative of "contamination" saw a direct causal connection between free trade and a loss of national sovereignty. Many Canadians, for example, were not completely persuaded by the extensive empirical findings of a major Royal Commission on the Canadian Economy, led by former Finance Minister Donald Macdonald, which urged Canadians to "take a leap of faith" in order to boost the economy by 3 to 8 percent GDP while creating jobs and lowering prices on consumer goods.

Newly elected Canadian Prime Minister Brian Mulroney was able to elicit sufficient political support to initiate free trade negotiations with the United States by advancing a new narrative of "hope" (his government argued that a new agreement would help lift Canada out of a deep recession by opening up new markets for Canadian goods and services in the United States). But he also made it clear that fears about a loss of independence in the contamination narrative of the government's critics were greatly exaggerated. He carefully stipulated that an agreement with the Americans would lead to "enhanced trade" (not "free trade") and would not, in his words, compromise Canada's "political sovereignty, our system of social programs, our commitment to fight regional disparities, our unique cultural identity, [and] our special linguistic character."

Mulroney assured Canadians that these were "the essence of Canada" and would not be "at issue in these negotiations." Even so, many Canadians were not convinced. When an agreement was finally concluded, the prime minister felt compelled to take the agreement to the Canadian people in the federal election of 1988. During the campaign, he defended the agreement against opposition Liberal party claims that "The Mulroney trade agreement sells out Canada's sovereign control over its economic, social, cultural, and regional policies [which will turn] Canada into a colony of the United States" (quoted in Hampson, 2018, p.31). After a hard-fought and, in some ways, cathartic campaign to convince voters that the agreement would not only serve Canadian interests but actually make Canada stronger and more self-confident as a nation and more globally competitive, Mulroney handily won the election.

Narratives also play into decisions not to prenegotiate. In 2002–2003 in the aftermath of 9/11, the United States worried openly about Iraqi president Saddam Hussein's acquisition of weapons of mass destruction (WMD) and his possible ties with terrorist groups, like al Qaeda. Within the administration, the president's key advisers, vice president Dick Cheney and secretary of defense Donald Rumsfeld, promulgated a narrative of "redemption" that only swift and decisive military action by the United States would eliminate the existential threat posed by Saddam Hussein once and for all and lead to democratic rule not just in Iraq but throughout the Middle East as the citizens of the Arab world emerged from the shadows of years of despotic rule (see: Keegan, 2004). As various commentators have pointed out, from the outset this was a self-rationalization for US military action and not based on any kind of genuine concern about the interests of the Iraqi people or an understanding about the deeper politics and culture of the region (see, e.g., Alkifaey, 2019; Moon, 2009; Zunes and Feffer, 2007).

The redemption narrative of the administration's hawks had little use for diplomacy and the resumption of negotiations with the Iraqi regime—even within a renewed prenegotiation framework—because diplomacy was seen as having further contaminated the situation by emboldening Saddam Hussein. (Negotiations had been underway for almost ten years prior under UN Security Council auspices to get Saddam Hussein to provide clear and unambiguous evidence that he did not possess WMD capabilities.) As President George W. Bush stated in his speech to the nation at the beginning of the war,

> The Iraqi regime has used diplomacy as a ploy to gain time and advantage. It has uniformly defied Security Council resolutions demanding full disarmament. Over the years, UN weapon inspectors have been threatened by Iraqi officials, electronically bugged, and systematically deceived. Peaceful efforts to disarm the Iraqi regime have failed again and again—because we are not dealing with peaceful men.
>
> *Bush, 2003*

Further, against the backdrop of the recent 9/11 attacks on the United States, the threat posed by the regime of Saddam Hussein was also viewed in stark, existential terms: "If Saddam Hussein attempts to cling to power," stated Bush,

> he will remain a deadly foe until the end. In desperation, he and terrorist groups might try to conduct terrorist operations against the American people and our friends. These attacks are not inevitable. They are, however, possible. And this very fact underscores the reason we cannot live under the threat of blackmail. The terrorist threat to America and the world will be diminished the moment that Saddam Hussein is disarmed.
>
> *Bush, 2003*

Narratives, BATNA, and reservation value

The BATNA is the "best" walk-away option if there is no agreement and is normally based on a calculation of the cost/benefit of "no agreement" versus an "agreement" (Blount and Neale, 1991; Fisher and Ury, 1981). However, deep political narratives can alter that calculus by raising the reservation value of the lowest offer one is prepared to accept while limiting what one is prepared to give up in return. In other words, a party's BATNA is tied to its identity and what psychologists refer to as "self-serving attributions," such as the need to protect the group's self-esteem and normative "core," which, in certain circumstances, may trump the value of any concessions, including contingent concessions, that might be available through a negotiated agreement (Mezulis et al., 2004; Zaccaro et al., 1987).

A classic illustration of how deep narratives reinforce BATNAs to the point where "no deal is better than any deal" is the Melian dialogue between Athens and Melos (see: Waelchli and Shah, 1994). In 416 BC Athens sent a landing force to the independent state island in an ill-fated bid to bring it into the Delian League against Sparta. The Melians were a proud people, however, and were reluctant to compromise their neutrality and independence. Generals Cleomedes and Tisias led the negotiations on the Athenian side while Melos was represented by 12 members of the Melian Council. For years, Athens had arrogantly believed in the unassailable righteousness of its own agency narrative that "might makes right." Athens believed that its BATNA, which was based on exercising its overwhelming military power, was self-evident, and would force the Melians into submission.

Athens therefore had little interest in offering Melos the kind of concessions that would recognize the independence and sovereignty demands of a small, weakly defended island state. "For ourselves," the Athenian generals remarked at the outset of negotiations,

> we shall not trouble you with specious pretenses—either of how we have a right to our empire because we overthrew the Mede, or are now attacking you because of the wrong you have done us—and make a long speech which would not be believed ... for you know as we do that right, as the world goes, is in question only between equals in power; while the strong do what they can and the weak suffer what they must.
>
> *quoted in Waelchli and Shah, 1994*

The Melians, in turn, also had an exaggerated sense of their own strengths and the legitimacy of their demands being, as they were, a proud, sovereign and independent people. Like the Athenians, they also thought that justice would ultimately prevail in their favor, that is, they would receive redemption by standing firm: "You may be sure that we are as well aware as you of the difficulty of contending against your power and fortune, unless the terms be equal," said its Elders.

> But we trust that the gods may grant us fortune as good as yours, since we are just men fighting against unjust, and that what we want in power will be made up by the alliance of the Lacedaemonians, who are bound, if only for very shame, to come to the aid of their kindred.
>
> *quoted in Waelchi and Shah, 1994*

This was a clear case of "irrational optimism" (Bazerman and Malhotra, 2007, pp.132–134) propelled by the belief that the Lacedemonians, who were too far away and lacked Athens' naval capabilities, would come to Melos' defence. The Melian mindset was that they were on the right side of the argument (and history) while Athens was not.

In the case of both Athens and Melos, deeply held agency and redemption narratives about the just nature of their respective positions led their negotiators to believe that they each had a strong BATNA and that their opponent would cave in to their demands. This reduced the incentive to engage in a genuine negotiation to reach a political compromise that would have avoided bloodshed and Melos's annihilation.

Narratives, networks, and social movements in negotiation

Most international negotiations are characterized by complexity—complexities regarding the range of issues under discussion, the large number of parties at the negotiating table, and the wide gamut of stakeholders who have a direct or indirect interest in the outcome of negotiations (Zartman, 1994). Issue and party consolidation via the formation of coalitions (usually state-based) are critical to managing this complexity. So too is design of the negotiation via issue-sequencing, agenda packaging, issue placement, and the careful management of the various institutional procedures and the rules of the negotiating forum (Hampson, 1995; Hopmann, 1998). However, in the setting of multilateral negotiations or even complex, multi-issue/multi-party bilateral negotiations, an effective negotiating strategy also requires a high degree of political mobilization at the societal level in support of negotiated outcomes through the formation of broad-based, supportive social networks or movements (Sikkink, 2011; Narlikar, 2020). The "members" of such movements or networks typically include nongovernmental organizations, civil society groups, epistemic communities, the private sector, and, at the most general level, the public-at-large (Hampson and Reid, 2003; Narlikar, 2020; Price, 1998).

Transnational social movements (and narrower, issue-based coalitions) do not form automatically. They have to be built—often from the ground up—and thus require a combination of both intrinsic and extrinsic agency (Giddens, 1979) (e.g., entrepreneurial leaders, mediators, team builders, effective communicators, bridge builders, and other champions) to mobilize different groups and construct a transnational political network whose members are willing to work together to achieve a particular negotiated outcome (Network Weaver, 2011; Totterdell et al., 2008). In order to operate efficiently and effectively, these social networks or movements need high levels of "closeness," "degree centrality," and the clustering characteristics of a "small world" network (Kadushin, 2012; Lamberson, 2016; McCarty et al., 2001; Scott, 2017; Stekette et al., 2015). But that is still not enough. They also require a deep narrative that creates an independent, collective identity and which converges on shared values and norms and allows for the sharing of information/experiences, building trust and social capital, providing mutual support, and the conjoining of material interests (Pentland and Feldman, 2007; Putnam, 2001; Stone, 2016; Van der Meer and Tolsma, 2014). Narratives of redemption, contamination, and/or agency help bring such groups together, solidify the network, and create focal points for collective action. In the absence of a deeply held narrative, these groupings will typically dissolve as conflicting interests over different issues that are subject of negotiation eventually drive the members of the network apart or cause it to split or fracture into much smaller, issue-based coalitions (Zartman, 1985). Narratives thus provide the normative "stickiness" or political glue that keeps a broad-based movement of diverse actors together during the course of lengthy and often difficult negotiations.

The global movement to ban the military use of anti-personnel landmines (APLs), which culminated in the so-called "Ottawa Process," offers a good illustration of the "stickiness" principle and the importance of a compelling contamination narrative to the formation of a powerful, global transnational movement of non-state actors that worked alongside a coalition state to secure a legally binding international agreement to ban APLs (see, e.g., Cameron et al., 1998; Hampson, 2002; Hampson and Reid, 2003; Price, 1998).

The origins of the movement to ban APLs began in the 1970s and was led by the International Committee of the Red Cross (ICRC), which tried to reinvigorate the century-old tradition in humanitarian law to reduce harm to noncombatant civilians who were being indiscriminately killed by these weapons (and hence victimized). For many years, ICRC officials had observed first-hand the devastating humanitarian consequences of landmines in different conflict settings in Africa, Asia, and elsewhere. The ICRC found other champions for the ban, including the Vietnam Veterans of America Foundation, Medico International, and other humanitarian NGOs who also had first-hand dealings with the devastating, indiscriminate consequences of these weapons. In 1992, the

International Campaign to Ban Landmines (ICBL) formed, headed by the well-known activist Jody Williams.

As Price notes, the formation of a transnational network to galvanize a coalition of states to negotiate a treaty banning the production, export, and use of these weapons required a compelling, moral narrative that reframed the APL issue as not just "another" humanitarian problem but instead as a catastrophic "weapon of mass destruction in slow motion" that was indiscriminately killing and maiming "more people than nuclear, chemical, and biological weapons combined" (Price, 1998, p.629). He argues that "moral persuasion and the social pressure arising from identity politics and emulation" in this broad-based, transnational society-state movement were crucial to securing the successful outcome of the APL treaty (Price, 1998, p.616). Further, it is arguable that the "stickiness" of this deeply held, contamination narrative (hundreds of thousands had been victimized by these indiscriminate weapons of warfare) not only helped keep a broad-based coalition of state and non-state actors together over the course of several years, but also generated widespread political support for a second negotiating track (the Ottawa Process) outside of the Conference on Disarmament arena, which was deadlocked, so that a total ban on APLs could be reached (Hampson and Reid, 2003).

Narratives are also important to increasing the political salience and relevance of so-called "epistemic communities," which are networks of scientific experts who have a shared causal understanding about the sources of a particular problem (Pisanty, 2014). On complex scientific issues like "ozone depletion" or climate change, which initially were not well understood by non-scientists, scientific arguments had to be couched in terms of a narrative that the public could readily understand and accept. The dangers of CFCs and their possible link with stratospheric ozone depletion were scientifically documented in the early 1970s, but only really got political traction when the public became aware of the growing risks of skin cancer from the depletion of stratospheric ozone (Benedick, 1998; Hampson, 1995). This contamination narrative converged on the dangers of CFCs as aerosol propellants in spray cans, including their use in nonessential products like hairsprays and deodorants (which led to the "ban-the-can" social movement), eventually forcing regulators to cut back on the use of CFCs in a wide variety of consumer products and eventually key production processes as well. In the late 1970s and early 1980s, the CFC-ozone issue moved from the national to the international arena when a UNEP-sponsored meeting of intergovernmental experts took on the task of developing a concrete action plan to protect stratospheric ozone in response to these pressures (Table 1.1).

Narratives and resolving formula in negotiation

The main purpose of any negotiation is to search for a formula that addresses competing interests and provides the foundation for an agreement. Zartman and Berman define a formula as "a shared perception or definition of the conflict

TABLE 1.1 Types of narratives

	Contamination	*Redemption*	*Agency*
Shallow	• "Project Fear" (Brexit)	• Theresa May's Brexit Agreement with EU Iraq War (2003) (rejection of diplomatic/ negotiation option)	• Oslo Peace Accords (1993) • Camp David Talks (2000)
Deep	• Opponents of Canada–US Free Trade • Ozone depletion (Vienna • Convention & Montreal Protocol) • Anti-Personnel Landmines social movement	• Melian Dialogue (Melos) • Supporters of Canada–US Free Trade (Mulroney Government)	• Melian Dialogue (Athens)

that establishes terms of trade, the cognitive structure of referents for a solution, or an applicable criterion of justice" on the grounds that a formula is more than just a concession or compromise based on a series of fixed moves or positions. To be effective, a formula or agreed solution must be "framed by a relatively simple definition or conception of an outcome" (Zartman and Berman, 1982, pp.95–105). But as Zartman and Berman are also at pains to point out,

> All perceptions are selective. No one perceives everything that there is about a situation or a relationship. Even those elements that each side may describe as "facts" can be perceived in quite different ways; the salience or meaning of facts may be different to different parties, a problem particularly pronounced in dealings between parties of different cultures. For the most part, perception is determined by needs, goals, and experiences of a party. The parties try to communicate their perceptions on these bases, but often they assume what needs to be expressed and the meaning of the facts they see never gets through to the other side.
>
> *Zartman and Berman, 1982, p.95*

This problem is compounded in intractable conflicts by contamination narratives that blame the other side for group victimization, exploitation and other abuses (Crocker et al., 2004, 2018, 2019). A "resolving formula" not only has to provide redress to actual (and perceived) injustices, but also be accompanied by a new narrative that is sufficiently persuasive, provides a distinct value proposition to the parties, does not threaten core group identities, and shifts social discourse away from a contamination narrative to one of redemption and/or joint agency. To be effective, these new narratives have to be conveyed by nodal actors who have genuine moral and political standing within their respective communities or social networks and can secure "buy in" from their constituents.

Finding a new political "equilibrium" that is grounded on a new narrative is no mean feat, especially when "sticky" contamination narratives present major psychological roadblocks to agreement and reconciliation. That is because

> [i]ntractable conflicts tend to take over the societies they affect. They permeate all societal institutions—politics, media, religion, education—and dominate political and social discourse. No one escapes from their impact, even in conflict where the level of violence is low.
>
> *Hampson and Zartman, 2012, p.123*

Mediators, for example, need to be aware that warning parties that they will be materially worse off without an agreement will generally tend to fall on deaf ears unless they can also change social discourse through the mobilization of new social networks and/or coalitions that promote a new narrative of redemption ("here is the path to a better future that will make us stronger if we join hands with the other side") and agency ("we can only change the situation for the better if we both take matters into our hands"). The same applies to the post-agreement phase where the activation of social networks around a new narrative is critical to public acceptance and implementation:

> The Oslo talks, a creative and committed exercise, fell victim to the key of its success: secrecy, just like Camp David. Neither side worked to sell the agreement to its home audience, nor even more so, to help the other side sell the agreement. Terrorism continued, culminating in the assassination of Rabin by a Jewish fundamentalist.
>
> *Hampson and Zartman, 2012, p.67*

A combination of what Hampson and Zartman (Hampson and Zartman, 2012, p.41,49) refer to as "Street Talk" and "Happy Talk" are useful negotiation "tools" of narrative transformation. Happy Talk focuses on working out a more pleasant future for all parties to replace "the unpleasant present ... A party that may be hurting now may have an eye on a glorious day in the future when all will be golden again." The challenge for negotiators is "to construct a common goal that can be beneficial to all sides" and "shake the parties from their zero-sum view of the conflict." Happy Talk must also be accompanied by Street Talk, which addresses "the needs of local communities who bear the deepest scars of conflict" and who must be involved if the negotiation enterprise is to succeed. Street Talk is a form of dialogue which, in Hal Saunders words, "engages representative citizens from the conflict parties in designing steps to be taken in the political arena to change perceptions, stereotypes, to create a sense that peace may be possible and to involve more of their compatriots" (Hampson and Zartman, 2012, p.19). Relevant examples include the Dartmouth Conference, which was a continuous dialogue and exchange between US and Soviet citizens during the Cold War; the Tajikistan Dialogue; and the Peace Process in Guatemala, which began with a meeting in Oslo organized by the Lutheran Church and evolved into a UN-supported Civil Society Assembly that engaged civil society and public participation to help end one of Central America's most brutal civil wars (Hampson and Zartman, 2012, p.50; also see: Saunders, 2009).

Street Talk and Happy Talk can also be useful accompaniments to economic negotiations under the right kinds of leadership. For example, one of the many difficulties that British Prime Minister Theresa May encountered selling her 585-page, November 2018 Brexit agreement with the European Union (EU) to her own party and Britons was that she could not offer a compelling political narrative via Street Talk or Happy Talk that would simultaneously appeal to both pro- and anti-Brexiteers to convince them that a better future lay in store for the entire country if her agreement was accepted (see, e.g., Wheeler et al., 2019). (One of the major criticisms of May was that she was too secretive and aloof.) Brexiteers thought her agreement was a sell-out and no better than the status quo, which, in their view, unduly compromised British sovereignty and political independence (theirs was a strong, contamination narrative about Brussels and the EU). Remainers worried that the proposed agreement would inflict major economic costs on Britain and did not deal properly with future EU-UK relations, especially regarding the status of Northern Ireland. Northern Ireland's Unionist Party (DUP), in turn, which propped up May's minority government, objected to the so-called "Irish backstop" provisions in the agreement on the grounds that any deviation from the existing status quo between Northern Ireland and Great Britain, such as border checks, would threaten the union.

Efforts to shock Britons about the dire economic consequences of Brexit through so-called "Project Fear," in which Bank of England's Governor Mark Carney played a prominent role, were derided in the press and ultimately proved unconvincing to many, not least because Carney flipflopped on his predictions about what lay in store. As Ferdinando Giuliano writes,

> After predicting a possible recession should Britain vote to leave the EU, the Bank adopted a more upbeat stance. In August last year, it raised rates to 0.75 percent as it warned that the economy was reaching its "speed limit," and planned more hikes. Last week, governor Mark Carney was much gloomier about the outlook again. The Bank's central forecasts show that Britain will avoid a recession in the first six months of the year, but there's a one in four chance of one happening. Most worrying, this prediction holds even if there's an orderly Brexit. With a "no deal" departure, the outlook would be worse still.
>
> *Giugliano, 2019*

(Arguably, Project Fear is as an example of a "shallow narrative" because it failed to credibly connect with the existential fears that many Britons on both the Remainer and Brexit side of the debate were feeling.)

Conclusion

Identity-based narratives form part of the broader social and political context of international negotiation processes. They shape positions on highly complex issues that may not be well understood by the public, but they are also the instruments or vehicles through which the complexities of any given issue are conveyed by negotiators and political elites to the public-at-large by playing on group identities and affiliations. The working hypothesis of this study is that coherent, deep identity narratives matter not only to the formation of intersubjective identities and broader transnational social movements, but also to the actual processes and outcome of complex international negotiations which, in today's world, may involve existential choices affecting the fate of nations.

The other chapters in this book are comparative case studies that explore how and why narratives contribute to negotiation failure or deadlock in some circumstances and why, in others, they do not because a new narrative that generates wider political support emerges through the process of negotiation and public engagement. In many respects, this book is intended to serve as an exploratory discussion about the role of identity-based political narratives in international negotiation processes and to stimulate further work in this area. Accordingly, we have taken a wide lens by examining the dynamics of identity-based narratives in different types of negotiation: civil and interstate conflicts, conflicts where there are two or more government actors, as well as those where there are non-state actors. In any negotiation there are power disparities, external allies, and extraneous third parties – all of which may (and undoubtedly will) influence negotiation narratives.

We also asked our contributors to explore the conditions under which specific identity-based narratives achieve a clear tipping point to become the dominant narrative and what it means for the negotiation. We also asked them to examine how narratives interact with negotiation principles (e.g., BATNA, interests, values) and how narratives alter the bargaining range of a negotiation, including the ability to make concessions.

It is important to stress that narratives are rarely static and competing narratives often interact with each other to affect the direction and ultimately the outcome of negotiations and the trading of concessions. Specifically, the case studies in the volume, which cover different kinds of disputes in international relations, explore the following issues:

1. Why different actors and organizational interests coalesce or diverge around particular narratives that underlie the negotiation;
2. How different actors and organizational interests come to define their BATNAs and resistance points (the point beyond which the negotiator is unwilling to settle) in negotiation through their respective narratives;
3. How different actors and organizational interests promoted their interests and values through their narratives in negotiations (including offering a

distinct value proposition in those narratives to their respective negotiating partners);

4. How narratives affect the parties' respective perceptions about the range of acceptable bargaining outcomes, including the critical ingredients of so-called "win-win sets," and the political legitimacy of a negotiated compromise;
5. How leaders use narratives to justify (or refuse) concessions at the negotiating table in order to secure support for a negotiated agreement (or explain why they are rejecting it); and,
6. Whether a new, political narrative emerges through the process of negotiation and is able to generate wider public/political support or not and if so, then why and under what conditions.

Note

1 In this chapter, our definition of "narratives" follows Brett Davidson (2016):

> A narrative consists of a collection or body stories of characters, joined in some common problem as fixers (heroes), causes (villains), or the harmed (victims) in a temporal trajectory (plot) leading toward resolution within a particular setting or context. These stories together or collectively convey a common worldview or meaning—an interpretation of the world and how it works. This worldview embeds within it particular power relationships.

Davidson also points out that,

> Narratives are reflected within cultural products, such as language and other forms of representation. Narratives operate at an emotional as well as cognitive level. Narratives cannot be evaluated or challenged empirically, but according to whether they are coherent and "ring true."

References

Adler, J. (2012) 'Living into the Story: Agency and Coherence in a Longitudinal Study of Narrative Identity Development and Mental Health Over the Course of Psychotherapy', *Journal of Personality and Social Psychology*, vol.102, no.2, pp.367–389.

Adler, J.M., Turner, A.F., Brookshier, K.M., Monahan, C., Walder-Biesanz, I., Harmeling, L.H., Albaugh, M., McAdams, D.P., and, Oltmanns, T.F. (2015) 'Variation in Narrative Identity Is Associated with Trajectories of Mental Health over Several Years', *Journal of Personality and Social Psychology*, vol.108, no.3, pp.476–496.

Akerlof, G. (2007) 'The Missing Motivation in Macroeconomics', *American Economic Review*, vol.97, no.1, pp.5–36.

Akerlof, G.A., and, Shiller, R.J. (2009) *Animal Spirits: How Human Psychology Drives the Economy and Why This Matters for Global Capitalism*. Princeton, NJ: Princeton University Press.

Akerlof, G.A., and, Shiller, R.J. (2015) *Phishing for Phools: The Economics of Manipulation and Deception*. Princeton, NJ: Princeton University Press.

Akerlof, G.A., and, Kranton, R. (2011) *Identity Economics: How Our Identities Shape Our Work, Wages and Well-Being*. Princeton, NJ: Princeton University Press.

Akerlof, R. (2017a) 'Value Formation: The Role of Esteem', *Games and Economic Behavior*, vol.102, pp.1–19.

Akerlof, R. (2017b) 'The Importance of Legitimacy', *World Bank Economic Review*, vol.30, Supplement, pp.157–165.

Akerlof, R. (2018, May 28) *Identity, Norms, and Narratives*, Presentation to the Global Solutions Summit, Berlin.

Alkifaey, H. (2019) *The Failure of Democracy in Iraq: Religion, Ideology and Sectarianism*. London: Routledge.

Anderson, B. (2016) *Imagined Communities: Reflections on the Origin and Spread of Nationalism*, Revised Edn. New York, NY: Verso.

Barnett, M. (2013) *Empire of Humanity: A History of Humanitarianism*. Ithaca, NY: Cornell University Press.

Bazerman, M.H., and, Malhotra, D. (2007) *Negotiation Genius*. New York, NY: Bantam.

Bazerman, M.H., and, Samuelson, W.F. (1983) 'I Won the Auction but Don't Want the Prize', *The Journal of Conflict Resolution,* vol.27, no.4, pp.618–634.

Bearman, P.S., and, Stovel, K. (2000) 'Becoming a Nazi: A Model for Narrative Networks', *Poetics*, vol.27, no.2–3, pp.69–90.

Benedick, R.E. (1998) *Ozone Diplomacy: New Directions in Safeguarding the Planet*. Cambridge, MA: Harvard University Press.

Benford, R.D., and, Snow, D.A. (2000) 'Framing Processes and Social Movements: An Overview and Assessment', *Annual Review of Sociology*, vol.26, pp.611–639.

Blount, S., and, Neale, M. (1991) 'Reservation Prices, Resistance Points, and BATNAs', *Negotiation Journal*, vol.7, no.4, pp.379–388.

Bonancich, P. (1987) 'Power and Centrality: A Family of Measures', *American Journal of Sociology*, vol.92, no.5. pp.1170–1182.

Brett, J.M., Adair, W., Lempereur, A., Okumura, T., Shikhirev, P., Tinsley, C., and, Lytle, A. (1998) 'Culture and Joint Gains in Negotiation', *Negotiation Journal*, vol.14, no.1, pp.61–86.

Bruner, J. (1998) 'What Is a Narrative Fact?', *The Annals of the American Academy of Political and Social Science*, vol.560, pp.17–27.

Bush, G.W. (2003, March 18) *Full text: Bush's Speech: A Transcript of George Bush's War Ultimatum Speech from the Cross Hall in the White House*, The Guardian.

Cameron, M.A., Lawson, R.J., and, Tomlin, B.W. (Eds.). (1998) *To Walk Without Fear: The Global Movement To Ban Landmines*. Toronto: Oxford University Press.

Cameron, M.A., and, Tomlin, B.W. (2002) *The Making of NAFTA: How the Deal Was Done*. Ithaca, NY: Cornell University Press.

Cohen, R.A. (1997) *Negotiating Across Cultures: International Communication in an Interdependent World*. Washington, DC: United Institute of Peace Press.

Collier, P. (2014, June) 'The Cultural Foundations of Economic Failure: A Conceptual Toolkit', *Journal of Economic Behavior and Organization*, vol.126, Part B, pp.5–24. www.sciencedirect.com/science/article/pii/S016726811500284X?via%3Dihub.

Cristackis, N.A., and, Fowler, J.H. (2011) *Connected: The Surprising Power of Our Social Networks and How They Shape Our Lives – How Your Friends' Friends' Friends Affect Everything You Feel, Think, and Do*. Boston, MA: Little, Brown, Spark.

Crocker, C.A., Hampson, F.O., and, Aall, P. (2004) *Taming Intractable Conflicts: Mediation in the Hardest Cases*. Washington, DC: United States Institute of Peace.

Crocker, C.A., Hampson, F.O., and, Aall, P. (2018) *International Negotiation and Mediation*. London: Routledge.

Crocker, C.A., Hampson, F.O., and, Aall, P. (2019) 'Mediation in the Emerging International Environment: From Hierarchy to Improvisation', In J. Wilkenfeld,

K. Beardsley, and D. Quinn (Eds.), *Research Handbook on Mediating International Crises* (pp.50–62). Cheltenham: Edward Elgar.

Crocker, C.A., Hampson, F.O., and, Aall, P. (Eds.). (2021) *Diplomacy and the Future of World Order.* Washington, DC: Georgetown University Press.

Cross, R., and, Prusak, L. (2002, June) *The People Who Make Organizations Stop and Go,* Harvard Business Review. https://hbr.org/2002/06/the-people-who-make-organizations-goor-stop.

Davidson, B. (2016, June 20) *The Role of Narrative Change in Influencing Policy,* On Think Tanks. https://onthinktanks.org/articles/the-role-of-narrative-change-in-influencing-policy/.

De Fina, A. (2006) 'Group Identity, Narrative and Self-Representations', In A. De Fina, D. Schiffrin, and M. Bamberg (Eds.), *Discourse and Identity* (pp.351–375). Cambridge: Cambridge University Press.

Dingwall, D. (2016) *Negotiating So Everyone Wins.* Toronto, ON: James Lorimer.

Dissanayake, W. (Ed.). (1996) *Narratives of Agency: Self-Making in China, India, and Japan.* Minneapolis, MN: University of Minnesota Press.

Fisher, W.R. (1984) 'Narration as a Human Communication Paradigm: The Case of Public Moral Argument', *Communication Monographs,* vol.51, no.1, pp.1–22.

Fisher, R., and, Shapiro, D. (2005) *Beyond Reason: Using Emotions as You Negotiate.* New York, NY: Penguin Books.

Fisher, R., and, Ury, W. (1981) *Getting to Yes: Negotiating Agreement Without Giving in.* New York, NY: Penguin Books.

Fleetwood, J. (2016) 'Narrative Habitus: Thinking Through Structure/Agency in the Narratives of Offenders', *Crime, Media, Culture: An International Journal,* vol.12, no.2. pp.173–192.

Fukuyama, F. (2018) *Identity: The Demand for Dignity and the Politics of Resentment.* New York, NY: Farrar, Stras and Giroux.

Giddens, A. (1979) *Central Problems in Social Theory: Action, Structure, and Contradiction in Social Analysis.* Los Angeles, CA: University of California Press.

Giugliano, F. (2019, February 12) *Brexit's 'Project Fear' Has Just Become Reality,* Bloomberg Opinion.

Hall, P.A. (1993) 'Policy Paradigms, Social Learning, and the State: The Case of Economic Policymaking in Britain', *Comparative Politics,* vol.25, no.3, pp.275–296.

Hammack, P.L. (2008) 'Narrative and the Cultural Psychology of Identity', *Personality and Social Psychology Review,* vol.12, no.3, pp.222–247.

Hampson, F.O. (1995) *Multilateral Negotiations: Lessons from Arms Control, Trade, and the Environment.* Baltimore, MD; The Johns Hopkins University Press.

Hampson, F.O. (2002) *Madness in the Multitude: Human Security and World Disorder.* Toronto and Oxford: Oxford University Press.

Hampson, F.O. (2018) *Master of Persuasion: Brian Mulroney's Global Legacy.* New York, NY: Penguin/Random House.

Hampson F.O., and, Reid, H. (2003) 'Coalition Diversity and Normative Legitimacy in Human Security Negotiations', *International Negotiation,* vol.8, pp.7–42.

Hampson, F.O., and, Troitskiy, M. (2018) *Tug of War: Negotiating Security in Eurasia.* Waterloo, ON: Centre for International Governance Innovation for the Processes of International Negotiation Project of the Dutch Royal Institute of International Affairs (Clingendael).

Hampson, F.O., and, Zartman, I.W. (2012) *The Global Power of Talk: Negotiating America's Interests.* Boulder, CO: Paradigm.

Hart, M. (1994) *Decision at Midnight: Inside the Canada-US Free-Trade Negotiations.* Vancouver, BC: University of British Columbia Press.

Hopmann, P.T. (1998) *The Negotiation Process and the Resolution of International Conflicts.* Columbia, NY: University of South Carolina Press.

Kadushin, C. (2012) *Understanding Social Networks: Theories, Concepts, and Findings.* New York, NY: Oxford University Press.

Keegan, J. (2004) *The Iraq War.* New York, NY: Vintage.

Lamberson, P.J. (2016) 'Diffusion in Networks', In Y. Bramoullé, A. Galeotti, and, B. Rogers (Eds.), *The Oxford Handbook of the Economics of Networks* (pp.479–503). Oxford: Oxford University Press.

Lapsley, D. (2010) 'Moral Agency, Identity and Narrative in Moral Development', *Human Development,* vol.53, no.2, pp.87–97.

Lee, S., Brett, J., and, Park, J.H. (2012) 'East Asians' Social Heterogeneity: Differences in Norms among Chinese, Japanese, and Korean Negotiators', *Negotiation Journal*, vol.28, no.4, pp.429–452.

McAdams, D.P., and, Bowman, P.J. (2001) 'Narrating Life's Turning Points: Redemption and Contamination', In D.P. McAdams, R. Josselson, and, A. Lieblich (Eds.), *Turns in the Road: Narrative Studies of Lives in Transition* (pp.3–34). Washington, DC: American Psychological Association Press.

McAdams, D.P., and, McLean, K.C. (2013) 'Narrative Identity', *Current Directions in Psychological Research,* vol.22, no.3. pp.233–238.

McAdams, D.P., Reynolds, J., Lewis, M., Patten, A.H., and, Bowman, P.J. (2001) 'When Bad Things Turn Good and Good Things Turn Bad: Sequences of Redemption and Contamination in Life Narrative and Their Relation to Psychosocial Adaptation in Midlife Adults and in Students', *Personality and Social Psychology Bulletin*, vol.27, no.4, pp.474–485.

McCarty, C., Killworth, P.D., Bernard, H.R., Johnsen, E., and, Shelley, G.A. (2001) 'Comparing Two Methods for Estimating Network Size', *Human Organization*, vol.60, pp.28–39.

Mezulis, A.H, Abrahamson, L.H., Hyde, J.S., and, Hankin, B.L. (2004) 'Is There a Universal Positivity Bias in Attributions? A Meta-Analytic Review of Individual, Developmental, and Cultural Differences in the Self-Serving Attributional Bias', *Psychological Bulletin*, vol.130, no.5, pp.711–747.

Miskimmon, A., O'Loughin, B., and, Roselle, L. (Eds.). (2017) *Forging the World: Strategic Narratives and International Relations.* Ann Arbor, MI: University of Michigan Press.

Mokyr, J. (2017) *Culture and Growth: The Origins of the Modern Economy.* Princeton, NJ: Princeton University Press.

Moon, B.E. (2009) 'Long Time Coming: Prospects for Democracy in Iraq', *International Security,* vol.33, no.4, pp.115–148.

Morson, G.P., and, Schapiro, M. (2017) *Cents and Sensibility: What Economics Can Learn from the Humanities.* Princeton, NJ: Princeton University Press.

Narlikar, A. (Ed.). (2010) *Deadlocks in Multilateral Negotiations: Causes and Solutions.* Cambridge: Cambridge University Press.

Narlikar, A. (2015, March 12) *The Power of the Powerless: The Politics of Poverty at the Doha Round,* Foreign Affairs.

Narlikar, A. (2020) *Poverty Narratives and Power Paradoxes in International Trade Negotiations and Beyond.* New York, NY: Cambridge University Press.

Network Weaver. (2011, July 11) *Movements, Coalitions, and System Development Networks,* Network Weaver. http://networkweaver.blogspot.com/2011/07/movements-coaliti ons-andsystem.html?m=1.

Odell, J.S., and, Tingley, D. (2013) 'Negotiating Agreements in International Relations', In J. Mansbridge and C.J. Martin (Eds.), *Negotiating Agreement in Politics* (pp.144–182). Washington, DC: American Political Science Association Task Force.

Ogunyemi, O. (2014) 'Perspective of Self-Narrative', In G. Tanzella-Nitti, I. Colagé, and A. Strumia (Eds.), *Interdisciplinary Encyclopedia of Religion and Science.* http://inters.org/selfnarrative-perspective.

Pentland, B., and, Feldman, M.S. (2007) 'Narrative Networks: Patterns of Technology and Organization', *Organization Science*, vol.8, no.5, pp.781–795.

Petzina, D., Stolper, W.F., and, Hudson, M. (1981) 'The Origin of the European Coal and Steel Community: Economic Forces and Political Interests', *Zeitschrift Für Die Gesamte Staatswissenschaft/Journal of Institutional and Theoretical Economics*, vol.137, no.3, pp.450–468.

Pisanty, A. (2014, May) 'Empowerment of Non-Governmental Actors from Outside the United States in Multi-Stakeholder Internet Governance', Paper delivered at The Hague Institute for Global Justice 2014 Global Governance Reform Initiative Conference on "The Future of Cyber Governance," The Hague, Netherlands.

Price, R. (1998) 'Reversing the Gun Sights: Transnational Civil Society Targets Land Mines', *International Organization*, vol.52, no.3, pp.613–644.

Putnam, R. (2001) 'Social Capital: Measurement and Consequences', *Canadian Journal of Policy Research*, vol.2, pp.41–51.

Raiffa, H. (2002) 'Decision Analysis: A Personal Account of How It Got Started and Evolved', *Operations Research*, vol.50, no.1, pp.179–185.

Raj, P. (2017, February 13) *The Role of Narratives in Economics*, ProMarket – Stigler Centre, University of Chicago Blog. https://promarket.org/role-narratives-economics/.

Rodan, S. (2011) 'Choosing the 'b' Parameter When Using the Bonacich Power Measure', *Journal of Social Structure*, vol.12, no.4, pp.1–23.

Saunders, H.K. (2009) 'Dialogue as a Process for Transforming Relationships', In J. Bercovitch, V. Kremenyuk, and, I.W. Zartman (Eds.), *The Sage Handbook of Conflict Resolution* (pp. 376–391). Thousand Oaks, CA: Sage.

Schiller, R. (2017) 'Narrative Economics', *American Economic Review,* vol.107, no.4, pp.967–1004.

Scott, J. (2017) *Social Network Analysis.* (4th Edn). Thousand Oaks, CA: Sage.

Sebenius, J.J. (2013) 'Level Two Negotiations: Helping the Other Side Meet Its 'Behind-the-Table Challenges', *Negotiation Journal*, vol.29, no.1, pp.7–21.

Sikkink, K. (2001) *The Justice Cascade: How Human Rights Prosecutions Are Changing World Politics.* New York, NY: W.W. Norton.

Slovic, P. (2010) 'If I Look at the Mass I Will Never Act: Psychic Numbing and Genocide', In Small, D., Lowenstein, G., and, Slovic, P. (2007) "Sympathy and Callousness: The Impact of Deliberative Thought on Donations to Identifiable and Statistical Victims', *Organizational Behavior and Human Decision Processes*, vol.102, no.2, pp.143–153.

Smith, E.E. (2017, January 12) *The Two Kinds of Stories We Tell About Ourselves,* TED Talks.

Stein, J.G. (Ed.). (1989) *Getting to the Table: The Processes of International Prenegotiation.* Baltimore, MD: The Johns Hopkins University Press.

Steketee, M., Miyaoka, A., and, Spiegelman, M. (2015) 'Social Network Analysis', *International Encyclopedia of the Social & Behavioral Sciences*, (2nd Edn) (pp.461–467). London: Elsevier.

Stone, R. (2016) 'Desistance and Identity Repair: Redemption Narratives as Resistance to Stigma', *The British Journal of Criminology,* vol.56, no.5, pp.956–975.

Suganami, H. (1999) 'Agents, Structures, Narratives', *European Journal of International Relations*, vol.5, no.3. pp.365–386.

Totterdell, P., Holman, D., and, Hukin, A. (2008) 'Social Networkers: Measuring and Examining Individual Differences in Propensity to Connect with Others', *Social Networks*, vol.30, pp.283–296.

Van der Meer, T., and, Tolsma, J. (2014) 'Ethnic Diversity and Its Effects on Social Cohesion', *Annual Review of Sociology*, vol.40, pp.459–478.

Waelchli, H., and, Shah, D.V. (1994) 'Crisis Negotiations Between Unequals: Lessons from a Classic Dialogue', *Negotiation Journal*, vol.10, no.2, pp.129–146.

Wahman, J. (2003) 'Illusions and Disillusionment: Santanaya, Narrative, and Self-Knowledge', *The Journal of Speculative Philosophy*, vol.17, no.3. pp.164–175.

Wendt, A.E. (1999) *Social Theory of International Politics*. Cambridge: Cambridge University Press.

Wheeler, B., Seddon, P., and, Morris, R. (2019, May 10) *Brexit: All You Need to Know About the UK Leaving the EU*, BBC News.

Wydick, B. (2015, January 9) *How Narratives Influence Human Behaviour,* World Economic Forum. www.weforum.org/agenda/2015/01/how-narratives-influence-humanbehaviour/.

Zaccaro, S.J., Peterson, C., and, Walker, S. (1987) 'Self-Serving Attributions for Individual and Group Performance', *Social Psychology Quarterly*, vol.50, no.3, pp.257–263.

Zartman I.W. (1985) 'Negotiating from Asymmetry: The North-South Stalemate', *Negotiation Journal*, vol.1, no.2, pp.121–138.

Zartman, I.W. (1989) 'Prenegotiation: Phases and Functions', In J.G. Stein (Ed), *Getting to the Table: The Processes of International Prenegotiation* (pp.1–17). Baltimore, MD: The Johns Hopkins University Press.

Zartman, I.W. (1994) *International Multilateral Negotiation: Approaches to the Management of Complexity*. San Francisco, CA: Jossey-Bass.

Zartman, I.W., and, Berman, M. (1982) *The Practical Negotiator*. New Haven, CT: Yale University Press.

Zunes, S., and, Feffer, J. (2007, March 9) *Iraq: The Failures of Democratization*, Foreign Policy in Focus. https://fpif.org/iraq_the_failures_of_democratization/.

2

BARGAINING IN MUSLIM ARABIA

Narrative lessons from the Qoran, Hadith, and 1001 Nights

I. William Zartman[1]

Introduction

We create our past; we are prisoners of our future. Out of the myriad sources that lie behind us, we find legitimization in those collected for the purpose; we then act in function of the destiny we have designed for ourselves. Orwell (1948, p.32) wrote, "Who controls the present controls the past. Who controls the past controls the future." As Caesar wrote, "The general tendency of people is to believe what they hope for," and he could have added, "and remember what they want to believe" (West, 2003, p.1). "Memories create our narratives, but our stories also create our memories," wrote psychologists (Tavris and Arnson, 2008).

We follow the future and create our past. We call that process our narrative, the story of our self-image, past, and future.[2] Narrative is used broadly here to refer to speech acts that, by encompassing specific frames and references, serve as a cognitive framework to assess action and events (Autesserre, 2012; Roig, 2019). As such, our narrative serves to guide what we do by giving meaning to what we have done. It covers our own self-perceived self and our actions in relation to others, when parties are standing alone, intrapersonally, and in conflict, interpersonally (Toolan, 1988, p.xii,7; Monk et al., 1996; Winslade and Monk, 2000). A society lives within a meta or historic or master or deductive or deep narrative (Haspeslagh, 2021, p.364; Orpad, 2010; Kalyvas, 2008, p.23; Narlikar and Hampson, in this volume), a whole image and identification of itself, defining what is done and acceptable in the society and excluding what is not, the "quality of norms as structuring and constraining" (Wiener, 2004, p.191). Understanding the parties' existential narratives from the past helps understand the intractable elements of conflict and enables focus on those elements that clash, preventing both continuity and reconciliation (West, 2003, p.2). In negotiation, each party's narrative serves to contain its behavior in interaction;

DOI: 10.4324/9781003203209-3

conflict is overcome when competing narratives are reconcilable and intractable when they are not. It is curious that there is little conflict- and negotiation-analysis in terms of narratives.[3]

Societies and groups have their formative myths and legends, which they can shape to inform a reliable foundation and are used as fits their purpose, and have been known to construct their stories out of whole cloth (Anderson, 1991). They set up their stories and experiences, and then organize themselves to live by them. Thus it would be enlightening to examine the construction of a meta-narrative at some moment in some context, as "their construction involves conscious or unconscious elements of selectivity—acts of suppression, inflation, and substitution, all meant to fashion the sequencing and coloration of events into an instrument that conveys what the narrator wants us to see and believe" (Epstein, 2019). As suggested, it is hard to distinguish a redemption from a condemnation (contamination) character since the two are opposite faces of the same coin of identity, indicating the two sides of agency according to the narrative.

But there is another narrative that crops up, from the bottom rather than from the top, a future-driven narrative created out of the position of the present situation in the projected outcome and not derived from the imagined past. This is an inductive or shallow narrative that explains, justifies, and determines current actions in terms of a party's declared destiny and established future. Inductively, these elements can be understood within each side's picture of the current context, not as a deep pre-established template but as an understanding that takes its meaning out of the face value of the events themselves. This is a common day-to-day practice, where parties do not seek deeper or older meanings of events in stories drawn from the distant past but take meaning out of the immediate context. There may be a coherence in these circumstantial mini-narratives, or they may each be an induced relation of the events to each other to be predetermined from the image of the future that has been established. The point is that, important as the big narrative picture is for a society, it may not always be determinant for an agent's view of events. The way in which narratives of different levels come together forms the subjective or narrative rationality, as differentiated from objective or traditional rationality, to provide the basis of decisions in negotiation (Fisher, 1984).

Narrative is also a function of agency. Actors have their own narratives, which may or may not reflect the meta-sense of society and may be tailored to fit the event, taking the future out of the hands of the past. Narratives are refracted by the perspective of observers and participants, whose actions then contribute to the evolving formulation of narrative (Kalyvas, 2003, p.479). Targets may discern a narrative quite differently from those who constructed it and may use their interpretations in ways not intended by the narrator. The event-based narrative may then eventually play into the broader story, as feedback feeds the basic flow. As always, the long term is made of many short terms, but also vice versa. The subject of this inquiry is to investigate the relation between the deductive meta-narrative of a society and any possible inductive contextual narrative that may compete with it. It examines the influence of the meta-narrative and compares it with more immediate levels and sources, with the hypothesis that it should be formative the more it retains the historic roots of the acting groups. But if the hypothesis is nullified, what takes its place?

For the national or meta-level to exist presupposes that there is a coherent past, constructed by will and evidence. The more established and tangible the evidence from the past, the more the job of creation has something to work with, with competing and contradicting pieces of past challenge the task of creation.[4] The clearest case has been developed by the analysis of the Mahabharat as the bedrock of Hindu Indian identity and its reflection as the narrative basis of current Indian negotiation (Narlikar and Narlikar, 2014). India may not be unique in the clarity of its antecedents, but it nonetheless does not meet many other societies providing as clear a past root on which a contemporary narrative could be grounded. Arguably the most striking exception is the Arab-Muslim world, standing firmly on two (and perhaps more) traditional sources that come from the 8th–9th century Golden Age of the civilization's historic (even if not ancient) culture. The following material will synthesize a meta-narrative from basic Arabo-Muslim tradition in Part I, and then compare it to involved parties' own narratives in an intrasocietal conflict in Part II, in the search for a link between the two.

The societal narrative from tradition

"History is the Muslim community on the march" (Smith, 1977). The oldest source of a historical basis of Muslim society is the 8th-century Qoran, which sets up an immutable basis and provides existential relevance for the identity and practice of the *umma* (Muslim community), complemented by the *hadith* of the same period, containing sayings of and about the Prophet. The Qoran has 114 *surat* (chapters), arranged in the book by length. The *hadith* is not canonized but the fullest collection is by Mohammed Ismael al-Bukhari (846a), containing 7563 sayings, many repetitive, of which a selection of 3269 (al-Bukhari, 846b) has mainly been used here. The other source from a slightly later period are the 9th-century (but also earlier) stories of *Thousand and One Nights*, translated by Edward William Lane (1930) in 1388 8pt-type pages. The Qoran is occasionally quoted (and God frequently invoked) in the 1001 stories. Exegeses of these works have been performed many times, but they have not been analyzed as the meta-narrative of Arabo-Muslim relations with special attention to conflict management and negotiation, as this brief effort will attempt to do. The resulting meta-narrative from the three sources will be then related to participants' narratives in a current puzzle of the 21st century, as a comparison and application.

Limiting the analysis to "negotiation" would provide little information. In fact, the word does not exist in Arabic, the closest being *mufawada,* referring to commercial dealings, much as *negotio* (*négoce*) initially had a purely commercial meaning in Western languages. In fact, the Qoran says only a little about negotiation, being primarily occupied with the establishment of proper belief and the interpretation of justice in judgment over disputes: "those who declare that they believe...can have no Faith unless they make Thee judge in all disputes between them." (S4:60,65). However, it does also emphasize reconciliation among Believers, implicitly by arbitration (Pilotti et al., 2020, pp.335–338, 340). "If two parties among the Believers fall into a fight, make peace between them... with justice and be fair, for God loves those who are fair (and just)" (S49:9). It also recognizes the sanctity of treaties of alliance, in an oblique historic reference (S8:72). Most of the relevant stories in the *hadith* also refer to judgments by the Prophet (arbitration) rather than conflict resolution worked out to be the parties themselves; "[Mohammed said,] 'Let us go and bring about a reconciliation'" in a dispute within a Muslim tribe (al-Bukhari 846a, 54:2693). There is less concern about reconciliation with non-Muslims but still enough need to establish principles for there to be some general references: "Strike terror into (the hearts of) the enemies...but if the enemy incline toward peace, do thou (also) incline toward peace and trust in God" (S8:60–61). A historical commentator noted, "The pagans asked to meet the Prophet Mohammed (GBPUH) in order to talk about reconciliation and other worldly interests. This all happened through the channels of negotiation" (al-Zuhaili, 1998). Nonetheless, out of these pieces of the narrative some cultural principles for negotiating behavior can be distilled (Pilotti et al., 2020).

The tales that Shahrazad told to the Sultan to save her (and many others') life are also only indirectly rich in advice for Arab negotiators. They are mainly concerned with making one's way through the adversities of life, spiced with many sexual adventures (with women as either the object or as a wily adversary). Although "merchant" is the most frequently referenced non-political profession in the stories, there is little treatment of behavior in commercial dealings and nothing on the typical Arab market bargaining (Khuri, 1968); offers are either taken, most frequently, or rejected. Yet enough material can be gleaned from the source to provide some behavioral characteristics of relevance.

The resulting meta-narrative provides a basic understanding available to Arabo-Muslim society reflecting a coherent story of societal relations through negotiation. It incorporates fundamental values and associated behaviors drawn from traditional interaction to paint a story of life in the Golden Age derived from divine revelation and human deviation in search for good guidance. These stories, legends, admonitions, and other relevant material will be examined here, first in relation to the three modes of negotiation: concession (zero-sum, win-lose, divide), compensation (win-win, exchange), and construction (reframing, redefining), and then in regard to two other important elements of negotiation behavior—consideration of alternatives to negotiated agreement and of the opposing party (Narlikar and Narlikar, 2014). Concessions are a mode of compromise in distributive bargaining where the disputed item is split in some proportion between/among the parties. Compensation or trading comes from integrative bargaining and provides a more satisfactory, positive-sum mode since parties buy their favored outcome in exchange for the other's favored outcome and a Nash (1950) or Homans (1961) solution is obtained. The other integrative mode is obtained by redefining the conflict in a way that provides benefits for both sides. In addition to these standard negotiation modes, the concept of alternatives, used both as a measure of negotiating power (best alternative to a negotiated agreement [BATNA]) and as a threat, bears examination, as do attitudes toward other parties, two concepts important in negotiation analysis.

Concession

According to the Qoran, in settling disputes by division, parties should be guided by the same principle of equality that Mohamed uses in making his arbitration judgments, basically applying some guiding value of justice (3:550, 3:534, 3:631); no other standard principle appears other than following God's ways (Pilotti et al., 2020, p.340). "Be just; that is next to piety" (5:8). In one of the few references to a negotiation in the *hadith*, unclear at best, two parties had apparently negotiated to reduce a debt in half, and the Prophet endorsed the decision, supporting a principle of split the difference. In the crafty world of 1001 Nights, there are a number of occasions in which heirs equally divide their inheritance or brothers split their common holdings, following an accepted pattern of allocation that obviated negotiation.

Compensation

The same value of fairness hovers over the idea of exchange in the religious literature, although in compensation the exact meaning of fairness is in the eye of the beholder (Zartman et al., 1996). While no specific injunctions are offered, the spirit of exchange is noted in the Qoran and illustrated in the *hadith*. Indeed, true faith is presented as the ultimate "bargain or trade" or "supreme triumph" in which "striving (your utmost) in the cause of God with your wealth and your person" is the payment for forgiveness of sins and admission "to a garden beneath which rivers flow and to beautiful mansions in gardens of eternity" (S61:10–12), in other words, a real deal. The only instance in the *hadith* where the details of an exchange are recorded is in negotiations for the 628 Hudaibiya ten-year truce between Mohammed's forces at Medina and the Quraish in Mecca (3:891). Negotiations began with an exchange of prisoners (no record is given about any equivalence of numbers). In the process, Mohammed demanded appropriate reference to himself and to God, refuge for a Muslim captive, and permission for Muslims to make a pilgrimage to the Ka'ba in Mecca, among others. He gave in on the names, kept the returnee, and got permission to visit the Ka'ba but delayed a year (the latter aroused complaints from Muslims but Mohammed's companion, Abu Bakr, pointed out that they had been promised a pilgrimage but the Prophet had not said when!). In exchange the Quraish got a ten-year truce, at the cost of some changes in wording.

Compensation and exchange appear much more often over the *Thousand and One Nights*. Indeed, the series begins with a deal of compensation—a story in exchange for a night of life—and continues with further tales of compensation which covers the first three nights (L 15–28) in the story of the Merchant and the Jinn, who sells away a part of his revenge in exchange for a good story, leaving him revengeless but shaking with delight. Marid the Fisherman made a charitable exchange with another Jinn, who agreed to do a service that would enrich Marid forever if the Jinn were liberated from the bottle, in the sixth night's story (L47).

A basic rule for fixing value in exchange was enunciated by Joodar's mother around the 615th night: "When plenty is wanting, man is content with the smallest thing, but when plenty is at hand, man desires to eat [a lot] of what is good" (L961). On closing the fifth night's story, the poet suavely ties exchange to the virtue of fairness: "Had they acted equitably, they had experienced equity; but they oppressed, wherefore fortune oppressed them...and fortune is blameless" (L46). In an unusually charitable interpretation of equity in exchange, Abu-Seer, who introduced the idea of a hammam to a city, convinced its king to charge only what each individual could pay, in the tale around the 937th night (L1272).

Construction

Framing an issue for negotiation provides the crucial setting for the process to continue; it identifies a new terrain or formula on which the interaction will take place (Zartman et al., 1996). The Qoran actually refers to the earliest recorded case, historically, in which a formula is established to permit subsequent bargaining over details, in the destruction of Sodom (although the Qoranic version misses the point). The account is scattered throughout the Qoran in pieces (7:80–84; 11:74–83; 15:51–77; 26:160–175; 27:54–58; 37:133–138; 51:31–37; 54:33–39), but it actually is only in the Biblical version, in Genesis 18, that the bargaining is recounted. The towns of Sodom and Gomorrah had been practicing unseemly acts to which the town gave its name (no longer unseemly in our day) and God vowed to destroy them; Abraham, however, a good man, pleaded that the few righteous souls in Sodom not be destroyed with the rest. He began by reminding God that as "Judge of all nations" his defining quality was to "do right" and that "far be it from Thee...to slay the righteous with the wicked" (Gen. 18:25; cf Qoran 11:74). Having thus framed the debate in terms of righteousness, Abraham turned from formula to detail and began to bargain over numbers to be spared: 50 righteous souls, then 45, then 40, then, then 20, and finally 10 (of which only one family was found and the city was destroyed). By establishing the negotiation on the formula of righteousness, which opened the way to bargaining over details in the form of numbers, Abraham (and God) established a basic model of negotiations, an insight missed in the Qoranic account of the same event. The Qoran (S29:46) urges believers to "dispute not with people of the Book, except in the best way," which the exegesist has commented to mean "finding true common grounds of belief to overcome incompatibility of positions." Other than in that one elusive passage, neither God nor Mohamed offers any advice about reconstructing conflict in a way so as to make it manageable.

Shahrazad is more helpful in illustrating the possibilities of reframing. Indeed, her very deal with sultan redefines the original of bargain of "one night in exchange for martyrdom" to "another night in exchange for a story" and no longer about martyrdom at all. Lady Dunya, finally around the 137th night (L401–402), when confronted with an altruistic story about men and birds, changes the reference for her image of men, and reframes her entire view of the opposite sex. Similarly, Zubeydeh disdained Ala ed-Deen when told he had elephantiasis, but when she heard him sing, she found a reframing referent, formed a different image of him, and marrying him, in a story around the 250th night (L604). Reframing the argument and the image is typical in the stories. Although the literature is not rich in advice or examples, the treatment of the three modes of negotiation provides basic ingredients in the culture's narrative on conflict management.

The other

The attitudes toward other parties in the scriptures and the stories are complex. In principle, they are divided between attitudes toward fellow Muslims (*dar al-islam*) and attitudes toward infidels (*dar al-harb*). Among Believers, the purpose of dispute settlement is to restore the cohesion of the Community *umma*) based on forgiveness and justice (Pilotti et al., 2020, p.337, 341). By some surat, Jews are literally beyond the pale, evil and condemned (S2:65, 5:60, 7:166). In reality, the division is not that manichean. Believers are urged to stick together: "The Believers, men and women, are protectors one of another; they enjoin what is just and forbid what is evil." (S9:71); "Be not like those who are divided against themselves" (S3:103) and the *hadith* (3:594) echoed. "Don't differ, for nations before your differed and perished." Believers are also repeatedly advised not to seek friends among unbelievers (S3:118, 4:144, 5:57; 60:13). Yet there can be alliances and agreements between the two *dar*s (al-Zuhaili 199x). "God forbids you not—with regard to those not of [your] faith...from dealing kindly and justly with them, for God loves those who are just." (S60:8). As a general injunction on conflict management,

> If two parties among the Believers fall into a fight, make peace between them, but if one of them transgress beyond bounds against the other, then fight against the one who transgresses until it complies with the command of God. But if it complies, make peace between them with justice and be fair, for God loves those who are fair.
>
> *S49:9*

This will be especially important in examining contemporary behavior in the case below.

In the Nights, behavior toward other Believers varies according to whether they are honest, fair, *shari'a*-abiding, respectful of authority, or not, and the tales are full of all sorts of behavior toward fellow Believers. Miscreants are decapitated freely, whether Muslim or not; Blacks, Christians, and Jews are regarded variously but frequently on a par with Believers. The situations are numerous enough and diverse so as not to bear enumeration; suffice it to note that there are no tight ascriptive categories that contain no internal variation or external separation in behavior.

So what behavior does the narrative prescribe in regard to an opponent? What matters instead of ascriptive distribution are achievemental characteristics, notably the fairness and justice already noted. One who acts fairly and justly is entitled to good treatment, and those who do not are not, whatever the substance of their disagreement. Repeated stories echo the distinction discussed above as enunciated in the Qoran. Following closely the good advice given, above, most interaction is among Believers but it is as varied as interaction with non-Believers (who are generally not friends, to be sure). Any attempt to pull out a single story beyond fairness as an illustration would not pay justice to the variations, but basic ideas about any other would seem to provide a helpful ingredient for reconciliation.

Alternatives

Generally, actors in the Arabo-Muslim literature make their offers straightforwardly, with little reference to BATNAs regarded as a measure of power where the party with the more favorable alternative to a negotiated outcome has the strongest position (Zartman and Rubin, 2005), or as a tactical threat, where the parties bargain against or worsen each other's BATNA in order to make it change its position. When there is a choice, the alternative usually is a punishment: "The recompense for an injury is an injury equal thereto, but if a person forgives and makes reconciliation, his reward is due from God;" and "Life for life, eye for eye, nose for nose, ear for ear, tooth for tooth, and wounds equal for equal. But if anyone remits the retaliation by way of charity, it is an act of atonement for himself," from the Qoran (5:45).

However, few negotiating dynamics are associated with alternatives in the literature. In the one brief instance where some negotiating exchanges are recorded, in the establishment of the Hudaibiya treaty with the Quraish, noted above, there were no threats or alternatives offered, and the BATNA was renewed war: positions were stated, countered, and a compromise accepted by the negotiators, although the Prophet had some trouble having the agreement accepted by his followers, a frequent agency problem (3:891).

The record

Together, the dictations, traditions, and narrations of the traditional sources provide a basic narrative for conflict management behavior that is standard and useful, a meta-narrative since it covers the whole *umma*. It is not full of tactical wiles or strategic insights but it provides a basis for positive relations. Fundamental values of fairness and justice are enunciated, with the details left up to the interpreter; judgments in the *Nights* tales are sometime hasty but even Haroon al-Rashid and the Prophet were human. The opponent is to be judged by such achievemental criteria rather than ascriptive characteristics, although some biases do emerge on occasion. The three modes of negotiation are recognized and practiced without any further behavioral elaboration. In all this, the narrative resembles early negotiation Book of Proverbs, treatises from those of de Callières (1716), Pequet (1737), and de Felice (1778) of the 18th century in France to Ury, Paton, and Fisher (1982) in 20th century America, although the narrative comes armored with religious dicta (Pilotti et al., 2020, p.335). The underlying dynamic to the process is judgment: God's judgment of actions, the Prophet's judgement as a guide, and the actors' judgment of others, rather than a dynamic process, which even in the contemporary world took a while to take root as an analytical approach. Members of the *umma* could find in these writings a general narrative on how they should regard the conflict management and negotiation processed as their Book of Proverbs but without much tactical or analytical advice.

The intrasocietal narratives of modern negotiation

So many things can weigh in on the influence of a traditional meta-narrative on modern society and its actors that it becomes difficult to explain the impact of the inheritance other than by coincidence. It is not evident how literally or exactly individual actors could be expected to translate general guidelines into specific actions, and mechanical application of the traditional meta-narratives reduced in size to fit the specific event is unlikely. More direct evidence would be through specific citation, but admittedly not all inherited traits are explicitly admitted. Whether it is due to a millennial time gap, to unheard signals and transmission noise, a level of analysis shift, or to modern context, corruption opens further inquiry but does not furnish further evidence. In a given context actors may operate within their own narratives, rooting their actions in a story of their own, drawn from past lessons and legends but also from future purposes and projects and what has to be done to accomplish them.

Parties in a conflict or other relationship begin with a micro-narrative of themselves, a story of who they are (Cassan and deBailliancourt, 2019, pp.35–68; Trakic et al., 2019). They then turn to the relationship with the other party, made to fit the beginning of the story and project it on the story of the other party, the substories of the other branching out from the initial self-story (Cassan and deBailliancourt, 2019, pp.69–1020). The narrative from each side meets and overlaps with the image of self and the relationship held by the other. The more that overlap harmonizes, the more likely or the easier the resolution of the conflict and the reconciliation of the parties (Winslade and Monk, 2000). If the harmonization does not naturally occur, effort is needed to make the two stories fit together. But the more coherent the individual narratives in their disharmony, the more obdurate the conflict. In this process, the meta-narrative can be useful. It can serve as the basis for the micro-narratives, providing the basic ingredient, differently interpreted for each party, or as the common table for bringing the opposing micro-narratives together. Or it can wilt in the heat of the moment and cede full place to the micro-narrative (Trakic et al., 2019).

Saudi Arabia and Qatar, both absolute monarchies, whose citizens with civil rights constitute only a part of their population (60% and 17%, respectively), have squared off in a vitriolic confrontation since 2017, forewarned since 2013. The confrontation is a family squabble, clothed in status rivalries, based on competing modernization strategies, and involving major policy realignments in the Middle East and beyond (Serwer and Zartman, 2019; al-Jaber and Neubauer, 2018; Nuruzzaman, 2015; Krieg, 2019; Ehteshami and Mohammadi, 2017). The two countries are founding allies in the Gulf Cooperation Council (GCC), established in 1981 under the predominance of Saudi Arabia, but since then they have taken different paths. Although the roots of the conflict run deep through the intertwined family relations, it was the Arab Spring beginning in 2011 that caused the rift to sharpen, as Saudi Arabia supported the authoritarian rulers (except in Syria), and Qatar supported Muslim Brotherhood affiliates and then developed more radical allies, notably Turkey, to cover its escape from Saudi predominance. In response to this split, Riyadh declared an embargo on all Qatari relations in 2017, and the measures that both sides have taken to entrench that status quo have only hardened and widened the gulf. The conflict is objectively resolvable with a grain of tolerance—mediation was tried by Kuwait and the United States and failed—but is subjectively frozen. Objectively stalemated, the parties have reached out to their external relations to remove the pain, a mutually unpainful stalemate (Serwer and Zartman, 2019). What is the narrative lens through which each side views the situation?

The following narratives are constructed out of quotations from interviews with Saudi and Qatari officials conducted in Riyadh and Doha on 14–17 January and 20–23 January 2019, respectively, and in Washington at the end of 2018. They are presented as raw data rather than being edited as a single statement, with the sources indicated in brackets, much as the quotations in the first part of this study were presented but as longer citations in order to keep the flavor. A synthesis will be given at the end.

Saudi Arabia

"National unity is promoted through dialogue. The culture of dialogue and coexistence should be spread, to bring people together. Saudi Arabia is made up of a diverse society with many tribes, regions, religious sects, and regions. It used to be very isolated but now is reaching in, to bring national pride and unity, and reaching out, to come together with its neighbors. People must be prepared for how to deal with conflict by learning how to accept ideas of tolerance. Initially, this idea focused on elites, but now opened up more to youth. Conservatives are always against change, afraid that change is coming from the outside, as a threat to one's own identity. Some misunderstandings persist, but we no longer seek comfort in isolating anyone. Family is very important; the family's views influence one's morals and values [Center for National Dialog]. We are part of the same tribes. It is definite that we are family. The crisis is not between the people, but rather between the governments. We are cousins. We share the same last names. They are our brothers and sisters, but we disagree [King Saud University]. The issue is with the government, not the people. Media war is a mistake from both sides [King Faisal Center for Research].

There have been so many years of tribes, people being divided, living in the desert. People are willing to give up some rights for stability and unity. There is no one model for change. Education is number one priority in Saudi Arabia [Human Rights Commission]. We are Bedouins, practical people. We just care if it works; the final product is most important [Ministry of Foreign Affairs]. Saudi Arabia is moving to be part of the world community; Qatar criticizes its efforts [King Saud University].

So why don't pragmatics work in the crisis with Qatar? Pride, Arab blood, and ego among the royal families and leaders are preventing rational behavior. It just takes someone to reach out, then things will fall in place [Prince Saud Al-Faisal Institute]. We did not start this crisis. After issues in 2014, we signed an agreement, but they broke their word. The crisis is not simply confined to politics. There is concern for social repercussions, namely relations between people even if/after the conflict is settled. Saudis and Qataris attack each other on social media. Even if the governments settle, the gap of hostility between the people will remain [*Al Riyadh*].

[The Gulf Crisis] is not a mutual conflict. One side [Qatar] did wrong. Qatar does not have [legitimate] grievances against Saudi Arabia. Saudi Arabia is not doing anything proactive: simply not dealing with them. We did not do anything wrong, they are the ones who need to fix it [MFA]. Why are they doing this? They are our cousins. We signed an agreement, but they broke it. They need to understand that there is a limit. Is there a strong leader in Qatar that can confront the Muslim Brotherhood? Some family members and leaders have left from the Al-Thani [the tribal leadership of Qatar] and have established organizations against Qatar. Where did family relations go wrong? All families have good and evil, but the Al-Thani Qataris are twisted. Al-Thani is not the same tribe as Al-Saud [Minister of Education]. Qatar broke the [2013] agreement not to support terrorists, not to support Yemeni insurgent, and not to interfere in internal affairs [KSU].

It is the pride and ego of the Qataris that has prolonged the crisis. Saudi Arabia and West agree that what Qatar is doing is wrong, but there is disagreement on how Saudi Arabia is going about the situation. The negative cost aspect for Saudi Arabia is the negative publicity. It is an uphill battle due to ingrained perceptions. It is not Saudi Arabia's objective to create turmoil in Qatar. Our destinies are intertwined, whether we like it or not. Qatar is moving in the right direction. The crisis will be solved, just unsure when. It depends on ego and gestures. The crisis will not be solved from outsiders being involved [MFA]. There has been no progress since the beginning: it is a stalemate and it will not be resolved quickly. Qatar is full of contradictions and double standards. Saudis are trying to stabilize region. Brothers, family, same tribes, feel unsafe when a friend is working against you. It was an unclear picture. Saudi Arabia drew the line, now is a clearer picture with camps established. Only political pressure (not economic) will change Qatar's behavior [KFCR]. This is an oversimplification, but why this perception [Prince Mohammed ben Nayaf]?"

Qatar

"The Gulf Crisis is the story of a small neighbor—big neighbor. Saudi Arabia is the hegemon that wants to continue to dominate. After 1971 Qatari independence, Qatar followed in line with Saudi policy. Emir Khalifa bin Hamad al-Thani went to Saudi Arabia every year to kiss the hand of the Saudi King. His sons did not like this show of subservience, perceived as meddling by Saudi Arabia [Georgetown University in Doha]. Everyone was shocked that a son could challenge father, and the 1995 change in power is the root of the crisis. The new emir, Hamad bun Khalifa al-Thani, emerged with a different vision to change in the status quo that Saudi Arabia has always been defending. The initial Saudi reaction was to stand with the father because they were comfortable with him and knew his policies. The Saudi impression of Hamad was that he was very outspoken; they saw the coup as betraying the Gulf. Family relations have been good as long as Qatari families fall in line with the Saudis. Some al-Thanis were not happy with Hamad and plotted a countercoup a year later, with attributed Saudi and UAE [United Arab Emirates] support; everyone interferes with everyone here [al-Jazeera Center for Studies].

Hamad put Qatar on the world map, carved out a presence. With ambition, drive, and determination to change, he wanted to not simply follow Saudi Arabia. He turned gas into liquid [LNG] with help of the Japanese, built a sustainable economy, locked in US support with the US at al-Uneini air base and made Qatar more self-sufficient and stable [Doha Institute for Graduate Studies; GUD]. Sheikh Hamad abdicated in 2013 in favor of his son, Tamim bin Hamad al-Thani, new Emir [Hamad bin Khalifa University]. The withdrawal of the GCC ambassadors followed in 2014: how can you do that in the Gulf? They are part of same family [DIGS]. Personal bad blood between King Salman and King Hamad? Yes, plays a role. What role? Why does this question keep being avoided? [al-JCS].

There have always been differences and different views in the Gulf. Crisis would not have occurred without dynamics impact from Arab Spring. Change comes from within. The question for Saudi Arabia is to maintain hegemony through force or leadership? Qatar wanted change; leadership is idealistic. Qatar supports stability through good governance [Qatar University]. Qatar stopped interference after the 2014 agreement and made offers to come to the table and negotiate, but the blockading countries [of the GCC] say no, we must meet their demands first [al-JCS]. Qatar cannot be bound by GCC or Saudi Arabia [DIGS].

Those in power making decisions in Saudi Arabia do not understand Qataris and do not have the right networks [GUD]. Qatar has a different approach to the region than Saudi Arabia: inclusive versus authoritarian/repressive. Saudi Arabia wants to control the region. Saudis are archaic and conservative; Qatar is deepening its strategic ability by hedging bets and diversifying relationships [GUD]. The two states have competing perspectives on security in the region. Saudi Arabia wants to be protected only by external powers. Qatar believes sustainable security is shaped by the region itself [al-JIS]. Qatar will continue down the path of self-sufficiency and keep new relations open with outside countries from Africa, Southeast Asia, etc. We have never thought of the self-sufficient model/strategy before. We have always been very relaxed, why replicate what Saudi Arabia has? We needed to diversify our supply chains. We transformed our consequences into gains [FM].

We, as a group, have failed institutionally in the region. These are demands for capitulation, not discussion. They are impossible to meet. Yes, we had a 2014 agreement and signed it. To my understanding, the agreement was fulfilled. There was an issue with the agreement, but the solution should not be a blockade. The quartet asked Qatar to sign a blank check. It was not an agreement, but rather Qatar had to agree with everyone else. How can you cooperate if basic elements of communication do not exist? This crisis will take time, there is no indication of it ending soon [FM].

The situation is being managed ridiculously, stupidity at its best. This is not 21st century diplomacy. We are modern countries, but [the crisis] is run by a middle age feudal system. Families do not like each other. People are tired of the policies of leaders. This is not a logical conflict, it is a personal one [HbKU]. There needs to be a united goal. Maintaining dialogue, itself, is a value. The severing of ties with Qatar is negative [Rasanah]. Social media, twitter, deep animosity, fraying of kinship bonds, same last names tweeting against each other—it's a question of kinship/family identity versus national identity [GUD]. Nobody wants this crisis to continue [Al-JCS].

Saudi Arabia is the big brother, yet poses as a threat at times [Saudi Crown Prince]. Mohammed bin Salman is now stable domestically, he eliminated/suppressed all of his rivals. But he is not stable externally/internationally, success depends on his relationship with Trump [Al-JCS]. The UAE are the brains. Saudi Arabia is the muscle. Why are they doing this? Political change in Saudi Arabia and the UAE is driving this action. They want a success story. Adventurous, rogue policies of a young leader who easily miscalculates his influence? Too much of an oversimplification. The Saudis want Qatar to be like a Bahrain [who follows obediently]. There is a double standard. They commit human rights violations. This crisis will take time, there is no indication of it ending soon [FM].

It was an act of war. We are very inter-related socially, half of the families here are connected with Saudi Arabia. It's political, so let us sit at the table and talk/resolve. Why don't you [Saudi Arabia] accept that we have a different point of view. Disagreeing does not mean that we cannot work together. It is a battle of sovereignty. We have reached out politically. The one red line on demands/concessions is sovereignty. We are willing to come to the table before any preconditions. Let us have a dialogue. We believe that Kuwait is the right mediator. Even if this crisis is settled and borders reopen, things will never be the same [FM]. Family connections will not repair overnight. At the people level, the damage is done. Even when the crisis is solved, it will take a generation to move on [Brookings Doha Center]. The main social issue is the ties between families: revisionists [Qatar] versus the status quo.

Hope that the government finds a solution by [the World Cup scheduled for Doha in] 2022. Irrational leaders, petty. The Arab world has a common identity, but with intricate details and differences. Complex society in Qatar that is split into three: ultra conservatives, moderate conservatives, and absolute liberals. Qataris more excited after blockade, 100% support now, not held back anymore [Supreme Committee for Delivery and Legacy]. Each country has used the crisis to increase a sense of nationalism, rallying behind the leader [BDC]."

The record

The narratives that emerge from this mosaic of statements are largely internally coherent. Saudi Arabia nurtures an injured hegemony, Qatar an insulted sovereignty. Saudi Arabia sees agreements broken; Qatar sees opportunities to strike out on its own. Saudi Arabia sees a conservative path to modernization; Qatar sees secular openings. The sides of the dichotomy could be extended. Agreement comes only in that the conflict has split a large family, led by two (or three) young impetuous leaders, and is intractable for a long future even though it should not be. The two narratives are not amenable to mutual alignment or coming into joint focus, and a portion of each specifically rules out concessions or compensation. Interactions are all distributive, with little room for integrative exchange. Reframing is open for consideration because it is not alluded to; there are plenty of new frames available—notably GCC cooperation, the mega-family, *khaliji* heritage, as well as Qoranic injunctions—but their pursuit is ruled out. In a word, the conflict has created its own unbridgeable narratives, centered on rich young upstarts as absolute monarchs in the midst of court intrigue.

In the heat of practice, the two narratives are drawn from the conflictual relation itself rather than guiding it, locked into the present/future rather than drawing on the past. Remarkably, neither draws any meaning or guidance from the meta-narrative of the civilization in which it is rooted. Neither makes any reference to the millennial past, and neither is troubled by its frequent transgression of the guidance it provides. Except for overhanging mentions of family, there are no more general references to undergird it. There is no place or grounding in the meta-narrative, no coincidence or correlation of elements between the meta and the immediate, and certainly no citation of the former by the later. In fact, it would do the parties good to go back and read their Qoran and study their *hadith*, let alone their Night reading.

It is tempting to stop here as a conclusion, but it is also inviting to push the inquiry a bit further. Do the immediate narratives have no roots other than the immediacy? If not roots, each can find a comfortable sitting in each side's not too distant past and present situation. Although there are no Wahabi quotations or references, Saudi Arabia's story draws on its Wahhabi past and the movement's rivalry with the Sublime Porte of Ottoman Istanbul, Qatar's ally today, and more recently its peninsular and petroleum hegemony, but these are much more recent—by a millennium—than the mega narrative of the Qoran and the Thousand Nights. It would be, literally, out of character for Riyadh to suddenly switch to another story, to locate a new narrative with which it would feel comfortable. Qatar's middle-level story is marked by the fact that it precisely has very shallow roots, leaving the current narrative free to roam. While wandering youth tends to settle down when mid-life sets in, it takes a while and tends to find its roots in its own immediate experience and its imagined future rather than in inherited more distant stories. (As of May 2021, the dispute had been papered over and the embargo at least partially lifted).

In a time of change, an examination of other countries of the Middle East would probably come to the same conclusion, that current self-stories find their sources in recent memories and reflect what they want to project, rather than in a shared meta-narrative from a common heritage. Like the conclusions of any study, this would be a fine subject for further studies. "The results of the battlefield reinforced preconceived notions of warfare. People learned the lessons that they were inclined to learn, and even those were strongly affected by their political implications" (Lorge, 2005, p.86). We create our past to fit our current needs and are locked in by our views of our prospects. We imagine the past and recall our future.

Notes

1 I am grateful for the thorough assistance of Patrick Makles in the collection of Saudi and Qatari data.
2 For a related study, see I.W. Zartman, (Ed.). (2001).
3 One has to go back to Kelman's (1965) seminal collection on *International Behavior* to find a long section—half the book—devoted to "images"; however, after a few chapters, that discussion veers off into social structure, external effects, ad public opinion. Since then, the approach has been eschewed, although other terms may pick up pieces of the concept insightfully (Campbell and Docherty, 2004).
4 Arguably, some recent countries, such as the United States, have not much sense of distant past at all and no national narrative, and that absence itself forms part of an eclectic pragmatic narrative quite unlike these with coherent evidence. As a ^country^, of course, America has a long history, but has been unable to come to its antecedents

before the national era; native American history could provide an enriching ingredient for a narrative, although reference myths and stories are difficult to pull together in a coherent whole. Strikingly, Algeria, Morocco, and now tentatively Saudi Arabia, have made efforts to incorporate the long pre-national history. The warped "1619" project is an attempt to fabricate an alternative narrative (Mezran, 2007).

References

Anderson, B. (1991) *Imagined Communities: Reflections on the Origin and Spread of Nationalism.* London: Verso.

Autesserre, S. (2019) 'Dangerous Tales: Dominant Narratives on the Congo and their Unintended Consequences', *African Affairs*, vol.111, no.443, pp.202–220.

al-Bukhari, M.I. (n.d.) *Sahih al-Bukhari.* Islamic Finder, 846a.

al-Bukhari, M.I. (2008) *Hadith al-Bukhari.* Forgotten Books, 846b.

Al-Jaber, K., and, Neubauer, S. (2018) *The Gulf Crisis: Reshaping Alliances in the Middle East.* Gulf International Forum.

Al-Zuhaili, W. (1998) 'Negotiation in Islam', *PIN Points: The Process of International Negotiation Project*, vol.12, pp.1–4.

Campbell, M.C, and, Docherty, J.S. (2004) 'Framing: What's in a Frame? (That Which We Call a Rose by Any Other Name Would Smell as Sweet)', *Marquette Law Review,* vol.87, no.4, pp.769–781.

Cassan, H., and, deBailliencourt, M.P. (2019) *Traité pratique de négociation.* Larcier.

De Callières, F. (1716, translated in 2002) *De la manière de négocier avec les princes.* Paris, France: Dalloz.

De Felice, B. (1778, translated in 1976) 'Negotiations, or the Art of Negotiating,' In I.W. Zartman (Ed.), *The 50% Solution: How to Bargain Successfully with Hijackers, Strikers, Bosses, Oil Magnates, Arabs, Russians, and Other Worthy Opponents In This Modern World.* Garden City, NY: Anchor.

Ehteshami, A., and, Mohammadi, A. (2017, June) 'Saudi Arabia's and Qatar's Discourses and Practices in the Mediterranean', *MEDReset* Working Papers, no.6.

Epstein, J. (2019, November 29) 'Politicians' Abuse of Language Is a Trend, Not a 'Narrative', *Wall Street Journal.*

Fisher, W.R. (1984, March) 'Narration As a Human Communication Paradigm: The Case of Public Moral Argument', *Communication Monographs,* vol.51, no.1, pp.1–22.

Haspeslagh, S. (2021) 'The 'Linguistic Ceasefire': Negotiating in an Age of Proscription', *Security Dialogue,* vol.52, no.4, pp.361–379.

Homans, G.C. (1961) *Social Behavior: Its Elementary Forms.* New York: Harcourt, Brace & World.

Kalyvas, S.N. (2003, September) 'The Ontology of Political Violence', *Perspectives on Politics*, vol.1, no.3, pp.475–494.

Kalyvas, S.N. (2008) *The Logic of Violence in Civil Wars.* Cambridge: Cambridge University Press.

Kelman, H. (1965) *International Behavior: A Socio-Psychological* Analysis. New York, NY: Holt, Rineheart and Winston.

Khuri, F. (1968) 'The Etiquette of Bargaining in the Middle East,' *American Anthropologist*, vol.70, no.4, pp.698–706.

Krieg, A. (Ed.). (2019) *Divided Gulf: The Anatomy of a Crisis.* London: Palgrave MacMillan.

Lane, E.W. (Trans.). (1930) *The Thousand and One Nights or Arabian Nights Entertainments.* London: Chatto & Windus.

Lorge, P. (2005) *War, Politics and Society in Modern China, 900–1795.* New York, NY: Routledge.

Mezran, K. (2007) *Negotiation and Construction of National Identities.* Leiden, Belgium: Martinus Nijhoff Publishers.

Monk, G., Winslade, J., Crocket, K., and, Epston, D. (Eds.). (1996) *Narrative Therapy in Practice: The Archaeology of Hope.* San Francisco, CA: Jossey-Bass.

Narlikar, A., and, Narlikar, A. (2014) *Bargaining with a Rising India: Lessons from the Mahabharata.* Oxford: Oxford University Press.

Nash, J. (April 1950) 'The Bargaining Problem', Econometrica, vol.18, no.2, pp.155–162. www.jstor.org/stable/1907266.

Nuruzzaman, M. (2015, November) 'Gulf Cooperation Council, Qatar, and Dispute Mediation', *Contemporary Arab Affairs,* vol.7, no.4, pp.1–19.

Orpad, L. (2010, October) 'The Preamble in Constitutional Interpretation', *International Journal of Constitutional Law,* vol.8, no.4, pp.714–738.

Orwell, G. (1948) *1984.* New York, NY: Penguin Books.

Pequet, A. (1737, re-published in 2019) *Discours sur l'Art de Négocier.* Paris, France: Hachette Livre-BNF.

Pilotti, M.A.E., El Alaoui, K., Hasan Salameh, M., Singh, S., and, Al Mulhem, H. (2020) 'The New and the Old: A Qualitative Analysis of Modes of Conflict Resolution in the Kingdom of Saudi Arabia', *International Negotiation,* vol.25, no.2, pp.329–344.

Roig, J. (2019) *Engaging Narratives for Peacebuilding.* PartnersGlobal: Alliance for Peacebuilding.

Serwer, D., and, Zartman, I.W. (Eds.). (2019) *Saudi Arabia and Qatar: A Non-Hurting Stalemate.* Baltimore, MD: SAIS-Johns Hopkins University.

Smith, W.C. (1977) *Islam in Modern History.* Princeton, NJ: Princeton University Press.

Toolan, M.J. (1988) *Narrative: A Critical Linguistic Introduction.* London: Routledge.

Tavris, C., and, Arnson, E. (2008) *Mistakes Were Made (But Not by Me): Why We Justify Foolish Beliefs, Bad Decisions, and Hurtful Acts.* Eugene, OR: Harvest Books.

Trakic, A., Benson, J., and, Agmed, P.K. (2019) *Dispute Resolution in Islamic Finance: Alternatives to Litigation.* London: Routledge.

Ury, B., Paton, B., and, Fisher, R. (1982) *Getting to Yes: Negotiating Agreement Without Giving in.* New York, NY: Penguin Books.

West, D.L. (2003) *Myth and Narrative in the Israeli-Palestinian Conflict,* World Peace Foundation. www.belfercenter.org/sites/default/files/legacy/files/wpf34mythandnarrative.pdf

Wiener, A. (2004) 'Contested Compliance: Interventions on the Normative Structure of World Politics', *European Journal of International Relations,* vol.10, no.2, pp.189–234.

Winslade, J., and, Monk, G. (2000) *Narrative Mediation: A New Approach to Conflict Resolution.* San Francisco, CA: Jossey-Bass.

Zartman, I.W. (2001, January) 'Negotiating Identity: From Metaphor to Process', *International Negotiation,* vol.6, no.2, pp.137–140.

Zartman, I.W., Druckman, D., Jenson, L., Pruitt, D.G., and, Young, H.P. (1996) 'Negotiation As a Search for Justice', *International Negotiation,* vol.1, no.1, pp.79–98.

Zartman, I.W., and, Rubin, J.Z. (Eds.). (2005) *Power and Negotiation.* Ann Arbor, MI: University of Michigan Press.

PART II

Narratives of foreign policies and economic negotiations

3

GERMANY, EUROPE, AND THE POWER OF NARRATIVES

Thomas Bagger

Introduction

As a country that literally had to "reinvent" itself after the abyss of the Nazi years, Germany is a particularly interesting case study to explore the invention, dynamic evolution, and remarkable power of newly constructed narratives – whether we understand them as expressions of self-constructed identity or as products of externally driven "re-education" (Winkler, 2007; Münkler, 2009).

Leaving aside more domestically oriented narratives such as "hour zero" or "Stunde Null," referring to the unconditional surrender of May 8, 1945 as an absolute and radical break with the past that allowed individuals to disassociate themselves – and German society as a whole – at least partly from the crimes and horrors of the Nazi years, possibly the most powerful narrative of post-war (West) Germany developed around the twin notions of "Never Again" (Auschwitz, Holocaust, racism, nationalism, war) and "Never Alone" (a strong emphasis on international institutions and Germany's integration into a rules-based system of international relations: NATO, European Union, United Nations, International Criminal Court; multilateral diplomacy as post-war Germany's "DNA," etc.). Over time, both of these notions became perfectly encapsulated in the evolving process of economic and political integration across Western Europe.

William Paterson and Simon Bulmer in their recently released volume on *Germany and the European Union*, the most comprehensive and balanced account of German perspectives of Europe and of Germany's role within Europe, remark on what they call the "semi-sovereign period" of West Germany 1955–1990: "The European framework for Germany's politics and economics commanded support from a public that was in search of identity during this period of a divided Germany and after the traumas of the Nazi period" (Bulmer and Paterson, 2019, p.240).

DOI: 10.4324/9781003203209-5

The European Economic Community that started with the integration in 1950 of industrial sectors widely perceived as key to the warfighting efforts of the past, that is, coal and steel, emerged as the perfect institutional frame for a narrative that focused on economic recovery, moral rehabilitation, political re-integration but also post-national identity after the catastrophe of nationalism.

A federal vision of Europe – indeed the "United States of Europe" – seemed to many Germans the natural solution to the "German question" of a country too small to dominate the continent but too big and too central to be just one among many. It also promised an escape from the symbols, the ambitions, and the rhetoric of the nation-state that were so thoroughly contaminated by their abuse during the 12 years of Hitler's rule. Thirty years after the fall of the Iron Curtain and the re-unification of Germany it is instructive to remember the widespread hesitation of large segments of the German public. The narrative of redemption adopted since the 1950s pointed to a post-national European Germany, not toward regaining national sovereignty in a bigger, more powerful Germany. This explains the reluctance of many Germans to embrace unification when the opportunity suddenly and unexpectedly presented itself.

Chancellor Helmut Kohl, who secured his place in Germany's history books by quickly realizing the historic significance of the moment but also by astutely managing the process of unification against concerns and opposition of some European partners, instinctively understood the need to integrate these dramatic events into the story of Germany's redemption after 1945. In his public speeches he interpreted henceforth German unification and European integration as two sides of the same coin. The first had only become possible because of the latter. The latter would now only become stronger because of the former.

Briefing papers for German officials in those days routinely included the notion of "the irreversible process of European integration." This was indeed both an analytical and a normative statement. What should happen would happen. This firm conviction also shaped Germany's definition of its own interests and the policies it pursued. The European interest and the national interest were seen as literally synonymous – but using the former in public discourse was clearly preferable, and not simply for reasons of disguise. In the negotiations leading to the creation of the European Economic and Monetary Union in Maastricht 1991/1992 Chancellor Helmut Kohl was able to "sell" the introduction of the single European currency to the German public as a contribution to forge a more integrated European Union, thus overriding those who wanted to preserve the "D-Mark" for reasons both of monetary stability and of its value as a symbol of successful reconstruction after the war. The Euro was the price to pay for a united but European Germany, and beyond a few economics professors that was widely accepted then.

"If the Euro fails, Europe fails"

A closer inspection of German public and political debates over the course of the Eurozone crisis since the Spring of 2010 reveals the enduring power but also the contestation of the dominant German narrative on Europe. It also reveals some of the ambivalent uses and effects of strong strategic narratives.

After fueling an economic boom through much lower public and private borrowing costs the Eurozone crisis developed in several phases as a consequence of the world financial crisis of 2008. Initially the massive bailout operations and the creation – almost overnight on May 10, 2010 – of the European Financial Stability Mechanism (EFSM) and the European Financial Stability Facility (EFSF) were presented to the German public as an exceptional and temporary fix. This was important to secure parliamentary approval in Germany including the support of those members of the conservative-liberal coalition that were deeply skeptical of cross-border bailouts, which they saw as explicitly excluded in the founding documents of the Monetary Union. After the exceptions began to multiply – besides Greece, also Ireland, Portugal and Spain required emergency liquidity provided by EMU partners – Chancellor Angela Merkel changed her rhetoric. She increasingly resorted to a much broader framing she had first used in May 2010: "If the Euro fails, Europe fails." After the risk of financial contagion across the Eurozone reached new heights in late summer of 2011, this formula became the core of her impassioned plea for more solidarity with Germany's European partners.

Thus Merkel was able to mobilize broad public support and massive resources for an otherwise unpopular policy of bailouts and even the creation in 2012 of the European Stability Mechanism (ESM) as a permanent institution replacing the temporary EFSM/EFSF. She tapped into the vast reservoir of positive connotations of European integration in the wider German public by enlarging the issue. If indeed Europe as we knew it was at stake, then even unpopular or controversial policy decisions could be justified. Who in his right mind would risk the very foundations of Germany's postwar success – and redemption?

It is instructive to contrast this with the British reaction. Then-Foreign Secretary William Hague (who had famously compared the Euro to "a house on fire with no exit") was shocked. The British had always stayed away from Monetary Union and were battling opposition within the Tory party and large parts of British media questioning the wisdom of Britain being a member of the European Union by carefully distinguishing between the Single Market and the perceived folly of a single currency. By deliberately conflating the two to shore up support in Germany, Chancellor Merkel had made the lives of British "remainers" (as they were not yet known then) in the already toxic intra-Tory debate about Europe far more difficult.

But the successful mobilization of public support to steer through the most critical months of the Eurozone crisis is only half the story. The parallel narrative of Germany as the EU's "lender of last resort" that emerged over the course of the Eurozone crisis progressively hardened into the more pejorative notion of the EU as a potential "transfer union," requiring permanent fiscal transfers from Germany to other EU (and more specifically EMU) member states.

While European integration included an element of fiscal transfers from the start, for example, through the Common Agricultural Policy favoring rural areas over industrial and urban regions but also through Structural and Cohesion Funds intended to shore up the infrastructure of less developed regions across the Union, the notion of a "transfer union" in the context of EMU had much deeper resonance in the German public than earlier disputes about Germany as a "net payer" to the EU's budget.

First, the fears of "transfer union" and the concerns about a "stable currency" hark back to another powerful German narrative, the lessons drawn from the traumatic experience of hyper-inflation in 1923 during the years of the Weimar Republic. It was in the framing of the lessons of those days that Bundesbank orthodoxy about monetary stability as the one and only legitimate focus and mandate of an independent central bank was shaped.

Secondly, the specter of a "transfer union" involved not only potentially much greater sums of money but also inflamed public sentiment by bringing in cultural stereotypes. The "dolce vita" charm of the European South that was the envy of a first generation of German Europhiles in the 1950s and 1960s was suddenly seen in a very different light. Here was the lazy South, living on borrowed money, with dysfunctional tax collection and lack of discipline, now asking the Germans to foot their bill.

It is worth remembering that the "Alternative für Deutschland" (AfD) was founded in 2013 by Economics professor Bernd Lucke on a platform of anti-Euro positions, mobilizing public opposition to fiscal transfers – before it discovered anti-immigrant, anti-refugee, and anti-Islam sentiment as more powerful mobilizing forces.

Even the German liberals, the FDP, which for decades was an engine for deeper European integration in the German political spectrum, with a proud history of four foreign ministers in charge of European affairs within the German cabinet, almost split in 2011 over deep disagreements on Eurozone policies. Disagreements that contributed to a devastating election loss in 2013 when the party failed to re-enter parliament after four years in government.

Chancellor Merkel sensed this opposition early on in the crisis, both in her own party and among deputies of her coalition partner FDP. She moderated the skepticism by pushing strongly at the European level for a set of policies focusing on fiscal stabilization (widely criticized as "austerity" abroad) and structural reforms. Pushing European partners and the so-called "program countries" that were the recipients of massive liquidity assistance to adopt a set of policies inspired by the German tradition of economic thinking was both a result of Germany's economic prowess and of the need to present a framework, which would look sufficiently "German" to shore up support with skeptical German deputies at home.

Angela Merkel undoubtedly navigated very skillfully the narrow path between convincing her own coalition deputies that denying bailouts could bring down the entire – very popular – edifice of united Europe, and on the other hand cajoling the debtor countries into often harsh structural reforms because otherwise she could not muster the required parliamentary majority at home in Germany. And yet by presenting new bailout packages – strictly conditioned – as inevitable ("alternativlos") to save European integration, forcing partners both at home and across Europe to stare into the abyss time and again in order to make them fall in line she also presided over the emergence of a significant counter-narrative to Germany's master story on European integration.

Today the narrative warning against the EU becoming a "permanent transfer union" resonates not only at the fringes of Germany's political spectrum and discourse but deep within the larger parties of the center-right and center-left, CDU/CSU and SPD, which embodied Germany's dominant pro-European narrative over six decades. It has over time grown into an almost insurmountable hurdle to mobilize public and political support for those further steps of structural economic and monetary integration deemed necessary by most economists to ensure sustainability of the Union.

Some conclusions

Looking at the German approach and policy responses during the Eurozone crisis provides a number of interesting observations on the power – and pitfalls – of deep narratives.

1. The dominant pro-EU integration narrative clearly helped the German government's ability to mobilize political support at home for desired outcomes. It set a high bar for articulating opposition to government policies on Eurozone stabilization and bailouts. It also shaped Germany's negotiating position vis-à-vis negotiation partners in Brussels and Germany's perception outside the EU.
2. Broadening the frame in the summer of 2011 with the notion of "If the Euro fails, Europe fails" increased the sense of urgency within Germany – it moved the crisis from the discussion of complex, even arcane financial technicalities to the level of existential tenets of post-war German success. It allowed a far more open appeal to deep-seated convictions and emotions. And it provided the German government with far greater room of maneuver in its difficult negotiations with EU partners. At the same time, it challenged domestic opposition to not just argue on a technical level against the government's course of action but to fundamentally challenge the broad consensus that "European integration is good for Germany." And in the perception of analysts abroad Germany's economic power perhaps for the first time directly translated into a political leadership role within the EU. Berlin became the place to watch and to follow.
3. This deliberate use of a broadly uncontested narrative for a controversial set of policies, however, clearly contributed to a fragmentation of the consensus, a polarization of public debate and an eventual dynamic evolution

of the narrative itself. Early on, the "transfer union" narrative (far closer to a "contamination narrative" than to the "redemption narrative" European integration provided over decades) was acknowledged but integrated into the government's negotiation position by demonstrating to EU partners that there was only limited negotiation space. While "good Europeans" the government was prepared to lead and contribute to bailout and stabilization measures, but in order to placate the skepticism at home these packages needed to reflect German economic policy preferences, that is, strict conditioning, budget cuts, structural reforms, a strong focus on increasing competitiveness, etc. This negotiating position was of course backed up by a de facto veto power as Germany was widely seen by financial market actors as the "lender of last resort."

4. Competing narratives – of the redemption type as well as the contamination type – thus shaped Germany's negotiation position during a decade of Eurozone stabilization efforts. The battle around Germany's European commitments was repeatedly taken to the Constitutional Court in Karlsruhe. Bailout packages and fiscal solidarity measures were challenged by those political actors that saw German "ordoliberal" traditions violated. But Karlsruhe, while strengthening parliamentary oversight powers significantly in the process, never challenges the government's commitments outright. The Constitutional Court did not want to make itself culprit of "failing Europe." Interviews given by judges of the court after the controversial ruling on the ECB asset buying program on May 5, 2020 only confirmed their hesitation to limit the space of political discretion (while explicitly justifying the limitations set forth vis-à-vis the European Court of Justice).
5. With the benefit of hindsight, it also seems plausible to conclude that the policies adopted over time influenced and transformed the narratives that shaped the policies in the early days of the crisis. The "transfer union" narrative is nowadays far from a mobilizing tool in negotiations in Brussels. It can obviously be used to deny resources in negotiations and serve as justification for a hard-line stance, but in reality, it is rather boxing the German government in, limiting its room for compromise, for example, in current discussion about the future of the EU's banking union project, despite the obvious need for a more flexible position. Thus, narratives shape policies but policies also in turn shape narratives, even if in unintended directions.

These observations support the notion that "narratives are a dynamic and ever-negotiated social product based on states' interactions both with their societies and with external significant others." (Miskimmon et al., 2013, p.8). They also beg the question of the broader dynamic of Germany's post-war master narrative and its evolution post-unification. On the one hand, German post-Wall identity is still closely tied to European integration. The summer 2019 edition of the regular Eurobarometer polls found that 78% of Germans believe that membership in the European Union benefits Germany – significantly higher than the 68% average of the EU-28.

But it is hard not to notice that the power of the "never alone" narrative that dominated Germany's foreign policy since the federal Republic's inception is fading. Increasingly "never again" carries the day. Being surrounded only by friends for the first time in its history, as Chancellor Helmut Kohl observed of unified Germany, not only turned the country into a status quo power, but it also reduced public threat perception to zero. Put differently, a Germany that – other than before 1989 – feels comfortably safe and prosperous in the heart of Europe without any sense of urgency about potential disruptions – be they monetary, economic, or security-related – no longer perceives the need for a "European insurance policy" like divided West-Germany did.

The "post-national" idea of Europe has faded from German public discourse. The emergence of a European identity is no longer seen as a preferable (and morally superior) version of national identity but both are increasingly perceived as complementary. The reconciliation of Germans with their own nation-state, while still more ambivalent than elsewhere and far from "normal," has made significant progress since reunification. The camp of "European federalists" has dwindled. There is more than one reason why the "net payer" narrative and its younger, more powerful, and dangerous sibling, the "transfer union" narrative gained traction post-1989. But one of them undoubtedly is that the stronger and more central Germany's role within the EU is perceived the more difficult it gets to argue and to mobilize for substantial compromises. Better to be "right" – even if it means to be alone. The challenge of "leading the EU" thus becomes ever more difficult at home. The country is in danger of re-constructing its European narrative in a way that potentially leads to self-isolation despite presenting itself as very pro-European.

In should not come as a surprise, then, that most Germans perceive themselves as the most generous country across the EU. Others, in turn, look at Germany as pursuing rather more narrowly defined self-interests (Stokes, 2013). While a gap between self-perception and the perception by others is all but human, this gap can become politically consequential and even dangerous if it grows too large and can no longer be moderated.

Finally, and on a more general note of caution with respect to the German experience, narratives are by definition grand generalizations. They provide a sense of meaning but not knowledge, the have "Verständniswert" but not "Erkenntniswert." They help to organize complex political processes, they instill a sense of purpose to political action, they help to build consensus in a society. But they also carry an inherent risk of providing the wrong frame in a rapidly changing environment, they might lead countries and government into perception traps, and may even create self-fulfilling prophecies (Mair, 2019).

Post-Wall united Germany firmly believed in finally being on the right side of history precisely at the moment of the "end of history." What started out as a narrative of post-war rehabilitation and redemption – post-nationalist, pro-integration, broadly anti-military – suddenly became a powerful "avant-garde" narrative. The future belonged to the trading state. Rules and institutions would replace military might and the use of force as the arbiters of conflicting interests. The creation of the International Criminal Court in 1998 can be seen as a high-water mark of this type of optimism. Accountability would be the norm also in the "anarchical society" of international relations (Bull, 2002). But reality defied these optimistic expectations. That "avant-garde" frame is no longer up to the reality of military conflict in Europe as it unfolds in Crimea and Donbass since 2014 or the former US president's vision of the world as an arena of nation-states competing for power and influence.

Will Germany be capable of realizing that the post-1989 period – in which its own post-war historical lessons and its sense of historical inevitability ran together – was not the beginning of the end of history, but rather a brief and unusually happy historical moment, a "golden quarter of a century?" That it risks being "out of sync" with its partners if it stubbornly clings to defending a status quo that is no longer viable? (Bagger, 2019). A grand strategic narrative that is out of touch with reality but too powerful to be adapted can inflict massive harm on the international negotiating position of a country. Such a "Melian mindset" (Hampson and Narlikar in the introduction to this volume) can lead to a dangerous "irrational optimism" but also to self-isolation through self-righteousness.

Shaping Germany's future narrative

So what could and should a new narrative for Germany look like that would enable the country to adapt to a rapidly changing international environment while staying true to deeply held collective lessons from its past? The German perspective these days often lacks a dynamic idea of the future and a sense of agency.

The debate on German foreign and European policy is only just beginning (Holmes and Krastev, 2019; Maull, 2019; Rödder, 2018). It will be a debate in which arguably the direct link between the catastrophe of nationalism and the construction of an integrated Europe is weakened by simple lack of personal experience in the generation now moving into positions of power.

Sometimes this debate is framed as a competition between the narrative of united Europe as a "peace project," still successfully taming and overcoming nationalist inclinations and rivalries that have led to ever more devastating wars on the continent, and the narrative of "global Europe," focusing on political and economic integration as the only way to stay relevant in the 21st century. Whether understood through the prism of the radically new concept of supra-national integration embodied in the creation of the European Commission and its rule-making role, or through the evocation of Europe's heavily dotted landscape of large military cemeteries as reminders of past confrontations, the narrative of integrated Europe as an enduring peace project remains potent. While it loses in resonance with another generation that knows little about the horrors of the last war, it retains an emotional resonance – particularly in Germany – that the more forward-looking robust idea of Europe as a global actor has not been able to generate. The latter is still a rather amorphous set of more or less sound arguments why Europe needs to pool its resources and political weight to have a seat at the table and have its voice heard in shaping the rule of today and tomorrow, from regional conflicts in Syria or Africa, to combating climate change and setting the rules of the digital age. None of it wrong but lacking in rhetorical and emotional persuasion.

When looking at Germany today, however, the struggle over whether Europe needs a new or simply an updated or expanded narrative is not the most consequential debate. Far more critical is the debate about Germany's own role within this European project. How central the European project will be seen to its own future and how central Germany's own contribution will be perceived to Europe's future?

Two qualities are required above everything else. First, a rediscovered sense of humility that recognizes the limits of our own ability to shape the world in our own image. We tend – understandably but wrongly – to over-universalize our rather unique historical experience. Our experience is not the template everybody else is destined to follow – within and even less outside Europe. The assumption of a grand global convergence around our own ideals and preferences is producing a crisis of exaggerated expectations that clouds our vision of what is realistically achievable. Secondly, once we bid farewell to this illusion, we should rediscover the curiosity that made Germany into a capital of knowledge about the world in all its diversity in the days of Alexander and Wilhelm von Humboldt. Grand generalizations have no use for the nuances of different cultural traditions, historic experiences, social fabrics, and political preferences. But without this curiosity Germany will progressively lose sight of the different traditions, expectations, and needs even of its European neighbors in the integration project that has kept peace between its members over seven decades and provided unparalleled prosperity. None of this is meant to suggest a course of cultural relativism. To the contrary, only a Germany that places the highest priority on political compatibility and economic convergence with its European partners will be able to provide and to use the power of Europe's successful own example to radiate its universalist normative ideals beyond its borders.

In a nutshell, then, Germany's idea of itself will undoubtedly change with the advent of a new generation that is being politicized in the struggle against climate change and other risks of the "Anthropocene" rather than in the horrors of the last World War or the threat of mutually assured nuclear destruction during the Cold War. But whatever precise form this new narrative will take, historical experience and geopolitical context suggest that it can only be successful if it places an integrated Europe at the heart of any idea of Germany's future.

The traditional narrative has not yet lost its appeal as was on full display when Chancellor Merkel and French President Emmanuel Macron put forward their French-German initiative for the European Recovery from the Coronavirus Crisis on May 19, 2020. Timing, sheer size, and political messaging of their suggested Recovery Fund sought to link as explicitly and directly as possible the future of Germany and of the European Union. Merkel's commitment to a fund based on fresh capital raised jointly through the European Commission was interpreted by some as a breakthrough to a future mutualization of fiscal policy, as a "Hamiltonian moment" for Europe. Merkel herself instead stuck to her story: This was an exceptional situation that required exceptional measures but her set of principles rejecting Eurobonds (or "Coronabonds") would remain intact. In the midst of the political fluidity created by an unprecedented crisis, the Chancellor – on the back of a surge in reputation and poll numbers – managed to "move the goalposts" of the German debate on European solidarity. Criticism in Germany was muted, explicit support for her bold move reassuringly broad. Once again, she managed to master and refine the narrative rather than being constrained by it.

The German narrative about European integration as a story of Germany's redemption had a remarkable cognitive and emotive resonance over decades. It helped to shape Germany's post-war perception of its interests in an enlightened way that saw the interests of its European partners as necessary ingredients of its own interests. It came close to what Alexis de Tocqueville famously called "self-interest rightly understood." Few developments are more worrying than a progressive narrowing of the definition of Germany's interests. None more so than a German idea of its future that can do without the narrative of being part of an integrated, united Europe (Steinmeier, 2020).

References

Bagger, T. (2019) 'The World According to Germany', *Washington Quarterly*, vol.41, no.4, pp.53–63.

Bull, H. (2002) *The Anarchical Society: A Study of Order in World Politics*. New York, NY: Columbia University Press.

Bulmer, S., and, Paterson, W. (2019) *Germany and the European Union. Europe's Reluctant Hegemon?* London: Macmillan.

Holmes, S., and, Krastev, I. (2019) *The Light that Failed*. London: Allen Lane.

Mair, S. (2019, August 1) *Das Risiko der sich selbst erfüllenden Prophezeiung*. Cicero. www.cicero.de/wirtschaft/sicherheitspolitik-usa-russland-china-eu-krieg.

Maull, H. (2019) 'Das Leid des Leaders', *Internationale Politik*, vol.74, no.5, pp.138–142.

Miskimmon, A., O'Loughlin, B., and, Roselle, L. (2013) *Strategic Narratives: Communication Power and the New World Order*. New York, NY: Routledge.

Münkler, H. (2009) *Die Deutschen und ihre Mythen*. Berlin, Germany: Rowohlt.

Rödder, A. (2018) *Wer hat Angst vor Deutschland? Geschichte eines europäischen Problems*. Frankfurt, Germany: S. Fischer.

Steinmeier, F.W. (2020, February 14) *Speech at the Opening of the 56th Munich Security Conference*, Der Bundespräsident. www.bundespraesident.de/SharedDocs/Reden/EN/Frank-Walter-Steinmeier/Reden/2020/02/200214-Munich-Security-Conference.html.

Stokes, B. (2013, May 13) *The New Sick Man of Europe: The European Union*, Pew Research Center. www.pewglobal.org/2013/05/14/the-new-sick-man-of-europe/.

Winkler, H.A. (2007) *Germany: The Long Road West* (Vol. II: 1933–1990). Oxford: Oxford University Press.

4

ST. GEORGE TRIUMPHS

The Brexit narrative and negotiations

Brendan Vickers[1]

Introduction

On June 23, 2016, the electorate of the United Kingdom (UK) of Great Britain and Northern Ireland voted by 52 per cent to leave the European Union (EU). However, delivering the outcome of the historic Brexit referendum proved to be far more challenging, even chaotic at times. In the post-referendum politics that engulfed an increasingly disunited Kingdom, two Prime Ministers resigned, two general elections were held in June 2017 and December 2019 – the first resulted in a minority government led by Theresa May while the second delivered a decisive majority for Boris Johnson to "Get Brexit Done" – and the date of departure from the EU was delayed twice. The UK Parliament on three occasions rejected May's Withdrawal Agreement, which ended her premiership. Johnson secured ratification of his renegotiated deal with Brussels albeit on terms May personally believed were unacceptable to any Prime Minister because it created a border between Britain and Northern Ireland for the first time in modern history and required the province to align with EU customs rules. And so, on January 31, 2020, almost three-and-a-half years after the Brexit referendum, the UK finally ceased to be a member of the EU.

Britain's exit from the EU marks the end of nearly a half-century's membership of the European integration project, including more than 20 years in the Single Market, which has delivered continued peace and prosperity to the nations of Europe. Overnight Britain went from full membership of the EU with a voice, rights and obligations to assume a new identity as an outside "third country" in the EU's external relations. A transition period until the end of December 2020 helped avoid a damaging cliff edge while London and Brussels negotiated their future relationship, including a Trade and Cooperation Agreement (TCA),[2] which was finalised on Christmas eve and implemented on January 1, 2021.

DOI: 10.4324/9781003203209-6

Narratives about Britain's past, present and future have played a pivotal role in shaping the entire Brexit enterprise – from the rhetoric of the Leave campaign to the notion of Britain's exceptionalism that shaped the government's win-set and best alternative to a negotiated agreement (BATNA) during the withdrawal negotiations with Brussels. As Glencross (2016) argues, there was nothing inevitable about the referendum's outcome and the campaign mattered profoundly. In that discourse, the Brexit narrative of contamination and redemption about Brussels and the EU was persuasive. The Leave campaign rallied populist concerns about sovereignty, identity and EU overreach, as well as immigration and jobs. This narrative appealed directly to the existential reality, core identity and visceral mindsets of disaffected groups, especially in smaller English cities and towns, rural areas and the heartlands of post-industrial Britain left behind by globalisation. When couched in English folklore, "The vote on whether Britain should leave the European Union was sold to the electorate as a St George moment, a swordthrust in the dragon's heart that would end the suffering of all good people" (Meek, 2019, p.9). By comparison, the Remain campaign's technocratic warnings about economic risk and recession – derided as Project Fear for its scaremongering tactics – offered no compelling alternative to the heroic narrative and purgative act of St. George triumphing over a beastly Brussels.

Brexit was generally considered a victory for English nationalism and specifically for a provincial polity of "England-without-London"[3] (Barnett, 2017). The pattern of voting to leave the EU generally reflected the bifurcated politics of "Two Englands" (Jennings and Stoker, 2016):

> In cosmopolitan areas we find an England that is global in outlook, liberal and more plural in its sense of identity. In provincial backwaters we find an England that is inward-looking, relatively illiberal, negative about the EU and immigration, nostalgic and more English in its identity.
>
> *Jennings and Stoker, 2016, p.1*

With Scotland and Northern Ireland, as well as the Welsh-speaking counties of Wales having voted for continued EU membership,[4] the politics of Brexit are nationalist and a far cry from a unified UK-wide project. Indeed, Brexit has strained the bonds and imperilled the 300-year-old union between the four nations (O'Toole, 2018). Even as the UK Parliament ratified the Withdrawal Agreement in January 2020, all three devolved legislatures in Northern Ireland, Scotland and Wales withheld their assent. As a result, wittingly or otherwise, Brexit may yet script the epilogue to the UK's island story: the potential reunification of the island of Ireland and the possibility of a second Scottish independence referendum, which ironically invokes the same narratives of sovereignty and taking back control from Westminster. Yet for many hard-line Brexiters, the act of reclaiming the UK's perceived loss of sovereignty from the EU, the European Court of Justice and so-called "unelected bureaucrats" in Brussels was worth any price, including some diminished prosperity or even the constitutional breakup of the UK (Matthews, 2019).

This chapter focuses specifically on the negotiation of the Withdrawal Agreement between the UK and the EU as required by Article 50 of the 2007 Lisbon Treaty.[5] It examines how some of the narratives of the Brexit campaign shaped the UK's approach to the negotiations. The chapter is divided into two parts. The first part examines the role of narratives during the Remain and Leave campaigns, and why Leave won the vote. The second part extends this analysis to the negotiations with Brussels, and why May's deal foundered while Johnson's deal succeeded. The chapter concludes with some observations about the persistence of narratives beyond Brexit, namely the negotiations for the EU-UK TCA.

The tale of two narratives

Following the 2010 General Election, David Cameron became Prime Minister of the UK, albeit as head of a coalition government between his own Conservative and Unionist Party, where Eurosceptic and even outright Europhobe backbenchers formed one wing of the party, and the pro-European Liberal Democrats. Ever since Britain joined the European Economic Community (EEC) in 1973 – with continued membership affirmed in a 1975 referendum – there had been a lingering question about Britain's identity, destiny and role in a post-imperial world, whether as an integral member of Europe with significant carve outs, or looking towards the Anglosphere as embodied in the 54-member Commonwealth of Nations (Reynolds, 2019). In 2013, confronted by rising Euroscepticism in his own parliamentary party, as well as the growing popularity and electoral success in European Parliamentary elections by the nationalist UK Independence Party (UKIP), Cameron offered a referendum to try settle the "Europe Question" (Glencross, 2015) and reconcile the factions within his own party. Cameron pledged that if the Conservative Party won the 2015 General Election, he would renegotiate the terms of Britain's EU membership and put this to the public in an "in/out" referendum. With an election manifesto premised on his three R's – reform, renegotiate, referendum (Reynolds, 2019) – Cameron contained UKIP and the Conservative Party won a parliamentary majority. However, his underwhelming negotiations with Brussels only secured an opt-out for the UK from the commitment to "an ever closer union among the peoples of Europe." On some of the existential concerns for British voters – such as immigration and jobs – the EU held firm to the principle of free movement, permitting only some small caveats.

The campaign to remain

The government's position was that Britain should remain in the EU. There was also an element of personal exceptionalism to the campaign. Buoyed by the success of the Scottish referendum, which opted to retain the status quo of the union, and the need to sway only moderate voters, Cameron believed he could personally deliver a Remain vote (von Tunzelmann, 2019). This overconfidence meant no contingency plans were made for the possibility of a majority Leave vote. Cameron, together with George Osborne, then Chancellor of the Exchequer, played the pivotal roles of narrators-in-chief, making the case that Britain was "Stronger in Europe." The government sought to persuade voters using a shallow narrative based on a cost-benefit argument for EU membership while offering no bold and visionary storytelling about the role of European integration in an age of discontents (Glencross, 2016). Moreover, the narrative was cognitive and technocratic: Remain represented the economically beneficial and stable status quo whereas Leave represented economic self-harm and multiple risks, including the peace in Europe. This was backed up by economic forecasts of post-Brexit recession from the Bank of England and other dire warnings from the International Monetary Fund and other international agencies, while influential external narrators – most noticeably then-United States President Barack Obama – were also enrolled to argue the case for Remain.[6]

Glencross (2016) calls this agenda "Project Trust," namely that the government's advice was reliable, credible and should be heeded. However, this approach only reinforced the growing backlash against the establishment, elites and experts in Britain and elsewhere (Nichols, 2017). By contrast, Brexiters assailed the government's scaremongering tactics as "Project Fear" and offered an alternative heroic story about Britain as a small yet plucky nation with a proud history of punching above its weight in the world.

Interestingly, a similar Project Fear narrative had helped Harold Wilson win the 1975 referendum to remain in the EEC – almost two to one – although the common market was very different from the EU. It was entirely economic, a less political organisation and not concerned with the free movement of people and immigration. In 1975, rational persuasion resonated with the electorate because it had some existential validity for voters. As Saunders (2016) suggests, Wilson's warnings about the dangers if Britain left the common market were not abstract forecasts by economists but resonated with an entire generation's collective memory and lived experience of economic crisis, food rationing and war. The EEC referendum was held just 30 years after the end of the Second World War (1939–1945). In the case of the Brexit referendum, there was no such comparable experience: the war had ended more than 70 years before, while even the First World War (1914–1918) was closer in time to 1975 than the Second World War was to 2016. Moreover, the late 1960s and 1970s was a time of decolonisation, stagflation and distress over the country's balance of payments, meaning the EEC seemed to offer some economic refuge and redemption (Gross, 2017). The economic arguments ultimately prevailed over other concerns, including appeals to sovereignty by the opposite side. Voters opted to remain in the EEC, viewing membership in transactional terms ever since (Saunders, 2016). By comparison, in 2016, Europe was mired in multiple crises, from the Eurozone to migrants, and this fed the contamination narrative about Brussels and the EU. Moreover, while polling results suggested voters expected post-Brexit Britain to be poorer, they did not envisage adverse consequences for themselves.

The referendum gamble turned out to be a great miscalculation for Cameron and demonstrated how the government had misread the public mood by offering only a pragmatic cost-benefit argument (Glencross, 2016). For example, more than half of Leave voters (52 per cent) cited immigration as important to making their voting decision, compared to 18 per cent who cited the economy (Ipsos/MORI, 2016). Cameron's resignation paved the way for Theresa May to become Prime Minister and responsible for leading the UK out of the EU despite having supported Remain.

The campaign to leave

The official and unofficial Brexit campaigns have been sweepingly portrayed as a "toxic form of nationalism combining racism, xenophobia, and imperialist nostalgia for the heyday of the British Empire" (Handa, 2019). While some voters certainly expressed such views – UKIP party leaders like Nigel Farage and the unofficial campaign did engage in egregious nativist scaremongering about immigrants – this crude caricature is misleading. It is more correct that the Leave campaign mobilised a broad and somewhat contradictory coalition of outward globalists, inward nationalists and disillusioned voters who felt left behind by globalisation, which included minorities and immigrants. In some respects, Brexit was a vote against globalisation in its current form. The Leave campaign tapped into deeper narratives that globalisation, technological change and austerity had shifted economic opportunity and prosperity to London and the south-east of England while economically depressing the north of England, Wales and Cornwall. The persuasiveness of the Leave narrative was evident in the cognitive dissonance of some voters: EU regional spending, which has been substantial in these economically deprived regions of Britain, did little to sway how they voted in the referendum (Huggins, 2018). Meanwhile, the UK was experiencing the largest public spending cuts in post-war history and the longest fall in living standards since records began (Gross, 2017). Overall, the Brexit mantra was of taking back control of money, borders and laws – not just from Brussels but from the political establishment and elites. The chief narrator was Boris Johnson, supported by pro-Brexit politicians of the Conservative Party and UKIP and a vociferous conservative media.

Unlike the Remain campaign, the Brexit narrative was sentimental rather than cognitive. Narrators often took positions that lacked convincing or credible data, while deploying populist rhetorical devices based on fear, hatred and lies to scapegoat "the other," whether immigrants or even Britons who wanted to remain in the EU. For outward looking globalists, Brexit offered a narrative of redemption: "Global Britain," once unshackled from the EU's protectionism, would bask and prosper in sunlit uplands, forge its own trade deals and reassert its rightful role in international institutions, including the World

Trade Organization (WTO), where the country would champion free trade. As Saunders (2019) argues, many Leavers invoked the past – "curated memories of war and empire" – to imagine a bright and prosperous future outside the EU. To validate their narrative about redemption, they presented de-historicised stories about British history and exceptionalism in the world (Reynolds, 2019). Past, present and future were connected in one grand narrative: first, Britain was recast as having been a benign global power rather than an expansive and coercive military empire; and second, free trade, innovation and entrepreneurialism replaced imperialism as the factors that had made Britain a great nation. This is most egregious in the case of the Commonwealth, which Brexiteers cherish as "some of the world's oldest and most resilient friendships and partnerships" (Fox, 2017) rather than being connected by a shared history of imperialism, slavery and mass migration. Indeed, some media, bureaucrats and commentators derided the focus on bolstering post-Brexit trade links with the Commonwealth as Empire 2.0 (Gruenbaum, 2017).

For inward-looking nationalists, Brexit offered a strong contamination narrative about Brussels and the EU and their complicity in unchecked immigration, loss of jobs, corrosion of identity, diminished welfare and changing demographics in Britain (Sobolewska and Ford, 2020). Factual evidence to the contrary – for example, immigration to the UK since 2000 has been of substantial net fiscal benefit (Dustmann and Frattini, 2014) – did little to alter the visceral mindsets of disaffected groups, especially given growing disdain for expert knowledge. The Leave campaign tapped into this deep-seated angst and made two promises during the referendum: first, to spend more money on the public National Health Service – they claimed that £350 million-a-week was paid to Brussels, which was dishonest and misleading; and second, to shut out an (entirely imagined) influx of migrants from Turkey, which they claimed would soon join the EU (Glencross, 2016).

Overall, the Brexit mantra was about taking back control and reclaiming sovereignty and independence. Many narrators also framed this narrative with a set of primal myths, deeper histories and political folk-legends that appealed especially to globalists and nationalists in England as the most populous of the four nations:

> The [Brexiters] succeeded because they shared the dream-vision of enough of the voters to offer a story that fitted right onto their map provided by their psyche. They found a ready-made myth. That myth was the myth of St. George.
>
> *Meek, 2019, p.7*

Brexit was presented as a St. George moment of victory and redemption, whereas the Remain camp lacked any similar folk myth. This resonated with the other great battles of Britain's glorious past: from "Waterloo, Agincourt and Crécy,"[7] to the victory against the existential threat posed by Nazism. It is this narrative about British exceptionalism as an island nation, and the myths and memory constructed around the history of empire and the Second World War (von Tunzelmann, 2019), which partly explain the UK's handling of the Brexit process and its negotiating positions.

The Brexit process and negotiations

The Leave campaign had a single-minded focus: to mobilise a broad coalition of voters for victory in the June 2016 referendum. Little consideration or attention was given to the more complex post-referendum process of negotiating the UK's exit from the EU (while Cameron had made no contingency plans either).[8] Indeed, during the pre-negotiating period, Brexiters were over-optimistic about the task of extricating the UK from an arrangement of more than 40 years. They had campaigned on the prospect that the UK could retain most of the advantages of remaining in the Single Market without any of the costs. Emboldened by the notion of Britain's exceptionalism, one leading campaigner claimed, "The day after we vote to leave, we hold all the cards and we can choose the path we want" (Henley and Roberts, 2018). Liam Fox, the Secretary of State for International Trade, later claimed that negotiating a free trade agreement with the EU "should be one of the easiest in human history" (Henley and Roberts, 2018). The spurious claims and lofty promises of the official and unofficial campaigns set expectations that were near impossible to fulfil without tough trade-offs, most notably regarding the EU/UK border on the island of Ireland. Warnings from Brussels about the complexity of the issues – the final deal would be almost 600 pages – and the UK's contradictory positions were dismissed as validating the Brexit narrative of contamination and redemption while introducing another dimension, namely retribution. Brexiters framed Brussels and the EU, particularly France and Germany, as intent on punishing the British people to prevent a domino reaction of further defections from the club. Indeed, many politicians and campaigners have compared Brexit to the Second World War, which remains engrained in the national psyche through books, movies and popular culture about the nation's curated "finest hour," and rallied the Blitz spirit against the EU's presumed retribution.

In November 2018, two-and-a-half years after the referendum, May finally struck a deal with the EU in the form of a legally binding Withdrawal Agreement[9] and a political declaration on the future relationship. However, the date of departure from the EU had to be delayed[10] because May could not secure domestic ratification of the agreement, ending her premiership. Her successor, Boris Johnson, having won a landslide 80-seat parliamentary majority in the December 2019 general election, secured passage of his renegotiated deal with the EU, albeit on terms that create a customs border in the Irish Sea. May's failure – and Johnson's success – highlight three issues in the two-level games of international negotiations (Putnam, 1988). These are the importance of constructing a viable domestic win-set; clear understanding of resistance points and BATNA; and compelling narratives to sell the deal, especially if it is not the optimal outcome.

The UK's domestic win-set

In international negotiations, win-sets are the possible outcomes that are likely to be accepted by domestic interest groups who either must ratify the agreement or provide some other form of government backing. In the end, securing the Brexit agreement at home and its passage through Parliament was much more challenging for May than the actual negotiations with the EU. This is because there was no consensus in Britain on the Brexit win-set, whether a hard break or a gentle decoupling from the EU, while pressure mounted for a People's Vote on the final deal.

May's management of Brexit was idiosyncratic and centralised, with little consultation beyond her inner circle of advisers (Seldon, 2019). Her initial pursuit of a hard Brexit approach rather than seeking the middle ground or a cross-party win-set for the negotiations reflected two political imperatives: to reassure English nationalists that she would deliver the referendum result despite having supported Remain; and internal party management given the increasing divisions within the Conservative Party over the terms of Brexit. The narrative about Britain's exceptionalism framed May's definition of the win-set. She proposed a bespoke deal with the EU – a "deep and special partnership" that retained selected commercial benefits of the Single Market but without any obligations – and insisted on parallel negotiations of the exit treaty and the future relationship. Von Tunzelmann (2019) highlights that Prime Ministers Cameron, May and Johnson all approached the EU with this deep narrative and belief that Britain deserves preferential treatment, more-than-equal status and the right to cherry-pick the Single Market's obligations, especially carving out the freedom of movement.

It was symbolism and hubris that led the UK to prematurely trigger Article 50 to formally notify the EU about withdrawal. This initiated the two-year negotiating period without any agreed win-set or negotiating strategy in place; and this would become even more challenging once May lost her majority and relied on the votes of the conservative Northern Ireland Democratic Unionist Party (DUP), a pro-union party that had opposed the 1998 Good Friday Agreement that brought peace to the island. This irrational optimism and lack of preparedness deprived the UK of considerable bargaining leverage in two ways.

First, the EU and its member countries, especially the Republic of Ireland (Connelly, 2017), were extremely well prepared; and this enabled Brussels to set the rules of the game from the outset of the negotiations and control the process. For example, the EU insisted there would be no pre-negotiations: Britain should trigger Article 50 before any discussions would commence. Once formal negotiations started, the UK conceded to the EU position on sequencing, namely settling the divorce issues first and negotiating the future relationship thereafter.[11] This removed the possibility for grand bargaining between the two phases and compelled the UK to agree to the Irish backstop in order to proceed to the second phase on economic and security cooperation. Second, the UK's BATNA of no-deal without contingency planning would have little credibility to force any major EU concessions, especially during May's premiership. As McTague (2019) writes, "The story that emerges is of a process in which the EU moved inexorably forward as Westminster collapsed into political infighting, indecision and instability."

By the negotiating endgame, May's win-set had shifted significantly. In January 2017, her Lancaster House speech spelled out a hard Brexit through a bespoke deal with the EU and BATNA of no deal. By July 2018, her Chequers Plan envisaged a softer Brexit through closer alignment with the EU. May was forced to recalibrate her win-set because there was insufficient support in the UK Parliament, as well as business and civil society, for a hard Brexit[12]; and so, May belatedly reached out to other parties to help ratify her deal. More importantly, the issue of the Irish border, which had not featured in the campaign narratives, had created irreconcilable resistance points for May. To the Irish Republic, May promise to maintain an open border to preserve the Good Friday Agreement that ended 30 years of political violence; to her DUP governing partners, she promised no regulatory divergence from the UK; and to Brexiters, she committed to leaving the customs union, which implied the need for a hard border for checks on goods. May's Chequers Plan envisioned the whole of the UK remaining in the EU's Single Market for goods until an alternative arrangement was agreed to maintain an open border on the island of Ireland. This deal cost her the political support of hard-line Brexiters in her party and the DUP.

By contrast, Johnson's premiership revived the Brexit narrative of Britain's exceptionalism by seeking a hard break from the EU. He undertook to renegotiate May's agreement, specifically the controversial Irish backstop, even as Brussels insisted the deal could not be reopened. Johnson's solution was Chequers for Northern Ireland: the province will remain aligned to the EU Single Market for goods by creating a customs border in the Irish Sea.[13]

Compared to the UK's fraught domestic politics, the EU – the institutions (i.e., the Council, the Commission and the Parliament) and the 27 member states – formally presented a united front throughout the negotiations despite May's attempts at side-deals to diplomatically divide the bloc. Unity was maintained though precise, transparent and legalistic negotiating mandates and extensive consultations and communication, especially between the EU's chief negotiator, Michel Barnier, and the EU Parliament, which would have to ratify the final deal (Desmet and Stourton, 2019). Unlike the UK, which sought to frame the negotiations in win-win terms, Brussels regarded the negotiations as lose-lose for all the parties because Brexit created no new value. The negotiations instead aimed to mitigate the damage and disruptions caused by the UK's decision to replace the unfettered benefits of the Single Market with less optimal economic terms (Desmet and Stourton, 2019; Barnier, 2021). The priority for the EU was to safeguard the integrity of the Single Market, which meant the indivisibility of the four freedoms. This ruled out the prospect of "cherry-picking" for May's bespoke deal. Brussels insisted that only existing third country models, like Canada or Norway, would be available for post-Brexit arrangements, although none of these appeared to be compatible with the UK's desired win-set.

BATNA and resistance points

May and Johnson sought a deal with the EU. However, both were willing to countenance a BATNA of no-deal if the terms were unacceptable or as an attempt to strengthen their bargaining position. No-deal involved the UK's unilateral withdrawal from the EU without a transition period and trading on the WTO's most-favoured nation terms. Hardline Brexiters, many in thrall to de-historicised narratives about Britain's buccaneering past and free trade (Reynolds, 2019), believed no-deal validated their narrative of contamination and redemption and actively encouraged this outcome. However, there was little political convergence on the UK's BATNA despite evidence of the potential economic costs (Tetlow and Stojanovic, 2018). The government's own assessment suggested that the UK would be worse off under every post-Brexit scenario (HM Government, 2018), but this was downplayed as an extension of Project Fear. May's cabinet was divided: it knew, but could not admit, that the best economic BATNA was full EU membership (Hayes, 2018); Parliament later held indicative votes on BATNAs, including no-deal, a customs union and a second referendum; while civil society clamoured for a People's Vote. Johnson later suspended Parliament because a majority opposed his negotiating positions and BATNA of no-deal.

May's perceived BATNA, like her win-set, evolved over time. In 2017, May declared "no deal is better than a bad deal" although no urgency was given to planning for such an outcome. This tough message was intended for a domestic audience, particularly the hardliners in her party, because she reportedly never raised or threatened no-deal in the negotiations (Desmet and Stourton, 2019). Towards the endgame, May's perceived BATNA had gone from no-deal is better than a bad deal to any deal is better than no deal. She had miscalculated by insisting that Brussels always compromised at the end (Seldon, 2019). This misreads the legal nature of the EU and its own BATNA of safeguarding the EU project:

> For many in Britain, EU membership has always been a transactional arrangement, a matter of money; for most EU members the European project is existential – the Union is the guarantor of peace and security on a continent that has been ravaged by war and tyranny for much of the past century.
>
> *Desmet and Stourton, 2019, p.3*[14]

By contrast, Johnson held firm to the BATNA of no-deal and this was deemed sufficiently credible for the EU to renegotiate the Irish backstop and replace it with a new Protocol on Northern Ireland. Johnson – who draws inspiration from his political icon, Winston Churchill (Johnson, 2014) – tapped into the Brexit narratives to declare in war-like terms that Britain would leave the EU "do-or-die" by the end of October 2019.[15] This implicit threat was supported by explicit cross-government civil contingency planning for no-deal, such as Operation Yellowhammer.

The personal beliefs of elites like May and Johnson have also framed perceptions of their BATNA and their resistance points in the negotiations. This relates specifically to the backstop to maintain an open border on the island of Ireland until an alternative arrangement is agreed. There were only two options: the entirety of the UK would have to abide by EU rules (something hardline Brexiters would never accept), or Norther Ireland would be subject to different laws from the rest of the country (something the DUP would never accept). At the point of domestic ratification, May's deal foundered on the first, while Johnson's deal succeeded on the second.

May had a strong aversion to commercially partitioning the UK market to deliver Brexit. This was partly driven by her deep personal belief about the "precious bond" between the four nations as she was a "unionist to her fingertips" (Seldon, 2019). She therefore proposed the UK-wide backstop, which effectively kept the country aligned to the EU in order to preserve the constitutional integrity of the union. This also delivered on her promise to the DUP to ensure no regulatory divergence between Britain and Northern Ireland. In contrast, Johnson had a lower resistance point and was prepared to put the province into play to achieve Brexit. With a parliamentary majority that relieved him of the need for the DUP's support, Johnson acceded to Brussels' favoured Northern Ireland-only backstop, which keeps the province aligned to the EU Single Market.

Political narratives

To secure domestic ratification, May and Johnson had to sell their deals to their own party, persuade the opposition and convince the electorate. They had to construct a compelling narrative about the benefits and trade-offs to reassure both pro- and anti-Brexiters that the deal offered better prospects than the BATNA of no-deal.

May struggled with this part of the ratification process because she approached Brexit as a damage limitation exercise, while her mechanical leadership style and few displays of emotion to the public earned her the nickname "Maybot" (Seldon, 2019). Unlike Brexiters, and especially Johnson's passionate storytelling, "She offered no vision of the future relationship between Britain and the EU, because she *had* no clear vision, seeing Brexit as a problem to be solved rather than a historic opportunity to reimagine Britain's future in a new world" (Seldon, 2019, p.xvii). Brexiters assailed May's agreement as a sell-out by reducing Britain to a "vassal state" of the EU together with the call to #chuckchequers. The Irish backstop was denounced as "anti-democratic" and rejected by the Conservative Party and the DUP despite the concessions and reassurances from Brussels that Britain would not be locked indefinitely into the customs union. It was also impossible for May to talk up the economic benefits – the government's forecast suggested the UK economy could be up to 3.9 per cent smaller after 15 years than if the UK had remained in the EU (HM Government, 2018). Moreover, May's case for ratification was not helped by external narrators, like US President Donald Trump, who declared that the agreement "sounds like a great deal for the EU" (Borger et al., 2018).

In comparison, Johnson was able to secure passage of his deal because of several factors. First, unlike May, Johnson is a passionate storyteller and master at setting a narrative, as evidenced by his two London Mayoral victories, his Vote Leave leadership and his landslide victory in the 2019 general election. In his first speech as Prime Minister on July 24, 2019, Johnson spoke of hope and optimism amid the parliamentary deadlock about a deal and the resulting economic uncertainties:

> At this extraordinary moment in our history and after three years of unfounded self-doubt it is time to change the record to recover our natural and historic role as an enterprising, outward-looking and truly global Britain, generous in temper and engaged with the world.

Second, his campaign message for the 2019 general election was simple, namely to "Get Brexit Done" and lead "Global Britain" (Happy Talk) while "levelling up" regions outside of London, especially the economically deprived north of England (Street Talk). This message appealed to a majority of the electorate, including voters exhausted by the interminable Brexit process and the failure of the political class to deliver the referendum result. Indeed, the action-oriented "Get Brexit Done" rallying cry was part of a broader narrative about the people (represented by Boris Johnson) versus an intransigent parliament suppressing the *vox populi* (Seargeant, 2019). The Conservative Party's electoral victory with the largest parliamentary majority since Margaret Thatcher in the 1980s strengthened the democratic case for respecting the Leave vote and ensured easy ratification of Johnson's deal.

The irony is that May had envisaged the Irish backstop being a fallback position, whereas Johnson declared victory by transforming it into the definitive future arrangement for Northern Ireland during the first four years after the transition period (O'Carroll, 2019). At the same time, he promised the people of Northern Ireland that there would be no border with Great Britain, although his negotiated Protocol would introduce barriers across the Irish Sea. Contrary to Johnson's assurances, customs checks are now implemented on freight entering the province from elsewhere in Britain. These post-Brexit arrangements have angered loyalists and partly contributed to the worst riots in years in Belfast (Sargeant, 2021). In other words, narratives that blithely discard facts and details for political expediency can have serious consequences.[16]

Third, Johnson's upbeat narrative was able to cast Brexit as a positive restart for Britain, even though economic forecasts of his deal suggested Britain would be worse off. While Johnson could claim victory with his deal, the divisiveness of Brexit and rising separatist sentiment in Scotland led him to adopt a less triumphalist and more conciliatory tone:

> We can now move forward as one country – with a government focused upon delivering better public services, greater opportunity and unleashing the potential of every corner of our brilliant United Kingdom, while building a strong new relationship with the EU as friends and sovereign equals.

Conclusion

Through the prism of Brexit, this chapter has demonstrated that narratives – stories about past, present and future – matter enormously for mobilising political constituencies and framing win-sets in negotiations. There was nothing inevitable about the outcome of the June 2016 referendum; for example, as late as December 2015, only 1 per cent of UK voters cited the EU as the issue most important to them (New Statesman, 2020). The Vote Leave campaign used emotionally engaging storytelling to mobilise a broad coalition of voters to win the day. Their narrative of contamination and redemption about the EU tapped into populist concerns about sovereignty, identity and EU overreach, as well as immigration and jobs, which resonated most strongly with English nationalists. In the end, however, it took almost three-and-a-half years for Britain to finally leave the EU. This was partly because the lofty promises and spurious claims of the Brexit campaign set expectations that were near impossible to achieve in the negotiations with Brussels without making tough trade-offs.

The post-Brexit negotiations for the future EU-UK relationship were framed by similar narratives. From the outset of the TCA negotiations, the UK prioritised sovereignty over market access. That meant imposing new barriers to existing free trade, championing the Brexit cause of fisheries (rather than services, which comprise 80 per cent of the UK's economy) and rejecting the EU's demands for a level playing field. With a BATNA of no-deal, Johnson's approach was confrontational with threats to walk away and refusing to extend the transition period despite the disruptions and devastation of the Covid-19 pandemic.

From "Take Back Control" to "Get Brexit Done," deep narratives have swayed voters on issues of identity and emotion rather than rational persuasion. Brexit has now fundamentally reshaped the UK's politics and even imperilled the three-centuries-old union between the four nations. Beyond Brexit, new and inclusive narratives may be necessary to build the case for preserving the UK. The same can be said for strengthening and unifying the EU.

Notes

1 Any views expressed in this chapter are those of the author and do not necessarily represent those of the Commonwealth Secretariat or its member countries.
2 The TCA is a free trade agreement covering all goods and limited services that leaves scope for regulatory regimes to diverge over time.
3 With the exception of Birmingham and Sheffield, all the major cities in the UK – London, Manchester, Liverpool and Newcastle, among them – voted to remain in the EU. They were outvoted by Leavers in smaller English cities and towns and in rural areas.
4 Wales voted for Brexit by a majority of just 82,000. However, an analysis of the voting reveals that the more genuinely Welsh areas, especially Welsh-speaking counties such as Gwynedd and Ceredigion, voted to continue EU membership. It was English settlers in border towns that swayed the vote (Perraudin, 2019).
5 Withdrawal from the EU is a right under Article 50 of the 2007 Lisbon Treaty: "Any member state may decide to withdraw from the Union in accordance with its own constitutional requirements." The two-year period for the withdrawal negotiations may only be extended with the unanimous agreement of the EU27 (union members, excluding the UK).
6 Obama (2016) argued that EU membership enhanced Britain's global leadership. He also cautioned that Britain would be "back of the queue" for any future trade deal, thus dealing a blow to the Brexiters' claims of burnishing the trans-Atlantic special relationship (Calamur, 2016).
7 Attributed to Jacob Rees-Mogg, leader of the pro-Brexit European Research Group within the Conservative Party (von Tunzelmann, 2019).
8 The position of the official Vote Leave campaign had been to use the time after the referendum to prepare and plan for the negotiations and not to trigger Article 50 pre-emptively (McTague, 2019).
9 The Draft Agreement on the Withdrawal of United Kingdom from the European Union.
10 The UK should have left the EU on March 29, 2019. This deadline was extended to October 31, 2019 and then January 31, 2020.
11 The first phase of the withdrawal negotiations focused on three areas: the settlement of the UK's financial obligations, safeguarding EU and UK citizens' rights and maintaining an open EU-UK land border on the island of Ireland. In December 2017, EU leaders agreed that sufficient progress had been made to move to the second phase of the negotiations, which focused initially on transitional arrangements and then on the framework for future economic and security cooperation.
12 There was a majority in the House of Commons in favour of a customs union arrangement.
13 The Withdrawal Agreement replaced the backstop with a new Protocol on Northern Ireland/Republic of Ireland. The Protocol provides the option for the Northern Ireland Assembly to vote after four years on whether to terminate or retain the arrangement.
14 In 2012, the EU was awarded the Nobel Peace Prize for advancing the causes of peace, reconciliation, democracy and human rights in Europe.

15 This was not to be the case and Johnson was compelled by parliament to ask for an extension to the deadline.
16 Johnson also threatened to legally override the Northern Ireland Protocol with the UK's Internal Market Bill, which was widely criticised for violating international law.

References

Barnett, A. (2017) *The Lure of Greatness: England's Brexit and America's Trump.* Unbound.

Barnier, M. (2021) *La Grande Illusion. Journal Secret du Brexit (2016–2020).* Paris, France: Gallimard.

Borger, J., Boffey, D., and, D. Sabbagh (2018, November 27) *May's Brexit Deal Sounds Like a 'Great Deal for the EU', Says Donald Trump,* The Guardian. www.theguardian.com/us-news/2018/nov/26/trump-brexit-deal-theresa-may-great-deal-for-eu

Calamur, K. (2016, April 22) *Obama's 'Brexit' Plea,* The Atlantic. www.theatlantic.com/international/archive/2016/04/obamas-brexit-plea/479469/

Connelly, T. (2017) *Brexit and Ireland: The Dangers, the Opportunities, and the Inside Story of the Irish Response.* Dublin: Penguin Ireland.

Desmet, L., and, Stourton, E. (2019) *Blind Man's Brexit: How the EU Took Control of Brexit.* London: Simon & Schuester.

Dustmann, C., and, Frattini, T. (2014) 'The Fiscal Effects of Immigration to the UK', *The Economic Journal,* vol.124, no.580, pp.565–568.

Fox, L. (2017, March 9) *Speech to Commonwealth Trade Ministers Meeting: Towards a Free Trading Future,* Government of the United Kingdom. www.gov.uk/government/speeches/commonwealth-trade-ministers-meeting-towards-a-free-trading-future

Glencross, A. (2015) 'Why a British Referendum on EU Membership will not solve the Europe Question', *International Affairs,* vol.9, no.2, pp.303–317.

Glencross, A. (2016) *Why the UK Voted for Brexit: David Cameron's Great Miscalculation.* London: Palgrave MacMillan.

Gross, S.G. (2017, June 23) *The Brexit Vote, One Year Later: The Historical Roots of the Decision to Leave the EU,* Foreign Affairs. www.foreignaffairs.com/articles/europe/2017-06-23/brexit-vote-one-year-later

Gruenbaum, O. (2017) 'Commonwealth Update. United Kingdom: Empire 2.0', *The Round Table. The Commonwealth Journal of International Affairs,* vol.106, no.2, pp.129–130.

Handa, S. (2019) *Can Brexit End the Scourge of British Nativism? Dominic Cummings Thinks So,* Foreign Policy. https://foreignpolicy.com/2019/08/10/can-boris-johnsons-brexit-guru-banish-nativist-populism-from-british-politics/

Hayes, T. (2018, March 3) *#Brexit: The UK Government's BATNA Dilemma,* BEERG Brexit Blog. https://beergbrexit.blog/2018/02/10/brexit-batna-dilemma/

Henley, J., and, Roberts, D. (2018, March 28) *11 Brexit Promises the Government Quietly Dropped,* The Guardian. www.theguardian.com/politics/ng-interactive/2018/mar/28/11-brexit-promises-leavers-quietly-dropped

HM Government. (2018, November) *EU Exit Long-Term Economic Analysis.* https://assets.publishing.service.gov.uk/government/uploads/system/uploads/attachment_data/file/760484/28_November_EU_Exit_-_Long-term_economic_analysis__1_.pdf

Huggins, T. (2018) 'Did EU Regional Spending affect the Brexit Referendum?', *Regional Studies, Regional Science,* vol.5, no.1, pp.388–397.

Ipsos/MORI (2016, June 16) *Immigration Is Now the Top Issue for Voters in the EU Referendum,* IPSOS. www.ipsos.com/ipsos-mori/en-uk/immigration-now-top-issue-voters-eu-referendum

Jennings, W., and, Stoker, G. (2016) 'The Bifurcation of Politics: Two Englands', *The Political Quarterly*, vol.87, no.3, pp.372–382.

Johnson, B. (2014) *The Churchill Factor: How One Man Made History*. London: Hodder & Stoughton.

Matthews, J. (2019, November 18) *Breakup of UK a Price Worth Paying for Brexit, Say Leave Voters in Poll*, Sky News. https://news.sky.com/story/breakup-of-uk-a-price-worth-paying-for-brexit-say-leave-voters-in-poll-11863830

McTague, T. (2019, March 27) *How the UK Lost the Brexit Battle,* Politico. www.politico.eu/article/how-uk-lost-brexit-eu-negotiation/

Meek, J. (2019) *Dreams of Leaving and Remaining*. London: Verso.

New Statesman (2020, January 29) *Leader: Britain After Brexit*. www.newstatesman.com/politics/brexit/2020/01/leader-britain-after-brexit

Nichols, T. (2017) *The Death of Expertise: The Campaign Against Established Knowledge and Why it Matters*. Oxford: Oxford University Press.

Obama, B. (2016, April 23) *As Your Friend, Let Me Say That the EU Makes Britain Even Greater,* The Telegraph. www.telegraph.co.uk/news/2016/04/21/as-your-friend-let-me-tell-you-that-the-eu-makes-britain-even-gr/

O'Carroll, L. (2019, October 17) *How Is Boris Johnson's Brexit Deal Different from Theresa May's?* The Guardian. www.theguardian.com/politics/2019/oct/17/how-is-boris-johnson-brexit-deal-different-from-theresa-may

O'Toole, F. (2018) *Heroic Failure: Brexit and the Politics of Pain*. London: Apollo.

Perraudin, F. (2019, September 22) *English People Living in Wales Tilted It Towards Brexit, Research Finds*, The Guardian. www.theguardian.com/uk-news/2019/sep/22/english-people-wales-brexit-research

Putnam, R. (1988) 'Diplomacy and Domestic Politics: The Logic of Two-Level Games', *International Organization*, vol.42, no.3, pp. 427–460.

Reynolds, D. (2019) *Island Stories. Britain and its History in the Age of Brexit*. London: William Collins.

Sargeant, J. (2021, April 15) *The UK Government Must Take Responsibility for Making the Northern Ireland Protocol Work*, Institute for Government. www.instituteforgovernment.org.uk/blog/northern-ireland-protocol-tensions

Saunders, R. (2016, July-September) 'A Tale of Two Referendums: 1975 and 2016', *The Political Quarterly*, vol.87, no.3, pp.318–322.

Saunders, R. (2019, October 11–17) 'Myths from a Small Island', *New Statesman*, pp.23–27.

Seargeant, P. (2019, December 20) *Get Brexit Done: Why Storytelling Is So Important for Electoral Success*, Diggit Magazine. www.diggitmagazine.com/column/get-Brexit-done-storytelling

Seldon, A. (2019) *May at 10*. London: Biteback Publishing.

Sobolewska, M., and, Ford, R. (2020) *Brexitland: Identity, Diversity and the Reshaping of British Politics*. Cambridge: Cambridge University Press.

Tetlow, G., and, Stojanovic, A. (2018) *Understanding the Economic Impact of Brexit*. London: Institute for Government. www.instituteforgovernment.org.uk/sites/default/files/publications/2018%20IfG%20%20Brexit%20impact%20%5Bfinal%20for%20web%5D.pdf

Von Tunzelmann, A. (2019, August 12) *The Imperial Myths Driving Brexit*, The Atlantic. www.theatlantic.com/international/archive/2019/08/imperial-myths-behind-brexit/595813/

5

A WIN-WIN COMPROMISE

How Canada won at home while America came first in NAFTA renegotiations

Meredith Lilly

Introduction

When the United States, Canada and Mexico reached a new agreement to replace the North American Free Trade Agreement (NAFTA) on September 30, 2018, Canada and the US issued a terse joint statement of confirmation. It marked the conclusion of 13 difficult months of negotiations in which talks nearly collapsed. The process was triggered on May 18, 2017, when US Trade Representative Robert Lighthizer notified Congress of the administration's intention to renegotiate NAFTA. Formally launched on August 16th the same year, negotiations were initially productive, as the three countries quickly reached consensus on areas of shared interest. However, tensions rose in the months that followed as controversial areas such as rules of origin on autos were tabled.

Separate tit-for-tat trade action between Canada and the US escalated, spilling over to stymy progress on the deal. The US had imposed punitive duties on Canadian softwood lumber exports, leading Canada to retaliate shortly thereafter with a WTO claim on trade remedies. Rumors of clashes between the US and Canada during the Montreal negotiating round in January 2018 were blamed on Canadian fringe proposals that neither Mexico nor the US prioritized, and were interpreted by the Trump administration as obstructionist (ICTSD, 2018). Not long after, American lawmakers speculated about sidelining Canada from negotiations to focus on progress with Mexico alone (Panetta, 2018). By the time Trump imposed steel and aluminum tariffs against both Canada and Mexico in May of 2018, trilateral negotiations had effectively ceased. However, motivated by Mexico's looming electoral calendar, the US and Mexico continued to negotiate bilaterally through the summer, excluding Canada. When the two reached an agreement-in-principle at the end of August, Canada was invited to return to trilateralized talks, dramatically increasing pressure on the northern country

DOI: 10.4324/9781003203209-7

to make concessions or face being left out altogether. Around-the-clock sessions continued for the next month, concluding on the US-imposed deadline of September 30, 2018.

Concurrent to policy developments at the negotiating table, national leaders developed political messaging about the events that were transpiring, and which they hoped media in their respective countries would propel more broadly. This chapter addresses the narratives that American and Canadian political leaders conveyed to citizens about the renegotiations.

The chapter is less about the messages that each government directed at one another, yet it is acknowledged that the content of a government's messaging to its home audience is often directed at the other side of the negotiations as well. Yet, through personal experience of participating in such negotiations at the highest levels, I know that the narratives conveyed to the public are usually a very simplified version of much longer and more complex private discussions between political leaders. Those exchanges are different still from the technical negotiations that consume most time and effort, and which represent the lion's share of any final agreement. Thus, the chapter is also not a record of the final outcomes achieved by any party in the NAFTA renegotiations, although the alignment and realignment of narratives to potential outcomes are addressed in several places.[1]

A deliberate decision was taken to omit Mexico's NAFTA narrative in this chapter. This was in part because the author is not a specialist on Mexico, and a strong understanding of language and culture is necessary to analyze narratives well. However, it is also due to the unique political context in Mexico during NAFTA renegotiations. The country's 2018 presidential election campaign period overlapped directly with the negotiations, meaning the US-Mexico-Canada agreement (USMCA) was negotiated primarily by outgoing President Enrique Peña Nieto. Populist candidate Andres Manuel Lopez Obrador (AMLO) was widely expected to win and his goals for the economy were completely different. Thus, although Peña Nieto's Economy Minister, Ildefonso Guajardo, was the public face of Mexico's negotiating team, AMLO's representative Jesús Seade also participated actively in the final months of negotiations before AMLO took office (Graham, 2018). Given these factors, it is difficult to assert either the origins or authenticity of any single Mexican narrative for the negotiations from publicly available sources.

Finally, for simplicity, this chapter will refer to the new agreement negotiated in 2018 as the USMCA. It is acknowledged that both Canada and Mexico use their own legal names for the agreement, represented as CUSMA and T-MEC, respectively. However, in alignment with the argument advanced in this chapter, the "America First" acronym will be used unless referencing a direct quote.

US presidential campaign rhetoric set the stage

Prior to his election as US president, Donald Trump had attacked NAFTA as the worst deal in US history and vowed to renegotiate it if elected. Throughout the 2016 campaign, Trump attributed American manufacturing job losses in the early 2000s directly to NAFTA, reminding audiences that it was Bill Clinton who signed the deal. During their first televised debate, Trump told Hillary Clinton the following:

> Your husband signed NAFTA, which was one of the worst things that ever happened to the manufacturing industry … You go to New England, you go to Ohio, Pennsylvania, you go anywhere you want, Secretary Clinton, and you will see devastation where manufacturing is down 30, 40, sometimes 50 percent. NAFTA is the worst trade deal maybe ever signed anywhere, but certainly ever signed in this country.
>
> *Blake, 2016*

Trump's opposition to free trade was not unique among presidential candidates: Hillary Clinton also adopted a campaign position opposing NAFTA, as had Barack Obama in his own presidential race. Instead, it was Trump's status as a Republican that made his opposition to NAFTA both unusual and newsworthy. More problematic, Trump's failure to soften his strident stance following the election also made him unique. For example, Bill Clinton had agreed to support NAFTA if elected, conditional on Canada and Mexico agreeing to the addition of labor and environment side letters (Behr, 1993). Similarly, Obama decided against reopening NAFTA shortly after meeting Mexican President Calderon and Canadian Prime Minister Harper, who both urged Obama to build on the agreement's strengths (Knowlton, 2009). In fact, Obama grew to embrace trade agreements as an important geopolitical tool, eventually leading the negotiation of the 12-country Trans-Pacific Partnership (TPP) that would have replaced NAFTA had Congress approved it. Many observers expected Trump to also moderate his fire and brimstone campaign rhetoric once in office. Instead, Trump doubled down, signing the Executive Order to withdraw the US from the TPP as one of his first official acts (White House, 2017).

The new president's approach was very threatening to Canadians, who had benefited greatly from NAFTA. Unlike in the US where half the population regarded the deal negatively in 2017, three-quarters of Canadians viewed the agreement as positive (Stokes, 2017; Gallup, 2017). Canada's optimism about free trade generally, and NAFTA specifically, has been largely attributed to the original Canada–US trade deal of the 1980s, which became a ballot box item for Conservative Prime Minister Brian Mulroney. In order to bolster his mandate to sign the agreement and counter domestic concerns about American domination of Canada under a trade pact, Mulroney waged his 1988 re-election on support for the deal. Dubbed Canada's "free trade election," Mulroney's subsequent victory largely settled the question of Canadian support for free trade for more than a generation (Hampson, 2018).

Given Canada's economic reliance on free trade with the US, it surprised many when the Trudeau government cheerfully agreed to renegotiate NAFTA the morning after Trump's election, rather than seeking to use the transition period to convince the incoming administration otherwise. Instead, on November 9th, 2016, Canadian Ambassador to the US David McNaughton sketched the outline of Canada's narrative that would persist for two years:

> If they (the US) want to have a discussion about improving NAFTA, we're ready to come to the table to try and put before the new administration anything that will benefit both Canada and the United States and obviously Mexico also.

In the weeks and months that followed, this "win-win-win" narrative would take hold in the Trudeau government, repeated by its leadership at every opportunity.

This chapter argues that the Trump administration consistently advanced a singular narrative to *Make America Great Again* (MAGA) by repeating simple messages to support it. Set in the framework of Hampson and Narlikar [in this volume] , the American narrative began as one of *contamination*, whereby the US needed to erase NAFTA, the "worst trade deal ever," and restore fair trade with other countries. As negotiations reached their conclusion, the US narrative transitioned to one of *redemption*, whereby Trump's unique commitment to putting America first would restore greatness. This US narrative, fully outlined below, was also a *deep* one (Hampson and Narlikar, [in this volume]) that elicited strong emotions of anger and victimization to explain America's decline under previous administrations.

By contrast, it is argued that Canada pursued a "win-win-win" narrative to benefit all three countries. As conceptualized by Hampson and Narlikar, Canada's approach reflected a *collective agency* narrative, appealing to all three countries to work together to make a good agreement even better. However, the Canadian approach was *shallow*, using intellectual messaging to advance complex policies that both failed to resonate with Canadians and were at odds with the Trump administration's goals. Thus, as predicted by Hampson and Narlikar, when Canada's shallow narrative inevitably clashed with Trump's deep one, Canada was forced to back down. At that point, Canada managed to articulate a new narrative of Standing up for Canadian Values, pivoting away from its shallow *collective agency* narrative toward a *redemption* theme. This shift resonated much more *deeply* with Canadians, enabling the government to both claim victory at home, while still allowing America to come first.

This chapter proceeds as follows. The key players for each country and their chosen methods for advancing their respective narratives are outlined. Next, the competing narratives presented by the US and Canada are fully described, with particular attention to shifts as negotiations advanced. Finally, an analysis is undertaken of how the two countries' narratives interacted, and the overall success of each.

Chief narrators and their communication tools

Although some elements of the two countries' narratives had already taken shape in 2016, both spent the early months of 2017 preparing for negotiations.

Long-time trade lawyer and former advisor to the Reagan administration, Robert Lighthizer, was appointed US Trade Representative in May 2017. With decades of experience advancing the interests of US steel and autos, Lighthizer was a major proponent of the president's America First approach (The White House, 2017). Yet despite his clear technical leadership on the file, Lighthizer rarely gave interviews or spoke publicly (Panetta, 2018). Instead, Trump himself was the US's chief narrator on NAFTA, continuing the storyline he advanced during his presidential campaign.

On the Canadian side, Prime Minister Justin Trudeau shuffled his government in early January 2017 to prepare for the Trump administration. Chrystia Freeland, who had been trade minister since 2015, became Canada's foreign minister and would also be given responsibility for all aspects of the Canada–US relationship including bilateral trade and NAFTA. Chief Negotiator Steve Verheul would head the technical negotiations, but Freeland would act as political lead and chief spokesperson. Freeland was given broad latitude by the prime minister and, as a former journalist, she engaged the press extremely effectively. She convened press conferences regularly throughout negotiations, delivering carefully rehearsed speeches followed by long Q&A sessions.

Normally, it would be problematic for countries to select representatives at different levels of seniority, as represented by the Trump-Freeland match. However, this asymmetry likely worked in Canada's favor. Trump's loud and bombastic threats did not need to be challenged directly by Prime Minister Trudeau, who could then play "good cop" with Trump throughout much of the negotiations (though there were ripples including following the G7 in Quebec). As a subordinate, Freeland was constrained in her capacity to play "bad cop," enabling her to confront the substance of Trump's threats without mentioning him directly. In this way, her criticism received broad domestic media coverage, without gaining much attention in the US. Although she was clearly on Trump's radar, and he once indicated "we don't like [Canada's] representative very much"(McCarten, 2018), he generally ignored her publicly.

Analysis of the key elements of the negotiating narratives advanced by the US and Canada is focused on the primary tools of communication used by each country's chief narrator. As has been well documented, Trump's preferred method of communication is via twitter. An "authentic outsider" (Gallagher, 2019; Enli, 2017), Trump was able to use the communication platform to reach voters directly, unfiltered by either traditional media or Republican party operatives. The @RealDonaldTrump account offers a raw and unconstrained source of data about the president's storytelling intentions for the negotiations (McKechnie, 2017). Some experts suggest that Trump used the twitter medium effectively to frame issues rhetorically to his own benefit by connecting emotionally with the public (Gallagher, 2019). Importantly for his political base, the president's frequent use of capitalized text and rudeness denote "authenticity markers" that further validate Trump's outsider credentials (Enli, 2017). Using the online tool, <trumptwitterarchive.com>, which provides a complete history of the president's tweets since inauguration (Brown, n.d.), all of the president's tweets related to NAFTA and trade with Mexico and Canada over a three-year period were analyzed for themes (January 20, 2017 to January 20, 2020).

By contrast, Freeland's leadership style embraces the establishment narrative of the international rules-based order (Lamp, 2020) and her preferred communication style is the carefully crafted public speech. Throughout negotiations, her addresses were the subject of intense interest from the Canadian press gallery. Unlike major American media outlets that reported on negotiation developments only sporadically, Canadian broadcasters televised every public meeting between Freeland and Lighthizer. Aligned with key phases of the negotiations, analysis focuses on four of Freeland's major public events: the launch of negotiations in August 2017; testimony to Parliament in February 2018; comments at the conclusion of Round Seven in Mexico; and the announcement of the conclusion of negotiations on October 1, 2018. Prime Minister Trudeau joined Freeland for that final press conference and his comments are also reflected (Global Affairs Canada, 2017; Global Affairs Canada, 2018a; Global Affairs Canada, 2018b; C-Span, 2018).

Competing narratives collide

From the outset, the US and Canada pursued different goals for the renegotiation of NAFTA. Figure 5.1 provides an overview of the negotiating narratives presented by both countries at different stages, which are described in detail below.

USA's overarching narrative: Make America great again

For Trump, NAFTA's renegotiation represented a signature policy in his broader MAGA narrative. Over three phases, the narrative morphed from one of *contamination* to *redemption* (Hampson and Narlikar, in this volume). While the end

Phase		Pre-negotiation and launch	Mid-phase confrontation	Endgame and conclusion
American	Primary	Make America great again!		
	Sub-theme	Erase NAFTA (*contamination*)	Fair trade	America first (*redemption*)
Canadian	Primary	Win-win-win! (*collective agency*)	(*Reorientation*)	Standing up for Canadian values (*redemption*)
	Sub-theme	Building on success	Progressive trade	Polite but strong

FIGURE 5.1 American vs. Canadian negotiating narratives

goal of the narrative was to restore American greatness through the negotiation, the president first needed to name the enemy (NAFTA) and demonstrate how he personally would rebuild American dominance. Thus, the broader MAGA narrative can be divided into three sub-themes or phases: (1) Erase NAFTA; (2) pursue Fair Trade; and (3) put America First. The simplified narrative can be stated as follows:

> To *Make America Great Again,* the US must *Erase NAFTA* and negotiate *Fair Trade* with other countries by putting *America First.*

Although the complete narrative was introduced early in negotiations, each sub-theme would be prioritized at different stages and are described below.

Erase NAFTA

The first sub-theme, *Erase NAFTA*, focused on further vilifying the already much maligned acronym and threatening to terminate the agreement altogether if Canada and Mexico did not work with the Americans to negotiate a better deal. During the first three years of Trump's presidency, the term "NAFTA" appeared 33 times and virtually every reference was negative:

> I received calls from the President of Mexico and the Prime Minister of Canada asking to renegotiate NAFTA rather than terminate. I agreed … subject to the fact that if we do not reach a fair deal for all, we will then terminate NAFTA.
>
> *@realDonaldTrump, 2017, April 27*

> We are in the NAFTA (worst trade deal ever made) renegotiation process with Mexico & Canada. Both being very difficult, may have to terminate?
>
> *@realDonaldTrump, 2017, August 27*

> NAFTA is a bad joke!
>
> *@realDonaldTrump, 2018, January 18*

In the early phase of negotiations, Trump's goal was to establish NAFTA as a contaminating force in the US by highlighting the agreement's "deficiencies and mistakes" (@realDonaldTrump, 2018, October 1). Success in establishing this first sub-theme would then enable Trump to move on to the second sub-theme, negotiating "fair trade" with the other two countries.

Fair trade

In Trump's articulation of the MAGA vision, the US is a winner. Thus, where the US has fallen behind, it must be because other countries have "cheated" or "stolen" from it. Trump has articulated this victimization sentiment across many files, including NATO and trade policy with China (Lamp, 2020). In NAFTA negotiations, Trump often focused on the concept of fairness, asserting that Canada and Mexico had treated the US unfairly under NAFTA, and his intervention would restore American dominance.

This sub-theme triggered a shift away from the theme of *contamination* and toward *redemption* (Hampson and Narlikar, in this volume), wherein Trump began to articulate how his intervention would reset relations with the two other countries. For Canada specifically, the President was preoccupied with eliminating its protectionist supply management system for dairy:

> Canada charges the U.S. a 270% tariff on Dairy Products! They didn't tell you that, did they? Not fair to our farmers!
>
> *@realDonaldTrump, 2018, June 8*

> Fair Trade is now to be called Fool Trade if it is not Reciprocal. According to a Canada release, they make almost 100 Billion Dollars in Trade with U.S. (guess they were bragging and got caught!). Minimum is 17B. Tax Dairy from us at 270%. Then Justin acts hurt when called out!
>
> *@realDonaldTrump, 2018, June 10*

> PM Justin Trudeau of Canada acted so meek and mild during our @G7 meetings only to give a news conference after I left saying that, "US Tariffs were kind of insulting" and he "will not be pushed around." Very dishonest & weak. Our Tariffs are in response to his of 270% on dairy!
>
> *@realDonaldTrump, 2018, June 9*

By emphasizing "fairness," the president's goal was to advance the application of quotas, tariffs and trade remedies to develop managed trade solutions the US "deserved," rather than promoting free trade solutions for all parties based on reciprocity. The following examples demonstrate how the president combined this stance with aggressive threats of additional tariffs to protect American interest groups in the new agreement:

> We have large trade deficits with Mexico and Canada. NAFTA, which is under renegotiation right now, has been a bad deal for U.S.A. Massive relocation of companies & jobs. Tariffs on Steel and Aluminum will only come off if new & fair NAFTA agreement is signed. Also, Canada must … treat our farmers much better. Highly restrictive.
>
> *@realDonaldTrump, 2018, March 5*

> Farmers have not been doing well for 15 years. Mexico, Canada, China and others have treated them unfairly. By the time I finish trade talks, that will change. Big trade barriers against U.S. farmers, and other businesses, will finally be broken. Massive trade deficits no longer!
>
> *@realDonaldTrump, 2018, June 4*

In addition, the president's attention to specific winners and losers is consistent with recent research demonstrating that citizens support trade agreements they perceive to benefit them personally, not their country as a whole (Brutger and Rathbun, 2017). While this *Fair Trade* sub-theme persisted throughout, once talks entered the end game, the president shifted his focus again to winning.

America first

After completing the first two phases of negotiations and their corresponding sub-narratives, Trump turned his sights to demonstrating how the US had won at the expense of the other two partners, thereby completing the shift to a *redemption* narrative (Hampson and Narlikar, in this volume). The *America First* sub-theme, focused on winners and losers in the NAFTA negotiations; while the US may have been losing under the unfair NAFTA deal, Americans would again be winners following renegotiations. This was exemplified in the new USMCA name, that effectively erased NAFTA and rightfully put America first.

> Late last night, our deadline, we reached a wonderful new Trade Deal with Canada, to be added into the deal already reached with Mexico. The new name will be The United States Mexico Canada Agreement, or USMCA. It is a great deal for all three countries, solves the many … deficiencies and mistakes in NAFTA, greatly opens markets to our Farmers and Manufacturers, reduce Trade Barriers to the U.S. and will bring all three Great Nations closer together in competition with the rest of the world. The USMCA is a historic transaction!
>
> *@realDonaldTrump, 2018, October 1*

> The terrible NAFTA will soon be gone. The USMCA will be fantastic for all!
>
> *@realDonaldTrump, 2018, November 30*

> Great reviews on the USMCA – sooo much better than NAFTA!
>
> *@realDonaldTrump, 2018, November 30*

Trump continued to advance this dichotomy following Congressional midterms when the Administration was forced to renegotiate aspects of USMCA to gain support of House Democrats:

> Nervous Nancy Pelosi & the Democrat House are getting nothing done. Perhaps they could lead the way with the USMCA, the spectacular & very popular new Trade Deal that replaces NAFTA, the worst Trade Deal in the history of the U.S.A. Great for our Farmers, Manufacturers & Unions!'
>
> *@realDonaldTrump, 2019, June 8*

Summarizing the American approach

Trump earned his reputation as an erratic and unpredictable president, but his NAFTA tweets reflected a remarkably consistent narrative. For example, he never referenced the term "free trade" with respect to the negotiations. Also, since the narrative was never intended to reach American trade or foreign policy experts, the president also successfully maintained simple, non-technical language and never made detailed assessments of progress. Furthermore, his use of strong, negative language, threats and actions were geared to his own political supporters, for whom the *Make America Great Again* narrative is so deeply felt they wear the slogan proudly on their clothing.

Canada's overarching narrative: Win-win-win

The Canadians' "win-win-win" NAFTA narrative reflected the Liberal government's broader "sunny ways" approach to governing (Liberal Party of Canada, 2016). Specifically, the Trudeau government believed that all three countries could benefit from modernizing and improving NAFTA to reflect 21st century realities. While there were elements of the agreement that Canada wanted to revise (particularly around procurement and *Buy America*), the Canadians focused on emphasizing the gains that all countries could make through expanding and further liberalizing trade between them. On the whole, this win-win-win narrative was intellectual, reflecting the use of collective agency to promote the liberalized trading order. The narrative was also a shallow one that largely failed to resonate with the public (Hampson and Narlikar, in this volume).

Within this broader framework, Freeland's team articulated three sub-themes as negotiations progressed: (1) Build on Success; (2) Progressive Trade; and (3) Polite, but Strong. All three were introduced early in negotiations, but they did not all endure, nor did they fit together neatly to create a clear overall picture of Canada's intentions. Unlike the US' MAGA narrative, which remained consistent throughout, Canada's win-win-win narrative became less prominent as talks soured and public hostility rose toward Trump. By the time negotiations concluded, Canada was forced to abandon its original, shallow narrative in favor of a more forceful one that resonated with citizens: "Standing up for Canadian Values."

Build on Success

Consistent with its "win-win-win" approach, Canada's primary goal was to *Build on Success* by modernizing NAFTA to cover new areas of trade such as digital and e-commerce provisions, and to broaden in scope existing chapters in such areas as temporary entry to be even more liberalizing (Lilly, 2019). This sub-theme also reflected the messages being sent by corporate leaders in all three countries who were very concerned about a potential US withdrawal from NAFTA. Business associations advocated a trilateral "first, do no harm" approach that focused on preserving market access above all else (Canadian Chamber of Commerce, 2017). Entering into talks, Freeland repeated that message:

> Canada, the United States, and Mexico have a powerful shared interest in reaching a mutually beneficial agreement. Strong economic fundamentals are a compelling argument for bolstering what works, and improving what can be made better.
>
> *Global Affairs Canada, 2017*

In the same speech, she reiterated the value-creating narrative underpinning Canada's strategy:

> We pursue trade, free and fair, knowing it's not a zero-sum-game. When innovators on both sides of a border are free to produce and sell their best wares to a wider market, while also getting access to goods and services from the other side, everyone wins.
>
> *Global Affairs Canada, 2017*

Thus, in the early days, Freeland appealed to *collective agency* to advocate for even broader and more open trade between the three countries (Hampson and Narlikar, in this volume). Not only did this approach fall flat with the Trump administration, the progressive arm of Trudeau's own government and its supporters in the organized labor movement also had concerns with the wholesale adoption of the previous Harper government's expansionist trade agenda. Thus, the Trudeau government began to introduce a second phase to its narrative focused on progressive trade.

Progressive Trade

As evidenced by Trudeau's ambiguous treatment of the TPP during the 2015 election campaign and through his first year in office, left-wing groups and Canadian labor organizations supporting the government had serious policy discomfort with further liberalizing global trade, pointing to the distributional consequences of globalization for the middle class. Freeland's proposed solution was to advance a progressive trade agenda that would ensure the benefits of trade could benefit "everyone" rather than a narrow class of "elites" (Lilly, 2018, pp.127–130). In NAFTA talks, these were expressed as the *Progressive Trade* sub-theme.

Freeland's original vision for the agenda was far-reaching. In her speech to launch NAFTA's renegotiation in August 2017, Freeland stated:

> Now, as we extol the benefits of global trade, we shouldn't be under any illusions that we have perfect trade deals, or a perfect economy. We do not. That

> is what makes this such an important moment. Too many working people feel abandoned by the 21st Century global economy, and have voted accordingly, abandoning the modern liberal vision of trade and growth and openness to the world. Too many towns and too many lives across the industrialized world have been blighted by factory closings and precarious work.
>
> *Global Affairs Canada, 2017*

Later in the speech, Freeland outlined Canada's core objectives for the NAFTA negotiations, including four chapters focused on progressive trade: labor, environment, gender and indigenous. She then outlined the redistributive purpose of that focus:

> One reason that these progressive elements, particularly on the environment and labour, are so important is that they are how we guarantee that the modernized NAFTA will not only be an exemplary free trade deal, it will also be a fair trade deal. Canadians broadly support free trade. But their enthusiasm wavers when trade agreements put our workers at an unfair disadvantage because of the high standards that we rightly demand.
>
> *Global Affairs Canada, 2017*

The theme would become problematic, both politically and from a policy perspective. First, it was ineffective as a narrative, and reflected instead a set of policy proposals the government was seeking to advance and awkwardly explain to a disengaged public. Second, the agenda became simplified into a "box-checking" exercise focused around negotiating the four above-mentioned chapters. In the process, the progressive trade agenda failed to retain the key aspect that resonated with the largest group of voters: fairness for the middle class. Third, the agenda represented a policy problem due to its conflicting orientation with the *Building on Success* theme. As conceptualized by Lamp (2020), *Building on Success* reflected an establishment narrative that prioritized maintaining the status quo, while *Progressive Trade* offered a critical narrative that required radical change. How could the Trudeau government both believe that NAFTA was successful, and also be in need of a complete overhaul because its economic gains had not been "fairly" or "broadly shared" among Canadians (Global Affairs Canada, 2017)?

Defending progressive trade became even more politically difficult for the Liberals during the winter of 2018 when Trump was lobbing his own phase-two *Fair Trade* grenades at Canada. The impression left among many Canadians was that their government was chasing butterflies while Trump was waging trench warfare. At that point, the Canadians were forced to downplay their progressive agenda, and increase attention to the middle class. For example, in February, Freeland stated:

> President Trump has said his most important goal is to help American workers and to help the American middle class. We in Canada have exactly

> the same goal for our workers and our middle class. This can and should be a shared project.
>
> *Global Affairs Canada, 2018b*

By renewing its original focus on middle class workers in this way, Canada effectively identified a shared priority of the Trump administration. This pivot away from progressive trade represented an important realignment of the Canadian narrative.

Polite, but Strong

Despite Freeland's initial optimism, she was keenly aware that Canada was in a precarious position with the Trump administration. Canada depended on the US for roughly 75% of its exports, and even Obama's relatively friendly administration took advantage of the asymmetrical power dynamics when negotiating with Canada over market access in TPP and softwood lumber (Lilly et al., 2020). Given that Trump had campaigned on tearing up NAFTA, Freeland knew that negotiations would be very difficult.

Thus, from day one, she advanced the *Polite but Strong* sub-theme. In her 2017 speech to launch negotiations, Freeland began by noting that during the war of 1812, the Canadians had erected a sign at the border "depict[ing] an American eagle and a British lion with the slogan, 'if you don't scratch, I won't bite' (Global Affairs Canada, 2017)." Later in the same speech, she reminded the audience of the history of tough actions by previous Canadian negotiators, and their willingness to walk away rather than accept sub-standard deals:

> Our approach in these talks will be in keeping with our national character; hard-working, fact-based, cordial, animated by the spirit of goodwill and the pursuit of compromise. We also know that there is no contradiction between being polite, and being strong. It is no accident that hockey is our national sport.
>
> *Global Affairs Canada, 2017*

Unlike Canada's overarching win-win-win narrative or the other two sub-themes, the *Polite but Strong* pillar was downplayed initially but would grow in importance as negotiations became challenging. By the end of negotiations, it had morphed into Canada's rearticulated overall narrative, *Standing up for Canadian Values.*

Freeland's 2.0 narrative: Standing up for Canadian values

As hostilities grew in the spring of 2018 and Canada found itself excluded from negotiations by early summer, it was clear that changes were necessary to Canada's overall negotiating strategy, including its narrative. Freeland needed to downplay Canadian expectations about what a successful agreement might look like, conscious that if Canada was invited back to the table, her government would be forced to accept a series of concessions. In a worst case scenario, there would be no agreement, and so a secondary narrative was also required to reassure Canadians that a no-deal outcome could be preferable (a so-called "BATNA" narrative – "best alternative to a negotiated agreement").

Thus, in summer 2018, the Canadian side was forced to pivot and prepare the ground for either eventuality. It was at this point that Freeland presented a new, reimagined narrative, *Standing up for Canadian Values*, which focused on confronting the administration and defending middle class jobs by working to achieve a "good deal":

> As the Prime Minister said yesterday in Chicago, our objective is a good deal, not just any deal. At the negotiating table, Canada always takes a facts-based approach. We are always polite and we are adept at seeking creative solutions and win-win-win compromises, but we are also resolute. Canada will only accept an agreement if it is in our national interest and respects Canadian values.
>
> *Global Affairs Canada, 2018a*

In this way, the government worked to reinforce the idea that some deals may not be worth accepting, and if negotiations failed, it was because the agreement on offer did not reflect Canada's economic interests or values.

As expected, when Canada was invited back to join the bilateral agreement-in-principle between the US and Mexico at the end of August, Canada was under enormous pressure to capitulate. In those final weeks of negotiations, the Canadians ramped up their references to the need to retain two specific policy outcomes in any final deal: (1) Chapter 19, the dispute settlement system; and (2) the cultural exemption for Canadian creative works (Tunney, 2018). Both tapped into deep Canadian fears about American domination over Canadian cultural and economic interests, and were red line items in the original Canada–US talks (Hampson, 2018). By underscoring the importance of these two outcomes, the Canadian side was seeking to exploit those longstanding domestic fears in order to prepare Canadians for the idea that a failed negotiation could only have resulted because the government could not accept such infringements on Canadian sovereignty.

Interestingly, in substantive terms, Chapter 19 was genuinely believed to be in jeopardy during those final weeks, both due to the 11th hour history surrounding the chapter in the original Canada–US agreement (Hampson, 2018), but also because its elimination was a longstanding personal goal of Secretary Lighthizer. However, close observers did not believe that retaining NAFTA's cultural exemption was ever a contentious topic.[2] Thus, while the first item was advanced to prepare Canadians for a potential no-deal, some have suggested that the cultural exemption was raised specifically to placate Quebec, the province most wedded to it. When Canada made dairy concessions to finalize USMCA, which hurt

Quebec's economic interests more than any other province, the government was able to point to its efforts to stand up for Quebec's values via the cultural exemption as a consolation prize (McGregor, 2018).

Despite the flurried effort underway to finalize a trilateral deal in September, the Canadian public's appetite for a fight with Trump was strong. Thus, it was essential for Freeland and her team to demonstrate they had not simply folded under pressure. For example, during the final press conference to announce the conclusion of USMCA, Trudeau opened with a reference to Canada's determination and strength:

> A year and a half ago, with rising questions about the future of NAFTA, I was asked how we would respond. My answer was that we'd respond as Canadians always have in uncertain times. We'd be constructive and reasonable, but we'd also be firm. We'd protect our interests and promote our values. We'd show determination and also flexibility and we would remain united. And ultimately, we'd emerge stronger. And that is exactly what we did.
>
> *C-Span, 2018*

To demonstrate success at pursuing Canada's national interests, he then championed Canada's retention of dispute settlement rules in the final agreement, aligning the outcome with Canadian values:

> [W]hen your trading partner is ten times your size, you need rules. You need a level playing field. Unless the new agreement achieved those objectives, we would not sign it. Simply put, the new agreement had to be good for Canada and for Canadians.
>
> *C-Span, 2018*

But more than anything, Trudeau referenced the preservation of NAFTA's market access, and the restoration of stability to the trading relationship. In this way, retaining status quo access to American markets was reframed as a victory:

> We kept our focus and resolve even when some were recommending we capitulate … Free and fair trade in North America … is in a much more stable place than it was yesterday … NAFTA will be preserved, updated, modernized and stabilized for the 21st century.
>
> *C-Span, 2018*

Finally, in thanking Canadians, Trudeau was able to demonstrate that the resolve shown by his team reflected the desire among Canadians to stand up to Trump: "I have to thank every Canadian – and there were thousands of them – who wrote letters and emails and stopped me on the street to say 'keep at it. Stay strong. We are with you." (C-Span, 2018)

Analysis: A winning compromise

How did the American and Canadian narratives interact with each other, and who advanced a more successful narrative? Regardless of the content of the final agreement, it is clear that the US conveyed and controlled its narrative very well. Trump launched a narrative to *Make America Great Again*, stuck with three simple messages to reinforce the narrative, and declared victory just over a year later. As promised, Trump successfully erased NAFTA and replaced it with USMCA, which literally put America first. Or, placed in the framework outlined by Hampson and Narlikar in the introduction, Trump articulated a contamination narrative, followed by a redemption narrative that only his leadership could achieve.

The Canadians, on the other hand, were forced to react, pivot and revise the shallow "win-win-win" narrative that was on a collision course with Trump's deep narrative. It would soon become apparent that Freeland's early "Happy Talk" (Hampson and Zartman, 2012, p.41) was falling on deaf ears. Furthermore, after being forced to swallow several bitter pills via steel and aluminum tariffs and Trump's personal attacks on Trudeau in the summer, the Canadian public also grew impatient with Freeland's cheerful rhetoric and wanted her to come out swinging. Thus, when Freeland dropped her proverbial hockey gloves to adopt a more existential narrative, it resonated deeply with Canadians and earned Freeland respect for standing up to the American bully.

It should be made clear that this chapter does not take the position that the Trump administration negotiated better than Canada's team, or that America won and Canada lost. In fact, Canada successfully worked first with Lighthizer to gain concessions from Mexico on labor, and later with US House Democrats to further improve the labor chapter after the US mid-terms. In addition, Canada's "red line" goal of retaining Chapter 19 on dispute settlement was achieved, against Lighthizer's opposition. Furthermore, Canada conceded only 3.6% market access on dairy, despite Trump's personal passion for eliminating Canada's supply managed system entirely (Lilly, 2019). However, as the largest economy and the demandeur, Trump always had the upper hand of articulating what constituted a successful renegotiation. Similarly, as the smaller economy that was forced into negotiations, Canada was placed in the impossible position of needing to respond to American demands from the beginning. Thus, it should have been expected that Canada would be forced to redefine success as negotiations proceeded.

This chapter also does not assert that the Canadians made a critical error by initiating a collective agency approach that was set to fail, although it is possible. For example, Hampson and Narlikar identify the ways in which parties may ignore their own biases when advancing a particular negotiating style with the other side. Perhaps widespread public support for free trade in 2016 mistakenly led Canadian leaders to believe that building on NAFTA for even greater success could also serve as a winning storyline and negotiating strategy with the

Trump administration. If that was the case, the Canadians were mistaken. For it seemed obvious to many from the outset – including Canadian business leaders with their "do no harm" mantra – that the original NAFTA already represented Canada's "BATNA" under a leader such as Trump.

Nevertheless, Freeland's opening narrative was not necessarily the wrong one. Research evidence demonstrates that although the general public prefer their leaders to adopt value claiming styles, starting out with that orientation can also be perceived as divisive and may have backfired on Freeland (Brutger and Rathbun, 2017). Though gender has not been a focus of this chapter, research evidence also demonstrates that women leaders are often punished by the public for being aggressive or displaying typically "male" behaviors (Williams and Tiedens, 2016). Other research demonstrates that citizens (even partisans from an opposite political party) will come around to support a leader who changes their typical negotiating style in order to close a deal, as Freeland did in the third phase by standing up for Canadian values (Brutger and Rathbun, 2017). Furthermore, Rathbun (2014) has found that citizens are more likely to support a trade agreement if they believe their leader worked hard to achieve it, regardless of its substance. Given that Canada walked away from USMCA negotiations with the original NAFTA more or less intact, it would be unjustified to conclude that Freeland's narrative compromise was the wrong approach.

Conclusion: Winning narratives for a losing outcome

In their introduction, Hampson and Narlikar outline how social identity leads some negotiating parties to pursue outcomes that are clearly suboptimal. USMCA is a good example of this phenomenon in practice. The final agreement has now been assessed by economists in both American and Canadian governments who have found that, despite adding chapters that cover new areas of the economy, the USMCA is likely to have negligible impacts on their respective economies overall (USITC, 2019; Global Affairs Canada, 2020). However, independent economists have been quick to point out that both countries relied on unrealistic assumptions to ensure their models remained positive.[3] When those assumptions are corrected to reflect more likely scenarios, USMCA is likely to have a negative impact on both countries' GDPs (Manak, 2020; Ciuriak, 2020). Despite this, leaders in both countries have claimed victory for achieving what is now recognized to be a substandard final agreement to replace NAFTA.

Perhaps this has occurred because the policy details surrounding the new USMCA were less important to Trump than harnessing negative emotions for political gain in the polarized 21st century context of 280-character storytelling (McKechnie, 2017). This chapter has demonstrated how Trump applied those tools successfully to communicate a NAFTA negotiating narrative that was consistent with his broader governing agenda and resonated with his intended audience. Meanwhile, Freeland kept Canada on its rhetorical toes, pivoting and ducking to avoid Trump's swings. In effectively reorienting Canada's public narrative to reframe the final USMCA deal as a successful culmination of her efforts to stand up to Trump, Freeland won the approval of Canadians as well.

Notes

1 For a comprehensive trilateral overview of the objectives and final content of the renegotiated agreement, see Lilly et al. (2019).
2 Despite this, the two governments adhere to different interpretations of how the final USMCA carve-out applies to digital services.
3 The US inflated future investment based on the reduction in "policy uncertainty" while the Canadian government evaluated UMSCA relative to no NAFTA at all, and assumed that s. 232 steel and aluminum tariffs would remain in place.

References

@realDonaldTrump, Twitter, Accessed May 7, 2020. www.trumptwitterarchive.com.

Behr, P. (1993, September 19) *Clinton's Conversion on NAFTA,* Washington Post. www.washingtonpost.com/archive/business/1993/09/19/clintons-conversion-on-nafta/3a5b9cb5-dfc8-4b5c-9ae6-30781f0a99fc/.

Blake, A. (2016, September 26) *The First Trump-Clinton Presidential Debate Transcript, Annotated,* Washington Post. www.washingtonpost.com/news/the-fix/wp/2016/09/26/the-first-trump-clinton-presidential-debate-transcript-annotated/.

Brown, B. (n.d) *Trump Twitter Archive,* Accessed May 7, 2020. www.trumptwitterarchive.com.

Brutger, R., and, Rathbun, B.C. (2017, December 4) *Style over Substance: How Negotiation Process Affects Support for International Agreements in the Mass Public,* PEIO. www.peio.me/wp-content/uploads/2018/01/Style-over-Substance_PEIO_12-4-2017.pdf.

Canadian Chamber of Commerce. (2017, June 7) *Three National Chambers Create Alliance to Build a New NAFTA,* Canadian Chamber of Commerce. www.chamber.ca/media/news-releases/170607-three-national-chambers-create-alliance-to-build-a-new-nafta/.

Ciuriak, D. (2020) 'The Trade and Economic Impact of the USMCA: Making Sense of the Alternative Estimates', SSRN Scholarly Paper ID 3546292. Rochester, NY: Social Science Research Network. https://doi.org/10.2139/ssrn.3546292.

C-Span. (2018) *Prime Minister Justin Trudeau on U.S.-Mexico-Canada Trade Agreement,* C-Span. www.c-span.org/video/?452365-1/canadians-trade-deal-us-mexico.

Enli, G. (2017) 'Twitter as Arena for the Authentic Outsider: Exploring the Social Media Campaigns of Trump and Clinton in the 2016 US Presidential Election', *European Journal of Communication,* vol.32, no.1, pp.50–61. https://doi.org/10.1177/0267323116682802.

Gallagher, T. (2019) 'The Outsider on the Inside: Donald Trump's Twitter Activity and the Rhetoric of Separation from Washington Culture,' *Atlantic Journal of Communication,* vol.27, no.3, pp.183–199. https://doi.org/10.1080/15456870.2019.1610763.

Gallup. (2017, February 1) *Americans' Opinions of NAFTA,* Gallup.Com. https://news.gallup.com/poll/204278/americans-opinions-nafta-trends.aspx.

Global Affairs Canada. (2017, August 14) *Address by Foreign Affairs Minister on the Modernization of the North American Free Trade Agreement (NAFTA),* Speeches. www.canada.ca/en/global-affairs/news/2017/08/address_by_foreignaffairsministeronthemodernizationofthenorthame.html.

Global Affairs Canada. (2018a, February 9) *Speech by the Honourable Chrystia Freeland, Minister of Foreign Affairs, to the Standing Committee on Foreign Affairs and International Development.* Speeches. Gcnws. www.canada.ca/en/global-affairs/news/2018/02/speech_by_the_honourablechrystiafreelandministerofforeignaffairs.html.

Global Affairs Canada. (2018b, March 5) *Address by the Minister of Foreign Affairs at Round Seven of Negotiations on the Modernization of the North American Free Trade Agreement (NAFTA).* Speeches. Gcnws. www.canada.ca/en/global-affairs/news/2018/03/address-by-the-minister-of-foreign-affairs-at-round-seven-of-negotiations-on-the-modernization-of-the-north-american-free-trade-agreement-nafta.html.

Global Affairs Canada. (2020) *The Canada United States-Mexico Agreement: Economic Impact Assessment.* www.international.gc.ca/trade-commerce/assets/pdfs/agreements-accords/cusma-aceum/CUSMA-impact-repercussion-en.pdf.

Graham, D. (2018, September 25). 'NAFTA talks: How Trump could split Mexico and Canada in negotiations'. *Global News.* https://globalnews.ca/news/4484150/nafta-talks-donald-trump-mexico-canada/.

Hampson, F.O. (2018) *Master of Persuasion: Brian Mulroney's Global Legacy.* New York, NY: Penguin/Random House.

Hampson, F.O., and, Zartman, I.W. (2012) *Global Power of Talk: Negotiating America's Interests.* New York, NY: Routledge.

ICTSD. (2018, February 1) *NAFTA Parties Wrap up Anti-Corruption Chapter, Acknowledge Continued Divides,* International Centre for Trade and Sustainable Development. www.ictsd.org/bridges-news/bridges/news/nafta-parties-wrap-up-anti-corruption-chapter-acknowledge-continued.

Knowlton, B. (2009, April 20) *Obama Has No Plans to Reopen Nafta Talks,* New York Times. www.nytimes.com/2009/04/21/business/21nafta.html?auth=login-email&login=email.

Lamp, N. (2020) 'How Should We Think about the Winners and Losers from Globalization? Three Narratives and Their Implications for the Redesign of International Economic Agreements', *European Journal of International Law,* vol.30, no.4, pp.1359–1397. https://doi.org/10.1093/ejil/chz067.

Liberal Party of Canada. (2016, January 8) *The 'Sunny Way.'* www.liberal.ca/the-sunny-way/.

Lilly, M.B. (2018) "International Trade: The Rhetoric and Reality of the Trudeau Government's Progressive Trade Agenda." In P. Lagassé and N. Hillmer (Eds.), *Justin Trudeau and Canadian Foreign* (pp.125–144). New York, NY: Palgrave Macmillan. www.palgrave.com/gp/book/9783319738598.

Lilly, M. (2019) *A Canadian Perspective on the Future of North America's Relationship. The Future of North America's Economic Relationship: From NAFTA to the New Canada-United States-Mexico Agreement and Beyond,* CIGI. www.cigionline.org/publications/future-north-americas-economic-relationship-nafta-new-canada-united-states-mexico.

Lilly, M., McDaniel, C., and, Perezcano Diaz, H. (2019) *The Future of North America's Economic Relationship: From NAFTA to the New Canada-United States-Mexico Agreement and Beyond,* CIGI. www.cigionline.org/publications/future-north-americas-economic-relationship-nafta-new-canada-united-states-mexico.

Lilly, M., McDaniel, C., and, Perezcano Diaz, H. (2020, May) 'Hewers of Wood and Drawers of Water 2.0: How American and Chinese Economic Nationalism Influence Canadian Trade Policy in the Twenty-First Century,' *Canadian Foreign Policy Journal,* vol. 26, no.2, pp.1–15. https//doi.org/10.1080/11926422.2020.1750444.

Manak, I. (2020, February 28) *Canada Evaluates USMCA, Raises More Questions than Answers*, Cato Institute. www.cato.org/blog/canada-evaluates-usmca.

McCarten, J. (2018, October 1) *How Trump's Attack on Chrystia Freeland May Have Been the Catalyst That Clinched a New Trade Deal*, Financial Post. https://business.financialpost.com/news/economy/u-s-president-cheers-new-usmca-trade-deal-heralds-end-of-nafta-era.

McGregor, J. (2018, September 14) *Canada's NAFTA Stance on Culture Is All about Politics, Not Policy*, CBC News. www.cbc.ca/news/politics/nafta-culture-politics-1.4822117.

McKechnie, D.B. (2017) '@POTUS: Rethinking Presidential Immunity in the Time of Twitter. (President of the US)', *University of Miami Law Review*, vol.72, no.1, p.33.

Panetta, A. (2018, February 7) *Annoyed with Canada, US Trade Czar Floats Idea of Separate NAFTA Deals: Lawmaker*, CTV News. www.ctvnews.ca/politics/annoyed-with-canada-us-trade-czar-floats-idea-of-separate-nafta-deals-lawmaker-1.3793626.

Rathbun, B.C. (Ed.) (2014) 'Creating Value: A Psychological Theory of Diplomacy.' *Diplomacy's Value: Creating Security in 1920s Europe and the Contemporary Middle East* (pp.22–57). Ithaca, NY: Cornell University Press. www.jstor.org/stable/10.7591/j.ctt1287cbz.5.

Stokes, B. (2017, May 9) *US Views of NAFTA Less Positive, More Partisan than in Canada and Mexico*, Pew Research Center. www.pewresearch.org/fact-tank/2017/05/09/views-of-nafta-less-positive-and-more-partisan-in-u-s-than-in-canada-and-mexico/.

Tunney, C. (2018, September 4) *No NAFTA Without Cultural Exemption and a Dispute Settlement Clause, Trudeau Vows*, CBC News. www.cbc.ca/news/politics/trudeau-cultural-exemption-1.4806919.

The White House. (2017, May 15) *Robert E. Lighthizer, United States Trade Representative*, The White House. www.whitehouse.gov/people/robert-lighthizer/.

USITC. (2019) 'U.S.-Mexico-Canada Trade Agreement: Likely Impact on the U.S. Economy and on Specific Industry Sectors', United States International Trade Commission. 4889, TPA 105–003.

White House. (2017, January 23) *Presidential Memorandum Regarding Withdrawal of the United States from the Trans-Pacific Partnership Negotiations and Agreement*, The White House. www.whitehouse.gov/presidential-actions/presidential-memorandum-regarding-withdrawal-united-states-trans-pacific-partnership-negotiations-agreement/.

Williams, M.J., and, Tiedens, L.Z. (2016) 'The Subtle Suspension of Backlash: A Meta-Analysis of Penalties for Women's Implicit and Explicit Dominance Behavior', *Psychological Bulletin*, vol.142, no.2, pp.165–197. https://doi.org/10.1037/bul0000039.

6

THE 5G DEBATE

Competing narratives in the new tech war

Oliver Stuenkel

Introduction

This chapter seeks to analyze the narratives embraced and articulated by China, the United States and Brazil in the debate about 5G mobile technology, and how these impact domestic debates about the subject, using Latin America's largest country as a case study. The analysis is organized in four parts. The first part describes the global debate about the subject, and how 5G has become a key element of the growing geopolitical dispute between Washington and Beijing. The second part offers a brief overview of the debate about 5G in Brazil. The third part discusses how viewing the debate through the lens of narratives articulated by the three countries (in China's case, including Huawei) helps us gain a better understanding of the negotiation. The final section concludes.

The geopolitics of 5G

While most observers focus on the ongoing trade war between the United States and China, it is the incipient tech war and the emergence of separate geopolitical tech spheres of influence that are set to have far broader consequences for the future of global order. Rapid technological change, symbolized by the arrival of 5G mobile technology, artificial intelligence and quantum computing are likely to be the defining element in the emerging great-power standoff, marked by the battle for supremacy in cyberspace between the United States and China. There is significant evidence to suggest that our era will be shaped no longer of trade liberalization and open competition, but by the "geopoliticization" of the world economy and the race toward technological self-reliance.

This new logic is already shaping contemporary politics in regions such as Latin America, Europe and Africa, where governments have been subject

DOI: 10.4324/9781003203209-8

to US pressure to refrain from embracing the Chinese telecommunications giant Huawei as the provider of 5G technology – a step that policy makers in Washington regard as the first, and almost irreversible step in Beijing's efforts to establish unprecedented political influence around the world (Stuenkel, 2019). In response, both the Trump and the Biden administrations have taken active steps toward excluding China from US-American technological know-how, a move that is set to change the basic rules of globalization – and which is unlikely to be reversed by future presidents (Waters et al., 2019). A significant part of the global economy is likely to be intimately tied to new technologies – ranging from autonomous cars and drones used for transport and warfare, to communication and global finance – and all of them will be subject to the new geopolitical logic of the emerging tech war. Whoever controls these new technologies is expected to have a massive strategic advantage in global affairs over the next decades. 5G technology, as *The Economist* puts it, has become "a proxy for superpowerdom" (Ren Zhengfei, 2019).

While the global tech industry will be most exposed, the so-called tech-split is likely to accelerate and deepen the overall trend of "decoupling," the declining economic interdependence between the world's two largest economies, and Western companies' growing aversion to being exposed to geopolitical risk that operating in China implies. This development risks the emergence of two separate economic camps, reverting the tremendous economic globalization that has been the hallmark of global order over the past four decades; precisely the period during which the integration of China into the world economy and the growing interdependence between today's largest and second-largest economies defined globalization more than anything else.

From an economic point of view, even a partial reversal of this interdependence is set to be costly, considering how deeply intertwined China's and the United States' economy have become – after all, even the 5G networks in China heavily depend on critical components from the United States. In response to Trump's ban in 2019, Huawei announced that it had built its first 5G mobile network base stations without using any US parts (Kupchan and Triolo, 2019). Perhaps symbolic of this grown schism, US pressure on Huawei then led the Chinese technology giant to abandon Android, Google's smartphone operating system, to develop a separate platform. Cooperation between China and the United States is already declining in many other areas, such as academia, and obtaining Chinese student and conference visas for US scholars and vice versa has become far more difficult.

Short-term political trends – for example, initial attempts by the Biden administration to ease tensions with Beijing and refrain from asking US companies to leave China, a 13 trillion economy of 1.3 billion people – are unlikely to fundamentally change this trend (Fontaine, 2019). What is often overlooked is that key elements of the Tech Cold War have been in place for years, but they are only becoming more visible now to most non-specialized observers. Huawei and ZTE have effectively been banned from the United States, and

China is blocking US tech firms such as Google and Facebook from its market, establishing an "economic Iron Curtain" and creating a separate digital universe. For Chinese strategists, it has long been clear that the only way to assure technological security is to achieve near-total self-reliance, a conviction confirmed by former president Trump's decision to place Huawei on the so-called entity list – a move that initially posed an existential threat to the Shenzhen-based telecommunications firm.

The rise of the Tech War is not only likely to be the defining element of the bilateral relationship between the United States and China, it will also create complex challenges for third countries such as Brazil, Germany, the UK and Japan as they seek to articulate their foreign policy strategy over the coming years. While they, naturally, will all seek to maintain strong ties to both Washington and Beijing, the technological split between the two countries (and their respective spheres of influence) risks reducing overall interoperability and makes maintaining a neutral stance more difficult. For example, when Brazil's president Jair Bolsonaro visited Donald Trump in February 2019, the US president made clear that stronger bilateral ties would depend on Brazil's efforts to limit Chinese influence in Latin America, specifically asking the newly elected Brazilian leader not to allow Huawei to be part of the 5G network's rollout (Stuenkel, 2019b). US officials have threatened to suspend intelligence sharing if the Brazilian government does not exclude the Chinese company from the bidding process, even though there has been no clear evidence of Chinese state cyber activity through Huawei so far (Campos Mello, 2019; see: Taylor, 2019). Washington employs a similar strategy when dealing with its key allies around the world. In the same way, China has threatened to downgrade trade ties to countries that block Huawei as a component provider in the construction of their 5G networks, a worrisome scenario for many nations like Brazil, which have benefitted significantly from Chinese demand and investment over the past years.

The debate about 5G in Brazil

The combination of being one of the 5G-contest's main prizes – as the world's sixth most populous country – and being economically vulnerable and currently somewhat isolated diplomatically – has made the decision about how to respond to growing pressure from both the United States and China vis-à-vis 5G highly relevant for Brazil's future. In early 2020, US ambassador to Brazil Todd Chapman said the United States was ready to provide financial support, via the International Development Finance Corporation, a development bank launched in 2018 to counter China's financial power, if Brazil picked a non-Chinese company such as Nokia or Ericsson to provide the components for its 5G network (Stuenkel, 2020c). President Bolsonaro long projected himself the country's most pro-American leader in history and was long thought to be personally inclined to shun Huawei. His anti-Chinese stance was shared by his politically powerful son Eduardo, former Foreign Minister Ernesto Araújo and by his National Security

Advisor, General Augusto Heleno. In an announcement in early 2020, Bolsonaro said he would take concerns about "sovereignty, data security and foreign policy" into consideration when making the decision, comments which were widely thought to be a sign that he was largely aligned with the United States on the matter (Stuenkel, 2020c).

Yet the Brazilian government also understood that Brazil's economy was deeply dependent on China, and the departure of Ernesto Araújo, a self-professed "anti-globalist," was a result of growing concern among Brazilian agribusiness leaders that Araújo's anti-Beijing rhetoric would hurt the bilateral relationship to China. Despite President Bolsonaro's attempts to forge a strategic alliance with Trump – which produced mixed results – Brazil's dependence on the Asian giant has only grown during his presidency, a trend that is set to continue. About a third of Brazil's exports go to China, more than twice the amount of products headed to the United States.

China's diplomats have largely acted behind the scenes, but it has been no secret that blocking the possibility for Brazilian telecommunication firms to choose Huawei components – which are particularly attractive to developing countries because they are cheaper than competitors – would be seen as a hostile act by Beijing. In 2020, for the first time, Beijing decided to embrace a more aggressive tone after leading members of the Bolsonaro government attacked China. While Bolsonaro temporarily opted for a more prudent stance toward Beijing in public after being elected in 2018, his supporters have never stopped stoking sinophobia on social media since he became president. That is beginning to have an impact: pro-Bolsonaro groups on WhatsApp are now teeming with xenophobic, anti-China and anti-communist rhetoric, and the most fervent Bolsonaro supporters commonly describe the coronavirus as a Chinese plot against Bolsonaro, capitalism and the West (Stuenkel, 2020b).

The Bolsonaro government has been deeply divided between nationalist pro-Trump ideologues who dislike China and military officials and free-market advocates who are aware of its importance for Brazil's economy. Both Vice President Mourão and Minister of Agriculture Tereza Cristina, seen as a guarantor of solid Brazil-China ties, are regularly vilified by Bolsonaro supporters as closet communists (Alves, 2020). Despite their best efforts, both have failed to control anti-China rhetoric by high-level officials close to Brazil's president. Several of Bolsonaro's most radical cabinet ministers left after Trump lost the elections in the United States, yet Bolsonaro continued to show his support for the former president and was one of the last presidents in the world to congratulate Biden to his victory.

Aware that Chinese loans, investments and purchases of Brazilian goods would be crucial to help Brazil overcome one of its worst economic crisis in history, key decision-makers, ranging from Hamilton Mourão and Tereza Cristina to Minister of Science and Technology Marcos Pontes and former House president Rodrigo Maia, began to speak out against banning Huawei (Saxena, 2019). The CEOs of Brazil's largest telecommunication providers, such as Vivo, also defended Huawei, which has operated in Brazil for more than two decades, provides lots of equipment for the country's 3G and 4G networks, and promised to make a $800 million investment to build another assembly plant in Brazil by 2022 (*Huawei anuncia nova fábrica*, 2019). Maia repeatedly urged the government not to "politicize" the issue, warned against excluding Chinese companies from the construction process and said that any delays would make Brazil less competitive, particularly now that the pandemic is likely to push parts of many activities, such as education, medicine and retail, into the online realm.

Maia also questioned US ambassador Chapman's attacks on China and pointed out that Brazilian telecommunication companies had been working with Huawei for years without any concern related to spying or sovereignty. The comments also reflect a broader reality that complicated the United States' plans to exclude the Chinese giant from Brazil's 5G construction process, and which will be discussed below: Brazilian policy makers, both on the domestic and the foreign policy front, tend to be more concerned about US meddling than Chinese interference, and US warnings against the potential risk of Chinese spying was unlikely to be taken seriously considering the still fresh memories of revelations that the US National Security Agency spied on President Rousseff's cell phone, as well as on Petrobras, a company which, despite numerous corruption scandals, still evokes national pride (Roberts, 2015).

In taking a decision vis-à-vis 5G and Huawei, Brazil thus knew it would inevitably upset either the United States or China. The natural temptation for Brazil in such a high-stakes scenario involving two superpowers is to kick the decision down the road, and further delays – or even the reversal of key decisions – must be expected. Initially scheduled to take place in March 2020, the long-awaited 5G auction was postponed to December before being postponed to early 2021 (Exman, 2020), and by the time of writing in June 2021, the exact date of the auction was still uncertain.

5G, identity and narratives

As noted by Narlikar in this volume, narratives can have a significant impact on the overall dynamic of a negotiation, either by simplifying it, making it more complex or allowing one side to improve its negotiating position. Faced with a rival who, in one particular dimension, was technologically superior and offered a poor country such as Brazil gain access to 5G technology at a lower cost than any of its competitors, the United States decided to frame the decision over 5G as something that goes far beyond technology, but which involves sovereignty and national autonomy, issues that Brazil is traditionally more concerned about. More broadly still, by threatening to downgrade ties to Brazil on a multitude of issues, ranging from military cooperation, intelligence sharing and trade if the Brazilian government decided not to block Huawei components from being used in the construction process of the next-generation network, and by framing the 5G debate as a fight between Western democracy and Chinese communism, the

United States is seeking to transform Brazil's decision into an issue about the country's very civilizational identity.

Huawei and the Chinese government, on the other hand, sought to frame the debate as an apolitical one, focusing on the opportunities than the fast and relatively cheap installation of 5G technology offer to a country eager to catch up – largely because they understood that, based solely on technical assessments related to telecommunication itself, there was little doubt that the Chinese company had the most attractive offer. In addition, China has begun to explicitly embrace the narrative that choosing Huawei would help Brazil put an end to a long history of being subject to US interference (Bangar, 2020).

As Hampson and Narlikar write in the introduction to this volume,

> In traditional economic theory, motivations are derived from a priori assumptions about utility maximization. In identity theory, people are motivated by the stories they tell themselves at the time of their decisions. Such stories, or narratives, convey beliefs about who we are, how we should behave, what is important, and how the world works. The impact on policy depends on the stories that get told. Policies, in turn, can shape and change stories.

The competing narratives in the realm of 5G have not only long surpassed the boundaries of Brazilian foreign policy – rather, they have thrust Brazil's political elite into a far broader debate about the future of the nation and its role in the "New Cold War," involving sectors and topics such as agriculture, transport, telecommunication, border security, trade and human rights (Wintour, 2020). That could, to some extent, be considered to be a success of the US government's strategy, which first needed to gain time to allow this reframing and new narrative in Brazil to take hold. The longer the decision-making process was pushed back, the greater the chances for other stakeholders and constituencies to embrace a more holistic understanding of the case, involving issues that go beyond telecommunication.

How do the United States and China promote their interests and values through their narratives in negotiations, including offering a distinct value proposition in those narratives to their respective negotiating partners?

The US narrative vis-à-vis 5G in Brazil: National security, democracy and national identity

The United States' narrative in the context of 5G consisted of three main elements, namely national security, democracy and national identity – a remarkable reframing effort considering that, despite its broad implications, the next-generation telecommunication technology will take years to have an impact on people's lives in Brazil, where half the population has no access to sewage treatment and millions of citizens continue to lack access to the internet (Stuenkel, 2019).

The US strategy to focus on national security consisted of systematic efforts by US foreign policy makers to warn both Brazilian decision-making elites and the general public of the risks of depending on China, repeatedly stressing that Huawei could be obliged by the Chinese government to pass on strategically relevant information and data about users. Successfully promoting such a narrative was not easy, largely because Latin American policy makers' view of the United States continued to be shaped by fears of a return to the days of the Monroe Doctrine, the guiding principle behind a long and traumatic history of US interventions in Latin America. Indeed, the majority of Latin American initiatives in the realm of international law – including the emergence of sophisticated normative principles articulated through the Calvo Doctrine of 1896 and the Drago Doctrine of 1902 – can be traced back to concerns about US intervention in the region (see: Stuenkel, 2019).[1]

Due to this Brazilian narrative of a United States seeking to undermine the region's autonomy, it was no surprise that historically, most US initiatives for the region were not embraced whole-heartedly by governments in Latin America, even by leaders often seen as friendly toward the United States, such as Brazil's president Fernando Henrique Cardoso. The most ambitious economic initiative, the Free Trade Areas of the Americas (FTAA), presented at the Summit of the Americas in Miami in 1994, was given a polite but lukewarm reception in the region and was ultimately mothballed due to Latin American resistance; part of a strategy Diana Tussie refers to as "defensive regionalism" (Tussie, 2009).[2] The most important US-led security initiative in Latin America, *Plan Colombia*, was widely rejected in the region and contributed to Colombia's isolation in the region (Spektor, 2012). Despite the United States' remarkable soft power and cultural attraction across Latin America, the policy makers in Latin America generally considered Washington as the biggest threat to international peace and their national security. While many Latin American scholars and diplomats largely viewed a rules- and norms-based order positively, the United States were often seen, by both policy makers and scholars, not only as an important promoter, but also as the main violator of those very rules – producing a cautious ambiguity typical for the region that often has been on the hard end of liberal order. After all, the history of US-Latin American relations has been, above all, shaped by the vast power asymmetry between the two, US-American dominance over its weaker neighbors in the South and attempts by Latin American leaders to reduce the influence of the "Colossus of the North" (Long, 2015).

In addition to making national security a key theme of its narrative toward Brazil, the US government has sought to transform the debate about 5G into a question of how committed Brazil is to democracy, arguing that Brazil's technological dependence on an authoritarian regime could, in the context of a growing schism between the United States and China, place Brazil within the technological sphere of influence led by a dictatorship, making its cooperation with democratic regimes more difficult.

The broadest and perhaps most ambitious attempt by the United States to reframe the Brazilian debate about 5G is to make the decision not about telecommunication, but one about Brazil's national identity, place in the world and the question of whether it belongs to the West – an issue highly relevant to the so-called "ideological faction" of the Bolsonaro government. In this context, Brazil's former Foreign Minister Ernesto Araújo has referred to US president Trump as the "savior of the West" and argued that moving closer to the United States was a civilizational or even spiritual matter (Araújo, 2017).

Defending the narrative that the choice about the provider of 5G components was one of national identity helped the United States reduce the set of acceptable outcomes (to Washington) and created the perception among the Brazilian public and decision-making elites that the country faces two stark options. The United States' strategy was built on the understanding that despite historic skepticism vis-à-vis US designs in Latin America, Brazilian elites mostly consider the country to be founded on "Western values" and principles.

We can thus state that the United States sought to embrace these narratives and pursued a strategy of broadening the debate – and, in the process, making it more complex, to strengthen its negotiating position, while China sought to strengthen its negotiating position by seeking to limit the discussion about 5G to the technical realm.

China's response: Strategic autonomy from the United States and economic opportunities

The United States' aggressive promotion of its narrative seemed to have some impact in the Brazilian public debate, and concepts such as national security, traditionally rare in a country that faces virtually no classic security threats (Stuenkel, 2010), began to arise more frequently when 5G was being discussed. And yet, the US approach had several weaknesses, which China sought to exploit – above all that the United States' efforts to influence Brazil on an internal issue was yet another example of foreign meddling the Latin American country has long fought against.

Huawei chief executive Ren Zhengfei explicitly referred to these historical and geopolitical sensitivities in media interviews, saying, "The United States treats Latin America as its backyard … our goal is to help Latin America get out of this trap and maintain the sovereignty of each country" (Bangar, 2020). In the same way, China sought to systematically rally support for international norms of independence, sovereignty and territorial integrity. Latin America, whose view of the world has been shaped by its traumatic experience with US unilateral interventionism, is generally inclined to ascribe similar importance and meaning to these norms. China's charm offensive evidenced by President Xi's 2014 Latin America visit has also aimed to increase support for China's preferred model of multilateral internet governance (Swaine, 2014). To some extent, China's effort has been successful: Brazil, along with Argentina, has in recent years joined

China in its criticism of US leadership in the global internet governance regime embodied by ICANN (Trinkunas and Wallace, 2015). These strategies help explain why, so far, it remains unlikely that United States attempts to generate concern in Latin America about the rise of China and its impact on national security will resonate across the region.

An additional narrative promoted by China has been that of an unreliable United States versus a reliable China, a "story" that has been facilitated by perception, in Brazil, that Bolsonaro's bet on striking an alliance with Trump failed to produce the expected results (Stuenkel, 2019d). After Bolsonaro's election victory, the president had voiced hopes that the United States could yet again become Brazil's most important trading partner, a position it lost to China in 2009. Yet even early in Bolsonaro's presidency, key factions in the government's coalition saw their hopes dashed that Trump would make any meaningful concessions to Brazil in the realm of trade. Brazilian farmers who had wanted a free trade agreement soon realized that Trump would not allow them to directly compete with American farmers, a key constituency for the US president. The neoliberal faction of the Bolsonaro administration – led by Guedes, the economy minister – was likewise disappointed that Trump would not push harder for Brazil's entry into the OECD, something seen as an important seal of approval to attract more foreign investment. In a leaked letter to OECD Secretary-General Angel Gurría in August 2019, the US State Department gave preference to Romania and Argentina's accession, a move seen as especially humiliating to a Brazilian audience given that Alberto Fernández, Argentina's president-elect at the time, would most likely care less about OECD membership than Brazil's Bolsonaro (Stuenkel, 2019d).

China, on the other hand, adroitly used its economic strength to its diplomatic advantage. Aware that attracting foreign firms to place a bid in Brazil's much-anticipated early November 2019 oil auction would be difficult, Bolsonaro asked Xi for help. The Chinese president promptly delivered: CNOOC and CNODC, two Chinese state oil companies, ended up being the only foreign bidders, helping the Brazilian president save face after the auction failed to meet expectations. Beijing has also learned to provide diplomatic support to partners in distress. When Brazil found itself the target of global outrage for doing too little to combat the Amazon fires in August, the Chinese government took the opposite strategy and publicly lauded Brazil's environmental record. China, the underlying narrative was, is a true all-weather friend (Stuenkel, 2019c).

Countering the United States' attempt to defend the narrative that depending on a Chinese telecommunications provider represents a threat to Brazil's national security, Beijing and Huawei have defended the narrative that the United States is seeking to muddy the waters to hide China's technological superiority and more attractive option to China, which should, from Beijing's perspective, be decisive. As a consequence, Huawei has promoted its technology-focused narrative in the Brazilian social media, emphasizing the opportunities 5G presents to specific sectors of Brazil's economy, such as agriculture, self-driving cars and "smart cities." In addition, the Chinese company frequently promoted new partnerships with Brazilian cities opening "5G laboratories" open to the public, showcasing how the new technology can impact everyday life and the economy (*Primeiro laboratório de testes 5G*, 2020).

Indeed, the US narrative to make Brazil's 5G decision about far more than just telecommunication contains numerous risks and could end up involving political actors in the Brazilian debate that hinder, rather than help, the United States. As Thomas Bagger rightly points out in this volume, narratives are usually grand generalizations which provide a big, easy-to-understand frame for complex problems – but they may also lead observers and political decision-makers into perception traps, which in the case of 5G may make it impossible for policy makers to align with the US position.

After all, given its significant relevance in the Brazilian public debate, the United States leaves few actors across the political spectrum indifferent. US cultural influence and visibility stands unrivaled across Latin America. Chinese culture, by comparison, remains largely unknown and is usually met with indifference and a lack of interest. Brazil's mass media tends to report even minor events in US politics or cultural life, yet Chinese news is usually relegated to business papers (Stuenkel, 2018).

Indeed, while significant US visibility and soft power may provide some tangible economic benefits in Latin America, it has also shown to be a double-edged sword, particularly in the foreign policy realm. China's under-the-radar approach in Latin America, by comparison, also brings important advantages, some of which may, paradoxically, be of greater strategic relevance when it comes to 5G. That is because, in a region traditionally concerned about US meddling, strong cultural influence tends to inflate the perceived political and economic influence. While the United States' de facto influence in Latin America has declined significantly over the past decade – partly due to China's growing role in the region, but also because US policy makers generally do not see the region as a priority – this change is barely reflected in the public debate, where the US role remains outsized (Stuenkel, 2018b).

That often makes cooperating with the United States politically difficult and costly. When Brazil's former President Cardoso reached, in 2000, a groundbreaking space cooperation deal with the United States, which would involve US use of the Brazilian space agency's launch site in Alcântara in Northern Brazil (its equatorial location allows reducing fuel costs of satellite launches by 30 percent), the opposition saw an opportunity to whip up anti-American nationalist sentiment by mischaracterizing the technology safeguards agreement (TSA) as a threat to Brazil's sovereignty. Cardoso found himself accused of being an *entreguista* – a common term to describe those more concerned with US national interests than those of Brazil – and canceled the project, which would have allowed Brazil to develop expertise in the area. If the project partner had been China back then or today, it seems unlikely that the project would have faced as much political resistance (Stuenkel, 2018b).

Between the two superpowers: Brazil's negotiating position

Faced with competing narratives promoted by Washington and Beijing vis-à-vis the construction of its 5G network, the Brazilian government adopted a wait-and-see approach. The Bolsonaro administration only shifted the responsibility for 5G from mid-level technocrats to the presidential palace when both US and Chinese foreign policy makers had already publicly discussed the topic, reducing its capacity to frame the public discussion. An earlier effort to set the public agenda on the subject may have allowed Brazil to alter the overall structure of the negotiation process – for example by developing its own narrative about what the arrival of 5G means for the country.

Brazil's vulnerability has been aggravated by the fact that rather than taking the initiative and articulating its own cohesive narrative, different factions of the Bolsonaro administration have begun to publicly share their own views, at times contradictory to each other. While government officials with ties to the so-called "ideological faction" preferred to take a tougher stance vis-à-vis China, members of both the armed forces and the neoliberal faction of the government have argued in favor of allowing Huawei to participate, as a provider of components, in the construction process (*China é parceiro estratégico do Brasil*, 2019).

Pre-existing narratives in Brazil about US meddling and the need to contain outside influence not only dampened Washington's capacity to impose its "story" – it also limited Brazil's capacity to think strategically about an issue that is bound to have a significant influence on its foreign policy in the coming years. One example of how this narrative may limit Brazil is that the concern and pessimism in the United States about the end of unipolarity and the transition to a more complex and multipolar "post-western world" has not resonated in Brazil at all – quite to the contrary. According to many Brazilian observers, the emergence of a new major power – or several new major powers – could help reduce the United States' capacity to reshape the world in its image, a phenomenon that has long created instability. China's growing influence in Latin America is thus often seen, somewhat simplistically – given the complexity of the phenomenon – as a welcome development that is likely to reduce the region's vulnerability to US interference. This consensus, however, often marginalizes potentially meaningful concerns about what Brazil's growing ties to an authoritarian regime mean for its foreign policy and democracy.

Given the peculiar set-up of the negotiation between Brazil on the one side and China and the United States on the other, the room for compromise, which could allow Brazil to see neither its ties to Beijing or Washington negatively affected, is limited. While a partial ban on Huawei, limiting its components to a certain percentage of Brazil's 5G network – a proposal initially made by the UK government before reversing position and siding with the US, may be acceptable to China, it would most likely have a severely negative impact on Brazil-US ties. Due to Brazil's dependence on China, most political actors in the country – including those occupying the ideological center – have been reluctant to oppose Beijing. In early 2021, the Brazilian government suggested it would allow Huawei components to be used in the country's main 5G network, but considered building a separate 5G network for government officials without Huawei components, thus seeking to assuage fears that Beijing could spy on Brazilian decision-makers.

Finally, it is worth returning to a theme that has appeared in this analysis in several moments – the impact that narratives have on a negotiation's degree of complexity. While the US narrative vis-à-vis 5G in Brazil amplifies and complicates the decision-making process from Brazil's perspective, one also needs to take into consideration that the decision-making process is shaped by a large number of unknowns. That complicates the notion of parties being merely maximizing actors who compare costs and benefits. Not only are these hard to measure – for example, does a far cheaper construction of the 5G network with Chinese components justify being dependent on an authoritarian government which may force Huawei to pass on sensitive information? Are the United States a more trustworthy partner than China? Does that calculus change if Trump or a Trumpian candidate returned to the presidency in the future?

In addition to the technical complexities, another difficulty for Brazilian policy makers is the negotiation's timeframe since the decision about 5G is unlikely to affect the country during their time in office. Indeed, policy makers' main concern, from an electoral point of view, may not be the strategic implications of 5G itself, but rather the collateral damage the country may suffer from seeing ties to either its most important or second-most important trade partner negatively affected. That may explain why, in the end, Brazil's government may opt for the strategy that will produce the least short-term economic damage, basically seeking to compare the impact of the United Sates and Beijing's retaliation.

After all, the entire debate about 5G is based on expectations and long-term projections that may or may not come to pass. While new technologies such as self-driving cars and food-delivering drones may become a reality in industrialized nations in a matter of years – creating a host of strategic challenges for governments, to many citizens and policy makers in developing countries concerned about more immediate challenges, 5G is unlikely to matter much in the near future. The lack of technical expertise in the realm of next-generation mobile technology is another aggravating factor that makes developing countries often dependent on outside knowledge. That may explain why, in Brazil's case, a wait-and-see approach has been the preferred choice so that other countries such as Germany and the UK would make their decisions vis-à-vis 5G.

Conclusion

The coming tech split, symbolized by growing tensions between the United States and China about the future of 5G and Huawei, is set to accelerate and deepen "decoupling" – the declining economic interdependence between the world's two largest economies – and exacerbate Western companies' aversion to the geopolitical risk that operating in China implies. This trend may bring about the emergence of two separate technological spheres and even economic camps, reversing the tremendous economic globalization that has been the hallmark of international order over the past four decades.

For countries like Brazil, traditionally reluctant to taking sides or being tied down in alliances and always seeking to carve out a maximum amount of strategic autonomy, this new scenario is highly uncomfortable and will involve hard choices. While President Jair Bolsonaro and his closest advisers favored strengthening ties to the United States – a stance that became more complicated after Trump's defeat in 2020 and growing tensions between Bolsonaro and Biden in the realm of deforestation – Brazil is economically dependent on China, which has been its most important trade partner since 2009.

Brazil has long used its ambiguous geopolitical role in its favor, successfully remaining on relatively good terms with all sides. Over the past decades, it was one of few countries in the world that could, when its domestic political situation allowed it, play a relevant role within non-Western outfits such as the BRICS or the G77, as well as Western-led groups such as the OECD, where it currently seeks membership. Brazil is not the only Latin American country that is keen to continue this balancing act for as long as possible. Leaders like Chile's Sebastián Piñera have similarly sought to maintain strong ties to both the United States and China, despite growing tensions between presidents Donald Trump and Xi Jinping (Stuenkel, 2020).

Yet with the emergence of technological spheres of influence and a more permanent stand-off between China and the United States, third countries' wiggling room is set to shrink considerably. In their attempt to bring countries on their side, both Washington and Beijing have articulated a set of sophisticated narratives to make their case to decision-makers and the wider public.

The United States has sought to broaden the negotiation to make Brazil's 5G decision about far more than just about telecommunication but transform the case into a decision with broad long-term geopolitical ramifications about Brazil's place in the world. This narrative has now been broadly accepted by Brazilian elites. Until recently controlled by Brazil's agency for telecommunication, a technical body, the public debate about Huawei is now widely regarded as one of the Bolsonaro government's most consequential foreign policy decisions, and the ultimate decision will be made by the president himself. Frequent delays in making that decision have helped the United States gain more time to promote this narrative, in addition to imposing economic sanctions on Huawei that have led to doubts about the Chinese telecommunication company's future capacity to operate. Specifically, the US narrative in Brazil has focused on three core aspects, none of which are directly related to 5G itself. First, US foreign policy makers have argued that permitting a Chinese company to build Brazil's 5G network would be a grave threat to Brazil's strategic autonomy, providing Huawei with access to highly sensitive data that the company may pass on to the Chinese government (Campos Mello, 2020). Secondly, according to US foreign policy makers, creating such a wide-ranging technological dependence on an authoritarian regime would be a direct threat to Brazil's democracy. Finally, Brazil's decision about 5G was depicted as a decision about Brazil's national identity and willingness to be part of the democratic or "Western camp" in a world increasingly shaped by bipolarity.

The Chinese narrative, by contrast, has been two-fold: In addition to focusing on 5G as a means to escape the United States' sphere of influence, Beijing largely focused on economic considerations and 5G as a historic opportunity for Brazil to catch up and fulfil its potential, a narrative that seeks to seize on the deeply seated frustration among many Brazilian policy makers that, contrary to countries like South Korea and China, the Latin American giant failed to escape the middle-income trap over the past decades.

The above analysis shows that the study of narratives in foreign policy making allows us to gain a better understanding of negotiations that may be overlooked when merely analyzing rational interests and the distribution of power between those involved in the bargaining process. Countries' capacity to frame debates and promote narrative and "stories" may, as the above example with the United States' failed 1999 bid to sign a space rocket agreement with Brazil shows, significantly alter negotiation outcomes.

Notes

1 The Trump administration's fondness for the Monroe Doctrine repeatedly caused apprehension among Latin American foreign policy makers over the past years.
2 In this context, Tussie describes the origins of regionalism in Latin America as "multiple and Bolivarian solidarisitic instincts," and that "a strategic competition between these regional projects, a competition which is at times adversarial and at other times mere sidelining of US interests."

References

Alves, C. (2020, August 4) *Depois de elogiar empresa chinesa: Mourão é atacado por bolsonaristas*, UOL. https://noticias.uol.com.br/colunas/chico-alves/2020/08/04/depois-de-elogiar-empresa-chinesa-mourao-e-atacado-por-bolsonaristas.htm.

Araújo, E. (2017) 'Trump e o Ocidente', *Cadernos de Política Exterior*, vol.3, no.6, pp.323–358.

Bangar, R. (2020, July 27) *Will Huawei Weather 5G Storms in Latin America?*, Financial Express. www.financialexpress.com/world-news/will-huawei-weather-5g-storms-in-latin-america/2036098/.

Campos Mello, P. (2019, August 31) *EUA podem rever parceria de inteligência se Brasil permitir 5G chinês, diz diplomata*, Folha de São Paulo. www1.folha.uol.com.br/mundo/2019/08/eua-ameacam-rever-parceria-de-inteligencia-se-brasil-permitir-5g-chines-diz-diplomata.shtml.

Campos Mello, P. (2020, June 11) *Por 'segurança nacional', EUA já discutem crédito para 5G no Brasil, diz embaixador*, Folha de São Paulo. www1.folha.uol.com.br/mundo/2020/06/por-seguranca-nacional-eua-ja-discutem-credito-para-5g-no-brasil-diz-embaixador.shtml.

China é parceiro estratégico do Brasil, não ameaça, diz Mourão à Folha, (2019, April 6), Exame. https://exame.com/economia/china-e-parceiro-estrategico-do-brasil-nao-ameaca-diz-mourao-a-folha/.

Exman, F. (2020, July 20) *Em meio a pressões, leilão de 5G só em 2021,* Valor Econômico. https://valor.globo.com/empresas/noticia/2020/07/20/em-meio-a-pressoes-leilao-de-5g-so-em-2021.ghtml.

Fontaine, R. (2019, September 9) *Great-Power Competition Is Washington's Top Priority—but Not the Public's,* Foreign Affairs. www.foreignaffairs.com/articles/china/2019-09-09/great-power-competition-washingtons-top-priority-not-publics.

Huawei anuncia nova fábrica em SP. Investimento é de US$ 800 milhões, (2019, August 9), O Globo. https://oglobo.globo.com/economia/tecnologia/huawei-anuncia-nova-fabrica-em-sp-investimento-de-us-800-milhoes-1-23866438.

Kupchan, C., and, Triolo, P. (2019, November 26) *Distrust but Verify: How the U.S. and China Can Work Together on Advanced Technology,* Supchina. https://supchina.com/2019/11/26/distrust-but-verify-the-us-china-advanced-technology/.

Long, T. (2015) *Latin America Confronts the United States. Asymmetry and Influence.* Cambridge: Cambridge University Press.

Primeiro laboratório de testes 5G do Brasil será inaugurado no DF, (2020, July 23), Correio Braziliense. www.correiobraziliense.com.br/app/noticia/cidades/2020/07/23/interna_cidadesdf,874813/primeiro-laboratorio-de-testes-5g-do-brasil-sera-inaugurado-no-df.shtml.

Ren Zhengfei may Sell Huawei's 5G Technology to a Western Buyer, (2019, September 12), The Economist. www.economist.com/business/2019/09/12/ren-zhengfei-may-sell-huaweis-5g-technology-to-a-western-buyer.

Roberts, D. (2015, June 30) *Brazilian President's Visit to US Will Not Include Apology from Obama for Spying,* The Guardian. www.theguardian.com/world/2015/jun/30/brazil-dilma-rousseff-obama-nsa-spying-apology.

Saxena, S. (2019, November 23) *Brazil Is Caught in the U.S.-China Tech War,* The Hindu. www.thehindu.com/news/international/brazil-is-caught-in-the-us-china-tech-war/article30062886.ece.

Spektor, M. (2012, October 17) *Colombianas,* Folha de São Paulo. www1.folha.uol.com.br/colunas/matiasspektor/1170442-colombianas.shtml.

Stuenkel, O. (2010, September 30) *Strategic International Threats Surrounding Brazil,* KAS International Reports. www.kas.de/en/web/auslandsinformationen/artikel/detail/-/content/internationale-strategische-bedrohungen-fuer-brasilien.

Stuenkel, O. (2018, February 19) *A China sabe muito sobre o Brasil e o Brasil sabe muito pouco sobre a China,* EL PAÍS. https://brasil.elpais.com/brasil/2018/02/19/opinion/1519073429_518020.html.

Stuenkel, O. (2018b, May 1) *Most Latin Americans Can't Name a Chinese Singer: Why That's Great for Beijing,* Americas Quarterly. www.americasquarterly.org/article/most-latin-americans-cant-name-a-chinese-singer-why-thats-great-for-beijing/.

Stuenkel, O. (2019, May 10) *Huawei Heads South,* Foreign Affairs. www.foreignaffairs.com/articles/brazil/2019-05-10/huawei-heads-south.

Stuenkel, O. (2019b, May 21) *Can VP Mourão Fix Brazil-China Ties?,* Americas Quarterly. www.americasquarterly.org/content/can-vp-mourao-fix-brazil-china-ties.

Stuenkel, O. (2019c, November 11) *In Spite of Bolsonaro, China Quietly Deepens Its Influence in Brazil,* Americas Quarterly. www.americasquarterly.org/article/in-spite-of-bolsonaro-china-quietly-deepens-its-influence-in-brazil/.

Stuenkel, O. (2019d, December 6) *Bolsonaro Placed a Losing Bet on Trump,* Foreign Policy. https://foreignpolicy.com/2019/12/06/bolsonaro-losing-bet-trump-brazil-tariffs/

Stuenkel, O. (2020, January 15) *Brazilian 5G: The Next Battleground in the U.S.-China Standoff*, Americas Quarterly. www.americasquarterly.org/article/brazilian-5g-the-next-battleground-in-the-u-s-china-standoff/.

Stuenkel, O. (2020b, May 15) *China's Diplomats Are Going on the Offensive in Brazil*, Foreign Policy. https://foreignpolicy.com/2020/05/15/chinas-diplomats-are-going-on-the-offensive-in-brazil/

Stuenkel, O. (2020c, June 30) *Huawei or Not? Brazil Faces a Key Geopolitical Choice*, Americas Quarterly. https://americasquarterly.org/article/huawei-or-not-brazil-faces-a-key-geopolitical-choice/.

Swaine, M.D. (2014, October 21) 'Xi Jinping's Trip to Latin America Swaine', *China Leadership Monitor*, no.45. www.hoover.org/sites/default/files/research/docs/clm45ms-xi_jin pings_trip_to_latin_america.pdf.

Taylor, E. (2019, September 9) *Who's Afraid of Huawei?: Understanding the 5G Security Concerns*, Chatham House. www.chathamhouse.org/expert/comment/who-s-afraid-huawei-understanding-5g-security-concerns.

Trinkunas, H., and, Wallace, I. (2015, July) *Converging on the Future of Global Internet Governance the United States and Brazil*, Foreign Policy at Brookings. www.brookings.edu/wp-content/uploads/2016/06/USBrazil-Global-Internet-Governance-web-final.pdf.

Tussie, D. (2009) *Latin America: Contrasting Motivations for Regional Projects*. Review of International Studies.

Waters, R., Hille, K., and, Lucas, L. (2019, May 24) *Huawei v the US: Trump Risks a Tech Cold War*, Financial Times. www.ft.com/content/78ffbf36-7e0a-11e9-81d2-f785092ab560.

Wintour, P. (2020, June 22) *US v China: Is This the Start of a New Cold War?*, The Guardian. www.theguardian.com/world/2020/jun/22/us-v-china-is-this-the-start-of-a-new-cold-war.

7

NARRATIVES, IDENTITY, AND INTERNATIONAL NEGOTIATION

The 2012 World Conference on International Telecommunications and the battle of Internet governance narratives

Fen Osler Hampson and Paul Twomey

Introduction

International negotiation is typically viewed as a coalition-building exercise whether it be in the multilateral (i.e., intergovernmental) or multi-stakeholder setting (states and non-state actors). In global institutions, like the United Nations, which have universal membership, negotiation processes are advanced via "minilateralism," smaller group interactions that typically involve the most powerful actors in the international system (Hampson, 1995; Hopmann, 1998; Zartman, 1994). However, in recent decades civil society actors and so-called epistemic are playing an increasingly important—if not critical role—in many areas of international public policy, by helping to raise public awareness, set agendas, and press for the negotiation of new international treaties. Within the arena of international negotiation, entrepreneurial leadership, which can be exercised by conference chairs or groupings of middle powers, is also important and can play a decisive role in negotiation processes and the development of new equilibria to global problems. Underlying most models of the negotiation process is the notion of rational expectations: parties are seen as utility maximizing actors. Their cost-benefit calculations shape and are in turn shaped by the negotiation process through exchanges of information and learning.

This chapter argues that there is another important dimension to the negotiation process that warrants closer scrutiny. It involves the identity of the parties and the political narratives or "stories" that develop around their organizational identities and governance arrangements, which they use to advance their respective values and interests during the negotiation process. As we argue here, identity and policy narratives are important to understand revealed preferences and strategic behavior at the negotiating table, especially in a technical and scientific

DOI: 10.4324/9781003203209-9

multi-stakeholder environment where epistemic communities can play a disproportionately influential role in shaping negotiating agendas and outcomes.

Identity narratives carry their own powers of persuasion and normative political legitimacy. When properly articulated by key nodal actors at the negotiating table, they can become of a key instrument of political mobilization and the formation of supportive multi-stakeholder coalitions either to promote new norms or, when the institutional status quo is threatened, as in the case of the Internet, to defend an existing governance equilibrium from actors who are trying to upset it.

When the members of a political coalition share a coherent, normative belief system and can deliver their political narrative through an extended network of state and non-state actors, they can fend off rivals who want to change the rules of the game, especially if their rivals are not united by a common narrative and lack a robust, extended network capacity to deliver key messages and narratives of their own.

Using the case study of negotiations leading up and during the highly controversial 2012 World Conference on International Telecommunications (WCIT-12), this paper discusses the role that competing narratives played in those negotiations (and in the lead up to the conference) and how Western countries were ultimately able to stave off—at least for the time being—an attempt led by Russia, China, and their "allies" to acquire greater control over the Internet's content and social layers by developing a persuasive narrative that centered on the "redemptive" qualities of an open and multi-stakeholder–managed Internet and dangers of "contamination" if the Internet were to fall under the control of authoritarian regimes who were keen to exercise greater sovereign control over the Internet and its future development. As defined in the introduction to this volume, a redemption narrative is one that stresses the importance of growth, sustainability, freedom, and self-actualization whereas a contamination narrative is one that points to the dangers of abuse and exploitation.

The evolution of the Internet as system of identity through common values

From the pioneering efforts of, among others, J.C.R. Licklider, Barry Leiner, Vint Cerf, David Clark, Paul Baran, Frank Heart, Bob Kahn, Leonard Kleinrock, Daniel Lynch, Jon Postel, Lawrence Roberts, Thomas Merrill, Ivan Sutherland, Bob Taylor, Donald Davies, Roger Scantlebury, Stephen Wolff, and Steve Crocker, the Internet's evolution was guided by a group of technologists and research administrators and funders (Leiner et al., 1997). The first manifestation of the network, which we now call the Internet, was the ARPANET initiated in 1969. The true Internet evolved four years later.

This growing community took some time to go from a band of questing fellow travelers into a mature, broad-based "epistemic community" with its own distinctive identity and narrative that was centered on sustainability and growth of the Internet as a key. In 1979, the Internet Configuration Control Board (ICCB) was formed. Barry Leiner transformed the ICCB into the Internet Architecture Board in 1983. Three years later, the Internet Engineering Task Force (IETF) was formed. All these organizations were structured to allow the growing technical community to coordinate its development work. The epistemic community was expanded through the foundation of the more broadly oriented Internet Society (ISOC) in 1992. The Internet Society eventually being a home not only for technologists but also for business, legal, and other civil society participants.

The Internet community more or less implicitly, if not explicitly, agreed on a broad set of values and a redemptive causal narrative that associated technological innovation and prosperity (effect) with an "open" and inclusive governance model that was non-hierarchical, loosely coupled, efficient, transactional, and standards-based (cause). The Internet community operated under a number of common values, which included the following and which have essentially not changed substantially with the passage of time (Twomey, 2004):

- Ensuring a single, end-to-end interoperable Internet;
- Bottom-up technical policy making and decision-making;
- Participation opens to all who wish to do so;
- Legitimacy determined by open participation and the value of the contribution to the joint effort, rather than power—meritocracy. (It should be noted that interpretation of this value created later tensions when other disciplines and interests emerged as part of the community [e.g., legal, policy and even consumer interests].);
- Consensus-based decision-making, but not full "census-based" consensus;
- Cooperation, coordination, and consultation among participants and groups pushing forward initiatives;
- Swift decision-making, if possible;
- Private agreement or contract approach to creating and managing linkages among and to the network;
- Global efficiency in the allocation of resources, such as Internet Protocol addresses;
- A commitment to encouraging innovation, particularly at the edge of the network;
- Using a layered approach to development and respecting these layers;
- Building on layers of protocols to ensure the stability of the whole construct. Very importantly, turning evolving thinking into "Running Code." This was the engineering equivalent to "Walk the walk, not just talk the talk," and was the key to the successful "guerilla" development of the Internet, in contrast to the heavy discussion auras of such standard development as in the X.25 and OSI model; and,
- Standards to be respected until obsolete—reflected in the Request for Comment process.

Google's Internet Evangelist Vint Cerf summarized some of these values:

> The Internet is designed to be layered in its implementation so that different groups can create software at different layers, take responsibility for operating different parts of the network and build and operate a variety of applications more or less autonomously, while following the technical standards that permit widespread interworking of independently implemented software...Two things about the Internet should be abundantly clear. First, it is a vast collaboration of many components and second, that it cannot and will not function without the cooperation and collaboration of the entire range of entities with interest in its operation. There are literally hundreds of thousands of networks that make up the global Internet...It should be evident from these observations that the coordination, collaboration and cooperation of many distinct entities is vital to the Internet's successful operation and that this characteristic has been a part of the Internet's history from its earliest conception.
>
> *Cerf, 2003*

The emphasis for the move to regime formation came not with any failure, but rather with the problems of success. By the mid-1990s the Internet was swiftly moving from its origins as a U.S.-based research vehicle, to becoming an international infrastructure for commerce, education, and communication. The traditional means of organizing its technical functions, especially the Domain Name System (DNS) and the allocation of other unique identifiers, came under pressure for change from many different quarters, including the business community, civil society, and other governments. An increasing number of Internet users also resided outside of the United States and those stakeholders sought to participate in Internet coordination and management. Additionally, as the Internet became increasingly commercialized, it became less appropriate for U.S. research agencies to direct and fund these functions (United States Department of Commerce, 2000). Eventually, the proposal for the establishment of the Internet Corporation for Assigned Names and Numbers (ICANN) showed that the values of an original epistemic community could be sufficiently attractive, and at the same time flexible, to draw key new constituencies—business, governments, and broader civil society—into the process of regime formation.

After several meetings in different regions of the world, and extensive and noisy debate about several institutional models, the initial Internet Corporation for Assigned Names and Numbers (ICANN) organization was formed and recognized by the US government (and other governments) as the appropriate institution.

Evolution of the Internet's core identity narrative toward an "open Internet"

The start-up nature of the new organization, and the need for the international Internet community to show the stability and maturity to self-manage an international multi-stakeholder body, necessitated a managed handover process. This process, a little like a due diligence procedure, was embodied in the Memorandum of Understanding between the US Department of Commerce and ICANN. The mission of the ICANN was to coordinate, at the overall level, the global Internet's systems of unique identifiers, and, in particular, to ensure the stable and secure operation of the Internet's unique (in the mathematical sense of having single, non-duplicate, non-ambiguous values) identifier systems.

The values of the founding community were also reflected in the first Article of the new organization's Bylaws (ICANN, 1998), including *inter alia* preserving and enhancing the operational stability, reliability, security, and global interoperability of the Internet; respecting the creativity, innovation, and unrestricted flow of information made possible by the Internet by limiting ICANN's activities to those matters within ICANN's mission requiring or significantly benefiting from global coordination; seeking and supporting broad, informed participation reflecting the functional, geographic, and cultural diversity of the Internet at all levels of policy development and decision-making; and remaining rooted in the private sector, recognizing that governments and public authorities are responsible for public policy and duly taking into account governments' or public authorities' recommendations.

Other competing identity narratives

Much of the contention in ongoing negotiations over Internet governance, including the negotiations in WCIT-12 and the run-up to them, can be interpreted as response of at least two other competing political narratives to the dominant multi-stakeholder, Internet-identifier coordination narrative, which is centered on ICANN and its highly decentralized, global institutional architecture. As an APNIC brief explained,

> Instead of a yawn...the public debate quickly became about the values of the Internet and what the Internet represented in terms of desired objective... There was the argument that this regulatory instrument was no longer relevant. One side of the emerging debate proposed the "multistakeholder model" in its place, based around broad participation from the public and private sectors...On the other side was the view that governments are the only legitimate representatives of public, private, civil, and business interests that exist within a national context—i.e., a much more restrictive, "sovereign-agency" view of Internet governance.
>
> Furthermore, under this restrictive narrative of Internet governance, proponents argued that it is the exclusive role of governments to represent the entirety of different national interests in an international context. In this paradigm, communications are a national asset that operates as a public sector activity at the demand of the national government.
>
> *APNIC, 2012*

Larry Downes in *Forbes* magazine dramatically put it this way:

> The lead-up and melt-down of WCIT-12 brings into stark relief a political transformation that has been building for several years. A global community of Internet users organized to face off and face down national governments and legacy regulatory agencies determined to appoint themselves overseers of technologies that have become economic and political powerhouses. Regimes obsessed with control over their citizens and the parochial interests of slow-changing industrial economics had been worried for years about the success of the Internet. Many of these countries, including Russia, China, Iran and some Arab and African nations, were content to fight the Internet using technologies of surveillance, introducing chokepoints at key network nodes and by passing repressive local laws that masked their true intent under the banner of law enforcement, cybersecurity, and reducing spam and malware.
>
> *Downes, 2012*

The Economist bluntly posed the question whether the world was on the cusp of a new "digital Cold War" (The Economist, 2012).

Incumbent TELCO-owned network narrative

The incumbent Telco-owned network narrative stressed the importance of maintaining traditional, incumbent-owned networks in the interests of network stability and the desirability of national regulation and oversight. The key characteristics of this narrative are that networks are owned end-to-end, and interconnected only at national borders; this, in turn, has traditionally caused them to be regulated and molded by governments, Telcos, and big Telco suppliers. At the national level, some countries have had government regulators, which have given some avenue for public input. But the governance model has a top-down, large institutional decision-making format. The institutional expression or key nodal actor in the traditional incumbent-owned networks model is the International Telecommunications Union (ITU).

The ITU was created in 1932 by the merger of the International Telegraph Union (founded in 1865) and the signatories of the International Radio Convention of 1906. Peter Cowhey has written that the ITU regime was based on a political consensus among telephone operators and government officials who believed that "natural monopolies" existed in telecommunications and that this equilibrium of control should be maintained. He argues that the regime's norms and political narrative were supported by the following:

- The political consensus to retain national monopolies;
- The consensus that international telephone, telegraph, and telex services could be used to cross-subsidize local services of this sort; and,

- Access to networks and the availability of equipment were defined as technical issues, and hence under ITU influence, rather than trade or competition issues.

As Cowhey observes, the consensus around monopolies' telephone provision in national jurisdictions resulted in the ITU acting "as a virtual telephone cartel for the PTT's...They were the anchor of a regime that facilitated by natural monopolistic bargains, reinforced national monopolies, and limited the rights of private firms in the global market" (Cowhey, 1990).

Over time, the ITU regime underwent significant change in its operative governance norms and values. The initial narrative evolved in favor of a slightly more pro-competitive norm. However, it could be argued that some of the residual values and norms of monopoly or near monopoly behavior continue to be shared by some member states and their national telephone carriers. In the run up to WCIT-12, for example, the European Telecommunications Network Operators' Association (ENTO), which was led by Telecom Italia, Telefonica, France Telecom, and Deutsche Telecom called for

> sending party pays system that would have been mandated by law through the [ITU] treaty. In essence, this would have meant that any content provider on the Internet would need to pay to have their information delivered to the recipient—this would be in addition to the fees the service provider already pay to connect to the Internet and in addition to the fees that the user pays for their access.
>
> *Cerf et al., 2014, p.6*

The proposal was debated extensively prior to Dubai, but also was so controversial that is was punted to a "[non-binding] 'study group' to recommend further action" (Cerf et al., 2014, pp.6,22).

"Primacy of state sovereignty" narrative

A second competing narrative to the multi-stakeholder version had longstanding, diplomatic, and cultural origins. Because of its UN foundations, many countries are represented in key Internet forums, like the World Summit on Information Systems (WSIS), by diplomats from their foreign offices. Not only do most of these representatives have little technical or cultural understanding of the Internet, the bilateral and multilateral state interaction regime in which they operate has very different principles, rules, and decision-making procedures compared to those of the ICANN (and other so-called "I star" organizations[1])—centered, Internet-identifier coordination regime. In the diplomatic sphere, power is the main currency and state sovereignty is a cherished political value. In the UN system, consensus is often driven by complete consensus. But most narratives of appropriate interaction with non-state actors in the diplomatic arena are top-down where legitimacy derives from the sovereign state (or a collection of sovereigns). The narrative about the primacy of state sovereignty and the state as key agent of governance has acquired growing currency in the Internet space as powerful, generally autocratic states, like Russia and China, have tried to use international institutions and negotiation processes to promote the proposition of greater government control over the Internet.

World Conference on International Telecommunications 2012—the battle of Internet narratives

Pre-conference tensions

The anti-competitive, pro-monopoly, and pro-sovereignty narratives clashed with the open, multi-stakeholder, pro-competition narrative of the Internet community—a narrative that stressed the diffusion of knowledge and innovation via an open network (Lamberson, 2016). Many months before WCIT-12, in delivering its own comment to WCIT preparations, the Internet Society (ISOC) publicly noted that

> a number of the draft treaty proposals could [adversely] impact...upon the continued growth and innovation of the Internet. The Internet is different from the traditional communications systems governed by ITRs. This difference must be understood and respected in the Internet's benefits are ever to reach all of the world's people.
>
> *ISOC, 2012*

Two other leading nodal actors, which also played a leadership role, were the global coordinating body for the Trade Union movement, International Trade Union Confederation (ITUC), and Greenpeace International. They liaised with key organizations within the international human rights and civil rights movements, but also brought an influential new voice to the arguments deployed at WCIT. Their direct intervention with the senior leadership of the UN in New York drew attention to the unacceptable way in which the WCIT conference had been prepared, expressing deep concern about the intention of some members of the ITU to continue to restrict the participation of multi-stakeholder actors the conference proper. At least partly, and possibly primarily, as a result of these direct interventions with the UN Secretary General, who consistently said the Organization as a whole had to take greater account of non-state actors, the ITU Secretary General changed the rules of access to WCIT at the last minute. While only government delegations were allowed to speak during any part of the conference, or to participate in subgroups and negotiating teams, civil society and other multi-stakeholders were allowed access to the conference room during plenary sessions. Add to this the way in which a number of countries included multi-stakeholder representatives in their national delegations, the overall outcome was undoubtedly diverse than might have been expected.

Indeed, the conflict over the way WCIT-12 was organized served to coalesce key factions of the Internet community, which had strong differences around other issues, and strengthen the bonds of the network.

The business community in developed countries, as well as academic, social service, and a large variety of citizens' organizations, had principles and needs which remained unmet in the ITU-centered model of governance. For example, the statement by the ITU that it listed a number of non-governmental organizations as members belied the fact that the large majority of these were supply-side trade or industry associations, and others like the International Astronomical Union actually defended the opportunities for science from possible interference by an unregulated use of the electromagnetic spectrum.

The clash of narratives and values was also apparent at the governmental level. Indeed, there was a lack of consensus among member states when confronted with the ITU's role in general areas of Internet governance.

In general, Western countries supportive of market-based solutions going into the conference were sympathetic to the values of the Internet community and ICANN's relatively open governance arrangements. For example, the Organisation for Economic Cooperation and Development (OECD), an intergovernmental body of some 30 member states, observed that:

> When OECD countries allocate resources, they have certain common objectives irrespective of the method chosen. These can include efficient allocation of a resource and efficient use of that resource, transparency in the award of resource, non-discrimination, and the creation of appropriate conditions for market competition. There may also be other wider economic and social objectives. Through statements and actions, it is clear that ICANN shares the ideals inherent in these objectives.
>
> *OECD, 2004*

Negotiations during WCIT-12

Negotiations during the two-week conference of the WCIT that took place in December 2012 in Dubai, in many ways, marked a critical turning point in the growing battle for control of the Internet by competing interests and associated narratives. The purpose of the Summit was ostensibly to draft new rules for the ITU's International Telecommunications Regulations (ITRs) that hitherto had governed international telecommunications links. The focus of the Summit was to update the ITRs, which were seen as being out of date and the core provisions of which had only be reviewed some 24 years earlier (1988). In the run-up to WCIT 2012 some member states called for specific Internet transmission issues to be included in the regulations. Most sub-Saharan countries led by South Africa, Senegal and Ghana, were concerned that spam was taking up all of their bandwidth which was hurting their ISPs who were paying for international carriage. They were also concerned about Voice over Internet

Protocol (VOIP) providers eroding their accounting rate revenues for switched traffic (i.e., telephone revenues). Their views were to some extent aligned with the Incumbent Telco-network narrative, which, as noted above, in the run-up to WCIT-12 favored a "sending-party-pays" system that would have been mandated by law through the treaty.

The Russians sought to oppose perceived American control and power over the Internet, including ICANN's role, and threw up a whole series of issues around the Internet largely involving crime and content while arguing that they needed to be resolved in a multilateral, intergovernmental framework where state sovereignty is paramount. There was also a sub-narrative by some countries, notably Sudan and Iran, supported by South Africa, that all countries should have access to the Internet as a right. This was a particular argument that was being used to oppose US sanctions against the first countries. ICANN operated under US law but always negotiated successfully with OFAC in the US Treasury to ensure that all country codes were active in the root zone of the Internet and hence not subject to sanctions. However, US companies, like Google, were prevented from offering service to Sudan. The Chinese essentially agreed with the Russian position, but their position was independent and nuanced. They did not want to antagonize the Americans, but they were also concerned about not diminishing the chances of their deputy in the ITU being elected into the Secretary General position.

Many civil society organizations, including the Internet community, which had been monitoring the issue closely, sought access to the negotiations and ultimately were successful in securing observer status. The important role that civil society had played in WSIS 2003–2005 meant that UN leadership considered civil society involvement to be essential. This meant that the ITU in the WCIT grudgingly had to allow civil society participation, with much of that pressure coming from New York and the UN Secretary General himself. The ITU itself was under pressure from countries like China not to include civil society.

Western countries going into the negotiation were not supportive of the Internet being included in the negotiations because they strongly believed WCIT and its related International Telecommunication Regulations (ITRs) were not the regime under which to include the Internet. The weakness of the Western negotiating position was that the minimalist narrative was just to say "no" inside the ITU and not to invoke the more robust multi-stakeholder narrative because they did not want to bring any Internet-related issues to the table—a crack in the door would have meant that there would have pressure to open it further. However, key nodal actors in the Internet community and wider civil society did not feel quite so constrained and warned openly about the dangers of the conference and the threat it posed to Internet freedom.

On the first day of the conference, Vint Cerf, one of the fathers of the Internet, ran a post on the official Google blog with a plea to keep the Internet free and open. The narrative was clear: "Our protocols were designed to make the networks of the Internet non-proprietary and interoperable," he wrote.

> They avoided "lock-in," and allowed for contributions from many sources. This openness is why the Internet creates so much value today. Because it is borderless and belongs to everyone, it has brought unprecedented freedoms to billions of people worldwide: the freedom to create and innovate, to organize and influence, to speak and be heard.
>
> *Cerf, 2012*

The inventor of the World Wide Web, Timothy Berners-Lee, key Internet companies (Google, Mozilla among them), and advocacy groups echoed the same message. More than 1,000 organizations in 160 countries also signed a petition using the #freeandopen hashtag on social media and posted videos carrying the same message attesting to the global reach of the Internet technological community and its broader, supportive civil society network (Fitzpatrick, 2012).

When WCIT started, it quickly became clear that other countries with different perspectives were putting a variety of issues onto the negotiating table that posed a direct challenge to the multi-stakeholder and open Internet narrative championed by the Internet's founders and supported by its key technological and civil society global network.

The first week was the traditional stating of positions and very little negotiation or consensus building. Debate was over the scope of the ITRs', potentially dangerous introduction of terms such as "telecommunications/ICT" and "Recognized Operating agencies versus Operating agencies" (the latter being a much broader term) preoccupied everyone. Content issues, such as security and spam, were also part of the debate. All this despite the prior assurances of Secretary General Hamadoun Touré that WCIT was not about the Internet or freedom of expression.

Over the weekend, Russia, Arab States, China, and others then proposed a "compromise text" for the whole ITRs that was merely an aggregation of their own views. It was a ploy to distract and later be seen to back down and gain negotiating leverage. Touré was well aware of, not promoting, the tactic. As Cerf, et al., observe,

> countries and regions [wanted]...to use the ITRs as a wholesale opportunity to divest ICANN of its authority and bring domain-name administration within the scope of a government-only agency like the ITU. Specifically, [the] proposal introduced in Dubai by Russia, UAE, China, Saudi Arabia, Algeria, Sudan and Egypt would have required the following: "Member States should have equal rights to manage the Internet, including in regard to the allotment, assignment and reclamation of Internet numbering, naming, addressing and identification resources to support for the operation and development of basic Internet infrastructure."
>
> *Cerf et al., 2014, pp.12–13*

These countries never actually formally tabled the proposal, but then rather publicly withdrew it. The clumsiness of the tactic became obvious when the very angry Egyptian delegation formally disassociated itself from it, claiming that it had never been consulted on the text. The remaining group then re-floated it when it was too late.

The conference chair (from UAE) Al Ghanim and Touré then took it upon themselves to form an informal sub-group to negotiate a chair's text. (Again, fairly standard for this stage in a UN-type conference.) This devolved into two groups, with the slightly ludicrous titles of the big-small-group (about 24 with delegates from each region plus chairs and vice chairs) and the small-small-group of eight or so. All the deal making in the second week took place in private among these member states, and often brought to the plenary for approval when most member states did not know what had been supposedly been agreed on their behalf by regional "representatives." It was not a pinnacle of chairing skills. There was little sympathy among many for Touré and the chair when some member states expressed their disapproval with elements of the text that were being presented to them as a fait accompli.

This was particularly the case with the private deal done to take specific reference to the Internet out of the ITR text and put it into a non-binding resolution. This took many member states by surprise and was railroaded through by a combination of a threat by the Arab Group that if the resolution was not accepted, then all negotiations would have to start again, and by an unusual and confusing ploy by Chair Al Ghanim to close out this session by asking for the "feel in the room," a sort of vote when you are not having a vote. Having got what he wanted, he closed off debate. The problem was he had now set the precedent for what was really voting—it would come back and bite him. The ITU routinely cites its commitment to finding consensus among member states. Failing this, decisions are brought to a vote (which Touré had said never happens). But this may have been the first time in the institution's history that a decision was made based on a rough estimation of the so-called "temperature of the room" filled with confused delegates, many of whom did not understand what was being asked.

The resolution text cherry-picked language from the Tunis declaration and ITU Resolution 102 to present a more sovereign-should-control perspective. Entitled "To foster an enabling environment for the greater growth of the Internet," it resolved that the ITU SG should "continue to take the necessary steps for ITU to play an active and constructive role in the multi-stakeholder model of the Internet as expressed in §35 of the Tunis Agenda…support the participation of Member States and all other stakeholders, as applicable, in the activities of the ITU in this regard." One of the difficulties with the resolution was that, despite its non-binding nature, it left the path open for representatives of the sovereign-control member states to argue in future ITU meetings that "in Dubai we agreed that the ITU has a role in the Internet," just like the way the particular WSIS language was cherry-picked in this resolution to justify its adoption.

Negotiations for the rest of the week focused on the draft ITRs. From the perspective of many members of the Internet community, the draft document was far from perfect.

In subsequent negotiations, many of the worrying proposals were defeated or watered down during the conference, including the following: legitimizing government shutdowns of communication networks in order to preserve national security or "public order"; requiring changes to IP routing methods in order to allow governments to more easily track communications as they travel through networks; and instituting charging schemes for Internet traffic traveling from network to network and prohibiting national net neutrality regulations.

But there was still text in the draft ITRs that dealt with network security and spam. And there was still the resolution specifically dealing with the ITU and the Internet. The most contentious sections in the draft ITRs were that "Member States should endeavour to take necessary measures to prevent the propagation of unsolicited bulk electronic communications and minimize its impact on international telecommunication services. Member States are encouraged to cooperate in that sense." This measure expanded the treaty's scope to cover content issues, a move that many countries opposed on the grounds that the ITU was not the right entity to be making policies concerning content, particularly in the broader UN context of the Universal Declaration on Human Rights, and the role of the Human Rights Council. Several African nations pushed this proposal in the interest of mitigating what they saw as spam taking up bandwidth as noted above (although the facts about this, considering the bandwidth impact of video remained very uncertain) and presenting mobile phone users with unwelcome charges when receiving unwanted spam messages. These may have been legitimate concerns, but it was not clear how the relevant provisions would be implemented effectively, leaving open the problem of one person's unsolicited bulk electronic communications" as another's "right to free speech."

The Russian definition of spam went even further defining it as

> information transmitted in bulk over telecommunications as text, sound, image, tangible data used in a machine interface bearing indiscriminate advertising nature of having no meaningful message, simultaneously or during a short period of time, to a large number of particular addresses without prior consent of the addressee (recipient) to receive this information or information of this nature.
>
> *quoted in Cerf et al., 2014, p.13*

This proposal would have left it up to governments to decide what constituted a " 'meaningful message'...a clear case of censorship" (Cerf et al., 2014, p.13).

Another new article touched on security, encouraging nations to cooperate in ensuring the security of international telecommunication networks. As with the spam provision, the language of the article was far too vague to be interpreted as a requirement that countries monitor users on their networks in order to maintain security. However, it left open, the possibility that some countries might try to claim that the provision lent support for monitoring Internet traffic and content by states.

After nearly two weeks of debate between pro-Internet freedom nations, pro-sovereign control of the Internet nations, and a set of less-ideologically driven developing countries (mostly African) who wanted specific items to defend their Telco's international telecoms revenue and diminish the impact of spam on existing bandwidth, the conference had by its final evening cobbled together a text of a new ITRs and a plenary resolution, which looked like it would run the typical path of a UN conference with no one side getting what they wanted, but with enough vague wording in place that each side could claim some sort of victory. However, at the last minute, everything fell apart.

A group of African nations attempted to insert words about the rights of member states to access telecommunication networks. The actual origins of this phrasing in a section, which was supposed to be about Human Rights, were a bit murky. Chinese delegates had been seen walking around African delegations distributing wording prior to this point being raised. But its origins may have come from Sudan (a country with substantial Chinese investment), which was concerned about the impact of US and other countries' sanctions on Sudan's communications sector.

There followed a number of back-and-forth interventions from some African countries supporting the wording and some European countries countering that Human Rights applied to individuals and not governments, and that WCIT was not the appropriate place to discuss the rights of states (nor Human Rights for that matter).

Quite suddenly, the representative of Iran (a country also under sanctions) demanded that the proposed text be put to a vote. The chair (with Touré's obvious support) tried to avoid the request, but the Iranian forced the issue, quoting the ITU's rules. Firstly, the motion was put to close discussion of the overall text, which received nearly overwhelming support. And then the ITR text was put to the vote. Thirty-three-member states (mostly western/developed countries) did not vote for the text. Seventy-seven countries voted for it. The EU states voted against it: the European Commission representative was seen during the vote telling the EU member states that they could not vote for the ITRs because the new language ran counter to EU policy and sanctions against Iran.

A brief period of euphoria, especially among African delegations, imploded into depressed silence as the US, and then the UK, Canada, and Poland said they would not sign the new ITRs. Sweden indicated that it would check with its capital, but also was very negative. The Netherlands expressed its own support for the multi-stakeholder model and said it would take the recommendation back to its capital and parliament. Denmark also referred to the multi-stakeholder model as key and said it would not sign the ITRs. New Zealand said the text contained content, Internet, and other language with which it did not agree and would refer it to its capital. Costa Rica reserved the right not to sign the ITRs and said it would check with parliament, but also signaled that the text was beyond the scope of the ITRs. Czechs said they would not sign. South Africa said it was in favor while Kenya said that multi-stakeholder ambitions were not achieved and reserved its right to consult back to capital. Qatar also committed itself to a multi-stakeholder approach. France, Japan, and Australia declared that they too would not sign.

The final language pushed by Iran effectively gave the pro-Internet freedom countries an escape hatch and a way out of agreeing to the new ITR language on the basis of the new clause being beyond the mandate of the ITU. In the end, 55-member states did not sign the ITRs.

The Fallout

Touré and the ITU were damaged

The failure to maintain a consensus created a major split in the ITU membership. Touré's executives were very depressed after the meeting and considered the outcome the worst case scenario. In a bid to reverse the impact on ITU prestige, Richard Hill of the ITU reportedly continued lobbying member states to sign the ITRs, including urging African signatories to pressure Kenya to sign.

Growing public engagement and political mobilization on Internet governance issues generally and support for the multi-stakeholder narrative specifically

Key nodal actors at the center of the Internet community, who were also highly visible and with political influence, championed the virtues of the multi-stakeholder model and an Internet free from government control:

> Vint Cerf and Tim Berners-Lee—two of the founders of the Internet and the World Wide Web respectively—came out strongly against its ratification as did ISOC, the IETF, ITUC, Greenpeace, and the wider technology and civil society communities. Google ran an ad campaign against the treaty and the process that wanted to overhaul it, declaring, "A free and open world depends on a free and open Internet. Governments alone, working behind closed doors, should not direct its future."
>
> *Garber, 2012*

The political attention to the WCIT was in large measure due to intense community concern around the world, with millions of people signing petitions in support of an open, multi-stakeholder–managed Internet (including 100,000 union signatures and NGOs like Avaaz and AccessNow, which together secured about 1 million signatures) and major media attention. The narrative was a simple one—innovation, creativity, and freedom of expression of an open Internet would be stifled if the multi-stakeholder regime was replaced by one that would effectively place the Internet under the control of the ITU in a new treaty. All of this activity also meant that the ITU leadership was put on the defensive and forced to defend itself against accusations that it had tried to limit public comment, did not engage civil society, and had kept most of the really contentious issues hidden from public scrutiny.

Limited scope of agreement

Although 77 countries signed the new ITRs, because of the way ITRs were incorporated into agreements with Telcos, the new ITRs were only applicable to agreements between Telcos that were corporate residents of the signatory countries. Where there was an agreement between a Telco from a non-signatory and one from a signatory, the old ITRs were still applicable. Given the major role of Telcos from the 55 non-signatory states in international telecommunications (and Internet traffic), the practical implication of the new ITRs was limited, or, in the words of Forbes' Elise Akerman, "the gesture in many ways was hollow" (quoted in Garber, 2012).

Mounting international divisions

The Dubai conference revealed to the entire world the deep divisions between those countries which want an open, multi-stakeholder model of Internet governance, and those sought to have Internet communications controlled by governments against the interests of freedom of speech. However, the immediate threat of an ITU takeover of the Internet by authoritarian states was staved off by the network of multi-stakeholder Internet champions and its leaders who conveyed their narrative to governments and to so-called "swing states" in the period that followed WCIT-12 (Maurer and Morgus, 2014). Unlike Western democracies, Russia and China did not have the kind of broad-based reach of technologists and civil society activists to support its own narrative and carry their message forward to other states, especially those that were undecided in their support for different Internet governance models.

Conclusion

The call for the formal vote on the draft that emerged at WCIT 2012 actually gave Western countries an out, because it allowed them to formally express their opposition and underscore that there was no consensus on the proposed amendments to the IT regulations.

In the aftermath of WCIT, Western countries and Internet NGOs did a lot of outreach to swing states, especially in sub-Saharan Africa to promote the benefits of the multi-stakeholder model and to advance the benefits of this approach to the Internet in a positive way, and focus on its importance for economic growth, innovation, and social inclusion (Maurer and Morgus, 2014). These efforts carried into WSIS plus 10, the IGF, regional meetings on the Internet, and NetMundial, which was hosted by Brazil, which had hitherto been in African-Russian-Chinese camp (Pisanty, 2014). Brazil had run a multi-stakeholder process domestically, but also opposed the Americans in the ITU. Brazil actually had two narratives, one led internationally by their foreign ministry, the other domestically by their Internet regulating agencies that supported an open Internet and innovation. However, once Brazil was in the position of bringing together and driving a major, international conference on the future of the Internet, its domestic narrative became ascendant and has subsequently been their dominant international narrative (The Economist, 2014).

Note

1 ISOC (often representing the interests of the Internet Architecture Board and the Internet Engineering Task Force), the Regional Internet Registries, which take Internet resources allocated to them by ICANN and allocate them in smaller units to member operators (Asia Pacific Network Information Centre, American Regional Internet Registry, RIPE-NCC, Latin American Network Information Centre, African Network Information Centre) and many country code operators such as the members of the Council of European National Top-Level Domain Registries (CENTR).

References

APNIC. (2012) *Calling Stumps at WCIT: Win, Lose, or Draw?*, APNIC www.apnic.net/community/ecosystem/iorgs/calling-stumps/.

Cerf, V.G. (2003) Foreword to *Who Rules the Net? Internet Governance and Jurisdiction*. Washington, DC: Cato Institute.

Cerf, V.G. (2012, December 2) *Keep the Internet Free and Open*, Google Blog. https://googleblog.blogspot.com/2012/12/keep-internet-free-and-open.html.

Cerf, V., Ryan, P., and, Senges, M. (2014) 'Internet Governance Is Our Shared Responsibility', *I/S:A Journal of Law and Policy for the Information Society*, vol.10, no.1, pp.1–41.

Cowhey, P.F. (1990) 'The International Telecommunications Regime: The Political Roots of Regimes for High Technology', *International Organization*, vol.44, pp.169–199.

Downes, L. (2012, December 18) *Requiem for Failed UN Telecom Treaty: No One Mourns the WCIT*, Forbes. www.forbes.com/sites/larrydownes/2012/12/17/no-one-mourns-the-wcit/#66cc50895b2c.

Fitzpatrick, A. (2012, December 5) *Why Internet Advocates Hate Russia's Proposal to Change the Web*, Mashable. https://mashable.com/2012/12/05/russia-internet-proposal/?europe=true.

Garber, M. (2012, December 14) *How the UN's 'Game-Changing' Internet Treaty Failed*, The Atlantic. www.theatlantic.com/technology/archive/2012/12/how-the-uns-game-changing-internet-treaty-failed/266263/.

Hampson, F.O. (1995) *Multilateral Negotiations: Lessons from Arms Control, Trade, and the Environment*. Baltimore, MD: The Johns Hopkins University Press.

Hopmann, P.T. (1998) *The Negotiation Process and the Resolution of International Conflicts*. Columbia, NY: University of South Carolina Press.

Internet Corporation for Assigned Names and Numbers (ICANN). (1998) Bylaws for Internet Corporation for Assigned Names and Numbers: A California Nonprofit

Public-Benefit Corporation: As effective 6 November. www.icann.org/resources/unthemed-pages/bylaws-1998-11-06-en.

Internet Society (ISOC). (2012, February) Internet Society comment to WCIT Preparations: 27 February, Internet Society.www.internetsociety.org/resources/doc/2012/internet-society-comment-wcit-preparations-february-2012/.

Lamberson, P.J. (2016) 'Diffusion in Networks', In Bramoullé, Y., Galeotti, A., and, Rogers, B (Eds.), *The Oxford Handbook of the Economics of Networks*. Oxford: Oxford University Press.

Leiner, B.M., Cerf, V.G., Clark, D.D., Kahn, R.E., Kleinrock, L., Lynch, D.C., Postel, J., Roberts, L.G., and, Wolff, S. (1997) *Brief History of the Internet, Internet Society*. www.internetsociety.org/internet/history-internet/brief-history-internet/.

Maurer, T., and, Morgus, R. (2014, May) Tipping the Scale: An Analysis of Global Swing States in the Internet Governance Debate. Internet Governance Papers Paper No. 7. Waterloo, ON: Centre for International Governance Innovation.

Organisation for Economic Cooperation and Development (OECD). (2004, July) Generic Top-Level Domain Names: Market Development and Allocation Issues, Working Party on Telecommunication and Information Services Policies (Paris, France: OECD).

Pisanty, A. (2014, May) 'Empowerment of Non-Governmental Actors from Outside the United States in Multistakeholder Internet Governance', Paper delivered at The Hague Institute for Global Justice 2014 Global Governance Reform Initiative Conference on "The Future of Cyber Governance," The Hague, Netherlands.

The Economist. (2012, December 14) *A Digital Cold War*, The Economist. www.economist.com/babbage/2012/12/14/a-digital-cold-war?fsrc=scn%2Ftw_ec%2Fa_digital_cold_war_/.

The Economist. (2014, March 29) *The Net Closes: Brazil's Internet Law*, The Economist. www.economist.com/the-americas/2014/03/29/the-net-closes.

Twomey, P. (2004, August 23) 'Technical Coordination, Concepts of Governance and the Need to Support a Rapidly Globalising Internet', President and CEO, ICANN (Internet Corporation for Assigned Names and Numbers), Keynote Address to World Computer Congress, Toulouse, France.

United States Department of Commerce. (2000) Management of Internet Names and Addresses. Docket Number: 980212036-8146-02. Washington, DC. www.icann.org/resources/unthemed-pages/white-paper-2012-02-25-en.

Zartman, I.W. (1994) *International Multilateral Negotiation: Approaches to the Management of Complexity*. San Francisco, CA: Jossey-Bass.

8

THE TECHNOLOGY NEXUS OF AI

Narratives as agents of change and lock-in

Dan Ciuriak, Maria Ptashkina, and Vlada Rodionova

Introduction

In a world of sweeping technological progress, technology is becoming the cornerstone of geopolitics, and a ripe ground to form powerful narratives. Reaping the benefits of newly arising economic opportunities, China has emerged as a new strategic competitor of the United States, leading to the outbreak of a new "cold war" between the two powers. The change in geopolitical landscape has also created a new rift between the United States and the European Union, while undermining the institutional framework established under US hegemony in the post-World War II era particularly the trade arrangements under the General Agreement on Tariffs and Trade (GATT) and its successor, the World Trade Organization (WTO), which had served as the forum for negotiation of access to economic opportunity and the settlement of trade disputes for the postwar era. The narratives forming around the flaring technological rivalry are an important part of the toolkits of the parties engaged in the new "Great Game" that will determine who dominates the pivotal technologies of the age (Ciuriak and Ptashkina, 2021a).

Artificial intelligence (AI) – or the nexus of AI, machine learning (ML), and data – is at the core of these emerging narratives. AI (which includes ML and other data science methods) constitutes a general – and dual-purpose technology nexus that is the foundation for the data-driven economy (DDE) that emerged in the technologically advanced economies and sectors in the years following the Great Recession of 2008–2009 (Ciuriak and Ptashkina, 2021b). These new technologies open up major new sources of economic value and of societal and national security risk. The contest to dominate these technologies and capture the economic rents they generate structures the conflicts of the modern

DOI: 10.4324/9781003203209-10

era (Ciuriak, 2020) and the renegotiation of the rules of conduct (Ciuriak and Ptashkina, 2020).

These technologies disrupt in the first instance by introducing a new and irreducible form of information asymmetry between those with access to data and those without. The effects of information asymmetry are strongly amplified when it is accompanied by steep economies of scale in the acquisition of data, powerful economies of scope (which increase the value of data the more broadly data can be cross-referenced), and in many cases network externalities (Ciuriak, 2018). At the enterprise level, these conditions drive a "winner takes most" or "superstar firm" dynamic. The implications for data have-nots are existential: in a Darwinian "survival of the fittest" context, companies with a data disadvantage lose market share and either exit or get acquired by more technologically advanced competitors. The DDE thus promises to be an extinction event at the enterprise level (e.g., the "retail apocalypse"), or a market consolidation mechanism (whereby larger firms devour smaller innovative companies). Significantly, at the international level, this implies a world of *global* superstars rather than competing "national champions" – for example, outside of China, Google largely dominates search. This contrasts with the norms of the industrial era when star firms from many countries competed as global brands. The global superstar firm dynamic makes the DDE a natural incubator for strategic trade and investment policies (Brander and Spencer, 1985).

Second, these new technologies generate a new form of productive capital – machine knowledge capital – in the form of hypercompetent AI that will both complement and substitute for white collar work and intensify the competitive pressure of robotics on blue collar work (Ciuriak, 2018). The net outcome for society is uncertain. In terms of growth, some industry representatives argue that AI will boost labor productivity and ultimately accelerate economic growth (Accenture, 2016); others are doubtful in view of declining total factor productivity growth over the last two decades (Bergeaud et al., 2017). In terms of income distribution, the deployment of machine knowledge capital promises to increase the share of income going to capital within societies, thereby exacerbating the growing income and wealth inequalities that characterized the post-1980 knowledge-based economy era (Gutiérrez and Philippon, 2017; Autor et al., 2020; Furman and Orszag, 2015). In turn, this promises to intensify the internal political strife that these inequalities have helped to generate. This dynamic promises to make the DDE a natural incubator for domestic political tension as well.

Third, these new technologies shift the source of comparative advantage in innovation by industrializing it. This shortens the catch-up period for any economy that has the capacity to make the necessary investments in information technology, particularly at a time when both the global stock of data and the power of supercomputers are doubling roughly every two years (Koomey et al., 2019), accelerating the development of AI applications. Significantly, it was in 2018, when Huawei surged unexpectedly into a leading position on 5G telecommunications networks, including in terms of acquiring standards-essential patents, that the United States was galvanized into scaling up its response (Blustein, 2019).

Fourth, the new technologies restructure geoeconomic contests because data, the chief source of internationally contestable rents, and its operational product, AI, are intangible assets. Conventional military assets largely lose their value as a tool for rent capture with intangibles compared to when rents were captured by controlling physical resources such as land and raw material resources (recall the oil wars) or trading ports (recall the Opium Wars that opened the Chinese markets by gaining control of the major "treaty ports") (Ciuriak, 2020). There is, however, a material aspect to the new geopolitics: the infrastructure of the digital economy, which includes submarine cables, data storage facilities, geostationary satellites, and the continental telecommunications backbone networks, which are now upgrading to 5G technology. In all three areas, geoeconomics and geopolitical rivalry is fully engaged.

Fifth, these technologies create new national security vulnerabilities in multiple dimensions. As the Internet of Things (IoT) expands, it transforms the backbone infrastructure of an economy (transportation, telecommunications, energy, and finance) into a veritable "central nervous system" for the digitized economy, with uncountable vulnerable points of entry that can be exploited for cyberattacks. In the western-dominated information space, China's unwelcome entry through Huawei is meeting stiff resistance on national security grounds, both in 5G networks (Maizland and Chatzky, 2020) and submarine cables (The Economist, 2020). In addition, AI is being weaponized for kinetic warfare through the development of autonomous weapons systems (AWS) that introduce algorithmic warfare possibilities that might prove to be impossible to understand or control (Pandya, 2019).

Sixth, by enhancing prediction, these technologies serve as the handmaiden of quantitative social psychology, including in weaponized form for military purposes (psychological operations) and commercial or political exploitation (social and political manipulation), as surfaced in the Cambridge Analytica scandal in the context of Brexit (Cadwalladr, 2017).

Seen through the prism of AI and the structural changes to which new technologies give rise, the changing geopolitical landscape – with the rise of China and the multifront rivalries – provides a ripe setting for narratives to emerge as the parties seek to influence outcomes in their favor. The narratives that are forming around AI should, in principle, reflect the positions taken by the various parties, given the hands that they have been dealt in the new Great Game that is now unfolding (Ciuriak and Ptashkina, 2018). This chapter examines whether this is indeed the case and whether these narratives play a constructive role in paving the way for negotiated outcomes or are weaponized in the contest to dominate the new technological nexus.

The positioning of players

The Hegemon's tale

If we date the DDE to the recovery from the Great Financial Crisis (GFC), the United States entered this era as a comfortably established front-runner in the technology nexus of AI.

- The modern study of AI started in the United States in 1956, at a conference at Dartmouth College, New Hampshire, where the term "artificial intelligence" was coined. The first major headline breakthroughs were American – IBM's Deep Blue beating Russian chess grandmaster Garry Kasparov in 1997; IBM's question-answering system Watson beating reigning Jeopardy champions Brad Rutter and Ken Jennings in 2011; and Google's AlphaGo defeating 18-time Go world champion Lee Sedol in 2016.
- In ML, the developmental credits are more widely spread, but the United States was the epicenter of development: Google established the Kaggle platform for ML competitions in 2010; a Google neural net learned to recognize cat faces in 2012; Facebook's neural net system DeepFace achieved human face recognition with 97.35% accuracy in 2014; the same year, Google made public its massively parallel ML platform Sybil, which had been developed internally to make predictions about user behavior and provide recommendations.
- The United States also dominated information space as the founder of the Internet and being home to all the major Internet/e-commerce companies that were almost literally hoovering up data globally. It was also ground zero for the age of mobile apps at the dawn of the data-driven era proper with the iPhone released in 2007, Google's Android in 2008, and Apple coining the slogan "there's an app for that" in January 2009.

The one area that the United States did not dominate completely was hardware production for the digital economy. With the sale of Lucent to France's Alcatel in 2006, the United States largely exited hardware development for telecommunications networks. As this was followed by Canada's decision to let Nortel Networks go bankrupt, which eliminated North America's leading telecommunications equipment supplier, the field was ceded to Europe's Nokia and Ericsson and Korea's Samsung. Huawei was not yet on the radar. In satellite systems, rivals to the US Global Positioning System (GPS), which had been in place since 1983, emerged: Russia's GLONASS was completed in 2011, Europe's Galileo in 2013, and China's Beidou system in 2020 (Jones, 2020). Submarine cables were laid by private sector consortia (although US firms dominated the leaseholds). Computer chip development was globalized with important parts of the value chain in Taiwan (Taiwan Semiconductor Manufacturing Company, or TSMC), the United Kingdom (ARM, owned by Japan's Softbank), and the Netherlands (ASML, which builds the advanced semiconductor lithography tools needed to manufacture advanced computer chips).

Being comfortably ahead, the US' main objective was to secure access to global data to lock in its first mover advantages. The US negotiating position in trade agreements was thus focused on ensuring the free flow of data across borders and banning data localization. This was pursued in the Trans-Pacific Partnership (TPP) negotiations with Pacific Rim countries, with the European Union in the Transatlantic Trade and Investment Partnership (TTIP) negotiation, and in the plurilateral negotiations toward a Trade in Services Agreement. As for the regulation of AI, the stance was to leave this to self-regulation by the industry giants in the first instance on the argument that it was premature to regulate. This maximized the freedom to operate for its world leading firms. Beyond direct regulation, the US maintained a strong opposition to digital taxation.

These elements were complemented with an increase in the protection afforded to a type of intellectual property (IP) of vital importance in the digital economy and to AI in particular – trade secrets. Algorithms and data are protected by trade secrets rather than patents or copyrights. The United States introduced sweeping new trade secrets legislation domestically, the Defend Trade Secrets Act of 2016, and pressed for similar levels of protection in its trade agreements.

The US narrative thus had a familiar central focus on the sanctity of private property coupled with freedom of commerce and prevention of restrictions on the activities of US multinationals – a generalized version of the concept of "freedom to operate," which allows multinational firms to optimize their business approach to a given market without constraints posed by government policies or regulations (Ciuriak, 2017a).

On AI specifically, the US has indicated its intention to develop strategies to ensure that it dominates global AI markets. The US National Security Strategy of December 2017 (at p. 20), states:

> To maintain our competitive advantage, the United States will prioritize emerging technologies critical to economic growth and security, such as data science, encryption, autonomous technologies, gene editing, new materials, nanotechnology, advanced computing technologies, and artificial intelligence. From self-driving cars to autonomous weapons, the field of artificial intelligence, in particular, is progressing rapidly.

Moreover, because AI is an essential component of tools such as drones and robotics relied upon by the US military, a competitive edge in AI is seen as essential for national security reasons: "Continued American leadership in Artificial Intelligence is of paramount importance to maintaining the economic and national security of the United States" (White House, 2019). Aaronson (2020) describes the policy execution as "nationalistic, protectionist, and insular" and notes that the United States has "proposed export controls on AI, dramatically limited work and educational visas, and alienated close scientific partners such as Canada, France, and Japan." CRS (2019) provides a detailed overview of the national security issues raised by AI as perceived by the United States, for which national security takes precedence over other issues: as former United States Trade Representative Robert Zoellick wrote, "ever since the rise of 'national security' as a concept at the start of the Cold War, economics has become the unappreciated subordinate of U.S. foreign policy" (Zoellick, 2012).

The core themes of the US narrative – protection of private property, freedom of cross-border flows, removal of restrictions on private enterprise, and technological leadership as essential to national security – were already well established as part of the US narrative from previous eras; the transition to the DDE and the nexus of AI was therefore seamless.

China's tale

China entered the DDE era far behind in the new technologies and with virtually no electronic commerce, but with an established substrate for the development of technological capabilities in these areas by virtue of a concerted policy effort over previous decades that included the following:

- Heavy investments in tertiary education, which continued through the post-Great Recession decade (China was building on average a university a week in the mid 2000-teens), with a heavy focus on STEM programs; it surpassed the EU's top eight countries and the United States in total number of science and engineering graduates as early as 2003–2004 (AIP, 2018);
- Home-grown technology development capacity, initially through "introduction, digestion, absorption, and re-innovation" (Kwan, 2015);
- A welcoming attitude to inward foreign direct investment (FDI) while using its economic clout to obtain technology transfer commitments;
- As it opened up its capital account, investment abroad at scale, with technology acquisition a key objective;
- Establishment of overseas research and development (R&D) centers by its technology firms in the leading technology hubs to tap into technology developments abroad; and
- Through its "Thousand Talents" programs, a push to reverse the brain drain that had seen many Chinese researchers go abroad to study at elite universities and remain abroad as well as to attract leading foreign researchers.

While China's economic development trajectory was initially based on assembly of imported technologically advanced components (Van Assche, 2006), this nonetheless supported the development of a critical mass of large manufacturing companies that used technology (e.g., firms such as Lenovo and Haier) – and were in a position to acquire technology through acquisition of companies (e.g., Lenovo purchased IBM's personal computer manufacturing business) and to develop their own technologies and applications through R&D. By the start of the DDE, China's R&D expenditures had risen to levels approaching those of the leading technology nations (1.7% of GDP in 2010 versus 2.7% for the United States; OECD, 2020). And its R&D workforce, while still small as a share of employment (1.6 per 1,000 employed in 2010, compared to 8.5 in the United States; OECD, 2020), was large in absolute terms – China's R&D workforce was estimated to be in the four million range in the mid-2000-teens (Wong, 2016).

As well, China had developed a large technology consumer base. When Apple released the iPhone 3 in China in January 2008, China's mobile phone consumers transitioned en masse to smartphones, setting the stage for explosive growth in mobile e-commerce – and the generation of the data that would fuel China's AI development.

As China's national interests increasingly shifted to IP, it developed the infrastructure for IP expansion, including training thousands of patent examiners, raising the level of IP protection domestically, and instituting IP courts for enforcement, etc. (Ciuriak, 2017b), including a new national IP appeal court that began operation on January 1, 2019 (Ni Zhenhua, 2019).

In addition, it developed a doctrine of "Internet sovereignty," which involved comprehensive Internet regulation and supervision in the form of the Golden Shield Project; when completed in 2008, this was colloquially referred to as the Great Firewall. While the primary objectives of the Firewall were political control and national security, this administrative apparatus gave China the tools for industrial policy in digital space.

China was thus poised to rapidly climb the technological ladder in the DDE – and it did. The penetration of e-commerce in China's economy is a useful metric for this purpose. From a negligible share in 2009, China's e-commerce penetration as a share of retail sales matched the United States in 2013 and was 50% larger by 2016 (Figure 8.1).

Through this period, China's innovation consisted primarily of application of existing, mostly foreign technology. This is demonstrated by its international position in IP payments and receipts (Figure 8.2). Over the period covered by these data, China made a cumulative USD 292 billion in payments for technology while earning only USD 26 billion in receipts – and 65% of those receipts were realized in the period 2017–2019. Over the same time period, the US earned USD 2,098 billion in receipts. In 2019, China generated USD 6.6 billion in IP earnings, a small fraction of the USD 129 billion realized by the United States. While China had established the basis for breaking through the "middle income trap" and acquired the ability to scale technology, it still trailed the established technology leaders by a very long distance.

The evolution of China's narrative reflected this underlying technological development.

In the post-Cold War period, China's narrative followed Deng Xiaoping's 24-character statement: "Observe carefully; secure our position; cope with affairs calmly; hide our capacity and bide our time; be good at maintaining a low profile; and never claim leadership" (Chen, 2019). In line with this, China adopted

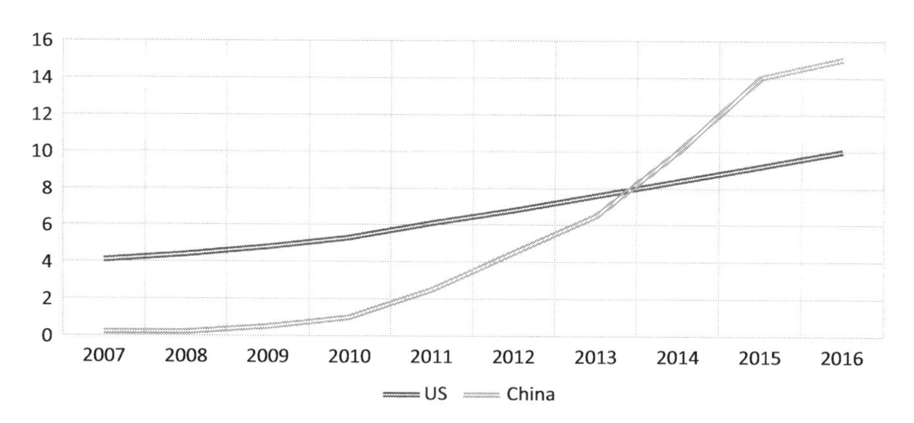

FIGURE 8.1 Share of e-commerce in total retail sales in the United States and China (%), 2007–2016

Source: Reproduced from Zhang and Chen (2019), based on Alibaba data.

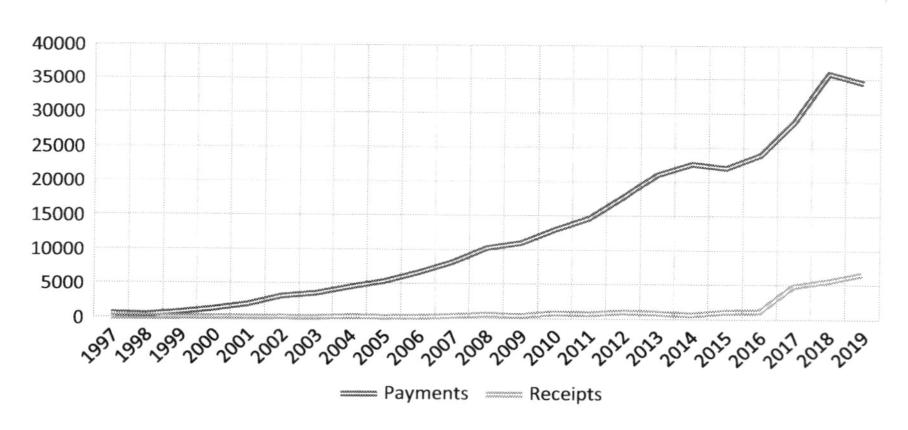

FIGURE 8.2 International payments and receipts for IP in China (million USD), 1997–2019

Notes: The data are presented in current USD, on a balance of payments (BoP) basis.
Source: World Development Indicators, The World Bank.

disarming slogans like "peaceful rise" and set modestly couched objectives like becoming a "moderately prosperous society."

The narrative China adopted for the "New Generation Artificial Intelligence Development Plan" (also referred to as "AI 2030") was more ambitious: to "seize the historical opportunity" offered by the emergence of a new technology sector that was not yet dominated by others, to "leapfrog" national technological competitiveness by aiming at these new emerging technologies, to build up "AI first mover advantage," and to accelerate "innovation-driven and globally advanced science and technology" development.

This strategy followed the adoption of the "Made in China 2025" (MIC2025) program, which aimed to move China up the technology ladder and avoid the "middle income trap" (Malkin, 2018). The strategy was modelled on industrial policies to take advantage of the so-called "fourth industrial revolution" pioneered initially by the United States (the 2011 Advanced Manufacturing Partnership; White House, 2012), and followed in short order by Germany (Industry 4.0), Japan (4.1J; Wu, 2016; and Connected Industries; METI, 2017), Korea (Connected Smart Factory; Park, 2016), and Taiwan (Smart Machine and Productivity 4.0; Wu, 2016), to name a few. MIC2025 abandoned Deng's cautious 24-character prescription and was infused with newfound ambition – to establish China as "the leader among the world's manufacturing powers" and to create the "capability to lead innovation and possess competitive advantages in major manufacturing areas."

The MIC2025 program (and to a lesser extent the AI 2030 program that accompanied it) fell under strict scrutiny abroad and was one of the ostensible triggers for the trade war launched by the United States (Ciuriak and Ptashkina, 2021b). By openly stating its desire to quit the sphere to which economic history had theretofore assigned it (the assembler of products based on advanced technology developed abroad), China abandoned the Deng philosophy of lying low. This point was raised in adversarial commentary abroad, after which China dropped the use of the term MIC2025 (although not the policy).

Deng's signature policy approach was no longer tenable once China's firms gained international prominence. This includes in areas such as 5G and smartphones (Huawei); the major Internet firms (Baidu, Alibaba, and Tencent), which have seen stock market valuations exceed USD 1 trillion; and unicorns where China's roster is second only to those of the United States (including well-known firms like Ant Financial, Bytedance, and Didi Chuxing, but also over a dozen AI unicorns; CB Insights, 2021). As well, some of China's main advances have come in highly visible applications (such as an AI news anchor, or TikTok) rather than largely invisible core technologies.

What the furor over MIC2025 shows is that China does not control the narrative outside of China. Similarly, its ambitions in AI face pushback.

The EU's tale

The EU missed out on the first major wave of Internet firms and it appears set to miss out on the next wave of AI firms. EU firms are not major users of AI in their businesses and hold only a small share of AI patents. Moreover, out of the 71 unicorns identified as AI firms, only two are in the EU27 (the UK has four; CB Insights, 2021). How and why this state of affairs came about calls for some soul-searching by EU policy makers – to have missed the boat once can be written off to circumstances; to have missed it twice starts to look systemic.

The EU confronts a situation in which the battle for domination of the technological heights of AI is, at least at the outset, mainly a contest between the

United States and China with the EU looking on. In this context, the European Commission has observed that each new wave of data brings with it new opportunities – and the next wave is now upon us with the IoT (European Commission, 2020). How does the EU play its hand?

In the first instance, the EU plays to its established strengths. With regard to the revenues generated by platform companies, the EU's position has been that a fair share of the rents should be allocated to the jurisdiction that generates them, regardless of whether the firm capturing the rents is domiciled there or has a physical presence there. The EU has also been a first mover on addressing the negative impacts on market competition of the market-failure-prone DDE; as well as on breaches of privacy, levying large fines, and introducing legislation to enable still greater fines in order to create the leverage to deter firms with trillion dollar market capitalization. The narrative that the EU has promulgated is that of fairness, good governance, and multilateral norm-setting – familiar territory.

At the same time, the EU has been working to develop its own economic stake in the DDE, protecting its own firms from foreign takeovers and implementing its own industrial policies.

All of these measures, both defensive and offensive, position the EU, which had been part of the narrative framework for the entire postwar period as a joined-at-the-hip ally of the United States, increasingly in an adversarial posture vis-à-vis the United States. These DDE-driven shifts amplify the geopolitical drift induced by other developments, including Brexit, the frictions generated by the extraterritorial reach into European economic relations of US geopolitical sanctions, and the Trump administration's attacks on the EU in terms of trade policies and the questions it raised about the future of the North Atlantic defense relationships (including withdrawing troops from Germany). The Trump administration's *alleingangs* (going alone) in the various clubs and multilateral fora served as a rude awakening to the EU, famously articulated by German Chancellor Angela Merkel, who stated, following a series of bruising G7 and NATO meetings:

> The times in which we could completely depend on others are, to a certain extent, over … I've experienced that in the last few days. We Europeans truly have to take our fate into our own hands.
>
> *Henley, 2017*

Following Brexit, the EU27 is increasingly looking East in a clear departure from the trans-Atlanticism that had been a pillar of its international posture throughout the postwar period – including for energy (e.g., continued support for the Nord stream II gas pipeline from Russia, despite US objections; Pistorius, 2021) and growth (through the EU-China Comprehensive Agreement on Investment or CAI, which was closed without consulting the incoming Biden Administration, to the dismay of the latter).

The EU has perforce developed a new narrative for itself around the concept of "strategic autonomy" (EEAS, 2020). Sabine Weyand, the Director General for trade in the von der Leyen Commission, stated as follows:

> Open strategic autonomy, if I have to sum it up in one sentence, I would say is a mindset which means we act together with others, multilaterally, or bilaterally, wherever we can. And we act autonomously wherever we must. And the whole of it adds up to the EU standing up for its values and interests.
>
> *Keynes and Bown, 2021*

While there is a lack of practiced assurance in the articulation, the tectonic plates have been set in motion and the pressures generated in the DDE promise to strengthen the momentum.

The dynamics of the contest

The Hegemon's tactics

The United States (particularly under the Trump administration) approached the contest over the new technology nexus with a strong revealed preference for preserving the confidence of equity markets; its best alternative to a negotiated agreement (BATNA) was to deploy tariffs, drive decoupling, and restrict Chinese access to US technology, but only to the extent possible. The "extent possible" was largely defined by the pain that this caused to its own firms – as objectively quantified by stock market performance. For example, if restrictions on sales of technology to Chinese firms resulted in declining stock values of US suppliers, the rules were loosened. The Biden administration has left the Trump measures in place while vowing to leverage the purchasing power of the federal government through the upgraded "Buy American" program to strengthen domestic manufacturing and create markets for new technologies (White House, 2021).

In terms of tactics, the United States offers the prospect of talks while preparing the ground for escalation. It uses a narrative built around how bad previous trade deals were (including allowing China into the WTO), the unfairness of bilateral trade imbalances, and the failure of previous administrations to enforce the terms of trade deals to press a one-sided negotiating agenda of take with no give. A telling feature of the US approach is that there is no value proposition offered to trading partners – it is all sticks and no carrots. This arguably reflects the exhaustion of US economic reserves – it has no carrots to offer.

Further, its escalating rhetoric on "China cheats" and the need to "confront China," coupled with the emphasis on "enforceability," paint the United States into a corner since it cannot be seen as compromising on such fundamental issues as national security which is claimed to be compromised by China's technological advance.

On technology, the line is hardening, with additional Chinese firms being added to the US "entities" list of proscribed firms and the reach of US extraterritorial prohibitions being extended ever deeper into supply chains. However, a full decoupling along the lines of the iron curtain between the west and the Soviet Union is extremely unlikely given the existing interconnections (Roach, 2020). One useful point to consider is that there are many firms in China. While the United Kingdom moved to exclude Huawei from its 5G buildout, it included China's Oppo. In setting the standards for 5G networks, Chinese firms were heavily involved – China Mobile alone submitted over 3,000 proposals or 30% of the total for the R16 standard as frozen on July 3, 2020 (Yibing, 2020).

In the public commentary, these technology-related issues tend to be conflated with the more conventional trade adjustment impacts experienced globally following China's accession to the WTO – the so-called "China Shock" – the statement that granting China "permanent normal trade relations" distorted labor markets and investment allocation in advanced economies because of China's massive and pervasive subsidies. While distributional consequences of trade shocks are still an active area of economic research, as Lincicome (2020) documents, if the outsourcing of manual labor had not been to China it would have been to another low-wage economy. From a narrative perspective, however, this conflation works to escalate the rhetoric.

China's tactics

In terms of tactics, China plays strict tit-for-tat, offering concessions when talks open or reopen but withdrawing them, if and when the United States escalates, and matching the escalation to the extent possible given the unbalanced relationship.

China's BATNA appears to be at all times prolonging the status quo, especially as regards delaying potentially lethal restrictions on US technology exports to Huawei and other exposed tech companies, buying time until the situation on the ground in terms of its own technological capabilities changes through its concerted domestic investment push to close the technology gap in critical areas (China has mobilized its technology investments to wartime footing to eliminate its exposure to US technology; given the dual use characteristics of AI, China is likely gearing up for a relatively high degree of autonomy).

In its external relations, China appears to be prepared to offer economic concessions, provided only that it is able to present the deal as "respecting dignity" and in some sense showing "balance" – China cannot come away entirely empty handed (e.g., a USMCA-type balance of a material transfer of benefits to the United States in exchange for token "wins" for the other parties would likely be accepted).

Given the risk of a relatively hard decoupling, China has prepared for a long-term conflict. Its narrative invokes the "unfair treaties" imposed on it following the Opium Wars to rally domestic support, and Mao Zedong's "Long March" to victory in China's civil war to stoke hope for eventual success. As regards the tone of commentary, China's business-facing press (Caixin) reports dryly and for the most part describes a world that is business as usual. However, when the main action shifts to pure foreign policy issues (reactions abroad to developments in Hong Kong, the South China Seas, and Xinjiang), the tone elevates and becomes much more confrontational, channeling the cinematic "wolf warrior" trope for domestic audiences, however badly this might play with foreign audiences.

The EU's tactics

The EU has redefined its relationship with China in terms of the latter being both a strategic partner as well as a strategic competitor, and without explicitly saying so, it appears to have done the same with the United States. This parallelism emerges from the EU's move to protect "vulnerable" assets from acquisition not only by Chinese entities but also (with regard to its telecommunications companies) by the United States, and its move to tax multinational corporations (which pits it primarily against the United States).

The EU's BATNA seems to be defined by maintaining global economic stability to allow it to develop its own technological capabilities – including in 5G and AI – for which China is an important partner while, at the same time, preventing a flare-up in its own trade relationship with the United States as it seeks a rebalancing of the benefits of the digital transformation in its favor.

The EU has established itself as a cautious player in the international digital realm, focusing on minimizing the potential adverse effects of the new technologies, and keeping the regulatory bar high. As such, the EU is focusing on protecting data privacy (through the implementation of General Data Protection Regulation), preserving net neutrality (e.g., emphasizing the point in the negotiations on the Comprehensive Economic Trade Agreement with Canada), and driving the development of taxation on digital services (Iacob, 2019).

Meanwhile, the EU works to preserve the framework of multilateralism (including, e.g., by partnering in the establishment of an alternative to the WTO Appellate Body while the latter is in a US-imposed hiatus) and to advance its own strong suit, which is regulation and addressing the ethical concerns that are at the center of discussions to AI development. In 2019, the EU-appointed High Level Expert Group on AI which addressed the waterfront of "AI and" issues, including respect for human value and individual freedoms; equality, nondiscrimination, and solidarity; social and economic rights; democracy; and the rule of law. This "human-centric" approach is adopted for the draft European Ethics Guidelines for Trustworthy AI. As the EU has been at the forefront of regulation, much of the future discussion of the ethical implications of AI is likely to be built around the EU's regulations.

The EU appears to be using its advantage in the "Art of the Compromise" to try and find a compromise on the regulation of AI. Legitimacy would depend largely on the result being broadly acceptable within the multilateral rules-based framework, the Commission being able to present the result as meeting at least some of the concerns of EU companies about competition from China and EU sovereignty and security being preserved as regards data privacy.

Discussion

The technological nexus of AI is presently an open contest to capture market share and future rents – there is no formal negotiation. The competing narratives are playing a central role by preparing the ground for an extended period of conflict rather than for the start of such negotiations. Thus, they harden rhetoric and prepare domestic audiences for the imminent costs of the trade and technology conflicts. In a sense, narratives lead to what in game theory is called a self-confirming equilibrium with beliefs: the narratives themselves help to form expectations that the negotiations would necessarily fall apart due to the "unbridgeable gap" of the initial positions.

Geopolitics is changing. The narratives that we use to explain back to ourselves what has happened and how things are changing are evolving. The DDE context of accelerated innovation has led to a "shoot first, ask questions later" approach to the contest over AI given the large stakes involved both in terms of economic rents and strategic advantage. Conflict has therefore perhaps unavoidably preempted negotiation; narrative construction has been accordingly dedicated to suit the adversarial purposes of conflict (by raising the temperature) rather than the constructive objectives of negotiation (by shedding light). In this context, the path to negotiations (e.g., toward a WTO 2.0; Ciuriak, 2019) thus must be on a parallel track that allows the many technical issues raised in the regulation of the digital economy and AI to be advanced, even as the Great Game over the future of AI plays out.

We are witnessing a natural experiment in progress. In the fullness of time, this will enable the testing of theories of how narratives are manufactured (to paraphrase the "manufacturing of consent"; Herman and Chomsky, 1988; and Lippmann, 1922), and of the role of narratives in shaping change. The analysis above suggests that the narrative framework for international relations that had evolved during the postwar era, as adapted to advance the interests of the digital economy powers, risks becoming a barrier to a cost-minimizing solution to the current trade and technology wars in which the technology nexus of AI play a pivotal role.

References

Aaronson, S.A. (2020) 'America's Uneven Approach to AI and Its Consequences', Institute for International Economic Policy, George Washington University, Working Paper IIEP-WP-2020-7.

Accenture. (2016) *Artificial Intelligence Is the Future of Growth*, Accenture. www.accenture.com/sk-en/insight-artificial-intelligence-future-growth#:~:text=The%20impact%20of%20AI%20technologies,efficient%20use%20of%20their%20time.

AIP. (2018) *Rapid Rise of China's STEM Workforce Charted by National Science Board Report*, American Institute for Physics. www.aip.org/fyi/2018/rapid-rise-china%E2%80%99s-stem-workforce-charted-national-science-board-report.

Autor, D., Dorn D., Katz, L.F., Patterson, C., and, Reenen, J.V. (2020, May) 'The Fall of the Labor Share and the Rise of Superstar Firms', *Quarterly Journal of Economics*, vol.135, no.2, pp.645–709.

Bergeaud, A., Cette G., and, Lecat, R. (2017, September 4) 'Future Growth: Secular Stagnation Versus Technological Shock Scenarios', *Vox CEPR*. https://voxeu.org/article/secular-stagnation-versus-technological-shock-scenarios.

Blustein, P. (2019) 'Schism: China, America and the Fracturing of the Global Trading System', Waterloo: Centre for International Governance Innovation.

Brander, J.A., and, Spencer, B.J. (1985) 'Export Subsidies and Market Share Rivalry', *Journal of International Economics*, vol.18, pp.83–100.

Cadwalladr, C. (2017, May 7) *The Great British Brexit Robbery: How Our Democracy Was Hijacked*, The Guardian.

CB Insights. (2021) *The Global Unicorn Club: Private Companies Valued at $1B+*, 30 September. www.cbinsights.com/research-unicorn-companies.

Chen, J. (2019) 'From Mao to Deng: China's Changing Relations with the United States', The Cold War International History Project Working Paper 92.

Ciuriak, D. (2017a) 'How Small Open Economies Can Leverage the Trade in Ideas', In R. Medhora (Ed.), *Special Report: New thinking on innovation* (pp.121–125). Waterloo, ON: Centre for International Governance Innovation.

Ciuriak, D. (2017b, March) 'Intellectual Property Proliferation: Strategic Roots and Strategic Responses', CIGI Paper No. 121, Centre for International Governance Innovation.

Ciuriak, D. (2018, March 5) 'The Economics of Data: Implications for the Data-Driven Economy', In *Data Governance in the Digital Age*. Waterloo, ON: Centre for International Governance Innovation. https://papers.ssrn.com/abstract=3118022.

Ciuriak, D. (2019) 'World Trade Organization 2.0: Reforming Multilateral Trade Rules for the Digital Age', CIGI Policy Brief No. 152, Centre for International Governance Innovation.

Ciuriak, D. (2020) 'Economic Rents and the Contours of Conflict in the Data-Driven Economy', CIGI Paper No. 245, Centre for International Governance Innovation.

Ciuriak, D., and, Ptashkina, M. (2018) 'Started the Digital Trade Wars Have: Delineating the Regulatory Battlegrounds', RTA Exchange, International Centre for Trade and Sustainable Development. www.cigionline.org/publications/toward-robust-architecture-regulation-data-and-digital-trade/.

Ciuriak, D., and, Ptashkina, M. (2020, April 15) 'Toward a Robust Architecture for the Deregulation of Data and Digital Trade', CIGI Paper No. 240, Centre for International Governance Innovation.

Ciuriak, D., and, Ptashkina, M. (2021a, March 14) 'The Data-Driven Economy and the Role of the State', In B. Haggart, N. Tusikov, and J.A. Scholte (Eds.), *Power and Authority in Internet Governance: Return of the State?*. London and New York: Routledge.

Ciuriak, D., and, Ptashkina, M. (2021b, March 8) 'Technology Rents and the New Great Game', In R.N. Choudhury (Ed.), *The China-US Trade War and South Asian Economies*. London and New York: Routledge.

CRS. (2019) 'AI and National Security', Congressional Research Service, Report R45178, https://crsreports.congress.gov.

EEAS. (2020, December 3) 'Why European strategic autonomy matters', Blogpost, European External Action Service. https://eeas.europa.eu/headquarters/headquarters-homepage/89865/why-european-strategic-autonomy-matters_en.

European Commission. (2020, February 19) 'On Artificial Intelligence – A European Approach to Excellence and Trust', White Paper. Brussels. COM(2020) 65.

Furman, J., and, Orszag, P. (2015, October 16) 'A Firm-Level Perspective on the Role of Rents in the Rise in Inequality', Presentation at 'A Just Society' Centennial Event in Honor of Joseph Stiglitz, Columbia University. http://tankona.free.fr/furmanorszag15.pdf.

Gutiérrez, G., and, Philippon, T. (2017, July) 'Declining Competition and Investment in the U.S.', NBER Working Paper No. 23583.

Henley, J. (2017, May 28). *Angela Merkel: EU Cannot Completely Rely on US and Britain Any More*, The Guardian. www.theguardian.com/world/2017/may/28/merkel-says-eu-cannot-completely-rely-on-us-and-britain-any-more-g7-talks.

Herman, E.S., and, Chomsky, N. (1988) *Manufacturing Consent: The Political Economy of the Mass Media*. New York, NY: Pantheon.

Iacob, N. and Felice S. (2019) 'Taxing the digital economy: Time for pragmatism', CEPS Brief, 02 December. *Centre for Economic Policy Studies*. www.ceps.eu/taxing-the-digital-economy/.

Jones, A. (2020, June 3) *China Launches Final Satellite to Complete Beidou System, Booster Falls Downrange*, Space News. https://spacenews.com/china-launches-final-satellite-to-complete-beidou-system-booster-falls-downrange/.

Keynes, S., and, Bown, C. (2021, January) *The EU's New Trade Policy, with Sabine Weyand of DG Trade*, Trade Talks, Episode 148. www.tradetalkspodcast.com/wp-content/uploads/2021/01/Episode-148-Transcript.pdf.

Koomey, J., Schmidt, Z., and, Naffziger, S. (2019) 'Supercomputing Performance and Efficiency: An Exploration of Recent History and Near-Term Projections', Report by Koomey Analytics, completed in collaboration with Advanced Micro Devices, Inc.

Kwan, C.H. (2015, February 4) 'China Aiming for Growth by Innovation: Private-Sector Companies as the Leading Force', RIETI, Fellows' Works: China in Transition.

Lincicome, S. (2020, July 8) 'Testing the "China Shock": Was Normalizing Trade with China a Mistake?' Cato Institute, Policy Analysis No. 895.www.cato.org/policy-analysis/testing-china-shock-was-normalizing-trade-china-mistake#

Lippmann, W. (1922) *Public Opinion*. New York, NY: MacMillan.

Maizland, L., and, Chatzky, A. (2020, February 12) *Huawei: China's Controversial Tech Giant*, Council on Foreign Relations. www.cfr.org/backgrounder/huawei-chinas-controversial-tech-giant.

Malkin, A. (2018, August) 'Made in China 2025 as a Challenge in Global Trade Governance: Analysis and Recommendations', CIGI Paper No. 183.

METI. (2017) 'Connected Industries', *METI*. www.meti.go.jp/english/policy/mono_info_service/connected_industries/index.html.

Ni Zhenhua B. (2019) 'China Established a Centralized IP Appellate Tribunal', *Blogpost, King & Wood Mallesons*, 15 January. www.chinalawinsight.com/2019/01/articles/intellectual-property/china-established-a-centralized-ip-appellate-tribunal/.

OECD. (2020, March 6) *Main Science and Technology Indicators*, OECD. www.oecd.org/sti/msti.htm.

Pandya, J. (2019, January 14) *The Weaponization of Artificial Intelligence*, Forbes. www.forbes.com/sites/cognitiveworld/2019/01/14/the-weaponization-of-artificial-intelligence/.

Pilling, D. (2018, August 13) *African Economy: The Limits of 'Leapfrogging'*, The Financial Times. www.ft.com/content/052b0a34-9b1b-11e8-9702-5946bae86e6d.

Pistorius, M. (2021, January 15). *Nord Stream 2: Europe Stays Quiet While US 'Tramples Over EU Sovereignty*, EURACTIV.fr. www.euractiv.com/section/energy-environment/news/nord-stream-2-europe-stays-quiet-while-us-tramples-over-eu-sovereignty/.

Roach, S. (2020, January 3) *The Myth of Global Decoupling*, Project Syndicate. www.project-syndicate.org/onpoint/the-myth-of-global-decoupling-by-stephen-s-roach-2020-01?barrier=accesspaylog.

The Economist. (2020, February 6) *The Digital Side of the Belt and Road Initiative Is Growing*, The Economist: Special Report.

Van Assche, A. (2006, July 1) 'China's Electronics Exports: Just a Standard Trade Theory Case', *Policy Options*, Institute for Research on Public Policy.

White House. (2012) *White House Advanced Manufacturing Initiatives to Drive Innovation and Encourage Companies to Invest in the United States*, Fact Sheet. https://obamawhitehouse.archives.gov/the-press-office/2012/07/17/fact-sheet-white-house-advanced-manufacturing-initiatives-drive-innovati.

White House. (2019, February 11) *Executive Order on Maintaining American Leadership in Artificial Intelligence*. www.whitehouse.gov/presidential-actions/executive-order-maintaining-american-leadership-artificial-intelligence/.

White House. (2021, January 25) *President Biden to Sign Executive Order Strengthening Buy American Provisions, Ensuring Future of America is Made in America by All of America's Workers*. www.whitehouse.gov/briefing-room/statements-releases/2021/01/25/president-biden-to-sign-executive-order-strengthening-buy-american-provisions-ensuring-future-of-america-is-made-in-america-by-all-of-americas-workers/.

Wong, J. (2016, November 1) *How China Is Fast Narrowing the Technology Gap with the West*, The Straits Times: Opinion. www.straitstimes.com/opinion/how-china-is-fast-narrowing-the-technology-gap-with-the-west.

Wu, M.J. (2016, May 30) 'Smart Machine and Productivity 4.0 in Taiwan: Now and Future', Presentation, Industrial Development Bureau, MOEA.

Yibing, Z. (2020) 'World's first complete 5G standard unveils future potential', CGTN Technology, https://news.cgtn.com/news/2020-07-04/World-s-first-complete-5G-standard-unveils-future-potential-RR7ElgdOsU/index.html.

Zhang, L., and, Chen, S. (2019) 'China's Digital Economy: Opportunities and Risks', *IMF Working Paper*, WP/19/16.

Zoellick, R. (2012, October 8) *The Currency of Power*, Foreign Policy. https://foreignpolicy.com/2012/10/08/the-currency-of-power/.

PART III

Narratives of peace and conflict negotiations

9

THE ROLE OF NARRATIVES IN NEGOTIATIONS

The case of the FARC and Colombia

Sophie Haspeslagh and I. William Zartman

Introduction

A narrative is a story, a cloud of identities and implications. It self-identifies the party and its view of the conflict and the opponent. Parties to a conflict begin with different stories, the difference preventing a resolution of the conflict. In fact, the difference often prevents negotiation itself as a way to resolving the conflict. Thus, the work of aligning the parties' narratives must begin before negotiation and continues during its practice. Parties in conflict have conflicting narratives of their own nature, of the conflict and of the others (nothing new there). Narratives on a collision course reflect (or undergird) the nature of the conflict itself, much as interests underlie positions. As the conflicting parties move toward negotiation, these narratives evolve, at least to the point of considering talking to each other.

But that evolution can occur in various degrees: (1) the narratives can come into focus in the way a binocular ends up with a three-dimensional appreciation of its object and making negotiation possible; (2) they can overlap in conflict, with mutual recognition and acceptance to allow an agreement to disagree and move in to a settlement on that basis; or (3) they can remain apart, resulting in a shallow unstable agreement or none at all. The subordinate questioning is when does this happen, before negotiations can take place, during the (self-diagnosis) phase or during the (mutual) formulation phase before agreement can take place. The third question then becomes why this happens. The job of adjusting narratives is usually left to each of the parties, as a result of internal and external changes. Internal changes can involve fatigue, leadership changes, reactions to cost, and evaluations of future prospect, among others. External changes include fortunes on the battlefield, and allies' reactions, among others. These are the working assumptions and hypotheses under which this study is undertaken.

DOI: 10.4324/9781003203209-12

The study examines the case of negotiations between the Revolutionary Armed Forces of Colombia (FARC for its Spanish acronym) and the Government of Colombia along these lines of inquiry. To analyze the narrative of the party and its view of the conflict and its opponent the paper analyzes statements made by the Colombian government and the FARC in the lead-up to the Havana negotiation as well as personal interviews.[1] The paper homes in on the process through which separate narratives got the parties to the Havana negotiations and argues that the narrative shift was not only an essential prerequisite for negotiations to start, but it was also central in answering the why question as it fostered ripeness between the parties because it allowed for a way out.

Government narrative

In the lead-up to the Havana negotiations the government narrative about the conflict identified it as a war against terrorists. There was an alignment between the international narrative about the Colombian conflict in a post 9/11 context of the war on terror, and the government's narrative under Álvaro Uribe. President Uribe set about reframing the public understanding and perception of the Colombian situation; there is no armed conflict (Uribe, 2002). In a speech in 2005 to the diplomatic corps in Colombia, Uribe made clear that if there is no conflict, then there are no combatants, just terrorists (Uribe, 2005). Before the UN General Assembly in September 2006, he said:

> For us, armed violence with fictitious political motives is terrorism and security is the path to peace. When there is a pluralist, vigorous democracy with guarantees, armed action against it is pure terrorism. Denying it would mean there is no difference between armed combat against dictatorships (...) and violent aggression suffered by our democracy, aggression that is terrorism.
>
> *Uribe, 2006*

By denying the existence of armed conflict and labeling the FARC as terrorists, Uribe could portray them as irrational, a bunch of criminals for whom change is not possible. A narrative of contamination. This made the idea of political negotiations with the group impossible in the eyes of the public. The conflict was in an intractable confrontation.

When Juan Manuel Santos took office as President in August 2010, he was already considering the possibility of initiating peace negotiations with the FARC, as will be explored below in the why section. But he was very aware that he could not suddenly embark in a negotiation with the armed group as portrayed. This challenge was also picked up by people following closely the dynamic at the time who commented that it would be challenging to shift perceptions when the armed group had actively been portrayed as "terrorists" for years. As the late Virginia Bouvier, head of the Colombia programme at the USIP, asked: "How to convince the public that the armed group can be negotiated with and can respond to rational thought?" (Bouvier, *Personal interview*, February 2014).

Retooling the government narrative

Reorienting the government narrative involved some deliberate changes in recognitions that had made part of the former, Uribe narrative. These concerned recognition of the conflict and recognition of the Other.

Recognition of the conflict

The seismic ingredient of the narrative shift in the lead-up to the Havana negotiations was President Santos' recognition of the armed conflict. Indeed, the major change in his discourse compared to President Uribe's was his explicit recognition of the existence of the armed conflict in Colombia. He explicitly changed the language he used, stating, for example, in the press in May 2011 that "It has been a while that there is an armed conflict in this country" (quoted in Parra, 2011). He went even further by enshrining this description in law through the Law on Victims and Land Restitution (Law 1448, 2011), which defined victims as:

> Those individuals who individually or collectively have suffered damage for events that occurred on or after 1 January 1985 as a result of violations of international humanitarian law or serious violations of international human rights standards that occurred during the *internal armed conflict*. [emphasis added]

By recognizing the existence of the conflict, he effectively recontextualized the FARC. And by Santos (2011a) argued that the "best way to end this conflict" was through dialogue. By shifting his description of the violence as an armed conflict instead of a "war against terrorists," he was shifting the image of the FARC publicly – nationally and internationally – and creating the conditions for a negotiation.

Recognition of the Other

President Santos was also sending direct signals to the FARC that he recognized them politically as a party to the armed conflict. According to a member of the FARC, the armed group was very conscious of this shift: "I know that at one moment they started recognizing this as a conflict. Under Uribe it was terrorists, which was absurd. Afterwards, with Santos they started talking about an armed conflict" (Alexandra Nariño, *Personal interview,* November 2015).

Looking at the words Santos used chronologically to describe the FARC, we see that he shifted first to using words such as "violent" instead of "terrorists." He then went further using words such as "subversive," "guerrilla," or "insurgent," which implied the group had a political agenda. This was a deliberate attempt to repoliticize the FARC. He started using the armed group's acronym "FARC" to address and describe them in a clear sign of recognition (Santos, 2010a, 2010b, 2010, 2011b). President Santos also started showing a form of respect for the group by acknowledging the structures of the organization using vocabulary such as "maximum leader" (Santos, 2011c), "number one" (Santos, 2011d,), or "Secretariat" (Santos, 2012a).

Another key element was to portray the FARC as a partner with which the government could do business. In February 2011, Santos said he "value[d] positively" (Santos, 2011) the freeing of five hostages by the FARC, a stark contrast to Uribe's refusal to even acknowledge previous releases. In April 2011, when the FARC released ten military and police officers and committed to no longer take hostages, Santos warmly welcomed this shift by stating that it was "a gesture that we value and appreciate in all its dimension" (Santos, 2012b). When Santos broke the news to the nation that authorities had been conducting exploratory talks with the FARC on August 27, 2012, he acknowledged that the FARC had "worked seriously" (Santos, 2012c). Later, Humberto de la Calle (2012), the government's chief negotiator, said the FARC had "fulfiled" the government's requirements. He was building an image of an opponent that was rational and should be trusted to start an official negotiation.

The FARC narrative

The reaction of the FARC against being labeled as "terrorists" was also very strong in the early years of the Uribe administration. The FARC demanded that the state and the government "exclude from the language of officials epithets of 'terrorists and narco-terrorists' to refer to our organization of political-military opposition against the State" (FARC-EP, 2002). In April 2003, they decried the usage of "pugnacious language" and "improper epithets" to describe them (FARC-EP, 2003a).

But the FARC also matched President Uribe's narrative of contamination with similarly negative and vilifying language. They describe him as a "paramilitary" (FARC-EP, 2004a), a "fascist" (FARC-EP, 2004a, 2009). The words "fascist" (FARC-EP, 2003b), "terror" (FARC-EP, 2008), or "military terror" (FARC-EP, 2010) were used regularly to typify government policy. The FARC demonized the Uribe administration implying it was without principles and irrational. The FARC also made regular references to the US role in Colombia, calling it "neo-colonial" (FARC-EP, 2004b), "US imperialism" (FARC-EP, 2004c), and "US intervention," implying a country that was "occupied" (FARC-EP, 2010a, 2010b) and in a subservient relationship toward the US, effectively implying the government was illegitimate.

Retooling the FARC narrative

In the lead-up to the Havana negotiations the FARC shifted their story about themselves in the conflict and the Other, just after the government shift of language.

Themselves in the conflict

The FARC always resisted and rejected the label of "terrorists" and offered a counter narrative. They described their struggle as the "universal legitimate use of the right to revolt" (FARC-EP, 2004c). In the years leading up to the Havana negotiations there are notable efforts at reframing their fight. The FARC's narrative started going beyond their classic historical account of class struggle and oppression. In their statements from 2010 onward, they start regularly describing their struggle as part of a broader movement of the masses. In a statement addressed "To the Colombian people," they refer to the strikes led by the indigenous, agrarian organizations, peasant farmers against fumigation, and truck drivers, in the summer of 2011, implying that they are part of the same struggle (FARC-EP, 2011d; Hernández Delgado, 2012). They tried to renew their ideology through social forums and mentioned issues as wide ranging as the minimum salary, LGBT rights, gender equality, the right to abortion, the protection of the environment, or unemployment (FARC-EP, 2011a). They were also trying to create an explicit link with the struggles of the poor and disenfranchised of Colombia, particularly the peasants, indigenous and afro-Colombian movements (FARC-EP, 2012a).

Moreover, by distancing themselves from certain practices deemed inhumane, the FARC started taking steps toward "devillainizing" themselves. This is particularly apparent in their public correspondence with *Colombianos and Colombianas por la paz (Colombian@s)* on the subject of hostage taking. Through an exchange of public letters the FARC committed itself to end what they described as "economic retentions" (Jímenez, 2012). *Colombian@s* succeeded in engaging the FARC in a public dialogue over a period of two years, which culminated in getting 40 hostages freed unilaterally. The FARC described these releases as a way of creating an atmosphere conducive to talks: "The releases of prisoners of war by the FARC are unilateral gestures to create an enabling environment to trigger the swap agreement for prisoners and clear the road for a political settlement to the conflict" (FARC-EP, 2011b). From the perspective of the government, this decision was seen as fundamental to show that the villain was willing to abandon its villainous ways. The fact that the FARC published a statement to end economic retention was seen as "very important to establish the process [i.e. the negotiation]" (Enrique Santos, *Personal interview*, June 2015).

Recognition of the Other

When President Santos was elected, the FARC were deeply skeptical and expected him to follow the course set by President Uribe. Santos had been Uribe's Minister of Defense and one of the leading figures in the government's military strategy. Initially, the FARC showed very little respect in the way they addressed him. The first mention does not even refer to him by name but as the "Minister of Defense of Uribe" (FARC-EP, 2010). In a video from Alfonso Cano addressing the President directly he refers to him as "Doctor Juan Manuel

Santos" (Cano, 2011). By 2011, FARC communiqués call him "Mister Juan Manuel Santos" (FARC-EP, 2011c), "Mister President" (FARC-EP, 2011c), and "President Santos" (FARC-EP, 2011b). This evolves to "President of the Republic" (FARC-EP, 2012b) when the negotiations with the government are announced in 2012. This evolution in characterization shows a clear effort at recognizing and respecting their opponent as well as a progression in how they perceived President Santos and his willingness to engage.

Though the FARC statements remained critical of Santos, they referred multiple times to his own expressions and statements such as using the sentence "President for Peace" (FARC-EP, 2011), or the fact that he claimed to be considered a "traitor to his social class" (FARC-EP, 2012) by stating his openness to dialogue. By using Santos' own words, even if it was done sometimes in a mocking or critical fashion, it showed that the FARC were paying close notice to what he was saying, they were taking on board the shifts in his tone and discourse, thereby acknowledging his efforts at shifting the narrative.

Moreover, instead of focusing on criticizing the government, the bulk of FARC statements in the period leading up to the Havana negotiations shifted to criticizing the role of business and the oligarchy. It showed an effort on the part of the FARC to uncouple the Santos administration from the broader Colombian establishment. This showed an effort on the part of the FARC to reassure parts of the armed group that were skeptical of the possibilities of negotiating.

Another development in FARC statements was the increase in language reflecting openness toward negotiations. They used language such as "finding the political solution to the conflict" (FARC, 2010c), "open paths to coexistence" (FARC-EP, 2010c), and "initiate dialogue" (FARC-EP, 2011c). It showed the FARC leadership making a deliberate and self-conscious effort to shift the narrative about their opponent but also themselves.

Meeting of the narratives: A story of redemption?

So how did these narratives meet and what story did they tell? A good place to look for signs of the parties etching a new narrative about their common future is the framework agreement signed between the Colombian government and the FARC on August 26, 2012, the culmination of the secret prenegotiation process.

The most striking thing about the framework agreement is that the "end of the conflict" becomes the overarching objective of the negotiations. This might seem unsurprising to negotiation scholars who expect this to be the case in any negotiation, but in the Colombian context after 60 years of protracted war and multiple negotiation attempts it was unprecedented. For the FARC, this was a momentous change for a group that had always described itself as a "party in arms," always fighting on both the military and political fronts. During previous negotiations, they never intended to give up arms and had still seemed convinced that the war against the Colombian state could be won militarily (Adviser, *Personal interview*, 2015). As he announced the start of public negotiations, President

Santos said "I am convinced that we are facing a real opportunity to definitively end the internal armed conflict; it is a difficult path, but it is a path that we must explore." The narrative emerging to explain why the government should enter into negotiations with the armed group was one of ending the bloodshed. This is what was being sold to Colombians.

But both the government and the FARC were also etching a future Colombia that was not only at peace but also fairer. Two of the points contained in the framework agreement show that the government embraced key points of the FARC's historical agenda around integral development of land and enhancing the political participation of marginalized sectors. This was essential for the FARC in bringing along their constituency.

These are the stories that were told to enter into the negotiation. It is only much later on, toward the end of the negotiation, when both parties were about to sign the peace agreement that we see a more ambitious story of redemption emerge. In February 2016, during a trip to the United States, six months before the signature of the peace accord, Santos said that

> Peace will help us consolidate a new nation, a country that will be safer, more prosperous, more just and equitable, better educated, and of course, happier. We'll be a confident nation that will continue to earn the trust and admiration of the entire world.

He was shoring up support both at home and abroad for the agreement he was about to sign. This vision was embraced by President Obama who, standing next to Santos said "That's a vision that we share (..) This is something that has to affect ordinary people in increasing their security and their opportunity. That's what we mean when we talk about building a truly peaceful, prosperous Colombia."

When does it need to happen?

There are clear differences between governmental and nongovernmental actors in terms of who had to do what and when in order to make the narratives negotiable. Because of the entrenched narrative of a war against terrorists during the eight-year Uribe administration, much work needed to be done by the government, to shift their narrative of contamination by acknowledging the existence of the conflict, dropping the terrorist label, and start recognizing the FARC as a potential negotiation partner, a process that can be described as a "linguistic ceasefire" (Haspeslagh, 2021). Much of the narrative changes in this regard took place before formal negotiations were launched. The government had to convince both a skeptical public at home and abroad that the FARC were an entity that could be negotiated with as well as send clear signals to the FARC that they recognized the existence of the conflict and their political nature.

In the lead-up to Havana, the narrative shift was incremental, and it continued evolving well into the negotiations and beyond, but the Santos government struggled to convince the media and large sections of public opinion that the FARC were no longer "terrorists.". In fact, well into the negotiations he was still pleading the media to stop describing the FARC as terrorists (Sierra, 2015).

The FARC on the other hand had to shift their narrative about themselves reframing their struggle and publicly abandon their villainous ways before a negotiation was possible. But most importantly, they had to shift their narrative of redemption and agree to a future without war. But it is only during the negotiations that the FARC started to shift their narrative acknowledging the pain they had caused. One year into the negotiation, in August 2013, the FARC made a first statement acknowledging their responsibility for generating victims in the armed conflict. And it was only toward the end of the negotiation, in September 2016, the FARC made a number of acts of contrition such as meeting the family members of the 11 Valle parliamentarians they had kidnapped and killed and asking for forgiveness.

Even though Timochenko, the leader of the FARC, received a standing ovation when he said "I ask for forgiveness for all the pain that we have caused during this war" during the signature of the peace accords in Cartagena, it was too little too late. The public was not convinced.

In fact, the rejection of the peace referendum in October 2016 by the Colombian public could be understood as the narrative shift failed to have an impact beyond the conflict parties themselves. It shifted just enough to allow the negotiations to take place but not enough to sell the peace agreement, and the concessions that both parties made to the Colombian public.

Why does it happen?

When President Santos said he held the "keys to peace" in his inaugural address, everyone was taken by surprise. Why did President Santos, who had been President Uribe's defense minister, decide to switch away from an all-out military strategy to contemplating peace negotiations with the FARC? And vice versa, why did the FARC get to the point of recognizing they would not win the war militarily and agree to negotiate an end to the war? Though both parties start feeling the pain of their mutual stalemate from 2008, they had no way out because of the government's terrorist framing of the Other. The narrative shift became essential to opening a way out both for the FARC and the government. This section explores ripeness and the parties' perceptions of their mutually hurting stalemate and way out (Zartman, 1989, 2000).

2008: The turning point

By taking on the global mantle of the fight against terrorism in Colombia, President Uribe was able to gain international and national recognition and legitimacy for his war against the FARC. Coupled with the refocusing of Plan Colombia on a fight against terrorists and the huge investment and modernization of the army, this had the effect of strengthening the Colombian government vis-à-vis the FARC. The government and large sectors of the Colombian population were convinced that the war could be and should be won and ended militarily.

The FARC was deeply affected by the military reversal during the two Uribe administrations. The Colombian military developed sophisticated techniques to identify the location of the FARC's top leadership and attack them. In 2008 a series of attacks against "high value targets" led to the killing of key leadership figures such as Raul Reyes and Iván Ríos. These assassinations of important commanders had a "very hard effect" on the FARC (de Roux, *Personal interview*, June 2015). Moreover, high rewards were given for internal treason. These rewards led to a number of internal betrayals that had a deep impact on the FARC. The most famous case was that of FARC Secretariat member, Ivan Ríos, who was killed in March 2008 by his bodyguard, who then cut off his hand as proof to claim the reward.

Between 2002 and 2010 the FARC lost five out of its seven Secretariat members. Though the FARC had a group leadership style, with a system to automatically replace fallen commanders, the sheer volume of deaths had an important impact at the leadership level of the armed group. But beyond that as well, the mid-ranking commanders and the rank and file of the armed group were also deeply affected by the military onslaught. According to the Group for Humanitarian Attention of Demobilized People, 15,500 FARC members defected between 2002 and 2010 (quoted in Jonsson, 2014).

As the Colombian military had been able to increase the frequency and precision of its bombardments on FARC camps, thanks to increased material and intelligence support, certain death became a reality for the FARC mid-ranking commanders and rank and file members. A number of interviewees confided that the increasing precision of the bombardments was affecting the FARC's moral (Colón, *Personal interview*, June 2015; similar point made by: Leyva, *Personal interview*, October 2015, who has deep knowledge of the FARC).

The FARC came to see a military victory as no longer within their reach. They no longer had the capacity to expand, "the guerrilla realizes it is much more weakened militarily" (González, *Personal interview*, June 2015). The year 2008, which was also marked by the (natural) death of Manuel Marulanda, the founder and leader of the FARC, became a "turning point" (Gross Stein, 1989) for the FARC. Most interviewees concur in saying that at this stage, in 2008, the FARC start perceiving that they cannot be defeated nor can they win (Peace and Development Advisor, *Personal interview*, June 2015; González, *Personal interview*, June 2015; de Roux, *Personal interview*, June 2015; Celis, *Personal interview*, June 2015).

It is the perception by the FARC that things had changed militarily that was important. Even though the Uribe administration had been saying for years that the FARC had been cornered and defeated, it is only from 2008 onward that the FARC *itself* show signs of recognizing and acting on it. The FARC's perception of the mutually hurting stalemate is epitomized in the words of Marcos Calarcá: "They haven't been able to win and we haven't been able to win – there are no winners, no losers" (Calarcá, *Personal interview*, May 2015).

Similarly, it is only between 2008 and 2010 that sectors within the government started perceiving that a military victory against the FARC remained elusive. Significantly, the nerve center of this shift happened in the military and the ministry of Defense, when President Juan-Manuel Santos was still President Uribe's Minister of Defence (between 2006 and 2009). The Colombian army itself started becoming aware of its limits. There was a growing realization that both the topography of Colombia and the nature and *modus operandi* of the FARC as an armed organization made the likelihood of a "military victory" elusive. The head of the armed forces, General Alejandro Navas, said that a military victory against the FARC was not possible. Every time a leader is killed, he is replaced by another: "Even though you are able to kill leaders and you move forward, there are still rising from the land and they will never end" (Colón, *Personal interview*, June 2015). So, while the targeted attacks against the leadership of the FARC deeply affected the group, as we saw above, the fact that the FARC had a group leadership system in its Secretariat gave the Colombian military the impression that new leaders would always arise.

A certain conviction started to emerge within the military and the Ministry of Defense that the war would not be won militarily. This got them thinking of different strategies and options. According to his brother, Enrique Santos, Juan-Manuel Santos "had the perception that the FARC was affected militarily but was still there, he realized that a military victory was not possible, Colombia is not Sri Lanka" (Santos, *Personal interview*, June 2015; de Roux, *Personal interview*, June 2015). He later took this perception along with him as he started his Presidency in 2010. As Francisco de Roux said, "Having been minister of defence [Santos] realized that even though you can put the FARC against the wall, weaken them, you cannot overcome them because of Colombia's complex circumstances" (de Roux, *Personal interview*, June 2015).

No way out

By 2008 both the FARC and the government were starting to feel the pain of a mutually hurting stalemate. But why did it take another two years for the FARC and the government to enter into prenegotiations and another two to enter into formal negotiations? Part of the answer lies in understanding that a party's feeling a hurting stalemate is not enough, it also needs to envision a way out. But with President Uribe's narrative and the framing of the conflict as a war against terrorists, there was no way out.

Even if the government had wanted to enter into peace negotiations with the FARC, it had no room for maneuver. It had created its own policy straightjacket by convincing the public and international opinion that the Colombian government should not negotiate with "terrorists." So, the government had no way out of the reliance on a military strategy, it was neither willing nor able to negotiate.

So, the FARC itself could not envision a political future under President Uribe. One of the FARC's four conditions vis-à-vis the government to initiate a peace negotiation was that the government should "Recognize our political character and stop signaling us as 'terrorists" (quoted in Villarraga Sarmiento, 2013, p.68). It had the effect of taking away their legitimacy, their political recognition externally. Their politics were banned and pushed further underground. They were increasingly isolated from broader Colombian society and internationally. There was no space for them to do politics. It is important not to forget that the decimation of the Unión Patriótica in the 1980s, the FARC's ill-fated attempt at creating a political party, is a deep wound they carried. It created much distrust in the possibility of political participation; they were not convinced they would receive the necessary security guarantees. This is especially the case in a context where being signaled as a "terrorist sympathizer" often led to the killing of individuals with political affinities with the FARC. The FARC believed they had no political future, so they had little incentive to enter into a dialogue process with President Uribe. The FARC *itself* could not see a way out.

Leadership change

It was only when President Santos came in with a new narrative about the conflict and the FARC that the armed group started envisioning a way out. People who have had close contact with the armed group or followed their evolution carefully confirm that the recognition of the armed conflict was central to the FARC's decision to engage in the negotiations with President Santos (Lozano, *Personal interview*, May 2015; Velandia, *Personal interview*, June 2015; Senior Analyst, *Personal interview*, May 2015).

Leadership change was an important element in the government's shift in perception of the stalemate. The new leader, in this case President Santos, was someone who had shifted his perception from the inside as Minister of Defence and carried this change into his Presidency. There was also a political component to the hurting stalemate. Once these military strategies had been in place for a while, the political costs associated with them become increasingly apparent. It is during President Uribe's second term that a number of scandals erupted, which shed light on some of the political, particularly human rights, costs associated with these strategies. The extrajudicial executions, the Departamento Administrativo de Seguridad (DAS) scandal, and parapolitics scandals, in particular, made the Colombian government lose a lot of national and international credibility.

While President Uribe did not appear to be hugely affected by these human rights concerns, President Santos was more sensitive to them, especially when these human rights concerns led to economic cost. A key moment occurred when the US Free-Trade Agreement was put on hold linked to concerns over human rights violations and the US started slowly reducing their unequivocal support to the Colombian military (Vásquez, *Personal interview*, May 2015). This slight shift in a key ally, and its main support in its war against "terrorists," had an impact on the Colombian government. President Santos started feeling the political pain of the war on terror. He was much closer than President Uribe to the international liberal business elite. There was also an increasing feeling within government ministries that the war was limiting their ability to act, both in terms of particular areas of the country that were "out of reach" but also in terms of developing infrastructure, roads, connectivity (Senior Analyst, *Personal interview*, May 2015; Colón, *Personal interview*, June 2015; Velandia, *Personal interview*, June 2015). There is a strong business component to President Santos' perception of the government's political stalemate: "Santos realized that the biggest obstacle for a stronger economic development in Colombia is war" (de Roux, *Personal interview*, June 2015). The government started feeling the political costs associated with their military strategy.

Leadership change also played a central role in shifting the FARC's perception. The generational changes within the organization compounded by the targeting and killing of key leadership figures and the desertion of key mid-ranking FARC cadres. The FARC leadership started to become painfully aware that the younger generations were not as political. They were struggling to fill the mid-level positions with the necessary political and military training and inclination. While the senior leadership of the FARC at this stage was mainly comprised of ideological Marxist-Leninist commanders who had joined the group in the 1960s and 1970s, the rank and file joined in the 2000s when the group had already compromised its ideological basis by depending substantially on drugs and kidnapping to fund their fight. Each FARC cadre had to have both political and military training – there was no separation between the two – and the armed group had found it increasingly difficult in practice because new recruits did not all have political inclinations: "For young people, managing weapons is much more attractive than political debate" (Ferro Medina and Uribe Ramón, 2002, p.82).

The possibility of a negotiated solution to the conflict became more appealing to the FARC in the context of trying to salvage what political capital they still had: "There is a big difference between the Secretariat and the rank and files. The ideological part of the FARC saw negotiations as the only way forward [they want to] leave with some kind of legacy." (Sánchez-Garzoli, *Personal interview*, April 2014). So, it is possibly more the risk of completely losing their political character that played an important part in the FARC Secretariat's assessment of its situation.

Here again leadership change played an important role in ripening the situation. Alfonso Cano played a central role. He led an internal process by consulting with others until he managed to get unity around the idea of entering peace negotiations. As one FARC leader noted: "I feel there was a shift towards peace through a strong debate" (de Roux, *Personal interview,* June 2015; similar point raised by Celis, *Personal interview*, May 2015). The FARC had a systematic discussion at the leadership level weighing-up their different options looking at their political and military reality, exploring their international and regional space. There was a complex shift of a quasi-relative minority who wanted to enter into negotiations led by Cano that had started strengthening with this thinking starting to trickle down to the rank and files. One member of the FARC remembers "an internal communiqué from Alfonso Cano in September 2010 where he gave some elements [of an openness to peace negotiations]" (Nariño, *Personal interview*, May 2016).

Before being elected, President Juan Manuel Santos had felt the political and military costs of the war against "terrorists" in Colombia. Now elected, he found the policy straightjacket, tailored during President Uribe's tenure, based on the idea that the Colombian government should not negotiate with "terrorists," itchy and tight fitting. He decided to unfasten it and slowly started fostering the way out. But in 2010, public opinion in Colombia and factions in the government and the military were completely against the idea of negotiating with "terrorists" as we saw above (Santos, *Personal interview*, June 2015). Undeterred, he started slowly shaping that possibility.

Conclusion

Exploring the stories of the Colombian government and the FARC showed that shifting the narrative was essential in setting the stage for the Havana negotiations. The government first had to shift its narrative of the conflict before both parties shifted their narrative toward mutual recognition ahead of the Havana negotiations though the evolution was incremental. But the narrative shift was not just a question of what happened, it was also essential in understanding the why it happened. It became instrumental in fostering a way out both for the government and the FARC.

It is important to recognize that the government did not just have a change in positions. Alone that could not be sustained by the other positions and policies in the government's sheaf. It was the whole narrative – or significant parts of it – that shifted to carry the policy shift with it. Particularly recognition of the Other, which carried with it recognition of the conflict as a conflict and the process, allowed for the story to shift.

This evolution also raises further questions, only some of which are answered here. What brings about that shift? How widespread does it have to be, both among adherents and in the coherence of the narrative. The explanation here is that the shift had an external cause, in the stalemate that developed between the two sides. As the ripeness syllogism expresses, it was the nature of the conflict that created the objective nature of relations between the sides. But that change had to be recognized as untenable by the tenets of the narratives – "we can't win" – and subjectively unbearable – "and it hurts us." Subjective recognition went hand in hand – chicken and egg – with another shift, the change in leadership on both sides.

But the matter of agency brings up another question of sociopolitical dynamics: Narratives are bodies of ideas that hang together. But they are vehicled by individuals and groups. What are the political dynamics of the way they change (and are carried). The story here shows that the change of perception at the leadership level actually led to a shift in narrative that was convincing enough to enable a negotiation to get off the ground. Its sociopolitical vehicularization and impact is another story. It seems that the normative stickiness of the terrorist label made it very hard to roll back.

But in its own focus, the story of how the FARC and the Colombian government went from an intractable deadlock to a remarkable breakthrough can give hope. Hope that words matter and that a profound symbolic shift in how adversaries characterize each other and the conflict can be the key to breaking a deadlock.

Note

1 The data used in this chapter, personal interviews and document analysis, was collected by Sophie Haspeslagh as part of the research for her book *Proscribing Peace: How Listing Armed Groups As Terrorists Hurts Negotiations* (Manchester: Manchester University Press, 2021a).

References

Cano, A. (2010, July 30) *Conversemos,* Al Jazeera.

De la Calle, H. (2012, October 18) 'Declaración de Humberto de la Calle, Jefe de la Delegación del Gobierno Nacional, durante la instalación de la mesa de conversaciones para la terminación del conflicto', Hurdal, Norway.

FARC-EP. (2002, May 15) 'Comunicado del Secretariado de las FARC-EP: Condiciones propuestas al nuevo Presidente para retomar la solución política, Montañas de Colombia.

FARC-EP. (2003a, April 27) 'Carta abierta de las FARC-EP a los expresidentes liberales', Secretariado del Estado Mayor Central de las FARC-EP.

FARC-EP. (2003b, July 12) 'Comunicado del Secretariado de las FARC-EP: proceso de paz pero con un gobierno dispuesto a concertar'. In A. Villarraga Saramiento (Ed.), *Gobierno-FARC: ni diálogo de paz ni "canje" humanitario. Propuestas de acuerdo humanitario* (pp.103–104). Biblioteca de la Paz 2002–2010, Tomo VIII: Bogotá, Colombia.

FARC-EP. (2004a, February 24) 'Comunicado.'

FARC-EP. (2004b, July 13) 'Comunicado', Secretariado del Estado Mayor Central, FARC-EP.

FARC-EP. (2004c, December 30) 'Secuestro en centro de Caracas', Secretariado del Estado Mayor Central.

FARC-EP. (2008, August 31) 'Comunicado', Bloque Iván Ríos y Martin Caballero de las FARC, Montañas de Colombia.

FARC-EP. (2009, May 9) 'Fascismo a la Criolla', Estado Mayor Central FARC-EP, Montañas de Colombia.

FARC-EP. (2010, January) 'Carta abierta a Señor Freddy Padilla de Léon', Jorge Suárez Briceño, Integrante del Secretariado del Estado Mayor Central.

FARC-EP. (2010a, February 22) 'Memorando del Secretariado delas FARC-EP: el conflict Colombiano, siempre hemos creído en una salida política.'

FARC-EP. (2010b, June 21) 'Comunicado', Secretariado del Estado Mayor Central, FARC-EP, Montañas de Colombia.

FARC-EP. (2010c, September 25) '¡Gloria eternal al comandante Jorge Briceño, heroe del pueblo en su resistencia contra el opresor!', Secretariado de las FARC-EP.

FARC-EP. (2011, March 7) 'Desde la trinchera', Jorge Briceño Suárez.

FARC-EP. (2011a, May 6) '47 Anos de batallas por la paz de Colombia desde la Resistencia armada', Estado Mayor Central.

FARC-EP. (2011b, July 16) 'El bombardeo mediático a Alfonso Cano', Jorge Briceño Suárez.

FARC-EP. (2011c, August 12) 'Saludo al encuentro nacional por la paz', Secretariado Nacional del Estado Mayor Central.

FARC-EP. (2011d, December 27) 'Al pueblo Colombiano', Secretariado del Estado Mayor Central de las FARC-EP.

FARC-EP. (2012, May 27) 'FARC-EP, 48 años de lucha armada rebelde', Secretariado Nacional del Estado Mayor Central FARC-EP.

FARC-EP. (2012a, July 22) 'Declaracion Publica', Secretariado del Estado Mayor Central de las FARC-EP.

FARC-EP. (2012b, September 5) 'La Mesa de Conversaciones, un triunfo del clamor nacional por la paz y la solución politíca', Secretariado del Estado Mayor Central.

Ferro Medina, G., and, Uribe Ramón, J.G. (2002) *Orden de la guerra. Las FARC-EP entre la organización y la política, El.* Bogotá, Colombia: Pontificia Universidad Javeriana.

Gross Stein, J. (1989) 'Getting to the Table: The Triggers, Stages, Functions, and Consequences of Prenegotiation', *International Journal*, vol.44, no.2, pp.475–504.

Haspeslagh, S. (2021) 'The 'Linguistic Ceasefire': Negotiating in an Age of Proscription', *Security Dialogue,* vol.52, no.4, pp.361–379. https://doi.org/10.1177/0967010620952610.

Haspeslagh, S. (2021a) *Proscribing Peace: How Listing Armed Groups as Terrorists Hurts Negotiations.* Manchester: Manchester University Press.

Hernández Delgado, E. (2012) *Intervenir antes que anochezca: Mediaciones, intermediaciones y diplomacias nonviolentas de base social el en conflicto armado colombiano.* Bucaramanga, Colombia: Universidad Autónoma de Bucaramanga.

Jímenez, T. (2012, March 3) 'Comunicado: Carta a la Señora Marleyna Orjuela, ASFAMIPAZ, Bogotá', Commandante del EMC.

Jonsson, M. (2014) *A Farwell to Arms: Motivational Change and Divergence Inside FARC-EP, 2002–2010.* Uppsala, Sweden: Uppsala Universiteit.

Parra, N.E. (2011, May 5) *Hace rato hay conflicto armado en este país,* El Tiempo.

Santos, J.M. (2010, August 30) 'Mientras las Farc persistan en el terrorismo.'

Santos, J.M. (2010a, September 17) 'Las Farc son un ratón.'

Santos, J.M. (2010b, September 26) 'Las puertas están abiertas para desmovilizarse.'

Santos, J.M. (2011, February 7) 'Alocución del Presidente', Bogotá, Colombia.

Santos, J.M. (2011a, May 4) 'Palabras del President Santos en el Foro 'La Reintegración, un negocio que apuesta a la paz', Bogotá, Colombia.

Santos, J.M. (2011b, July 20) 'Palabras del Presidente.'

Santos, J.M. (2011c, December 23) 'Las Farc se están desmoronando poco a poco', Tolemaida, Colombia.

Santos, J.M. (2011d, December 30) 'Alocución del President Juan Manuel Santos, de saludo de Año Nuevo', Barranquilla, Colombia.

Santos, J.M. (2012a, April 19) 'Declaración del Presidente Juan Manuel Santos sobre renuncia del general Óscar Naranjo a la Dirección de la Policía Nacional', Bogotá, Colombia.
Santos, J.M. (2012b, April 2) 'Declaración del Presidente Juan Manuel Santos luego de la liberación de los 10 militares y policías', Bogotá, Colombia.
Santos, J.M. (2012c, September 4) 'Alocución del Presidente de la República, Juan Manuel Santos sobre el 'Acuerdo General para la Terminación del Conflicto', Bogotá, Colombia.
Sierra, Á. (2015, July 30) *Y ahora, ¿a desescalar de este lado?,* El Tiempo.
Uribe, Á. (2002, August 7) 'Retomemos el lazo unificador de la ley, la autoridad democrática, la libertad y la justicia social', Bogotá, Colombia.
Uribe, Á. (2005, January 31) 'Saludo al cuerpo diplomático acreditado en Colombia', Bogotá, Colombia.
Uribe, Á. (2006, September 21) '61st General Assembly Speech', UN General Assembly, New York, N.Y.
Villarraga Sarmiento, Á. (2013) 'Imposibilidad de entendimientos entre el Gobierno y las FARC, propuesta de acuerdo humanitario'. In Á. Villarraga Saramiento (Ed.), *Gobierno-FARC: ni dialogo de paz ni 'canje' humanitario. Porpuesta de acuerdo humanitario* (pp.65–93). Bibliotecas de Paz 2002–2010, Tomo VII, Bogotá, Colombia: Fundación Cultura Democrática.
Zartman, I.W. (1989) *Ripe for Resolution.* Oxford: Oxford University Press.
Zartman, I.W. (2000) 'Ripeness: The Hurting Stalemate and Beyond', In P. Stern and D. Druckman (Eds.), *International Conflict Resolution After the Cold War.* Washington, DC: National Academy Press.

Personal Interviews Conducted by the Author

Haspeslagh, S. (2014, February) Interview with V. Bouvier, Director of the Colombia Program, United States Institute for Peace. Washington, D.C.
Haspeslagh, S. (2014, April) Interview with G. Sánchez-Garzoli, G., Senior Associate for Colombia, Washington Office on Latin America (WOLA). Washington, D.C.
Haspeslagh, S. (2015, May) Interview with C. Lozano, Director for *Semanario Voz* and Communist Party Member. Bogotá, Colombia.
Haspeslagh, S. (2015, May) Interview with L.E. Celis, Advisor for the Fundación Paz y Reconciliación.
Haspeslagh, S. (2015, May) Interview with Marcos Calarcá (L.A. Albán Burbano), Member of the FARC Negotiation Team and International Secretariat. Havana, Cuba.
Haspeslagh, S. (2015, May) Interview with a Senior Analyst, International Organization. Bogotá, Colombia.
Haspeslagh, S. (2015, May) Interview with T. Vásquez, Researcher for the Nacional de Memoria Histórica. Bogotá, Colombia.
Haspeslagh, S. (2015, June) Interview with an Adviser for the Colombian High Commissioner for Peace. Bogotá, Colombia.
Haspeslagh, S. (2015, June) Interview with C. Velandia, Former Commander of the Ejército Nacional de Liberación (ELN).
Haspeslagh, S. (2015, June) Interview with E. Santos, President Santos' brother and Government Negotiator. Bogotá, Colombia.
Haspeslagh, S. (2015, June) Interview with General R. Colón, Director for Acción Integral Contra Minas Antipersonal, Presidencia de la República. Bogotá, Colombia.

Haspeslagh, S. (2015, June) Interview with F. González, Coordinator of the Peacebuilding and Development Programme, CINEP/ Programa por la Paz. Bogotá, Colombia.

Haspeslagh, S. (2015, June) Interview with P.F. de Roux, Jesuit Provincial. Bogotá, Colombia.

Haspeslagh, S. (2015, June) Interview with a Peace and Development Advisor. Bogotá, Colombia.

Haspeslagh, S. (2015, October) Interview with A. Leyva, Conservative Politician and long-time FARC Intermediary. Bogotá, Colombia.

Haspeslagh, S. (2015, November) Interview with A. Nariño (T. Nijjmeijer), Member of the FARC Negotiation Team. Havana, Cuba.

Haspeslagh, S. (2016, May) Interview with A. Nariño, Member of the FARC Negotiation Team. Havana, Cuba.

10

THE MAKING OF WAR HEROES

Narratives, negotiations, and former warring parties in post-conflict societies

Julia Strasheim

Introduction

Intrastate armed conflict has long been considered as one of the greatest threats to human security worldwide. Since 1989, more than one million people have died as the result of direct combat between government forces and rebel groups – a number that does, however, not even begin to account for fatalities resulting from other types of violence typically associated with intrastate warfare, or for the vast indirect costs it bears for human development (Sköns, 2005).

To end armed conflict and reduce the risk of its recurrence, numerous scholars and practitioners have proposed strengthening state capacity, reforming state institutions, and rebuilding post-conflict political orders firmly in the hands of civilians (Paris and Sisk, 2009; Ansorg and Kurtenbach, 2017): If armed conflict occurs because groups rebel against their political or economic exclusion, the argument goes, then reforming state structures so that a post-conflict order is more inclusive and democratic should have a pacifying effect. Hence, peacebuilding endeavors have, since the end of the Cold War, typically advanced various reforms to achieve this transformation, such as by disarming and demobilizing warring parties, reducing their arms' stockpiles, reforming security sectors, or strengthening the integrity of post-conflict elections.

But despite these efforts, the former state- and non-state warring parties and the political organizations that directly descend them often continue to be very powerful in many post-conflict societies: their elites occupy core positions of government, control notable factions of the military, or are among the wealthiest members of society. Rwanda (Lyons, 2016), South Sudan (Brosché and Höglund, 2016), or El Salvador (Allison, 2010) are cases in point. Given the vast resources spent on transforming societies from wartime rule to post-conflict political orders, what explains this dominance of the former warring parties?

DOI: 10.4324/9781003203209-13

Past research tends to consult three sets of factors to explain the persistence of the former warring parties. As I detail below, it focuses on (1) how some institutions favor warring parties over other actors, (2) how internal structures reduce warring parties' political organization costs vis-à-vis other actors, and (3) how international donors help choose post-conflict elites.

The aspect I study instead is how narratives and negotiations help former warring parties manage to consolidate their power in post-conflict societies in the long run. The concrete aims of this chapter are threefold. *First*, I present a central narrative that we often see former warring parties advance in post-conflict peace processes and in places as diverse as Cambodia, Nepal, Kosovo, Bosnia, Ruanda, or Angola: a narrative that celebrates the members of a former warring party as courageous and spirited war heroes, glorifies those who died in war as martyrs and symbols of exceptional heroism, and villainizes critics as lacking gratitude. Of course this "war hero narrative" is not the only story that former warring parties can advance about themselves in post-conflict societies, nor are warring parties always successful in constructing warrior charisma, as Hensell and Gerdes (2017) or Bultmann (2018b) show for Liberia and Cambodia. But other case evidence reveals that it can be a symbolic resource of utmost importance in transitions to peace after war (Bultmann, 2018a; Samaratunga, 2019).

Second, I discuss a key factor in understanding the outcome of post-conflict peace processes: how warring parties use negotiations for the design of state institutions to stay in power. As I said above, peacebuilding has often pursued the goal of strengthening statehood and state institutions after war, but these institutions do not come into being at random: all institutions are negotiated. Who controls these negotiations – warring parties, other domestic actors without a history of war, or members of the international community – directly affects long-term distributions of power after war (Strasheim, 2019). Warring parties thus have a fundamental interest to shift power and control in these negotiations to their advantage.

Third, I then tie these two strands of my argument together. I show that one effective strategy for former warring parties to shift power to their advantage in institutional negotiations is to advance war hero narratives. In building my argument, I link research on narratives and peacebuilding practices to Max Weber's work on legitimacy, arguing that peacebuilding aims at creating post-conflict orders where legitimacy comes from what Weber termed *rational-legal authority*, but that warring parties manipulate this process by promoting a war hero narrative where legitimacy is instead linked to what Weber understood as *charismatic authority*.

The remainder of this chapter is structured as follows. I begin by discussing in detail the factors that previous research usually consults to explain why former warring parties often dominate post-conflict politics. I then make a case for why focusing on narratives and negotiations complements and expands this research. I present frequent components of war hero narratives and offer empirical illustrations to show what purpose the narrative serves in negotiations with international actors, how it defines a warring party's best alternative to a negotiated agreement (BATNA), and how it erodes or is coopted by other actors. The final section concludes.

Former warring parties in post-conflict societies

Why do former warring parties – that is, the government or any non-state opposition group "that uses armed force to promote its position" in war (Uppsala Conflict Data Program, 2019) – often remain such powerful actors in post-conflict politics? Past research offers three explanations.

Institutional explanations

Academics and practitioners alike often regard the purposeful design and reform of state institutions as an important remedy for intrastate war and key ingredient of post-conflict peacebuilding. Institutional reform can make post-conflict politics more just, but is also a tool to buy off former warring parties: by distributing government offices among these parties, institutions can make partaking in peace more profitable than war (Haass and Ottmann, 2017). In Sierra Leone, for instance, rebel leader Foday Sankoh was convinced into signing the 1999 peace deal by making him Vice President and Chairman of the Commission for the Management of Strategic Resources, National Reconstruction and Development, which gave him control over Sierra Leone's diamond trade (Binningsbø and Dupuy, 2010).

Institutional factors thereby help explain the power of former warring parties in post-conflict societies. The role of power-sharing interim governments in peace processes is another good example. Interim governments are the institutions exercising executive and/or legislative authority before first post-conflict elections, and power-sharing usually means offering warring parties guaranteed posts in these bodies. But power-sharing interim rule, which by design aims at easing access to politics for rebel groups with veto powers over a peace process, also affects "the longer-term distribution of power" after war (Manning, 2007, p.54): it impacts who gets early access to the spoils of a state, such as income from natural resources; writes the laws regulating politics for years to come; or enjoys the benefit of name recognition in an election. Thereby, institutions that guarantee warring parties a seat in office (even if only for the interim period) can entrench them in power in the long run (Roeder and Rothchild, 2005).

Internal explanations

In addition to institutional explanations, internal organizational features of former warring parties help understand their long-term power after war. In many peace processes, rebel groups are offered the chance to organize and compete as a political party in elections. The Alliance for the Future of Kosovo (AAK) and the Democratic Party of Kosovo (PDK), both descendants of the Kosovo Liberation Army (KLA), are cases in point. A potential downside of rebel-to-party-transformation processes is however that they can limit "the possibility for other actors [without a history of war] to emerge and influence the post-war political agenda" (Söderberg-Kovacs, 2008, p.135). Former warring parties tend to have easy access to arms and thus veto powers over a peace process. They also enjoy core advantages in organizational structures if they create local cells or political wings during war that they use in its aftermath.

Angola is a good example for this argument. In Angola's 1991 peace accord, the ruling People's Movement for the Liberation of Angola (MPLA) and the rebels of the National Union for the Total Independence of Angola (UNITA) agreed to let new political parties organize and compete in post-conflict elections. But neither the MPLA nor UNITA had previously allowed for organizational space outside their own party structures in the territories they controlled during war (Pearce, 2015). New parties thus only began to organize in 1991, a year before elections. Most had no real program despite being firmly opposed to whatever UNITA or the MPLA stood for. Limited resources meant few could set up campaign offices in Luanda (let alone elsewhere); even fewer could afford advertising in the time slot allotted each day on the MPLA-controlled national radio (Ottaway, 1998). As a result, new parties were unable to have a say in negotiations regarding electoral regulations or successfully compete in the 1992 elections.

International explanations

A third factor that helps explain the persistence of warring parties in post-conflict politics is the role of the international community. The international community – such as UN peacekeeping missions, aid agencies, nongovernmental organizations, or diplomats – plays an important role in designing and implementing important political reforms in many peace processes, and is at times even directly involved in selecting who gets to be part of a post-conflict elite: international actors "exercise unusually high influence and may attempt to use the opportunities this creates to exclude or include certain types of political actors while they can" (Manning, 2007, p.56).

In some contexts, this means picking and choosing candidates they deem fit to run for office while excluding others, such as in Bosnia. In other cases, international actors are unable or unwilling to "substantially alter" preexisting wartime distributions of power (Ottaway and Lacina, 2003, p.85). Reasons may include that they lack a detailed understanding of historic power relations, or that they suffer from rapid staff turnover, preventing them from inciting real change (Autesserre, 2012). Finally, international actors may also decide to entrench prominent warring party elites in power in order to ensure a degree of political stability. A good example is Kosovo, where diplomats quickly endorsed the KLA as the winner of the war and helped move influential KLA leaders, such as Hashim Thaci and Ramush Haradinaj, into politics. Their endorsements have allowed men like

Thaci, who has since twice been Prime Minister, in addition to serving as Foreign Minister and President, to dominate post-conflict politics and to obtain "de facto immunity from police investigations" (Hensell and Gerdes, 2017, p.179).

Narratives and negotiations in post-conflict societies

How can narratives help understand why former warring parties often control politics after war? I understand narratives as collections of stories joined in a common problem "as fixers (heroes), causes (villains) or the harmed (victims) in a temporal trajectory (plot) leading towards resolution within a particular setting" (Davidson, 2017). They help make sense of social situations but can also be strategic and efficient rhetorical tools that help actors claim power in negotiations. As Roselle et al. (2014, p.74) hold: conveying a simple, compelling narrative can be a great power resource in negotiations, as it helps build legitimacy in front of relevant audiences.

I outlined the building blocks of my argument above. *First*, peacebuilding in the post-Cold War era has often meant building peace by building states and reforming state institutions. This practice is linked to a Weberian understanding of statehood: it advances democratic structures, a functioning bureaucracy, and institutions to uphold the monopoly of the legitimate use of physical force where legitimate power rests on rational-legal authority – a reliance on rules and laws (Weber, 2019; Lottholz and Lemay-Hébert, 2016).

Second, post-conflict political orders and institutions, however, do not appear at random but come into being in negotiations between warring parties, other domestic actors, and members of the international community. Who gets to participate in these negotiations controls their timeframe or the issues up for debate, and who is most successful at promoting their interest or influencing perceptions of power to their advantage affects the design of institutions as such, and by extension the long-term distribution of power after war. Actors write rules that suit their own interests, and warring parties, who benefit from power distribution at the end of war, have incentives to use negotiations to increase their chances at maintaining their grip onto power.

Third, since custom, practice, interest, solidarity, or opportunism cannot provide a reliable basis for stable rule (Weber, 2019), narratives advanced by former warring parties in these negotiations must serve to establish them in front of negotiation partners as well as the broader public as the ones having secured the legitimacy to decide on the design of a post-conflict order. In the volatile, fast-paced, and resource-deprived post-conflict environments, the most powerful tool former warring parties have at their disposal to construct legitimacy is to promote a narrative that elevates them as courageous, protective, and experienced war heroes. As I show below, this narrative manipulates the post-conflict peacebuilding process by claiming a rival source of legitimacy as posited by Weber, that is, charismatic authority secured by a belief in the "special powers" of a ruler among a set of followers, such as in the sanctity, heroic quality, or knowledge of a person or a group of "fixers" (Weber, 2019, p.336). In Hampson and Narlikar's typology (this volume), war heroism is a deep narrative of redemption or hope: it is persuasive because it is easy to grasp and explains how entrusting a former warring party with building a post-conflict political order can help achieve a more positive state of affairs of peace, stability, and recovery. It does so by tapping into deep-rooted myths and glorifications, exaggerating the protective role of a warring party, or eliciting emotions of hope, such as for quick fixes for radical change.

Building blocks of the war hero narrative

In post-conflict societies, former warring parties can elicit either backward- or forward-looking stories that focus on heroism either at the group level or of a single exceptional leader.

At the group level, former warring parties can advance general political myths or stories about their important transformative role in a foregoing war and the sacrifices they made. These stories demonize enemies, exaggerate a party's protective role toward society, or advance emotional legends that honor and glorify the valor of its martyrs dying for the good of the people (Lyons, 2016). Warring parties may reproduce these stories rhetorically or through actions such as naming streets or buildings after fallen combatants, erecting memorials in their names, promoting veteran days, or calling national holidays linked to the war, all with a goal to "reinforce the unifying power of the master narrative" (di Lellio and Schwandner-Sievers, 2006).

The above-mentioned PDK and AAK in Kosovo are good examples of how former warring parties use war legends and martyrdom to create a simple, compelling war hero narrative. PDK and AAK leaders regularly evoke well-known KLA fighters, such as Adem Jashari, in their speeches in which they frame his death as one of the main causes for the freedom of Kosovo. For instance, in a ceremony commemorating the 20th anniversary of Jasharis killing by Serbian police forces, speaker of parliament (and one of the founders of the KLA) Kadri Veseli called his death "the beginning of the end" of Serbia's rule over Kosovo (Balkan Insight, 2018b). PDK and AAK have also supported creating memorials packed with KLA symbolism; including naming Pristina International Airport after Jashari. In another peculiar incident, long-time PDK leader Hashim Thaci was accused of falsifying a photograph of himself with Jashari to prove a relationship where, in fact, none existed (di Lellio and Schwandner-Sievers, 2006).

Martyrdom was also a prominent feature of how the Communist Party of Nepal (Maoist) rebel group constructed its war hero narrative. During the war, the Maoists regularly organized ceremonies to remember fallen combatants, founded an association of martyrs' families, and held minutes of silence before meetings and battles (Lecomte-Tilouine, 2010). After war, they erected martyrs' gates throughout the country and proclaimed 8,000 of their combatants martyrs of the struggle for the transformation of Nepal (cf. Lundqvist, 2019).

But former warring parties may also emphasize expertise rather than sacrifice, such as by promoting stories of how they have amassed through war the necessary professional political or military experience and thus legitimacy to decide over post-conflict orders. Professional expertise, experience, or credit frames portray actors without a history of war as inexperienced and international actors as unacquainted with local contexts. They link to Weber's idea of charisma by stressing the professional competence and special knowledge of a group.

An example of a former warring party highlighting military credit to construct a compelling narrative is the Rwandan Patriotic Front (RPF), which actively builds a heroic identity for Rwanda's army at home and abroad with stories of its hardworking "individual heroes, who serve as examples of how to behave, act, and think" (Kuehnel and Wilén, 2018, p.161). The RPF also stresses the army's military experience and the authority that derives from this experience ("We managed to stop the situation in '94, and build the country to this extent," Kuehnel and Wilén, 2018, pp.162–163).

Former warring parties can also advance more personal stories about a leader's exceptional heroism, by pushing tales about combat bravery or revolutionary appeal – much like *The New York Times*' obituary for Angola's Jonas Savimbi that called him one of the most "charismatic rebels on the continent," a "burly leader ... easily recognized by his lumbering gait, menacing scowl, combat fatigues, pistol and black beret" (Kaufman, 2002). Stories about leaders can also be more forward-looking and construct individuals as skilled guardians of peace or the ones most likely to bring about radical change, while villainizing critics as lacking gratitude. In Weber's terms, this constructs a charismatic leader who "goes against tradition, generates new things, and changes points of reference or frameworks" (Epley, 2015, p.7).

In Cambodia, for instance, Prime Minister Hun Sen has been in power ever since 1985 and throughout the post-conflict period by persuasively advancing a heroic image of himself as the sole guardian of peace. As Hughes (2006, p.470) writes, he forcefully cultivates a story of "innate and unassailable spiritual power" to elevate himself "to the status of natural power-holder and ... guardian of the national good." Doing so, he exploits the violent recent history of Cambodia to have citizens believe his electoral defeat would inevitably mean a return to war – and "strongman rule is a lesser evil than mass murder" (McCargo, 2005, p.106).

The war hero narrative in international negotiations

In negotiations with international actors about the design of post-conflict political orders, the war hero narrative can help former warring parties shift power to their advantage in two ways.

First, promoting a war hero narrative helps former warring parties create legitimacy vis-à-vis the more powerful or resourceful international players in negotiating post-conflict political orders. It allows them to take credit for achievements made in the course of war, selectively highlight their experience and reputation, starve off criticism by the international community, or even portray international actors as interventionist villains or outsiders.

When Nepal's civil war ended in 2006, a key feature of the peace process up for debate was the UN's presence in the country and the role it would take in disarming factions and reforming the Nepal Army. The UN had earlier articulated an interest for deeper engagement in the peace process and in 2003, the Secretary General had offered to facilitate peace negotiations under UN auspices, something the warring parties strictly refused (Westendorf, 2018). The warring parties – the Maoists, the army, and the political parties forming the government and controlling the security sector – had made clear that their interest was to considerably limit the role the UN would play in designing the post-conflict order and they only wanted a very light version of UN involvement. UN staff was, however, initially reluctant to depart from existing, more intrusive approaches to post-conflict peacebuilding (Westendorf, 2018).

To promote their interest against a much more powerful negotiation partner, the former warring parties advanced versions of the war hero narrative that focused on professional military experience. Especially prominent figures in the army began painting their institution as the most qualified and practiced actor to implement disarmament and reform; and they portrayed international actors questioning this expertise and their capability to manage the peace process as intrusive and insensitive to local realities. In my interviews in Kathmandu in 2015, for example, a high-ranking army general argued the UN did not understand that Nepal's state structure had not completely collapsed during war and that the army therefore had sufficient capacity to guide reforms: "We are not an African country" he said, and army "integration is our job." Army figures often reinforced this framing by stressing not only domestic professional credit, but that they also had long been one of the main troop contributors to UN peacekeeping. For these reasons, they said it would be disturbing, "humiliating," and a loss of prestige to see a strong UN presence in Nepal (Strasheim and Bogati, 2017).

Pushing this narrative, the former warring parties early on established the notion that an international role in designing Nepal's post-conflict political order needed to be limited, which soon "became the centerpiece in the political culture that surrounded the peace talks" (Suhrke, 2011, p.17). Gradually, this narrative not only affected the identities of the former warring parties, but became a powerful political story across societal and political spectrums, and many Nepalis took "justifiable pride in the fact that their peace process was their own, and not imposed or mediated by any external actor" (Martin, 2010, p.10). Today, this narrative still informs how the former warring parties interact with the international community, such as when pushing back against UN demands for a more thorough transitional justice process.

A second way by which the war hero narratives help shift power to the advantage of the former warring parties in negotiations is by constructing a war-torn and politically divided post-conflict society as a strong unitary actor. It does so by helping warring parties keep criticism at bay and strategically silence their critics at home; and it helps influence a country's image in front of an international audience. This links to what Hampson and Narlikar (this volume) call the "political glue" function of narratives that help keep diverse actors together.

In Kosovo, promoting war heroism has helped the PDK and AAK build an environment in which criticism of the KLA and its martyrs long amounted to blasphemy: for a long time, no "space for critical engagement" with the KLA existed (Ingimundarson, 2007, p.104). Memories of the war that did not fit the dominant narrative were suppressed and marginalized. For instance, when parties negotiated the creation of a memorial for fallen soldiers, an activist likened the atmosphere to North Korea, as opposition was seen impossible (di Lellio and Schwandner-Sievers, 2006). In 2018, a journalist was publicly villainized and called a "Serbian spy" after criticizing a government plan to award money to families of former KLA members who were convicted of involvement in a gun battle in Northern Macedonia (Balkan Insight, 2018a).

In international negotiations, such as talks with Serbia, the narrative has helped promote images of a unified "Albanianess" of Kosovo (cf. Obucina, 2011). Di Lellio and Salihu (2014, p.119) cite from Haradinaj's memoir to show that he often presents KLA values as national values: "I will not allow myself in any form to talk about KLA political values … as values of just one group. These were values of our people, I was just one of them." Ingimundarson (2007) makes a similar case, arguing that even though PDK and AAK are substantially more moderate in their language toward international actors than home audiences and try to project a modernist image of Kosovo on the world stage, war heroism is a powerful collective memory tool for them to promote claims for majority Albanian rule of Kosovo, while resisting plans of international actors to make multiethnicity a defining feature of the post-conflict order.

War heroism and a group's BATNA

As Hampson and Narlikar (this volume) argue, narratives may reinforce a group's BATNA to a point where "no deal is better than any deal" by affecting what a group is prepared to accept or give up and when to walk away if core identities or interests are threatened. This point is particularly salient for warring parties with a heroic, revolutionary identity that have villainized all other political forces as enemies, because to them, negotiations and deal-making with other political actors or the international community are risky by definition.

In Nepal, the Maoists' early post-conflict construction of war heroism meant projecting their leader Pushpa Kamal Dahal as an authoritative revolutionary. Until today, Dahal goes by his *nom de guerre* Prachanda ("the fierce one"), and right after the war, he was said to cultivate a mysterious, secretive image of himself. The media stylized him as "a man whose face, until a few weeks ago, was known only through a single photograph" (Haviland, 2006). And a Nepali UN official I interviewed in Kathmandu in 2015 remembered: "In 2008, who were these people? [They were] strangers, revolutionaries, their body language [was] different ... Prachanda was a brand new [politician], he had been active underground his entire life."

One aspect that arguably *was* "brand new" about the Maoists and substantially informed their identity was their attention to minority demands. During the war, they had mobilized various marginalized minorities into their ranks. Upon joining the post-conflict interim parliament in 2007, they named 9 women, 11 Dalits, 20 Madhesis, and 23 Janajatis among the 73 people that would represent them in this body – in a first for Nepal. Framing their struggle as a resistance against a greedy, feudal, incompetent political elite that would improve the livelihoods of minorities was key in their appeal throughout Nepal.

One task of the interim parliament was to write laws for upcoming national elections in 2008. But negotiations were soon deadlocked due to disagreements between the rebels and the other parties and in September 2007, the Maoists resigned from the interim bodies and walked away from negotiations in protest over not having their key demands met: an immediate proclamation of Nepal as a republic and a constitutional amendment that would alter the mixed electoral system so that proportional elements would be strengthened (Bhandari, 2007). The objection against the electoral system was purely based on concerns about their chances at the polls (Freedom House, 2008), but they framed it in terms linked to their revolutionary identity and their protective role toward "the people." It is likely that other parties assumed the Maoists would not dare to walk away from the talks because participating in the interim parliament was financially profitable for their leaders (Freedom House, 2008). But the Maoists had kept walk away options open and kept an unsatisfied and potentially violent group of ex-combatants in disarmament sites as a bargain for further negotiations (Bleie and Shrestha, 2012).

Following weeks of tensions and ultimately new negotiations, the parties struck a deal in December 2007 for the Maoists to reenter the interim government. This deal changed the text of the Interim Constitution considerably according to the demands of the Maoists, and the Maoists were also given two further minister portfolios in the interim cabinet. Maoist leader Badal described this as: "We thought this was a gain for the people" (Ogura, 2008, p.44).

Two caveats are in order with regard to these findings. *First*, my argument thus far has emphasized that the war hero narrative is about gaining power and manipulate negotiations and peacebuilding processes. But that does not mean that it always has to be hostile to peace. The dominance of warring parties after war is generally by no means always negative but can have benefits for peace processes, as it helps keep men with guns satisfied in power for a while or as armed groups may genuinely seek a better future for their society (Ingimundarson, 2007). The war hero narrative particularly has reconciliatory elements: it serves unity and nation-building after war and also offers a sense of dignity, meaning, value, and pride for (formerly) marginalized ex-combatants in post-conflict societies. This is why, when it loses resonance, ex-combatants can experience severe identity crises and shame, as Bougarel (2008) compellingly demonstrates for Bosnia, where evolving politics of the international community directly challenged hitherto official accounts and heroic images of the war. The resulting loss of prestige and symbolic societal status meant former combatants "no longer appeared to be heroes, but … naïve losers" (Bougarel, 2008, p.485). In Nepal, the war hero narrative helped parties claim power in negotiations with international donors – but this also meant that parties could not point to donors for delays in implementing the peace process, knowing that voters would blame any failures on the parties themselves. The narrative thus also helped build feelings of agency and responsibility.

Second and related, while my discussion has highlighted how warring parties may utilize the war hero narrative vis-à-vis international actors, the narrative itself is shaped by the actions and presence of the international community after war. For instance, a number of studies detail how trials of the International Criminal Tribunal for the former Yugoslavia and public screenings of these trials have contributed to the making of war heroes in the region. The conviction of Croatian general Ante Gotovina "turned into a celebration of a Croatian martyrdom" as he "was seen not only as a war hero, but also as an innocent victim now sacrificed for the sake of Croatian independence" (Ristic, 2019, p.180). In Kosovo, the warrior image of KLA commander Haradinaj may have been created independently of the presence of the international community – his biography already constructs a "heroic tale" of himself "from his successful defeat of Serbian forces" to his "leading role" in post-conflict politics (di Lellio and Salihu, 2014, p.117). But Haradinaj's repeated prosecution by the international community has added fuel to his image, and is seen as particularly harmful for the standing of donors in Kosovo (Lyck, 2007).

Life cycle of the war hero narrative

Narratives are not static but, as Hampson and Narlikar remind us in this volume, dynamic entities with life cycles: their strategic value in negotiations ebbs and flows. This is especially true for narratives constructing charismatic legitimacy through tales of war heroism. As Weber says, a key problem with charismatic authority as opposed to legal rule is its instability: charisma can only exist in the short term, before it becomes an everyday matter.

Of course, narratives do not have to be true to resonate, and claims about warrior legacy must not be rooted in evidence. In Kosovo, Ingimundarson (2007, p.105) says, the war hero narrative is full of contradictions and selective memories: due to the NATO intervention, the war "had little to do with masculine military values, such as risk taking, sacrifice and martyrdom" but was fought with precision-guided weapons and represented the "antithesis" to what the KLA wanted to project. In Nepal, the Maoists may have created stories of their revolutionary appeal to the minorities they wanted to mobilize into their ranks, but most of their leadership actually belonged to the very identity group who had for centuries formed Nepal's political elite and, thus, a structure the Maoists claimed to fight: high-caste, Nepali-speaking Hindus from the country's central hill region (Strasheim, 2019).

But the Maoist experience in Nepal also demonstrates that if narratives become too distant from reality, they are hard to maintain. As Hampson and Narlikar (this volume) argue, in order to flourish, narratives have to be articulated and conveyed by "nodal actors" who are not only politically influential within their respective communities but also have genuine moral standing in these communities. When the Maoists entered negotiations with other political parties and the international community shortly after the civil war in Nepal, this alone meant that they faced challenges in "maintaining their revolutionary image" (Ogura, 2008, p.42). At the same time, the Maoist leadership around Prachanda was accused of privately enriching themselves with state resources meant for the upkeep of their combatants, which hurt their revolutionary image and led to a "sense of betrayal" among ex-combatants (Adhikari and Gautam, 2014, p.80). Prachanda, in particular, lost his moral standing as a "nodal actor" and "compounded the resentment of some of his comrades" for acquiring a luxury mansion and seemingly adopting "the lifestyle of the billionaire royals he once loathed" (Nelson, 2012). Ultimately, these actions and the erosion of the narrative added to a split of the party in 2012, when a radical left-wing group argued Prachanda had hurt the credibility of the revolution (Subedi, 2014).

War hero narratives can also lose their value for the former warring parties if other actors successfully exploit them for own gain. In Kosovo, the Vetëvendosje student movement-turned political party actively sought association with the KLA's war heroism because this suited their own nationalist identity. For instance, Vetëvendosje leaders made "regular appearances at KLA commemoration ceremonies, such as ... when its leading representatives pay homage at the graves of Jashari" (Schwandner-Sievers, 2013, p.103). But Vetëvendosje turned the KLA's martyr cult against the descendants of the former rebel group. It presented the KLA as Kosovo's proud heritage and a "legacy to be cherished," but KLA leader Hashim Thaci as a "traitor of the KLA fight" and lackey of the international community (Schwandner-Sievers, 2013, p.100). This reasoning culminated in early 2020, when Vetëvendosje leader Albin Kurti, briefly Prime Minister of Kosovo, published a hitherto secret deal from 2013 between then Prime Minister Thaci and NATO, which he argued gave the latter veto powers over Kosovo's security forces.

Conclusion

How can narratives and negotiations help explain the long-term power of former warring parties in post-conflict societies? In this chapter, I argued that peacebuilding processes have typically aimed at strengthening state capacity, reforming state institutions, and rebuilding a post-conflict political order firmly in the hands of civilians: in Weber's terms, peacebuilding in the post-Cold War era has typically tried to promote peace by creating states where power rests on a rational-legal authority. But all institutions are negotiated, and to safeguard their power, warring parties can advance a rival source of legitimacy in this process: simple but compelling narratives that celebrate them as charismatic, courageous, protective, and experienced war heroes.

Drawing on empirical illustrations mostly from Nepal and Kosovo, I demonstrated that promoting a heroic warrior image can be a strategically effective rhetorical tool in negotiations with the international community that allows warring parties take credit for achievements made in the course of war, highlight their experience and reputation, starve off criticism by international actors, silence critics at home, and ultimately construct a war-torn and politically divided post-conflict society as a strong unitary actor in negotiations with the international community. In this way, their "emotive orbit of symbols, language and ritual practices" can help successfully construct an identity "that exists in parallel and opposition to the imported bureaucratic-universalist culture and its language" of post-conflict peacebuilding processes (Schwandner-Sievers, 2013, p.96). I argued that this must not only have necessarily negative consequences for peace processes – the war hero narrative also has reconciliatory elements, serves nation-building after war and offers a sense of dignity and pride for combatants in post-conflict societies. Finally, I showed that – in line with Weber's understanding of charisma that can only exist in the short term before it becomes an everyday matter – the strategic value of the war hero narrative in post-conflict societies ebbs and flows and can be coopted by other actors.

References

Adhikari, A., and, Gautam, B. (2014) *Impunity and Political Accountability in Nepal.* Kathmandu, Nepal: The Asia Foundation.

Allison, M.E. (2010) 'The Legacy of Violence on Post-Civil War Elections: The Case of El Salvador', *Studies in Comparative International Development*, vol.45, pp.104–124.

Ansorg, N., and, Kurtenbach, S. (2017) 'Introduction: Institutional Reforms and Peace Building', In N. Ansorg and S. Kurtenbach (Eds.), *Institutional Reforms and Peacebuilding: Change, Path-Dependency and Societal Divisions in Post-War Communities* (pp.1–18). New York, NY: Routledge.

Autesserre, S. (2012) 'Dangerous Tales: Dominant Narratives on the Congo and Their Unintended Consequences', *African Affairs,* vol.111, no.443, pp.202–222.

Balkan Insight. (2018a, February 1). *Kosovo Journalist Abused for Criticising Kumanovo Payout,* Balkan Insight. https://balkaninsight.com/2018/02/01/kosovo-journalist-insulted-over-his-reporting-01-31-2018/.

Balkan Insight. (2018b, March 5) *Kosovo Commemorates 'Beginning of End' of Serbian Rule,* Balkan Insight. https://balkaninsight.com/2018/03/05/kosovo-commemorates-beginning-of-the-end-of-serbian-rule-03-05-2018/.

Bhandari, S. (2007, September 18) *Maoists Quit Government in Blow to Nepal Peace Pact,* Agence France Press.

Binningsbø, H.M., and, Dupuy, K. (2010) 'Using Power-Sharing to Win a War: The Implementation of the Lomé Agreement in Sierra Leone', *Africa Spectrum,* vol.44, no.3, pp.87–107.

Bleie, T., and, Shrestha, R. (2012) *DDR in Nepal: Stakeholder Politics and the Implications for Reintegration as a Process of Disengagement*. Tromsø, Norway: Centre for Peace Studies.
Bougarel, X. (2008) 'The Shadow of Heroes: Former Combatants in Post-War Bosnia-Herzegovina', *International Social Science Journal*, vol.58, no.189, pp.479–490.
Brosché, J., and, Höglud, K. (2016) 'Crisis of Governance in South Sudan: Electoral Politics and Violence in the World's Newest Nation', *The Journal of Modern African Studies*, vol.54, no.1, pp.67–90.
Bultmann, D. (2018a) *The Social Order of Postconflict Transformation in Cambodia: Insurgent Pathways to Peace*. Lanham, MD: Lexington Books.
Bultmann, D. (2018b) 'Insurgent Groups During Post-Conflict Transformation: The Case of Military Strongmen in Cambodia', *Civil Wars*, vol.20, no.1, pp.24–44.
Davidson, B. (2017) 'Storytelling and Evidence-Based Policy: Lessons from the Grey Literature', *Palgrave Communications*, vol.3, no.1, pp.1–10.
di Lellio, A., and, Salihu, M. (2014) 'Albanian Personal Narratives of the Kosovo War and the Struggle for a National Narrative', *Култура/Culture*, no. 5, pp.115–124.
di Lellio, A., and, Schwandner-Sievers, S. (2006) 'The Legendary Commander: The Construction of an Albanian Master-Narrative in Post-War Kosovo', *Nations and Nationalism*, vol.12, no.3, pp.513–529.
Epley, J.L. (2015) 'Weber's Theory of Charismatic Leadership: The Case of Muslim Leaders in Contemporary Indonesian Politics', *International Journal of Humanities and Social Science*, vol.5, no.7, pp.7–17.
Freedom House. (2008) *Freedom in the World 2008: Nepal Country Report*. New York, NY: Freedom House. https://freedomhouse.org/report/freedom-world/2008/nepal#.VJgNef94OB.
Haass, F., and, Ottmann, M. (2017) 'Profits from Peace: The Political Economy of Power-Sharing and Corruption', *World Development*, vol.99, pp.60–74.
Haviland, C. (2006) *Meeting Nepal's Maoist Leader*, BBC News. http://news.bbc.co.uk/2/hi/south_asia/4707058.stm.
Hensell, S., and, Gerdes, F. (2017) 'Exit from War: The Transformation of Rebels into Post-War Power Elites', *Security Dialogue*, vol.48, no.2, pp.168–184.
Hughes, C. (2006) 'The Politics of Gifts: Tradition and Regimentation in Contemporary Cambodia', *Journal of Southeast Asian Studies*, vol.37, no.3, pp.469–489.
Ingimundarson, V. (2007) 'The Politics of Memory and the Reconstruction of Albanian National Identity in Postwar Kosovo', *History and Memory*, vol.19, no.1, pp.95–123.
Kaufman, M.T. (2002, February 23) *Jonas Savimbi, 67, Rebel of Charisma and Tenacity*, The New York Times.
Kuehnel, J., and, Wilén, N. (2018) 'Rwanda's Military as a People's Army: Heroes at Home and Abroad', *Journal of Eastern African Studies*, vol.12, no.1, pp.154–171.
Lecomte-Tilouine, M. (2010) 'Martyrs and Living Martyrs of the People's War in Nepal', *South Asia Multidisciplinary Academic Journal*, no.4, pp.1–21.
Lottholz, P., and, Lemay-Hébert, N. (2016) 'Re-Reading Weber, Re-Conceptualizing State-Building: From Neo-Weberian to Post-Weberian Approaches to State, Legitimacy and State-Building', *Cambridge Review of International Affairs*, vol.29, no.4, pp.1467–1485.
Lundqvist, M. (2019) 'Post-War Memorialisation as Everyday Peace? Exploring Everyday (Dis-) Engagements with the Maoist Martyrs' Gate of Beni Bazaar in Nepal,' *Conflict, Security & Development*, vol.19, no.5, pp.475–496.
Lyck, M. (2007) 'International Peace Enforcers and Indicted War Criminals: The Case of Ramush Haradinaj,' *International Peacekeeping*, vol.14, no.3, pp.418–432.

Lyons, T. (2016) 'From Victorious Rebels to Strong Authoritarian Parties: Prospects for Post-War Democratization', *Democratization*, vol.23, no.6, pp.1026–1041.
Manning, C. (2007) 'Interim Governments and the Construction of Political Elites', In K. Guttieri and J. Piombo (Eds.), *Interim Governments: Institutional Bridges to Peace and Democracy?* (pp.53–72). Washington, DC: US Institute of Peace Press.
Martin, I. (2010) 'All Peace Operations are Political: A Case for Designer Missions and the Next UN Reform', In Center on International Cooperation (Eds.), *Review of Political Missions 2010* (pp. 8–14). Boulder, CO: Lynne Rienner Publishers.
McCargo, D. (2005) 'Cambodia: Getting Away with Authoritarianism?', *Journal of Democracy*, vol.16, no.4, pp.98–112.
Nelson, D. (2012, January 30) *Nepali Maoist Leader Adopts Millionaire's Lifestyle*, The Telegraph.
Obucina, V. (2011) 'A War of Myths. Creation of the Founding Myth of Kosovo Albanians', *Contemporary Issues*, vol.4, no.1, pp.30–44.
Ogura, K. (2008) 'Seeking State Power: The Communist Party of Nepal (Maoist),' In *Resistance/Liberation Movements and Transition to Politics,* vol.3. Berlin, Germany: Berghof Research Center for Constructive Conflict Management.
Ottaway, M. (1998) 'Angola's Failed Elections', In K. Kumar (Ed.), *Postconflict Elections, Democratization, and International Assistance* (pp.133–152). Boulder, CO: Lynne Rienner Publishers.
Ottaway, M., and, Lacina, B. (2003) 'International Interventions and Imperialism: Lessons from the 1990s', *SAIS Review*, vol.23, no.2, pp.71–92.
Paris, R., and, Sisk, T.D. (Eds.) (2009). *The Dilemmas of Statebuilding: Confronting the Contradictions of Postwar Peace Operations*. London: Routledge.
Pearce, J. (2015) *Political Identity and Conflict in Central Angola, 1975-2002*. Cambridge: Cambridge University Press.
Ristic, K. (2019) 'The Legacy of the ICTY in Croatia, Bosnia and Serbia', In A. Ciampi (Ed.), *History and International Law. An Intertwined Relationship* (pp.168–190). Cheltenham: Edward Elgar Publishing.
Roeder, P.G., and, Rothchild, D. (2005) 'Power Sharing as an Impediment to Peace and Democracy', In P.G. Roeder and D. Rothchild (Eds.), *Sustainable Peace: Power and Democracy after Civil Wars* (pp.29–50). Ithaca, NY: Cornell University Press.
Roselle, L., Miskimmon, A., and, O'Loughlin, B. (2014) 'Strategic Narrative: A New Means to Understand Soft Power', *Media, War & Conflict*, vol.7, no.1, pp.70–84.
Samaratunga, J. (2019, February 10) *The Role of the 'War Hero' in Post-Conflict Sri Lanka*, Colombo Telegraph. www.colombotelegraph.com/index.php/the-role-of-the-war-hero-in-post-conflict-sri-lanka/.
Schwandner-Sievers, S. (2013) 'Democratisation through Defiance? The Albanian Civil Organisation 'Self-Determination' and International Supervision in Kosovo', In V. Bojicic-Dzelilovic, J. Ker-Lindsay, and, D. Kostovicova (Eds.), *Civil Society and Transitions in the Western Balkans: Societies and the Crisis of Globalization* (pp.95–116). New Perspectives on South-East Europe Series. London: Palgrave Macmillan.
Sköns, E. (2005) 'The Costs of Armed Conflict', In *Peace and Security: Expert Papers Series Five*. Stockholm, Sweden: International Tasks Force on Global Public Goods.
Söderberg-Kovacs, M. (2008) 'When Rebels Change Their Stripes: Armed Insurgents, Post-War Politics', In A.K. Jarstad and T.D. Sisk (Eds.), *From War to Democracy: Dilemmas of Peacebuilding* (pp.134–156). Oxford: Oxford University Press.
Strasheim, J. (2019) 'No 'End of the Peace Process': Federalism and Ethnic Violence in Nepal', *Cooperation and Conflict*, vol.54, no.1, pp.83–98.

Strasheim, J., and, Bogati, S. (2017, December 13) *Prestige, Dignity, and Job Security: How Army Integration Promotes Peace*, Political Violence at a Glance. https://politicalviolenceataglance.org/2017/12/13/prestige-dignity-and-job-security-how-army-integration-promotes-peace/.

Subedi, D.B. (2014) 'Ex-Combatants, Security and Post-Conflict Violence: Unpacking the Experience from Nepal', *Millennial Asia*, vol.5, no.1, pp.41–65.

Suhrke, A. (2011) 'Virtues of a Narrow Mission: The UN Peace Operation in Nepal', *Global Governance*, vol.17, no.1, pp.37–55.

Uppsala Conflict Data Program. (2019), "Definitions." www.pcr.uu.se/research/ucdp/definitions.

Weber, W. (2019) *Economy and Society: A New Translation*. Translated by Keith Tribe. Translation. Cambridge, MA: Harvard University Press.

Westendorf, J.K. (2018) 'Challenges of Local Ownership: Understanding the Outcomes of the International Community's 'Light Footprint' Approach to the Nepal Peace Process', *Journal of Intervention and Statebuilding*, vol.12, no.2, pp.228–252.

11

NARRATIVES AND NEGOTIATIONS IN FOREIGN AID

How post-genocide Rwanda uses narratives to influence perceptions of power

Haley J. Swedlund

Introduction

Foreign aid negotiations are characterized by a high degree of asymmetry. In 1995, immediately following the civil war and genocide, net official development assistance (ODA) as a percentage of gross national income (GNI) to Rwanda was 94.9%. Even now—more than two decades later—net ODA as a percentage of GNI is over 11%, with the World Bank estimating that over 59% of Rwanda's central government expenses come from foreign aid.[1] Despite claims to the contrary, Rwanda remains reliant on international donors. Nevertheless, it is widely acknowledged that the Rwandan government does not easily succumb to pressures from international donors. The current Rwandan President, Paul Kagame—a prolific "tweeter"—frequently pushes back at global superpowers with seemingly little regard to the consequences. If anything, Rwanda seems to have benefited from the tough stance it takes with donors. As Reyntjens writes, "Rwanda is a small, landlocked, and extremely dependent country without much of a real economy...And, yet, since 1994 it has tackled the rest of the world as if it were a global superpower" (2011, p.18). What makes this possible?

In this chapter, I make the case that narratives have been instrumental in enabling the current Rwandan leadership to push back against power asymmetries with international donors. More specifically, I argue that the Rwandan leadership uses a country-specific narrative of guilt and redemption combined with a broader narrative of agency and ownership in international development to increase perceptions power. In practice, neither of these narratives fundamentally alter the structural conditions governing foreign aid negotiations. Rwanda remains dependent on foreign aid. At the same time, both narratives are also strongly contested. Nevertheless, these narratives affect *perceptions* of power and therefore influence how each party makes calculations regarding their

DOI: 10.4324/9781003203209-14

BATNA and reservation price (Zartman and Rubin, 2000). Rwanda uses the two interconnected narratives of guilt & redemption and agency & ownership to increase perception of power and push for a more symmetrical negotiation space when it comes to aid.

The chapter is divided into two main sections. The first section focuses on foreign aid negotiations, explaining what these negotiations look like and how they differ from other types of international negotiations. In this section, I emphasize that a defining feature of aid negotiations is asymmetrical power relations. The second section focuses on how post-genocide Rwanda uses narratives to increase perceptions of power in their negotiations with international donors. I conclude with a short reflection on what this case study tells us about the role of narratives in international negotiations more broadly.

What do foreign aid negotiations look like?

Every day in developing countries throughout the world, donor agencies and recipient governments engage in negotiations about how foreign aid can and should be disbursed. These negotiations can be fierce and, like many other types of negotiations, are often cloaked in secrecy. Negotiations between donor agencies and recipient governments take place in the context of formal dialogues, but also through backdoor negotiations and informal discussions. These negotiations are so important that many cash-strapped ministries of finance in aid-dependent countries have a special department or unit whose sole job is to oversee these negotiations (Swedlund, 2017a, pp.64–65). For example, Tanzania's External Finance Department, which is responsible for liaising with foreign aid donors, has a staff of more than 40 people.

Despite the relevance and importance of aid negotiations, bargaining between donor agencies and recipient countries has long been overlooked in both the scholarship on international negotiations and the scholarship on foreign aid. Only recently, have some scholars begun to shine a light on what these negotiations look like and why they are important (Whitfield, 2009; Whitfield and Fraser, 2009; Swedlund, 2017a; Swedlund and Lierl, 2019). Foreign aid negotiations have been overlooked, at least in part, because of the large power asymmetries inherent in foreign aid. A common assumption is that, because they control the purse, Western donors determine how aid is allocated. Consequently, the space for negotiation is limited. In the language of international mediation, the assumption is that the BATNA of recipient governments is extremely low. Because developing countries only rarely walk away from aid money, the assumption is that there is relatively little negotiation in aid. This, however, is not true.

Foreign aid amounts are largely determined by donor governments. Recipient countries often have very little say about how much aid is being offered, and—facing highly constrained budgets—recipient governments are not often in a position to turn away foreign aid. However, how that aid is actually allocated and the conditions that are attached to aid are determined via intense negotiation and bargaining between recipients and donors (Swedlund, 2017a). For example, let us imagine that a donor country has allocated two million dollars to a recipient government to bolster the country's health sector. Donor agencies have to decide exactly how to spend that money. Will the funds be spent on medicine or infrastructure? What does the recipient government need to do to receive the funds? Do they, for example, need to promise to draft a new health sector development plan or promise to staff the hospital? Will the money be disbursed via non-state actors or through the recipient government? These details—which determined how and on what grounds aid is actually disbursed—are determined via negotiations with recipient governments.

Donors have to negotiate with recipients regarding the conditions surrounding aid for at least three reasons (Swedlund, 2017a, pp.23–24). First, recipients must at least tacitly consent to a donor being active in a country (Ostrom et al., 2002). While rare, there are examples of recipients throwing donors out. As I explain in greater detail below, Rwanda severed diplomatic ties with France for several years in 2006. In 1979, Tanzania threw the IMF out after it conditioned future support on the government implementing a macroeconomic adjustment program that the government opposed (Edwards, 2014, p.9).

Two, donors rely on recipients to effectively implement aid programs and projects. Almost all aid programs rely on some type of input from recipient governments to be successful. For example, if a donor wants to build a hospital, they need the permits to be able to do so, as well as commitments from the government to, for example, staff the hospital.

Three, donors rely on governments to carry out policies and reforms that they desire in exchange for aid. In exchange for their aid, sometimes donors may push for highly political things, like preferential trading status. More commonly, however, they seek more development-oriented commitments, like a commitment to overhaul the country's drug distribution network or a commitment to spend a certain percentage of the budget on poverty initiatives. Either way, because donors always want something in exchange for aid, they are forced to negotiate with recipients—even if there are strong power asymmetries between the two.

Thus far, the nascent literature on bargaining in foreign aid has focused on the structural conditions shaping aid negotiations, namely, (a) negotiating capital (Whitfield, 2009; Whitfield and Fraser, 2009) and (b) credible commitments (Swedlund, 2017a; Swedlund and Lierl, 2019). In an edited volume, Whitfield and her colleagues argue that the strategies pursed by recipient countries in aid negotiations are determined by structural conditions and recipient agency. What matters is how much negotiating capital or leverage the negotiators are able to derive from structural conditions. According to Whitfield and Fraser, a recipient government's negotiating strategy is largely determined by "given structural conditions and how it decides those conditions can be deployed in aid negotiations to meet its objectives" (2009, p.39).

In my own work, I argue that commitment problems—or the difficulty donors and recipients have keeping their promises to one another—affect the sustainability of negotiated agreements (Swedlund, 2017a; Swedlund and Lierl, 2019). Both donor agencies and recipient governments struggle to keep their promises to one another—often for reasons exogenous to foreign aid. For example, elections in a donor country often led to the realignment of development priorities, irrespective of past performance. The presence of commitment problems in foreign aid undermines the sustainability of negotiated agreements between donors and recipients, forcing the two parties to continually renegotiate foreign aid agreements. The result is an industry marred by fads and fashions where effectiveness does not guarantee longevity.

Narratives and negotiations in foreign aid: The case of Rwanda

Missing from the scholarship on foreign aid negotiations is a discussion of the potential role of narratives and identity-related factors.[2] Narratives are particularly interesting in the context of foreign aid negotiations, because of the inherent power asymmetries in these negotiations. Narratives have been shown to empower marginalized actors (Narlikar, 2015). In contexts where structural conductions heavily favor one party, how might narratives be used to empower marginalized actors—in this case, recipient governments reliant on foreign aid?

Below I make the case that narratives have been instrumental in enabling the current Rwandan leadership to push back against power asymmetries with international donors. In particular, I argue that the Rwandan leadership has used narratives of guilt and redemption specific to the 1994 genocide and broader narratives about the important agency and ownership in international development to increase perceptions of their bargaining power with international donors. Whether or not these perceptions are based on objective realities is to some degree irrelevant—perceptions are what matter in international negotiations (Zartman and Rubin, 2000). Even scholars that study power and negotiations in a highly rationalized way acknowledge that negotiators' perceptions of each party's BATNA and hence how they proceed with negotiations can depend on how social environments are interpreted (Kim et al., 2005, p.807). In this way, narratives have the potential to change the outcomes of negotiations, even if the structural conditions remain the same.

Narratives of guilt and redemption

According to David Mwambari, "Rwanda's violent past has become a platform for Rwanda not only to rise in prominence globally but also to argue its case on an international stage that has in the past been almost exclusively allocated to larger international players" (2020a, p.131). Not only is the genocide evoked in all major speeches by Rwandan representatives and diplomats, the memory of the genocide has also been used to oppose powerful states like France at the United Nations and elsewhere. But, how exactly do narratives of guilt and redemption related to the 1994 genocide playout when it comes to aid negotiations?

It is widely acknowledged that the current Rwandan government is keen to control the narrative around reconstruction and development in Rwanda, painting the current government, led by the ruling party the Rwandan Patriotic Front (RPF) and President Paul Kagame, as the moral saviors of Rwanda (Pottier, 2002; Thomson, 2018a). This narrative is justified in two ways. First, the RPF—a militia-force turned ruling party—effectively stopped the genocide when it captured Kigali and took power in 1994. Second, since the genocide, the RPF—led by Kagame—has overseen a period of significant economic transformation and growth.

A number of scholars have documented how the RPF goes to great length to control the narratives around reconstruction in order to preserve this moral high ground (e.g., Jessee, 2017; Longman, 2017; Mwambari, 2020b; Ingelaere, 2010; Ruzibiza et al., 2005; Reyntjens, 2011; Reyntjens, 2004).[3] Citizens are subject to a lengthy list of fines for things like having uncleaning clothing or body hygiene or not wearing shoes, and the government often (violently) suppresses evidence or people that challenge the narrative of progress. Common tactics include eliminating political rivals through assassination or forced asylum, and destroying and discrediting reports that poke holes at a seamless transformation.

In 2007, for example, a report by the United Nations Development Program (UNDP) identified some shortcomings and challenges for Rwanda, including a rise in absolute poverty and inequality. The report also included the claim that governance and democracy needed to be improved to facilitate long-term stability. Not only was the report rejected by the Rwandan cabinet, the minister of finance—despite having written the introduction to the report himself—was asked to refute the report, which he did. Moreover, UNDP was pressured to release a statement that the report contained unfounded and misleading information and the lead researchers were blacklisted by the government (Ingelaere, 2010).

A number of scholars have relatedly argued that the government uses a narrative of guilt and redemption to starve off criticism from the international community regarding authoritarianism and crimes committed by the RPF both during and since the civil war and genocide. The current government has, for example, been accused of supporting militias—in particular, the infamous M23—and instability in neighboring DRC (Charbonneau, 2012). A leaked UN report in 2010 even went so far as to suggests that Rwandan activities in the DRC may account to genocide (McGreal, 2010). The current regime has also been accused of targeted assassinations against the opposition, as well as former members of the RPF that have fallen out of favor with Kagame (Behuria, 2016; Burke, 2019).

As Pottier explains, the RPF, "as Rwanda's post-genocide spiritual guardian, displays exceptional skill at converting international feelings of guilt and ineptitude into admissions that the Front deserves to have the monopoly on knowledge construction" (2002, p.202). That is, the RPF uses guilt and their moral high ground as the "saviors" of Rwanda to fed of criticism and continue to receive vast amounts of aid. Reyntjens' calls this a "genocide credit," arguing that the genocide has become "a source of legitimacy astutely exploited to escape condemnation" (2004, p.199). Elsewhere colleagues and I have critiqued the argument that Rwanda is treated in an exceptional way by international community, arguing that ignoring damning accusations is not something unique to Rwanda (Desrosiers and Swedlund, 2018). Nevertheless, it is quite clear that Rwanda strategically uses a narrative of guilt and redemption to try and silence both domestic and international critics.

The guilt and redemption narrative plays on both realities and fears. The international community did stand back while Rwanda descended into genocide (Barnett, 1997; Barnett, 2002; Dallaire, 2005). Moreover, there is evidence that international donors not only didn't do anything to stop the terrifying events of the early 1990s, but actually contributed to fostering the system of systemic violence that allowed the genocide to take place in the first place. The book that most systematically advances this argument, *Aiding Violence: The Development Enterprise in Rwanda*, by Tufts University professor Peter Uvin (1998) is widely read by practitioners working in Rwanda (Hayman, 2011). As a result, there is often a (reasonable) fear among aid practitioners that peace in Rwanda is highly precarious and that they, as outsiders, don't fully understand the complex domestic dynamics at play. As a result, many are hesitant to " 'rock the boat" out of fear that violence will erupt once again.

How precisely does the narrative of guilt and redemption affect aid negotiations? In practice, this is difficult to systematically measure. However, a narrative of guilt and redemption appears to have empowered Rwanda to exert themselves with international donors, even though structural conditions suggest that the government should be hesitant to anger international donors. In the language of international negotiation scholars, the narrative of guilt and redemption appears to have affected Rwanda's BATNA and reservation price. As one Reuters headline from 2012 reads, "Defiant Rwanda calls West's bluff on aid" (John, 2012). The article then goes on to quote a US-based consultant who claims that Rwanda has "made the calculation that they won't be isolated or ostracized. And if they lose some donor support, they can support that."

Consistent with the narrative that they will not be pushed around by an international community that wasn't there for them when it mattered the most, Rwanda has taken a hardline against high-powered donor countries on a number of occasions. Most famously, Rwanda suspended diplomatic relationships with the French in 2006, after a French judge issued arrest warrants for nine current Rwandan political officers accused of being involved in the downing of the former President Habyarimana's plane in April 1994 (The New York Times, 2006).[4] Germany was also caught up in this scandal, when they—acting on a European arrest warrant—apprehended one of those accused, Rose Kabuye, after she was sent on a mission to Germany knowing she would be arrested. In response, the German ambassador in Kigali was expelled, and the Rwandan ambassador in Berlin was recalled (BBC News, 2008).

For their part, international donors have often seemed hesitant to play hardball with Rwanda, continuing to offer support to the country and often engaging with the government on its own terms. German foreign aid amounts increased rather than decreased after the aforementioned suspension of diplomatic relations. As Hayman (2011) explains, there is a general consensus among development workers that the government responds better to "a soft approach based on constructive dialogue" than criticism.

Twenty-years after the genocide, there is some evidence that patience with the regime may be waning (Beswick, 2014). A damning report from the UN in 2012 regarding Rwandan support for the violent rebel group M26 resulted in the suspending of direct assistance to the country (Smith, 2012). Moreover, the decision to change presidential constitutional term limits in 2015 in order to allow Kagame to seek reelection for an additional three terms (until 2034) was widely condemned (McVeigh, 2015). However, as of writing, despite these transgressions, the international community continues to extend vast amount of resources to Kigali, and Kagame continues to have a number of high-powered supporters.

Importantly, this narrative has been effective with donors, at least in part, because the current Rwandan government is widely seen as being a high efficient government. The narrative would almost certainly not be as effective if Rwanda didn't offer what donor agencies need—a successful African case (Zorbas, 2011). The streets of Kigali are clean and safe, the public buses have WIFI, and government offices are sweltering with a hub of activity and efficiency. Moreover, the government takes a very strong stance on corruption, providing assurance to donors that they will not be embarrassed by a corruption scandal. This shiny example of a country that has transformed within a generation is almost irresistible for a development industry that continually must defend its existence to a skeptical public. Accordingly, it perhaps should come as no surprise that Kigali goes to great length to project an image of development and growth. Without the ability to frame Rwanda as a successful case of economic development in Africa, donor attention and support would most certainly dwindle.

Narratives of agency and ownership

Deep-rooted narratives of guilt and redemption, couple nicely with a more general and widespread narrative in international development regarding "country ownership." In the early 2000s, consensus emerged among a group of donors (sometimes referred to as the "like-minded donors") that sustained poverty action requires effective governments that are accountable to their people. Consequently, the narrative that emerged is that aid donors should explicitly avoid using approaches that undermine accountability and ownership (Lawson et al., 2003, p.26). The importance of "country ownership" was solidified in the

2005 *Paris Declaration on Aid Effectiveness*, which was signed by more than 100 countries and put ownership front and center (Armon, 2007).

The ownership narrative contains all elements of a good narrative: victimhood, redemption, and agency. Take, for example, the opening lines of a 2009 report Oxfam America entitled, "Ownership in Practice":

> Why is it so important to improve US foreign aid? Because one billion people have been left behind by current global development trends. Aid, used in smart ways, can save lives and help people get themselves out of poverty. Better yet, smart aid can help make other local, national, and global economic and political forces work for poor people.
>
> Sixty years of foreign aid have shown that donors cannot fix the problems of poor people by themselves, no matter how well donors understand development. Donor-imposed solutions are often wrong for the context. Even when they're right, successes aren't maintained without local buy-in.
>
> It is because we believe in human rights and the responsibilities they invoke that Oxfam aims to strengthen local ownership of aid, such that foreign aid is delivered in ways that strengthen the voice of citizens and the responsiveness of the state.
>
> *Hufstader, 2009, p.2*

In this story, the poor are the victims of failed development. However, there is hope for redemption. By giving agency back to developing countries, we can force states to be responsive to the needs of their people and make development work.[5]

Over the past decade, the Rwandan government has used the concept of ownership in very strategic—as well as country-specific—ways in order to claim ground, often linking this narrative in clever ways with the aforementioned narratives of guilt and redemption. As Hayman writes, "Rwanda is a country which has grasped the opportunity to take ownership of aid" (2009, p.595). Kagame himself frequently asserts the need for Rwanda to stop being dependent, using this to push back at policies the regime disagrees with. In August 2002, for example, the US blocked an aid disbursement related to Rwanda's Poverty Reduction and Growth Facility with the IMF. Shortly after, Kagame pushed back, saying "Rwandans must stop being dependent" on the international community, whose attitude "that compounds our problems emerge[s] from indifference, ignorance and malice" (Reyntjens, 2011, p.20).

Kigali has also used the concept of ownership to facilitate concessions from donor countries, using global forums to push for more favorable aid commitments and exert weight on the global stage. For example, during the Fourth High-Level Forum on Aid Effectiveness in Busan, South Korea in 2011, Rwanda pushed hard for donors to commit to channeling more aid through national systems and to end so-called tied aid. Speaking at the opening ceremony, Kagame adeptly alluded to the previous failures of donors to justify his claims: "While donors may not be entirely to blame for bypassing these systems where they are weak, or non-functional, why not use aid to build up and strengthen such critical systems?" (Tran, 2011).

Rwanda has similarly skillfully used the ownership narrative at a domestic level (Keijzer et al., 2019). In the name of ownership, Rwanda pushed for all working groups related to aid disbursement to be "government led." This means a government representative is always supposed to be in the room and sign off on official correspondence—they are supposed to be in charge. [In other aid-dependent countries, development coordination meetings are frequently donor-only.] The ministry of finance also used the narrative of ownership to pressure donors into committing to a "Division of Labor," which required donors to commit to only being active in three sectors (i.e., health, education, agriculture) (Republic of Rwanda, 2010a). While most donors publicly supported the idea, in interviews, many expressed concerns with the proposal, telling me that they were backed into a corner by the government. Under the narrative of ownership, the government also implemented a "Donor Performance Assessment Framework" in 2009. The DPAF sought to shame donors into taking greater action on the Paris principles, such as more direct financing and less tied aid, using the narrative of ownership to shame or validate individual donors (Republic of Rwanda, 2010b).

Narratives ebb and flow, and gradually rhetoric and preferences at the global level for certain aid practices, like direct financing, have decreased (Keijzer and Black, 2020). Rwanda has adopted to these changes. Although the government continues to play on themes of ownership, the rhetoric is now less about reforming traditional aid and more about moving away from it entirely in the name of self-reliance and *Agaciro*—a Kinyarwanda word, which can be translated to mean dignity or self-worth (Behuria, 2016; Rutazibwa, 2014; Rutazibwa and Ndushabandi, 2019). As Behuria (2016) explains, the concept of *Agaciro* was already being developed in 2011, but took on particular meaning and strategic use following the 2012 freeze in foreign aid, which infuriated the government.

Over time, *Agaciro* has come to symbolize neoliberal principles of entrepreneurship and self-reliance, against a common enemy—donors—with a history of inaction (Behuria, 2016, p.437). Following the 2012 aid suspension, the Rwandan government established the domestically funded Agaciro Development Fund or ADGF (Manson and Wallis, 2012). The ADGF is supported by voluntary contributions[6] from wealthy Rwandans with self-stated vision of "improv(ing) the level of financial autonomy of Rwanda as a nation."[7] The ADGF, therefore, very symbolically and publicly challenges the traditional aid system.

At the same time, the government has pursued a number of economic initiatives in tourism and manufacturing that emphasize self-reliance and have pushed back hard at critiques of these initiatives. In 2018, for example, the government sponsored the English Premier League team Arsenal with a deal speculated to be worth 30 million pounds (Thomson, 2018b).[8] When Dutch Members of Parliament questioned the government's decision to invest so much money in this way, State Minister Ambassador Olivier Nduhungirehe replied on twitter "Dear MPs from

The Netherlands. This is NONE of your business. Rwanda uses revenues from National Parks to promote investment and tourism, aiming self-reliance."[9] The same year, the government also banned the import of second-hand clothing, despite strong protests and the suspension of duty-free privileges on Rwandan clothing by the United States (John, 2018). The ban was designed to boost local manufacturing and revitalize the local clothing market and was originally agreed to by several East African countries. Kenya, Tanzania, and Uganda, however, all reverse course after pressure from the US (Mumbere, 2018). In contrast, Rwanda held strong, emphasizing the need for dignity and self-reliance, and pursuing in tandem the "Made in Rwanda" campaign, which champions Rwandan-made goods, particularly in the textile and garment sector (Fashion Revolution, 2021).

Tied to this symbolic move away from traditional aid is the possibility of "new" sources of financing from nontraditional donors, including the UAE, India, Turkey, and of course China (Ferry and Swedlund, 2021). In a widely cited interview for the German newspaper *Handelsbatt*—titled "China Gives What Africa Needs"—Kagame is quoted as saying:

> Africa was neglected and even exploited for a long time. But now we have decided: We don't want this anymore, we want to have fair relations with the rest of the world. The odds are in our favour! There are new players, developing countries like China, India, Brazil and Russia. That opens new possibilities for new relationships. Suddenly, the Americans and Europeans discover that they don't want to be left out.
>
> *Rinke, 2009*[10]

Here Kagame is playing into another powerful and pervasive narrative in international development circles that alternative financing from China and other nontraditional in particular is upending traditional development assistance (Swedlund, 2017b). According to the rhetoric, China and other nontraditional donors provided African governments with more "policy space" or "the ability to make decisions to pursue their self-defined development objectives, not those of their donors, after decades of quasi-unilateral dependence on Western donors" (Reisen and Stijns, 2011). Nagire Woods of Oxford writes:

> By quietly offering alternatives to aid-receiving countries, emerging donors are introducing competitive pressures into the existing system. They are weakening the bargaining position of western donors in respect of aid-receiving countries, exposing standards and processes that are out of date and ineffectual. The result is a serious challenge to the existing multilateral development assistance regime.
>
> *2010, p.1221*

Important to the success of this narrative is the idea that China treats Rwanda and other African countries as an equal; that is, that Rwanda maintains agency in their deals with China. On the occasion of Chinese President Xi Jinping's state visit to Rwanda in 2018, Kagame is quoted as saying:

> The growing relationship with China is based as much on mutual respect as on mutual interest...China relates to Africa as an equal. We see ourselves as a people on the road to prosperity. China's actions demonstrate that you see us in the same way. This is a revolutionary posture in world affairs, and it is more precious than money.
>
> *Shaban, 2018*

To help maintain this image, China avoids the language of donor/recipient, emphasizes the principles of mutual respect and sovereignty in its communiques with African states, and takes what Benabdallah (2020) calls a more human approach to power.

Narratives on China itself are, of course, highly contested. China is alternatively portrayed as a provider of "rouge aid" or as a "pariah" who is only in Africa for exploitative purposes (Alessi and Hanson, 2012; Naim, 2007; Servant, 2005; Taylor, 2008; Tull, 2006). Empirically, it is also important to keep in mind that, despite the spotlight on China in recent years, many African countries—including Rwanda—still receive large amounts of traditional financing. China and other nontraditional donors fund very different types of development aid projects. They focus on productive sectors—rather than the social sectors—and the majority of their aid flows to Chinese (often state-owned) companies. Therefore, in practice, there is often much less competition between traditional and nontraditional donors than is commonly assumed (Humphrey and Michaelowa, 2019; Swedlund, 2017b).

This contestation notwithstanding, the narrative that China is upending the traditional aid system can be incredibly useful to African governments like Rwanda. The idea that money might—at any moment—flow in from China (without any conditions) helps Kigali project a stronger bargaining position. High-profile projects, like the construction of a 27 million dollar administrative home for the prime minster (Tasamba, 2019), help maintain the narrative that China is omnipresent in Rwanda and offers a real alternative to traditional aid. Kagame daftly uses the idea that China and other nontraditional donors provide a real alternative to traditional development aid; that is, he uses the growing presence of China to project the idea that Rwanda's BATNA has changed.

Concluding remarks

What can the Rwandan case tell us about the potential power of narratives in foreign aid negotiations—and in international negotiations more broadly? Two points are worth emphasizing. First, the example of Rwanda suggests that narratives can change perceptions of bargaining power—affecting how both parties see their BATNA. These changes in perceived power can occur *irrespective* of objective structural conditions. In the case of Rwanda, the government strategically uses narratives of guilt and redemption, as well as narratives of agency, to challenge long-standing power asymmetries in foreign aid. They are able to do so, even though structural conditions are not in their favor.

Second, given the inherent structural inequalities in foreign aid, narratives might be the strongest tool recipient countries have in their toolbox. While it is often assumed that negotiations are most effective when the two parties have equal power, asymmetric power relations are the norm in international negotiations (Zartman and Rubin, 2000). The structural conditions responsible for these asymmetric relations are deep-seeded and difficult to change. Narratives, on the other hand, are more malleable and open for reinterpretation. Governments like Rwanda that excel at capitalizing on narratives for their own ends can potentially change existing power dynamics, even if they cannot change existing structural conditions.

Notes

1 Figures are from 2019. Source: https://data.worldbank.org/.
2 Following Hampson and Narlikar, I define a narrative as: "collection or body stories of characters, joined in some common problem as fixers (heroes), causes (villains) or the harmed (victims) in a temporal trajectory (plot) leading towards resolution within a particular setting or context" (Davidson, 2016).
3 This literature also documents how the "official" narrative is routinely contested by both public figures and everyday citizens.
4 The report also implicates Kagame, accusing him of issuing the instructions to down the aircraft.
5 The concept of "ownership" has been widely critiqued by scholars (Harrison, 2001; de Renzio, 2006; Swedlund, 2013).
6 There is heavy social pressure to contribute to the fund (John, 2012).
7 http://agaciro.rw/index.php?id=12
8 During the 2018 season, the left shoulder of the jerseys for Arsenal's first, U-23 and women's teams were adorned with "Visit Rwanda" logo.
9 https://twitter.com/onduhungirehe/status/999926348071268352?lang=en (emphasis in original).
10 English translation available here: http://paulkagame.com/?p=33.

References

Alessi, C., and, Hanson, S. (2012) *Expanding China-Africa Oil Ties*, Councial on Foreign Relations. www.cfr.org/china/expanding-china-africa-oil-ties/p9557.

Armon, J. (2007) 'Aid, Politics and Development: A Donor Perspective', *Development Policy Review*, vol.25, no.5, pp.653–656. https://doi.org/10.1111/j.1467-7679.2007.00390.x.

Barnett, M.N. (1997) 'The UN Security Council, Indifference, and Genocide in Rwanda', *Cultural Anthropology*, vol.12, no.4, pp.551–578. https://doi.org/10.1525/can.1997.12.4.551.

Barnett, M.N. (2002) *Eyewitness to a Genocide: The United Nations and Rwanda*. Ithaca, NY: Cornell University Press.

BBC News. (2008, November 11) *Rwanda Expels German Ambassador*, BBC News.

Behuria, P. (2016) 'Countering Threats, Stabilising Politics and Selling Hope: Examining the Agaciro Concept as a Response to a Critical Juncture in Rwanda', *Journal of Eastern African Studies*, vol.10, no.3, pp.434–451. https://doi.org/10.1080/17531055.2016.1250871.

Benabdallah, L. (2020) *Shaping the Future of Power Knowledge Production and Network-Building in China-Africa Relations*. Ann Arbor, MI: University of Michigan Press.

Beswick, D. (2014, April 4) *20 Years on, Rwanda Exhausts Its 'Genocide Credit' with Donors*, The Conversation.

Burke, J. (2019, September 24) *Rwanda Opposition Leader Says Ally's Killing Was Act of Intimidation*, The Guardian. www.theguardian.com/world/2019/sep/25/rwanda-opposition-leader-victoire-ingabire-ally-killing-act-intimidation.

Charbonneau, L. (2012, June 27) *U.N. to Release Divisive Report on Rwanda Support for Congo Rebels*, Reuters. www.reuters.com/article/us-congo-democratic-rwanda/u-n-to-release-divisive-report-on-rwanda-support-for-congo-rebels-idUSBRE85P1JA20120627.

Dallaire, R. (2005) *Shake Hands with the Devil: The Failure of Humanity in Rwanda*. New York, NY: Carroll & Graf; Distributed by Publishers Group West.

Davidson, B. (2016, July 20) *The Role of Narrative Change in Influencing Policy*, On Think Tanks. https://onthinktanks.org/articles/On Think Tanksthe-role-of-narrative-change-in-influencing-policy.

Desrosiers, M.E, and, Swedlund, H.J. (2018) 'Rwanda's Post-Genocide Foreign Aid Relations: Revisiting Notions of Exceptionalism', *African Affairs*, vol.118, no.472, pp.435–462. https://doi.org/10.1093/afraf/ady032.

Edwards, S. (2014) 'Economic Development and the Effectiveness of Foreign Aid: A Historical Perspective', Working Paper 20685. Cambridge, MA: National Bureau of Economic Research.

Fashion Revolution. (2021, March 8) *An Evaluation of Made in Rwanda: A Policy Dialogue on Standards, Quality and Sustainability*, Fashion Revolution. https://issuu.com/fashionrevolution/docs/made_in_rwanda_policy_dialogue.

Ferry, M., and, Swedlund, H.J. (2021) 'Emerging Powers, Governance and Development', In W. Hout and J. Hutchison (Eds.), *Edgar Handbook on Governance and Development*. Cheltenham: Edward Elgar Publishing, forthcoming.

Harrison, G. (2001) 'Post-Conditionality Politics and Administrative Reform: Reflections on the Cases of Uganda and Tanzania', *Development and Change*, vol.32, no.4, pp.657–679. https://doi.org/10.1111/1467-7660.00221.

Hayman, R. (2009) 'From Rome to Accra via Kigali: 'Aid Effectiveness' in Rwanda', *Development Policy Review*, vol.27, no.5, pp.581–599. https://doi.org/10.1111/j.1467-7679.2009.00460.x.

Hayman, R. (2011) 'Funding Fraud? Donors and Democracy in Rwanda', In, S. Straus and L. Waldorf (Eds.), *Remaking Rwanda: State Building and Human Rights after Mass Violence* (pp.118–131). Madison, WI: University of Wisconsin Press.

Hufstader, C. (2009, September 21) *Ownership in Practice: The Key to Smart Development*, Oxfam America. www.oxfamamerica.org/explore/research-publications/ownership-in-practice-the-key-to-smart-development/.

Humphrey, C., and, Michaelowa, K. (2019) 'China in Africa: Competition for Traditional Development Finance Institutions?', *World Development*, vol.120, pp.15–28. https://doi.org/10.1016/j.worlddev.2019.03.014.

Ingelaere, B. (2010) 'Do We Understand Life after Genocide? Center and Periphery in the Construction of Knowledge in Postgenocide Rwanda', *African Studies Review*, vol.53, no.1, pp.41–59. https://doi.org/10.1353/arw.0.0307.

Jessee, E. (2017) *Negotiating Genocide in Rwanda: The Politics of History*. Cham, Switzerland: Palgrave Macmillan.

John, M. (2012, October 21) *Analysis: Defiant Rwanda Calls West's Bluff on Aid*, Reuters. www.reuters.com/article/uk-rwanda-aid/analysis-defiant-rwanda-calls-wests-bluff-on-aid-idUKBRE89K03M20121021.

John, T. (2018, March 28) *How the US and Rwanda Have Fallen out over Second-Hand Clothes*, BBC News. www.bbc.com/news/world-africa-44252655.

Keijzer, N., Klingebiel, S., and, Scholtes, F. (2019) 'Promoting Ownership in a 'Post Aid-Effectiveness' World: Evidence from Rwanda and Liberia', *Development Policy Review*, vol.38, no.S1, pp.32–49. https://doi.org/10.1111/dpr.12469.

Keijzer, N., and, Black, D. (2020, January) 'Special Issue Introduction Ownership in a Post-aid Effectiveness Era: Comparative Perspectives', *Development Policy Review*, vol.38, no.S1, pp.1–12. https://doi.org/10.1111/dpr.12490.

Kim, P.H., Pinkley, R.L., and, Fragale, A.R. (2005) 'Power Dynamics in Negotiation', *Academy of Management*, vol.30, no.4, pp.799–822.

Lawson, A., Booth, D., Harding, A., Hoole, D., and, Naschold, F. (2003, October) 'Evaluability Study Phase 1' vol.1.

Longman, T. (2017) *Memory and Justice in Post-Genocide Rwanda*. Cambridge: Cambridge University Press.

Manson, K., and, Wallis, W. (2012, September 6) *Rwanda Seeks to Reduce Reliance on Aid*, Financial Times. www.ft.com/content/57e6aea2-f75e-11e1-8e9e-00144feabdc0.

McGreal, C. (2010, October 1) *Delayed UN Report Links Rwanda to Congo Genocide*, The Guardian. www.theguardian.com/world/2010/oct/01/un-report-rwanda-congo-genocide.

McVeigh, T. (2015, December 19) *Rwanda Votes to Give President Paul Kagame Right to Rule until 2034*, The Guardian. www.theguardian.com/world/2015/dec/20/rwanda-vote-gives-president-paul-kagame-extended-powers.

Mumbere, D. (2018, April 4) *Rwanda Insists on Second-Hand Clothing Ban, Says U.S. Can Withdraw AGOA Benefits*, Africanews. www.africanews.com/2018/04/04/rwanda-insists-on-second-hand-clothing-ban-says-it-s-up-to-us-to-withdraw-agoa//

Mwambari, D. (2020a) 'Emergence of Post-Genocide Collective Memory', In E. Nyaga Muni, D. Mwambari, and A. Ylönen (Eds.), *Beyond History: African Agency in Development, Diplomacy, and Conflict Resolution* (pp.9–134). Lanham, MD: Roman & Littlefield.

Mwambari, D. (2020b) 'Music and the Politics of the Past: Kizito Mihigo and Music in the Commemoration of the Genocide Against the Tutsi in Rwanda', *Memory Studies*, vol.13, no.6, pp.1321–1336.

Naim, M. (2007) 'Rogue Aid', *Foreign Policy*, no.159, pp.95–96. http://foreignpolicy.com/2009/10/15/rogue-aid/.

Narlikar, A. (2015, March 12) *The Power of the Powerless: The Politics of Poverty at the Doha Round*, Foreign Affairs. www.foreignaffairs.com/articles/commons/2015-03-12/power-powerless.

Ostrom, E., Gibson, C., Shivakumar, S., and, Andersson, K. (2002) 'Aid, Incentives, and Sustainability: An Institutional Analysis of Development Cooperation', *Sida Studies in Evaluation 02/01*. Stockholm, Sweden: Swedish International Development Cooperation Agency.

Pottier, J. (2002) *Re-Imagining Rwanda Conflict, Survival and Disinformation in the Late Twentieth Century*. Cambridge: Cambridge University Press.

Reisen, H., and, Stijns, J.P. (2011, July 12) *Emerging Partners Create Policy Space for Africa*, VoxEU.Org. www.voxeu.org/article/how-emerging-donors-are-creating-policy-space-africa.

Renzio, Paolo de. (2006) 'Aid, Budgets and Accountability: A Survey Article', *Development Policy Review*, vol.24, no.6, pp.627–645. https://doi.org/10.1111/j.1467-7679. 2006.00351.x.

Republic of Rwanda. (2010a) *Donor Division of Labour in Rwanda*. Kigali, Rwanda: Ministry of Finance and Economic Planning.

Republic of Rwanda. (2010b) *Donor Performance Assessment Framework (DPAF), FY 2009–2010*. Kigali, Rwanda: Ministry of Finance and Economic Planning. www.africa-platform.org/sites/default/files/resources/rwanda_donor_performance_assessment_framework_2009-2010.pdf.

Reyntjens, F. (2004) 'Rwanda, Ten Years on: From Genocide to Dictatorship', *African Affairs*, vol.103, no.411, pp.177–210. https://doi.org/10.1093/afraf/adh045.

Reyntjens, F. (2011) 'Constructing the Truth, Dealing with Dissent, Domesticating the World: Governance in Post-Genocide Rwanda', *African Affairs*, vol.110, no.438, pp.1–34. https://doi.org/10.1093/afraf/adq075.

Rinke, A. (2009, November 10) *Ruandas Präsident: China Gibt, Was Afrika Braucht*, Handelsblatt. www.handelsblatt.com/politik/international/paul-kagame-ruandas-praesident-china-gibt-was-afrika-braucht/3278216-all.html.

Rutazibwa, O.U. (2014) 'Studying Agaciro: Moving Beyond Wilsonian Interventionist Knowledge Production on Rwanda', *Journal of Intervention and Statebuilding*, vol.8, no.4, pp.291–302.

Rutazibwa, O.U., and, Ndushabandi, E. (2019) 'Agaciro: Re-centering Dignity in Development', In A. Kothari, A. Salleh, A. Escobar, F. Demaria, and A. Acosta (Eds.), *Pluriverse: A Post-Development Dictionary*. New York, NY: Columbia University Press.

Ruzibiza, A.J., Vidal, C., and, Guichaoua, A. (2005). *Rwanda, l'histoire secrète*. Paris, France: Éditions du Panama.

Servant, J.C. (2005, May) *China's Trade Safari in Africa,* Le Monde Diplomatique. https://mondediplo.com/2005/05/11chinafrica.

Shaban, A.R.A. (2018, July 23) *'China Relates to Africa as an Equal'—Paul Kagame*, Africanews. www.africanews.com/2018/07/23/china-relates-to-africa-as-an-equal-paul-kagame/

Smith, D. (2012, September 27) *EU Partially Freezes Aid to Rwanda*, The Guardian. www.theguardian.com/world/2012/sep/27/eu-partially-freezes-aid-to-rwanda.

Swedlund, H.J. (2013) 'From Donorship to Ownership? Budget Support and Influence in Rwanda and Tanzania', *Public Administration and Development*, vol.33, no.5, pp.357–370. https://doi.org/10.1002/pad.1665.

Swedlund, H.J. (2017a) *The Development Dance: How Donors and Recipients Negociate the Delivery of Foreign Aid*. Ithaca, NY: Cornell University Press.

Swedlund, H.J. (2017b) 'Is China Eroding the Bargaining Power of Traditional Donors in Africa?', *International Affairs*, vol.93, no.2, pp.389–408. https://doi.org/10.1093/ia/iiw059.

Swedlund, H.J., and, Lierl, M. (2019) 'The Rise and Fall of Budget Support: Ownership, Bargaining and Donor Commitment Problems in Foreign Aid', *Development Policy Review*, vol.38, no.S1, pp.50–69. https://doi.org/10.1111/dpr.12463.

Tasamba, J. (2019, April 23) *Rwanda Inaugurates Chinese-Built Administrative Office Complex*, China Daily. www.chinadaily.com.cn/a/201904/23/WS5cbf1763a3104842260b7dd5.html.

Taylor, I. (2008) 'Sino-African Relations and the Problem of Human Rights', *African Affairs*, vol.107, no.426, pp.63–87. https://doi.org/10.1093/afraf/adm056.

The New York Times. (2006, October 24) *Rwanda Breaks Diplomatic Relations with France*, New York Times. www.nytimes.com/2006/11/24/news/24iht-rwanda.3660589.html.

Thomson, S. (2018a) *Rwanda: From Genocide to Precarious Peace.* New Haven, CT: Yale University Press.

Thomson, S. (2018b, September 12) *Rwanda's £30 Million Arsenal Sleeve,* Africa Is a Country. https://africasacountry.com/2018/09/rwanda-on-a-sleeve.

Tran, M. (2011, November 30) *Rwanda Steps up Campaign for Greater Ownership of Aid*, The Guardian. www.theguardian.com/global-development/poverty-matters/2011/nov/30/busan-rwanda-aid-effectiveness.

Tull, D.M. (2006) 'China's Engagement in Africa: Scope, Significance and Consequences', *The Journal of Modern African Studies*, vol.44, no.3, pp.459–479.

Uvin, P. (1998) *Aiding Violence: The Development Enterprise in Rwanda.* West Hartford, CT: Kumarian Press.

Whitfield, L. (Ed). (2009) *The Politics of Aid: African Strategies for Dealing with Donors.* Oxford: Oxford University Press.

Whitfield, L., and, Fraser, A. (2009) 'Negotiating Aid', In L. Whitfield (Ed.), *The Politics of Aid: African Strategies for Dealing with Donor* (pp.27–44). Oxford: Oxford University Press.

Woods, N. (2010) 'Whose Aid? Whose Influence? China, Emerging Donors and the Silent Revolution in Development Assistance', *International Affairs*, vol.84, no.6, pp.1205–1221. www.jstor.org/stable/25144989.

Zartman, I.W, and, Rubin, J.Z. (Eds.). (2000) *Power and Negotiation.* Ann Arbor, MI: University of Michigan Press.

Zorbas, E. (2011) 'Aid Dependence and Policy Independence: Explaining the Rwandan Paradox', In S. Straus and L. Waldorf (Eds.), *Remaking Rwanda: State Building and Human Rights after Mass Violence* (pp.103–117). Madison, WI: University of Wisconsin Press.

12

NARRATIVES, NEGOTIATION, AND THE IRAQ WARS

Rodger A. Payne

Introduction

This chapter examines and compares strikingly similar narratives employed strategically by United States foreign policymakers and diplomats in the international negotiations building up to the 1991 Persian Gulf War and 2003 Iraq War. In both cases, US officials sought to create sizeable coalitions of states in support of coercive diplomacy against Iraq to change its behavior. However, US officials relatively quickly abandoned coercive diplomacy in both instances and then sought to build multinational coalitions in support of major military operations.

For comparison purposes, the situations offer significant parallels. For example, during the many months in each instance when US negotiators were attempting to build strong coalitions, the target state, Iraq, was governed by Saddam Hussein and the US was led by a Republican president named George Bush. Moreover, key US foreign policymakers served in prominent positions in the administrations of father and son, including Dick Cheney (Secretary of Defense in 1991, Vice President in 2003) and Colin Powell (Chair of the Joint Chiefs of Staff in 1991, Secretary of State in 2003). More importantly for the purposes of this chapter, the narrative employed by US leaders, negotiators, and diplomats were also similar in the cases. In both instances, the US attempted to employ a narrative of redemption to explain the importance of a multilateral coalition to confront Hussein's Iraq and transform global politics for the better. However, the results of the coalition-building negotiations were ultimately quite different, suggesting either that the contexts were more unique than alike or that the narratives were not uniformly effective.

In 1990, Iraq invaded Kuwait and thereby contaminated international politics in a manner that nation-states collectively rejected long ago in the United

DOI: 10.4324/9781003203209-15

Nations charter, if not in the Westphalian system. President George H.W. Bush promoted a redemptive multilateral "new world order" to address this traditional threat to state sovereignty. US negotiators and statesmen achieved an impressive multinational coalition to fight the Persian Gulf War and the collective action those states pursued was widely viewed as legitimate in world politics. The size and political status of the assembled coalition allowed for the employment of a military strategy that quickly met almost all the limited policy objectives. In contrast, negotiators and statesmen working in the presidential administration of George W. Bush assembled a much less notable Iraq War coalition. Bush tried to convince world leaders that Saddam Hussein would contaminate their world in the future by connecting the material resources of his "rogue" state with the political vagaries of dangerous terrorists. The redemption on offer by the US did not appear to be especially multilateral and was not universally viewed as legitimate. The dearth of material and political support for the resulting "coalition of the willing" ultimately required a military strategy in Iraq that proved unable to meet its policy objectives quickly. Can these differences in outcome be at least partly explained by the appropriateness – or inappropriateness – of the strategic narratives employed in each circumstance?

The chapter begins with a brief discussion of the key politico-military background details justifying the US attempts to attract coalition partners in these anti-Iraq endeavors. Then, the narratives the leaders and diplomats employed strategically are outlined. The subsequent section evaluates the effectiveness of the coalition-building efforts and discusses how the suitability (or unsuitability) of the narratives factored into the outcomes. The final section offers some brief conclusions about the narrative employed in these cases.

Key politico-military background

Persian Gulf War

On August 2, 1990, Iraq attacked neighboring Kuwait. Iraqi forces quickly occupied the country and briefly set up a puppet government before simply annexing Kuwait. Though the US immediately condemned this action, an American-led international military response was certainly not foreordained. After all, Ronald Reagan's administration had backed Iraq during most of its nine-year war with Iran in the 1980s, restoring full diplomatic relations in 1984 and providing development loans and credits (Karabell, 1995, pp.29–30). The George H.W. Bush administration, after entering office in January 1989, pursued a policy of "conciliation" toward Iraq and even "approved the sale of advanced data-transmission devices" (Wilz, 1995, p.546) on August 1, the day before Iraq's invasion. Arguably, however, Bush's policy, also known as "constructive engagement," had for months been failing miserably given Iraq's dubious behavior. In the words of one scholar (Karabell, 1995, p.45), the Bush administration "pursued this policy in the face of overwhelming evidence that Iraq was violating human rights, using and producing chemical weapons, producing biological weapons, violating nuclear non-proliferation agreements, evading US export controls" and using loans illegally to buy arms. Contemporaneous critics on the right viewed the Bush conciliatory policy as "appeasement" in the face of "a series of escalating threats and actions" Iraq signaled toward Arab neighbors during this time (Gigot, 1990, pp.4,7; see also Wilz, 1995, pp.534–536).

In retrospect, a crisis seemed inevitable. In May 1990, Saddam Hussein declared at a meeting of Arab leaders that various neighboring states were violating OPEC production quotas, which constituted a "declaration of war against Iraq" (Wilz, 1995, p.538). Hussein also delivered a highly threatening radio address on July 17, the day after foreign minister Tariq Aziz sent a memo to the Secretary General of the Arab League charging that Kuwait had stolen Iraqi oil and built various military and economic outposts on Iraqi land, which altogether amounted to "'military aggression'" (Wilz, 1995, p.538). Consistent with these threats, Iraq amassed a substantial military force near the Kuwaiti border. Eight days prior to the attack, on July 25, US Ambassador to Iraq April Glaspie (*Transcript of Meeting*, 1990) met with Hussein to inquire about Iraq's intentions toward Kuwait given the "massive numbers of troops [deployed] in the south." The Iraqi leader replied that he remained willing to seek a settlement about long-disputed territories, but "if we are unable to find a solution, then it will be natural that Iraq will not accept death." In the same meeting, Hussein declared Iraq's intent "to defend our claims on Kuwait to keep the whole of Iraq in the shape we wish it to be" and asked the US Ambassador about "the United States' opinion on this?" Glaspie replied:

> We have no opinion on your Arab – Arab conflicts, such as your dispute with Kuwait. Secretary [of State James] Baker has directed me to emphasize the instruction, first given to Iraq in the 1960's, that the Kuwait issue is not associated with America.

Likewise, Assistant Secretary of State for Near East Affairs, John Kelly (Joseph, 1993, p.77), testified to Congress on July 31 that the US had "no defense treaty relationships with any of the [Gulf] countries. We have historically avoided taking a position on border disputes." Some analysts have argued that these statements and others emanating from administration officials signaled a "green light" to Hussein that Iraq could attack Kuwait without fear of US retaliation (Mearsheimer and Walt, 2003, p.54). However, Hussein may well have already made up his mind to attack and signaled an interest in diplomacy as an act "of tactical deception in order to retain the element of surprise" (Gause III, 2002, p.62). Moreover, Defense Secretary Cheney, Under Secretary of State Paul Wolfowitz, and various other figures indicated a US commitment to Gulf state sovereignty and warned Iraq to resolve its disputes peacefully (Stein, 1992, pp.150–151). Whatever message Saddam Hussein received from these communications, "While the crisis was intensifying, Washington's signals to Iraq were ambiguous and contradictory" (Stein, 1992, p.150) at best.

Constructive engagement clearly ended in August after the invasion and US policy almost immediately took a "180-degree shift" (Wilz, 1995, p.546). President Bush issued a stern warning just three days after the invasion that such aggression "will not stand" (Watkins and Rosegrant, 2001, p.184). Indeed, Bush (1990) soon publicly outlined "four simple principles" that would guide US policy throughout his administration's management of the Persian Gulf crisis – the unconditional and complete withdrawal of Iraqi forces from Kuwait, the restoration of Kuwait's government-in-exile, the protection of American citizens in Iraq and Kuwait, and a commitment to the security and stability of the Persian Gulf. Though Bush often emphasized these US goals, Canadian Prime Minister Brian Mulroney and British Prime Minister Margaret Thatcher (Smith, 1992, pp.63–72) also influenced Bush's thinking about the global implications of the crisis. Mulroney (Hampson, 2018, pp.195–202) successfully pushed for a response through the United Nations Security Council (UNSC) to gain broad international consensus. Thatcher (1993, pp.820–822) primarily focused on the need to confront Iraq forcefully, though she argued that this could be justified quite simply via Article 51 of the UN Charter, which upholds the right of individual or collective self-defense in the event of armed attack against a member.

The UNSC unanimously adopted Resolution 660 on August 2 condemning the Iraqi invasion, demanding immediate and unconditional withdrawal, Resolution 661 on August 4 implementing economic sanctions under Chapter VII of the UN Charter, and Resolution 665 on August 25 to authorize a naval blockade to enforce the sanctions.[1] Resolution 670 extended economic sanctions to civil aviation on September 25.[2] Bush (1990B) boasted to the General Assembly on October 1 that the world was witnessing "unprecedented unity and cooperation." Though the US had been rotating a large number of troops into Saudi Arabia to defend it against a potential Iraqi attack, a major practical step toward evicting Iraq from Kuwait was the announced deployment of 150,000 additional US troops to the Persian Gulf on November 8, roughly a doubling of the deployed US forces (Stein, 1992, p.172; Watkins and Rosegrant, 2001, p.198). The UNSC passed Resolution 678 authorizing "use of all necessary measures" to eject Iraq from Kuwait on November 29. Resolution 678 provided an ultimatum for Iraq compliance and set a deadline of January 15, 1991.[3] Throughout fall 1990, the US worked with dozens of partner countries to form the largest military coalition since World War II. Secretary of State Baker also sought substantial economic support for what the US called Operation Desert Shield and obtained substantial pledges from Kuwait, Saudi Arabia, Japan, and Germany to help offset the cost of the military deployments. The funds also eventually supported the use of force – codenamed Operation Desert Storm. Between the August invasion and the ultimatum deadline, Arab, French, and Soviet mediators also tried to achieve diplomatic resolution of the crisis, but in the end Iraq rejected all of their initiatives (Stein, 1992, p.171).

Aerial bombing of Iraq began on January 16, 1991 and continued for roughly six weeks. About 100 hours after a ground campaign was initiated on February

24, a ceasefire was declared, and victory was celebrated by the coalition partners. In his January 29 "State of the Union" address before Congress, Bush (1991) hailed the fact that the world had "answered Saddam Hussein's invasion with 12 United Nations resolutions" and that the ongoing war included "forces from 28 countries of 6 continents."

Iraq War

The Iraq War was launched on March 20, 2003, after the administration of US President George W. Bush spent just over six months alleging that Iraq's possession of weapons of mass destruction (WMD), support for international terrorism, and noncompliance with various prior UNSC resolutions justified collective action to disarm – and preferably end – Saddam Hussein's regime. The political context for this use of coercive diplomacy was shaped within the US and around the world by the devastating September 11, 2001 terrorist attacks on New York and Washington DC (Krebs and Lobasz, 2007). Indeed, President Bush and his administration ultimately framed the attack on Iraq as a critical element of the ongoing "war on terror" because Hussein's rogue regime in Iraq had pursued WMD and cooperated with transnational terrorists, allegedly including al Qaeda.

Extending the war on terrorism to Iraq was not an altogether unexpected decision. Through the 1990s, the US applied a containment strategy toward Iraq, viewing it as an outlaw state hostile to American interests and an array of international norms. In 1998, the US Congress passed and Bill Clinton signed the Iraq Liberation Act (1998), which simply declared "that it should be the policy of the United States to seek to remove the Saddam Hussein regime from power in Iraq and to replace it with a democratic government." A Washington-based think tank, the Project for a New American Century (PNAC), had publicly advocated for that law, as well as for adoption of a military strategy of regime change in Iraq (Schmidt and Williams, 2008, p.193). The January 1998 open PNAC letter to Clinton urging action was signed by many individuals who soon became prominent members of the Bush administration.[4] Throughout the 1990s, Iraqi WMD programs discovered after the Persian Gulf War were monitored with mixed success by the UN and International Atomic Energy Agency (de Jonge Oudraat, 2002). The international community met noncooperation during that era with punitive economic sanctions, intermittently bolstered by US bombing campaigns against various Iraqi targets (de Jonge Oudraat, 2002). In mid-December 1998, the "cat and mouse" (Fitchett, 1998) game Iraq had been playing with weapons inspectors ended. The US and UK conducted air strikes against Iraq for four days. However, Iraq then terminated its cooperation altogether and refused to allow weapons inspectors into the country for four years.

Soon after the 9/11 attacks in the US, President Bush lumped Iraq with North Korea and Iran as an "axis of evil." Specifically, in his annual January State of the Union address, Bush (2002) condemned "States like these, and their terrorist allies" who are "arming to threaten the peace of the world. By seeking weapons of mass destruction, these regimes pose a grave and growing danger." By that fall, the campaign to focus on Iraq in the war on terror was in full force both domestically and globally. In a September 2002 speech to the UN General Assembly, the President (Bush, 2002A) outlined the Security Council's many post-1991 Resolutions targeting Iraq and spoke about the need for the regime to end its pursuit of WMD, support for terrorism, and persecution of its domestic civilian population. However, the ultimatum Bush provided during that speech seemed to be directed at the UN itself:

> All the world now faces a test, and the United Nations a difficult and defining moment. Are Security Council resolutions to be honored and enforced, or cast aside without consequence? Will the United Nations serve the purpose of its founding, or will it be irrelevant? The United States... will work with the U.N. Security Council for the necessary resolutions. But the purposes of the United States should not be doubted. The Security Council resolutions will be enforced – the just demands of peace and security will be met – or action will be unavoidable.

After weeks of high-level diplomacy, the UNSC (2002) unanimously passed Resolution 1441 on November 5 offering Iraq "a final opportunity to comply with its disarmament obligations." The resolution required Iraq to allow new international weapons inspections and to report its WMD activities. On February 5, 2003, Secretary of State Powell delivered a presentation to the UNSC to share US intelligence about Iraq's alleged WMD programs and support for terrorism. Powell (2003) argued that Iraq was in "material breach of its obligations" and thus "in danger of the serious consequences called for" in 1441. However, that resolution explicitly did not include automatic triggers to use force and even the US Ambassador to the UN, John Negroponte (2002), acknowledged that Iraqi noncompliance would require "a return to the Council for discussions."

Nonetheless, in March 2003, the leaders of the US, Great Britain, Portugal, and Spain met and announced that their countries would enforce resolution 1441 against Iraq without a follow-up UNSC resolution explicitly authorizing the use of force. UK Prime Minister Tony Blair (Reynolds, 2003) called the situation "tragic" given that Iraq was playing "games" that divided the UN and NATO as many countries resisted action. At the same press conference, President Bush emphasized the futility of a second UNSC vote because France had already announced its intent to veto.

The war began on March 20, Iraq's military was quickly defeated in combat, and its government was readily toppled. By May 1, in fact, President Bush (2003A) famously helped land a naval Viking jet on the aircraft carrier *USS Lincoln*, changed from his flight suit to business attire, spoke in front of a large banner reading "Mission Accomplished," and declared that "major combat operations in Iraq have ended." However, despite this celebration, Iraq rapidly became the site of a prolonged insurgency and a devastating civil war. Thousands of anti-American foreign fighters were attracted to Iraq, leading the administration to label the evolving conflict in Iraq as the "central front in the war on terror" (Krebs and Lobasz, 2007, p.450). In many ways, subsequent conflict involving the Islamic State of Iraq and Syria (ISIS) was a continuation of the Iraq War, though the presidential administration of Barack Obama officially ended the US military presence in Iraq in 2011.

About 18 months into war, the Iraq Survey Group (DCI Special Advisor, 2004) reported that Iraq had halted its nuclear program in 1991, likewise unilaterally destroyed its undeclared chemical weapons stockpile in 1991, and had no interest in a biological weapons program after the destruction of its Al Hakam facility in 1996. In other words, Iraq had no active WMD program for many years prior to the war. Moreover, the 9/11 Commission (National Commission, 2004, p.66) found "no evidence" that Iraq and al Qaeda had a "collaborative operational relationship" or cooperated "in developing or carrying out any attacks against the United States." In retrospect, many observers argue that the Iraq War contends with the Vietnam War as the greatest foreign policy mistake in American history.

US narratives

The US narrative employed in both of these cases seems best explained by Richard N. Haass, who served President George H.W. Bush in 1990–1991 as National Security Council Senior Director for Near East and South Asian Affairs. Then, January 2001 to June 2003, Haass was George W. Bush's Director of Policy Planning in the State Department. In between those years of service, Haass (1997) wrote a book arguing that after the end of the Cold War, the US often serves as a "reluctant sheriff" in international politics, obliged to form a posse of likeminded states to accomplish a specific task, such as the extraction of Iraq from Kuwait. Haass (1997, p.93) argued that this kind of "foreign policy by posse" could be implemented via "coalitions of the willing." Haass considered the Persian Gulf War and Operations Desert Shield and Desert Storm "the model for the idea" (see also Gray, 2004, p.13) and the most famous instance of its use. However, Haass (1997, p.98) advocated this kind of multilateralism more broadly because it promotes burden sharing and provides "some measure of international legitimacy" to action without requiring formal ongoing institutionalization. In the following sections, I demonstrate that US leaders and policymakers in both Iraq cases sought to utilize this narrative strategically to shape the international response. The sheriff and posse narrative redemptively explained the nature and resolution of the crises, as well as what the postcrises landscape should look like.

Persian Gulf War

In its pre-war diplomacy, the George H.W. Bush administration relied upon a narrative borrowed from a common story employed about the American Old

West – a sheriff forms a posse to confront an outlaw. In this case, the US sheriff and international coalition posse assembled to remove the troops of the villainous Iraq rogue state from neighboring Kuwait. Establishing Iraq as the villain in the story was not especially difficult, given its invasion, but the Bush administration went to great lengths to assure that this point was made clear for all audiences, including the domestic public. In Bush's (1990) August 8 speech, the President claimed that "Iraq's tanks stormed in blitzkrieg fashion through Kuwait in a few short hours," an obvious reference to Germany's notorious World War II offensive tactic. Bush also described Iraq as a significant adversary, "a rich and powerful country" possessing "the world's second-largest reserves of oil" and "the fourth-largest military in the world." Moreover, at a midterm election campaign appearance, Bush explicitly compared Saddam Hussein unfavorably to Adolf Hitler (Raum, 1990). While Bush (1990B) did not mention Hitler in his October 1 UN speech, he did emphasize that "Iraq's unprovoked aggression is a throwback to another era, a dark relic from a dark time. It has plundered Kuwait. It has terrorized innocent civilians." In his August address, Bush (1990) had warned that "if history teaches us anything, it is that we must resist aggression or it will destroy our freedoms. Appeasement does not work."

These accusations not only underscored Iraq's treachery, but they also emphasized Kuwait's victimhood. Tapping into deeply shared international norms about nonintervention and the importance of state sovereignty, Bush named additional potential victims as part of the rationale for confronting Iraq. For instance, Bush's (1990B) August address emphasized that Iraq "may not stop using force to advance its ambitions" as it had already "amassed an enormous war machine on the Saudi border capable of initiating hostilities." White House spokesperson Marlin Fitzwater (Rosenthal, 1990) said Iraq posed "an imminent threat to Saudi Arabia." In his UN speech, Bush (1990B) also accused Iraq of waging "a genocidal poison gas war" against the nation's "own Kurdish villagers." Indeed, Bush (Raum, 1990) frequently accused occupying Iraqi forces of committing "outrageous acts of barbarism." For example, at least ten times during fall 1990, Bush referenced a horrific allegation that became widely publicized but was demonstrated two years later to be a false Kuwaiti public relations ploy. The fabrication concerned "Babies pulled from incubators [by Iraqi troops] and scattered like firewood across the floor" of Kuwaiti hospitals.[5]

While establishing the villain and victim in the narrative was not especially difficult given the circumstances, the U.S. emphasis on the importance of collective action through the UN solidified the American role as sheriff and the international community's position as posse. As President Bush (1990B) said to the UN General Assembly, his warning that "the annexation of Kuwait will not be permitted to stand" was "not simply the view of the United States; it is the view of every Kuwaiti, the Arab League, the United Nations. Iraq's leaders should listen: It is Iraq against the world." Moreover, Bush explicitly linked his vision of how to proceed in Iraq to a broader redemptive story about international life after the end of the Cold War. Bush (1990B) described a "new world order" that would, unlike the divided Cold War era, entail using the UN "as it was designed: as a center for international collective security."

Shortly after the war ended, Bush (1991B, p.161) efficiently summarized the narrative surrounding the events: "The recent challenge could not have been clearer. Saddam Hussein was the villain; Kuwait the victim. To the aid of this small country came the nations from North America and Europe, from Asia and South America, from Africa and the Arab world—all united against aggression." More than a decade later, scholar Colin Gray (2004, p.13) described the US as "the sheriff of the current world order" and noted that it successfully led "a large UN-blessed posse against Iraq in 1991."

Iraq War

The George W. Bush administration attempted to employ a very similar narrative in advance of the 2003 Iraq War, hoping to build a sizeable international coalition of states – a posse – under the leadership of the US sheriff and its top deputies, Australia and the United Kingdom. In Prague for a NATO summit in November 2002, Bush (Bumiller, 2002) claimed that "Contrary to my image as a Texan with two guns on my side, I'm more comfortable with a posse." Indeed, the US President clearly sought partners at that NATO summit visit to apply unified collective pressure against Iraq. He boasted about the 90 nations that were "joined in a global coalition to defeat terror" and claimed that "the world is also uniting to answer the unique and urgent threat posed by Iraq" (Bush, 2002C). As proof, he pointed to the return of UN weapons inspectors. Bush (2002C) declared that the US and the world shared the goal of "the comprehensive and verified disarmament of Iraq's weapons of mass destruction." However, Bush emphasized Iraq's short window of time to comply, warning that "Delay and defiance will invite the severest of consequences."

Certainly, the wider global war on terrorism, which began almost immediately after the 9/11 attacks on New York and Washington, was explicitly organized as a coalition of the willing and closely followed Haass' recipe for foreign policy by posse. A UK House of Commons Committee on Foreign Affairs (2002) report found that "the views articulated by Richard Haass" – Director of Policy Planning at the State Department – had "wide currency" among the US officials they interviewed. The report confirmed that "The international coalition that has been assembled to fight terrorism since September resembles in many ways Haass's 'posse.'" Moreover, from the beginning, President Bush's rhetoric about the global war on terror surely sounded like a prototypical western sheriff. In a speech to Pentagon employees soon after 9/11, Bush (Sanger, 2001) noted that "There's an old poster out west, as I recall, that said, 'Wanted: Dead or Alive.'" He added, "I want him [Osama bin Laden] – I want justice."

The Bush administration framed the war against Iraq as an extension of the war on terror (Krebs and Lobasz, 2007). During the buildup to war, Bush (White House, 2006) often implied that Iraq and the 9/11 attackers posed a unified contaminating threat:

> The danger…is that al Qaeda becomes an extension of Saddam's madness and his hatred and his capacity to extend weapons of mass destruction around the world. Both of them need to be dealt with…you can't distinguish between al Qaeda and Saddam when you talk about the war on terror.

Once the administration turned its full attention to Iraq in fall 2002, top officials told a familiar story about the nature of the villain and the needed collective response, echoing the narrative the US employed in the lead up to the earlier Persian Gulf War. For example, President Bush (2002D) declared in an October 2002 speech:

> I want to take a few minutes to discuss a grave threat to peace, and America's determination to lead the world in confronting that threat. The threat comes from Iraq. It arises directly from the Iraqi regime's own actions – its history of aggression, and its drive toward an arsenal of terror.

In numerous speeches, Hussein's Iraq was described as an evil international villain. Though Bush (2002E) did not directly compare Hussein to Hitler as his father had, he referenced "the harsh experience of 1938" and declared that "when great democracies fail to confront danger, greater dangers follow." Like his father, Bush (2003) also specifically employed the "Munich analogy" and warned against appeasing Iraq:

> In the 20th century, some chose to appease murderous dictators, whose threats were allowed to grow into genocide and global war. In this century, when evil men plot chemical, biological and nuclear terror, a policy of appeasement could bring destruction of a kind never before seen on this earth.

If Iraq was the clear villain in the narrative, the US itself was now an aggrieved victim because it had suffered the 9/11 attacks. However, Bush's rhetorical strategy also emphasized that the world could not wait to respond to future contamination in the form of devastating WMD attacks. Indeed, Bush (2002C) told the UN, "To assume this regime's [Iraq's] good faith is to bet the lives of millions and the peace of the world." Ultimately the "coalition of the willing" posse created for the Iraq War included almost 50 nation-states including Australia, Denmark, Italy, Japan, Norway, Poland, Spain, and the UK. However, the collective did not include notable 1991 partners such as Belgium, Canada, Egypt, France, Germany, Pakistan, Saudi Arabia, and Sweden. France and Germany, as well as Russia, openly opposed a UNSC resolution that would have authorized states to use force against Iraq and no such resolution was agreed.

This fact obviously did not stop the war and was never likely to prevent it. To reiterate the ultimatum Bush (2002C) directed at the UN in his September speech, the President repeatedly served notice that the US was willing to confront

Iraq alone if the world did not agree to be deputized into a posse. In October, President (Bush, 2002B) declared that

> America must not ignore the threat gathering against us. Facing clear evidence of peril, we cannot wait for the final proof – the smoking gun – that could come in the form of a mushroom cloud...we have every reason to assume the worst, and we have an urgent duty to prevent the worst from occurring.

These statements declaring a US intent to attack Iraq without UN authorization had profound implications for the sheriff and posse narrative, rendering it a shallow story that failed to bind the international community. As analyst Colin Gray (2004, p.55) explained, "a significant reason why the United States is able to function as sheriff is precisely because it usually behaves in a manner that serves the general good as well as its own interests." While Gray (2004, p.23) argued that "from time to time the United States will need to act as judge, jury, and even executioner," other observers had a much less sanguine perspective that helps explain the narrative's weakness. Bruno Tertrais, a senior fellow at a prominent French security research organization, explained why France did not view either the US or its leader as a sheriff: 'Despite the fact that Bush chose to go to the U.N. on Iraq, he is still seen as a cowboy with his finger on the trigger" (Bumiller, 2002). Indeed, many states critical of the war embraced an argument similar to the one later offered by retired senior law Lord Tom Bingham (Norton-Taylor, 2008) – an invasion "unauthorized by the Security Council" was itself "a serious violation of international law and the rule of law." Bingham continued, "The moment a state treated the rules of international law as binding on others but not on itself, the compact on which the law rested was broken." He then quoted Oxford legal scholar Vaughn Lowe who stated bluntly that this is "the difference between the role of world policeman and world vigilante."

Outcomes

Persian Gulf War

The sheriff and posse narrative seemingly worked quite effectively in the Persian Gulf War case. In terms of global politics, President Bush (1991B, p.161) declared immediately after the war that this was "a victory for every country in the coalition; for the United Nations; a victory for unprecedented international cooperation and diplomacy...It is a victory for the rule of law and for what is right." Domestically, much polling data from the time reveal that the US public generally supported the use of military force against Iraq for many months prior to the attack (Mueller, 1993). More importantly, all four of Bush's principles guiding US policy were arguably met. Iraqi forces were forced to leave Kuwait, the exiled Kuwaiti government was restored to power, and American lives in the region were protected. Granted, the commitment to security and stability of the Persian Gulf region was somewhat more ambiguously achieved. After all, Saddam Hussein remained in power and the US and the international community would eventually devote substantial resources to address ongoing threats to regional and international peace and security involving Iraq.

With British, Canadian, and French assistance, American negotiators successfully convinced UNSC members to support the use of force, or in the case of China, not to veto the key resolutions. In fact, as previously reviewed, prior to the start of the Gulf War UNSC members adopted several important resolutions largely at US urging. These resolutions initially condemned Iraq's attack on Kuwait, then imposed economic sanctions, and ultimately authorized the use of force. Thanks to UNSC support, the war was almost universally viewed as a legitimate multilateral operation – though US foreign policy advisor Haass (Watkins and Rosegrant, 2001, p.191) was "not filled with great confidence" about the implied precedent of requiring the UN's "Good Housekeeping seal of approval...before you could ever do anything." Nonetheless, the fruits of cooperation were important as the US provided about three-fourths of the military forces, but the coalition included members from 34 states and the burden of financing the war was largely assumed by coalition partners (Watkins and Rosegrant, 2001, p.194). Most funds were provided by Saudi Arabia, Kuwait's government-in-exile, and wealthy trading states Germany and Japan, both highly dependent on imported oil.

Iraq War

The Bush administration's primary original goals for the Iraq War could not be met because US weapons inspectors quickly concluded that Iraq did not have WMD after all. In hindsight, there was no need for WMD disarmament. While the war transformed Iraq into a host for insurgent terrorists, the post-facto condition could not justify the original coercive diplomacy or attack. The insurgency and civil war, moreover, led the US to adopt expansive military goals that proved difficult to achieve over a period of many years and at tremendous material cost.

Most importantly for the purposes of this chapter, the pre-war negotiations were not especially successful. Only three members of the Iraq coalition of the willing contributed materially to the invasion – Australia, Poland, and the UK. Rather than helping to finance the war, many coalition partners reportedly received increases in foreign aid or other tangible incentives from the US in exchange for their declared support, including allegedly India, Pakistan, and Turkey (Weitsman, 2009) – and Turkey nonetheless refused to allow the US access to military bases to launch the war in March 2003. The publicized list of coalition partners looked suspiciously padded as it included tiny nations such as the Marshall Islands, Micronesia, Palau, and the Solomon Islands. The overwhelming majority of the material costs for the Iraq War were paid by the US, including over 4,000 deaths. Economically, the war cost nearly $840 billion in dedicated defense spending (Crawford, 2020). The real total expense, including interest paid on debt used to finance the war as well as health care for wounded veterans, has been nearly $2 trillion. The UK, which provided the second largest military force, spent in comparison about £10 billion on the Iraq War (BBC News, 2010).

In contrast to the Persian Gulf War case, as previously noted, American negotiators were unable to gain UNSC authorization for the Iraq War. Prior to attack, US diplomats were merely able to convince the body to adopt a resolution giving Iraq a final opportunity to comply with disarmament obligations. After a period of weapons inspections and despite various diplomatic efforts, no follow-up resolution authorized the use of force. Moreover, major states that supported the Persian Gulf War, and thereby helped legitimize it via UNSC support, openly opposed the US case for war in 2003, including France, Germany, and Russia. The lack of Iraqi adherence to older UNSC resolutions may well have justified the use of all necessary means including force to compel Iraqi compliance. However, under international law, such a determination can only be made by the UNSC. Without such authorization, the use of military force to compel adherence to a UN resolution is itself widely viewed as a violation of basic non-intervention norms. UN Secretary General Kofi Annan (BBC News, 2004) declared that the war "was not in conformity with the UN charter."

Of course, neither the Bush administration's strategy nor narrative was tied to UN decisions. After all Bush (2001) had framed the international discussion about the global war on terror quite differently from the very start: "Every nation, in every region, now has a decision to make. Either you are with us, or you are with the terrorists." Seemingly, this same warning applied to the UN itself in the case of Iraq. At a September 2002 Camp David meeting with Italian Prime Minister Silvio Berlusconi days after delivering his UN address, President Bush (Associated Press, 2002) warned that the US would enforce Security Council resolutions whether the body agreed to act or not. Saddam Hussein, he declared, had "stiffed the world" sixteen times and did not deserve another chance. Bush argued that the UN deserved a chance to "show some backbone." The President continued, "Make no mistake about it. If we have to deal with the problem, we'll deal with it." Essentially, the US pinned the sheriff's badge on its own chest and openly declared a willingness to confront the villain it considered an international outlaw worthy of every state's attention – even if the townspeople disagreed.

Conclusions

The fruitful negotiations in advance of the Persian Gulf War, emphasizing the deeply shared norms of nonintervention and the redemptive promise of a new world order, translated directly into significant financial and other material support. Secretary of State Baker, working with other diplomats and allies, successfully achieved numerous UNSC resolutions condemning Iraq's attack on Kuwait and assembled a large multilateral coalition supporting the use of force to end Iraq's occupation. Years later, Baker (Frontline, 1996), told an interviewer that the administration could have legally justified an attack against Iraq based on Article 51 of the UN Charter, just as Margaret Thatcher had argued. Baker and Bush, however, wanted to conduct the operation in such a way "that it was not seen to be a cowboy operation." Haass' sheriff and posse narrative seemingly worked in this case and the war itself was widely celebrated as a meaningful victory.

The Iraq War that started in 2003 shared a similar narrative, again imagining a US sheriff rounding up a posse to attack outlaw state Iraq for its alleged WMD and support for terrorism. Negotiations for a resolution authorizing the use of force were not successful, but President George W. Bush often stated a willingness to attack without UNSC approval. Lack of American commitment to fundamental international legal norms of nonintervention made the sheriff and posse narrative seem shallow. While the story likely helped assure domestic support, the US failed to garner critical UNSC support and the coalition of the willing was notably less impressive. Ultimately, the paucity of multilateral partners cost the US tremendous financial and other material resources. Germany, France, and Turkey publicly challenged the US, which arguably signaled a crisis of multinational order. As noted earlier, the younger Bush openly promoted the idea that he was a western cowboy (West and Carey, 2006). In this instance, the cowboy appeared to be a reckless and angry vigilante attempting to rally a vengeful lynch mob rather than a legitimate representative of global law enforcement.

Notes

1. Yemen did not vote on Resolution 660. Cuba and Yemen abstained from votes on Resolutions 661 and 665.
2. Cuba voted against Resolution 670.
3. Cuba and Yemen voted against Resolution 678 while China abstained.
4. Signees included eventual Secretary of Defense Donald Rumsfeld, Deputy Secretary of Defense Paul Wolfowitz, Vice President Cheney, and Cheney's Assistant for National Security Affairs, Lewis Libby (Schmidt and Williams, 2008, p.193).
5. The 15-year-old daughter of the Kuwaiti Ambassador to the US posed as an on-site witness to atrocities and presented false testimony at a congressional hearing on October 10 (Walton, 1995, pp.771–772).

References

Associated Press. (2002, September 14) *Bush Calls on U.N. to Show 'Backbone' on Iraq*, New York Times.www.nytimes.com/2002/09/14/international/bush-calls-on-un-to-show-backbone-on-iraq.html.

BBC News. (2004, September 16) *Iraq War Illegal, says Annan*, BBC. http://news.bbc.co.uk/2/hi/middle_east/3661134.stm.

BBC News. (2010, June 20) *Cost of Wars in Iraq and Afghanistan Tops £20bn*, BBC. www.bbc.com/news/10359548.

Bumiller, E. (2002, November 22) *Threats and Responses: The Allies; Bush, at NATO Meeting, Firms up His 'Posse'*, New York Times.

Bush, G.H.W. (1990, August 8) *Address to the Nation Announcing the Deployment of United States Armed Forces to Saudi Arabia*, Bush Presidential Library and Museum. https://bush41library.tamu.edu/archives/public-papers/2147.

Bush, G.H.W. (1990B, October 1) *Address Before the 45th Session of the United Nations General Assembly in New York, New York*, Bush Presidential Library and Museum. https://bush41library.tamu.edu/archives/public-papers/2280.

Bush, G.H.W. (1991, January 29) *Address Before a Joint Session of the Congress on the State of the Union*, Bush Presidential Library and Museum. https://bush41library.tamu.edu/archives/public-papers/2656.

Bush, G.H.W. (1991B, March 6) *The World After the Persian Gulf War*, US Department of State Dispatch, pp.161–163.

Bush, G.W. (2001, September 20) *Address to a Joint Session of Congress and the American People*, White House, George W. Bush Archive. https://georgewbush-whitehouse.archives.gov/news/releases/2001/09/text/20010920-8.html.

Bush, G.W. (2002, January 29) *President Delivers State of the Union Address*, White House, George W. Bush Archive. https://georgewbush-whitehouse.archives.gov/news/releases/2002/01/20020129-11.html.

Bush, G.W. (2002A, September 12). *President's Remarks at the United Nations General Assembly*, White House, George W. Bush Archive. https://georgewbush-whitehouse.archives.gov/news/releases/2002/09/20020912-1.html.

Bush, G.W. (2002B, October 7). *President Bush Outlines Iraqi Threat*, White House, George W. Bush Archive. https://georgewbush-whitehouse.archives.gov/news/releases/2002/10/20021007-8.html.

Bush, G.W. (2002C, November 20) *President Bush Previews Historic NATO Summit in Prague Speech*, White House, George W. Bush Archive. https://georgewbush-whitehouse.archives.gov/news/releases/2002/11/20021120-4.html.

Bush, G.W. (2003, March 17). *President Says Saddam Hussein Must Leave Iraq Within 48 Hours*, White House, George W. Bush Archive. https://georgewbush-whitehouse.archives.gov/news/releases/2003/03/20030317-7.html.

Bush, G.W. (2003A, May 1) *President Bush Announces Major Combat Operations in Iraq Have Ended*, White House, George W. Bush Archive. https://georgewbush-whitehouse.archives.gov/news/releases/2003/05/20030501-15.html.

Committee on Foreign Affairs. (2002, June 12) *Foreign Affairs – Seventh Report*. https://publications.parliament.uk/pa/cm200102/cmselect/cmfaff/384/38409.htm.

Crawford, N. (2020, February 4) *The Iraq War Has Cost the U.S. Nearly $2 Trillion*, The Conversation. https://theconversation.com/the-iraq-war-has-cost-the-us-nearly-2-trillion-129617.

de Jonge Oudraat, C. (2002) 'UNSCOM: Between Iraq and a Hard Place', *European Journal of International Law*, vol.13, no.1, pp.139–152.

DCI Special Advisor. (2004, September 30) *Comprehensive Report on Iraq's WMD*, Central Intelligence Agency. www.cia.gov/library/reports/general-reports-1/iraq_wmd_2004/Comp_Report_Key_Findings.pdf.

Fitchett, J. (1998, December 22) *U.S. Plans to Keep Up Pressure on Saddam: 'Cat and Mouse' Over*, New York Times. www.nytimes.com/1998/12/22/news/us-plans-to-keep-up-pressure-on-saddam-cat-and-mouse-over.html.

Frontline. (1996) *Oral History: James Baker*, The Gulf War, PBS. www.pbs.org/wgbh/pages/frontline/gulf/oral/baker/1.html.

Gause III, F.G. (2002) 'Iraq's Decisions to Go to War, 1980 and 1990,' *The Middle East Journal*, vol.56, no.1, pp.47–70.

Gigot, P.A. (1990) 'A Great American Screw-Up: The US and Iraq, 1980–1990,' *The National Interest*, no.22, pp.3–10.

Gray, C. (2004) *The Sheriff, America's Defense of The New World Order.* Lexington, KY: University of Kentucky.

Haass, R.N. (1997) *The Reluctant Sheriff; The United States After the Cold War.* New York, NY: Council on Foreign Relations.

Hampson, F.O. (2018) *Master of Persuasion: Brian Mulroney's Global Legacy.* Toronto, ON: Signal/McClelland & Stewart. Iraq Liberation Act. (1998, October 31) Public Law 105–338. www.congress.gov/bill/105th-congress/house-bill/4655/text?overview=closed.

Joseph, P. (1993) *Peace Politics; The United States Between the Old and New World Orders.* Philadelphia, PA: Temple University Press.

Karabell, Z. (1995) 'Backfire: US Policy Toward Iraq, 1988–2 August 1990,' *Middle East Journal*, vol.49, no.1, pp.28–47.

Krebs, R.R., and, Lobasz, J.K. (2007) 'Fixing the Meaning of 9/11: Hegemony, Coercion, and the Road to War in Iraq', *Security Studies*, vol.16, no.3, pp.409–451.

Mearsheimer, J.J., and, Walt, S.M. (2003, January/February) 'An Unnecessary War', *Foreign Policy*, no.134, pp.50–59.

Mueller, J. (1993) 'A Review: American Public Opinion and the Gulf War: Some Polling Issues', *Public Opinion Quarterly*, vol.57, no.1, pp.80–91.

National Commission on Terrorist Attacks Upon the United States. (2004) *The 9/11 Commission Report.* Washington, DC: USGPO.

Negroponte, J. (2002, November 8) *Statement by Ambassador John Negroponte of the US*, Global Policy Forum. www.globalpolicy.org/component/content/article/168/36071.html.

Norton-Taylor, R. (2008, November 17) *Top Judge: US and UK Acted as 'Vigilantes' in Iraq Invasion*, The Guardian. www.theguardian.com/world/2008/nov/18/iraq-us-foreign-policy.

Powell, C. (2003, February 5) *Remarks to the United Nations Security Council*, U.S. Department of State Archive. https://2001-2009.state.gov/secretary/former/powell/remarks/2003/17300.htm.

Raum, T. (1990, November 1) *Bush Says Saddam Even Worse Than Hitler*, AP. https://apnews.com/c456d72625fba6c742d17f1699b18a16.

Reynolds, M. (2003, March 17) *Azores Summit Ends in Ultimatum to U.N.*, Los Angeles Times. www.latimes.com/archives/la-xpm-2003-mar-17-fg-azores17-story.html.

Rosenthal, A. (1990, August 8) *Bush Sends U.S. Force to Saudi Arabia as Kingdom Agrees to Confront Iraq; Seeks Joint Action*, New York Times.

Sanger, D. (2001, September 18) *Bin Laden Is Wanted in Attacks, 'Dead or Alive,' President Says*, New York Times.

Schmidt, B.C., and, Williams, M.C. (2008) 'The Bush Doctrine and the Iraq War: Neoconservatives versus Realists', *Security Studies*, vol.17, no.2, pp.191–220.

Smith, J.E. (1992) *George Bush's War.* New York, NY: Henry Holt and Company.

Stein, J.G. (1992) 'Deterrence and Compellence in The Gulf, 1990–91: A Failed or Impossible Task?', *International Security*, vol.17, no.2, pp.147–179.

Thatcher, M. (1993) *The Downing Street Years.* London: HarperCollins.

Transcript of Meeting Between Iraqi President, Saddam Hussein and U.S. Ambassador to Iraq, April Glaspie (1990, July 25), Global Research. www.globalresearch.ca/gulf-war-documents-meeting-between-saddam-hussein-and-ambassador-to-iraq-april-glaspie/31145.

United National Security Council (2002, November 8). S/RES/1441. www.un.org/Depts/unmovic/documents/1441.pdf.

Walton, D. (1995) 'Appeal to Pity: A Case Study of the *Argumentum Ad Misericordiam*', *Argumentation*, vol.9, no.5, pp.769–784.

Watkins, M., and, Rosegrant, S. (2001) *Breakthrough International Negotiation: How Great Negotiators Transformed the World's Toughest Post-Cold War Conflicts*. San Francisco, CA: Jossey-Bass.

Weitsman, P. (2009) 'With a Little Help from Our Friends?: The Costs of Coalition Warfare', *Origins*, vol.2, no.4. https://origins.osu.edu/article/little-help-our-friends-costs-coalition-warfare.

West, M., and, Carey, C. (2006) '(Re)Enacting Frontier Justice: The Bush Administration's Tactical Narration of the Old West Fantasy after September 11', *Quarterly Journal of Speech*, vol.92, no.4, pp.379–412.

White House. (2006. September 15) *The Rest of the Story: Iraq's Links to Al Qaeda*, George W. Bush Archive. https://georgewbush-whitehouse.archives.gov/news/releases/(20022006/09/20060915-4.html.

Wilz, J.E. (1995) 'The Making of Mr. Bush's War: A Failure to Learn from History?' *Presidential Studies Quarterly*, vol.25, no.3, pp.533–554.

13

MEMORY AND NARRATIVES OF HATE AND FORGIVENESS IN POST-CONFLICT SOCIETIES

Valérie Rosoux

> *"We have seen what men 'should' not see; it is not translatable into any language. Neither do hate and forgiveness address it".*
>
> Robert Antelme[1]

Introduction

The aim of this chapter is to better understand the interactions between narratives and negotiations in post-conflict settings. These particular settings are highly context-specific. The consequences of civil wars cannot be assimilated to those of international or colonial wars. Likewise, the type of actors, their respective resources and expectations vary greatly from one case to another. However, post-war societies have three features in common, which explain why they can be considered as archetypal in terms of both narratives and negotiations.

First, in the aftermath of international or inter-community conflicts, most individuals feel under threat and think of themselves particularly in a narrative mode (Wertsch and Billinsley, 2011). Unsurprisingly, post-setting contexts favour homogenized and stereotyped narratives that reinforce the "us" "them" dichotomy. These "deep" narratives usually resonate with pre-existing stories, meta-narratives, or even cultural myths about heroic destiny and/or victimhood (Harper, 2006, p.603). They are particularly persuasive, "sticky," and therefore hard to negotiate (Forsberg, 2003, p.73).

Second, post-conflict settings are inevitably times of transition that trigger negotiation processes at all levels. Leaders have to address economic, political, and social issues in a context which is often characterized by highly emotional dynamics and entrenched positions towards historical grievances. In this respect, one of the biggest challenges is to encourage forward-looking outcome

DOI: 10.4324/9781003203209-16

processes rather than backward-looking outcome processes (Zartman and Kremenyuk, 2005).

Third, post-conflict settings lead to extremely complex interactions between parties whose interests and narratives are often incompatible, and whose time-frames are rarely similar. Survivors, criminals, families, bystanders, outsiders, returnees, former combatants, religious associations, international donors, mediators, policy makers, all operate within their own time-frame and, within each of these groups, every individual may react in a unique and largely unpredictable way. This multiplicity of interests, narratives, and temporalities make most relationships extremely complex.

As is mentioned in the introduction to this book, the relationship between narratives and negotiations is a reciprocal one: narratives generate negotiations and vice versa. Accordingly, two main dimensions should be examined in this chapter. Firstly, we shall observe to what extent narratives determine the negotiation processes that take place after a war. Do narrative shifts actually impact the outcome of negotiations? If so, how? Secondly, it is vital to explore how negotiation processes influence the narratives passed on by former belligerents. Can negotiations effectively provoke a change of narratives? If so, in what conditions can such a change take place?

To address these questions, the chapter examines two emblematic case studies: the case of France and Germany and the case of South Africa. Aside from their specificities, both cases illustrate a dramatic shift in narrative templates. They show, in particular, how narratives of hate can gradually be replaced by narratives of cooperation and even forgiveness. The analysis is divided into three parts. The first underlines the research posture adopted in the study, and questions some premises shared by numerous scholars and practitioners working in the area of conflict resolution. The second focuses on the Franco-German case, which is frequently presented as a model of reconciliation after an international war (Gardner-Feldman, 2012). The third part examines the case of South Africa, most often depicted as a success story of reconciliation after an inter-community conflict (Bucaille, 2019). These two case studies allow us to analyze the move from a narrative of contamination to one of redemption and joint agency (see the introduction to this book), and to show that the impact of this narrative shift on negotiations is actually much more equivocal that we might initially think.

Research posture: Broadening the approach

Despite their obvious differences, narratives of hate and forgiveness share the same aim: to integrate the emotional consequences of a violent past into coherent stories. In designing social roles (such as heroes and villains, righteous and traitors), these narratives constitute a core element of stakeholders' identity (Anderson, 1983; Hobsbawm and Ranger, 1992; Zerubavel, 2003). After a war, most readings of the past are incompatible. One person's hero is another's villain. To address these contradictions, conventional wisdom holds that a shared understanding of the past leads to a shared understanding of the future (Maddison, 2016, p.262). Therefore, master narratives emphasized at national level should be examined closely. Yet an exclusive focus on State actors does not allow us to encompass the various processes that take place at the local level (where specific memory entrepreneurs, veterans' associations, victims' associations, or religious leaders can have an impact on negotiation processes), the transnational level (where NGOs and international organizations promote globalized reconciliation practices), and the individual level (where we can hear the "subordinate" voices that have been marginalized, silenced, or even excluded from the dominant discourse – see Dalsheim, 2014).

The broadening of the approach is not just a question of agency. It also stems from a wish to consider both interests and emotions. The transformation of relationships between former enemies cannot be properly understood without taking into consideration the (a)symmetry of power that characterizes each case. However, the balance of power is not the only factor in determining the future. Post-war shifts are not only determined by the pursuit of interests, as important as these are, but also by the emotional weight of the past. At the end of a war, suspicion, mistrust, and hatred remain strong, even many years later. Beside the interests and resources of each protagonist, these emotions are crucial to understanding post-war dynamics and deadlocks. Even if a rapprochement seems necessary to the representatives of all parties, it cannot be imposed by decree. As the French novelist George Bernanos wrote, "memories of war are like memories of childhood" (Bernanos, 2014, p.182). They leave a lasting emotional imprint. In post-conflict societies, emotions such as fear, shame, guilt, anger, or grief are widely shared and passed on in family circles.

Most studies devoted to the transformation of relationships between former enemies consider these emotions from a normative perspective (Krondorfer, 2018). They distinguish clearly between "radicalized" narratives based on hatred, anger, or resentment, and "better-formed" narratives that derive from openness, empathy, and forgiveness (Cobb, 2013, p.221). The former narratives are perceived as systematically divisive and therefore detrimental to negotiation. The latter are considered as inherently unifying, and thus directly contributing to integrative negotiation processes. The objective of this chapter, however, is not to distinguish between "bad" and "good" narratives. It is rather to stress the ambivalence of narratives, which are neither positive nor negative *per se* – meaning that their impact on negotiations fundamentally depends on the objective pursued.

The Franco-German case: Emphasis on an alternative narrative

There are a wealth of books describing post-war Franco-German relations and highlighting the shift from "hereditary enmity" to "reconciliation" – a complete turnaround symbolized by the signing of the Treaty of Friendship in January 1963. This teleological and State-centric description overlooks the multiplicity of cross-border exchanges and mutual influences that have always existed between the two interacting societies (Sangar, 2020). However, no one can deny that there has been a radical change of focus in the strategic narratives passed down on both sides of the Rhine. This shift was initiated in the immediate post-war years by individual citizens and politicians from both countries. The emergence of a new common enemy (the USSR) rapidly strengthened the focus on joint agency and led to a long series of multilateral and bilateral negotiations, all converging to foster cooperation.

Context: An ambiguous fascination

For centuries, the German enemy was a basic component of French national identity, and vice versa. In both strategic narratives, the *other* was the mirror-image of qualities that each nation attributed to itself. Three cruel wars (1870–1871, WWI, WWII), in addition to the Napoleonic era, made this antagonism seemingly irreversible. Mutual hate was particularly palpable after the end of the First World War. Stereotypes abounded and echoed the fears, frustrations, and resentments, which each country felt for the other. However, this hatred is not sufficient to depict the true depth of Franco-German relationships. One of the key facets of this case is the ambiguous fascination which captivated both peoples. Interestingly enough, this fascination was not incompatible with hatred of the enemy. A long line of French intellectuals and artists expressed their admiration for German writers and composers. Thus, Germaine de Stael painted an idealized picture of Germany as a land of poets and thinkers. Her study of German culture, *De l'Allemagne* (appearing in 1810), offering a positive view of the country, was banned as an anti-French work. Likewise, respect for French culture was commonplace among the German elite. This mutual fascination, although ambivalent, guaranteed a form of symmetry between the enemies despite the battlefields and even the defeats.

In 1945, Germany was not merely defeated – its very identity as a nation-state was invalidated. The revelations of the concentration and death camps meant that Germany had not only to face a military, but also a moral defeat. As the former *Wehrmacht* officer August von Kageneck explains, the "catastrophe of 1945" was symbolized by

> a mountain of deaths and ruins, the loss of one third of the national territory, the expatriation of 11 million fellow citizens from their ancestral lands in the East, but also the awful images of what Germans had done to other European peoples.
>
> *von Kageneck, 2004, p.126*

The crushing defeat of Germany changed the whole tone of its relationship with France, making this much more asymmetrical than it was before. The Germans were *the* losers of the war, while the French appeared among the "winners." This asymmetry made the rapprochement with France much easier. Rather than being stuck in a competitive struggle with their rival, French leaders could highlight a different narrative to depict their former enemy.

Process: Structural approach to reconciliation

Far from the myth of hereditary enmity, the Franco-German story gradually came to be associated with friendship and even brotherhood. This narrative was already circulating in the 19th century and was emphasized in the inter-war period by those who advocated rapprochement. The change of focus began at the very end of WWII, long before any official negotiations were launched between the two States.

From below. As early as in 1944, numerous members of the French *Resistance* stressed the urgent need to respect German prisoners after the war. Robert Antelme is a central figure in this regard. Rescued from Buchenwald and Dachau, he immediately denounced any attempt to take revenge and insisted on the undeniable dignity of any German prisoner: "Far from taking revenge on us, anyone who shoots down or hits a German prisoner actually insults us" (Antelme, 2005, p.10). Similarly, Joseph Rovan attempted to improve the conditions of German prisoners in France. Joseph Rovan was born in Munich on July 1918. After Hitler's rise to power, his family left Germany to live in Paris. He joined the French Resistance in 1940 and was arrested and sent to Dachau in 1944. In 1947, he was appointed head of adult education in the French Zone of Germany. One year later, he was among those who created the German-French Institute at Ludwigsburg, in order to promote cooperation between the two nations through group exchanges, lectures, and language instruction for men working in embassies, in ministries, on the staff of newspapers, in the leadership of the unions, political parties, and professional organizations of both countries.

In the same vein, some French and German historians quickly gathered in order to critically scrutinize the myths of a "hereditary enmity" between France and Germany. Non-governmental organizations in both countries also provided avenues by which victims and victimizers could address their collective grief. Such initiatives, for the most part sponsored by religious associations (both catholic and protestant), focused on collective mourning and forgiveness (Ackermann, 1994).

From above. The founding fathers of the European Union struggled to erase systematic anti-German feelings in France. Robert Schuman, a member of the French National Assembly, was arrested by the German Gestapo in September 1940 and escaped in 1942. German-speaking, he was born in Alsace-Lorraine when it was under German rule. Once a conscript in the Kaiser's army, he became an outspoken advocate of reconciliation after the war. In 1950, while foreign minister, he developed the Schuman Plan, which led to the formation of the European Coal and Steel Community (ECSC) two years later, and the European Economic Community (Common Market) in 1958.

Besides these multilateral initiatives, Charles de Gaulle and Konrad Adenauer undertook considerable efforts to persuade the public of the need for a rapprochement. Between 1958 and 1962, they worked to connect the two countries, carrying out frequent trips on both sides of the Rhine to help their populations overcome fears rooted in past events. In Ludwigsburg, in particular, General de Gaulle stoked the enthusiasm of young people by denouncing – in German – any form of collective condemnation, and denying Manichean readings of the past. For him, the great mistakes of the past could not erase the fact that Germany had "spread around the world fruitful waves of thought, science, art, philosophy; enriched the universe with countless of its inventions, its techniques, and its work; and displayed in works during peacetime and during the hardships of war the treasures of courage, discipline, and organization" (September 9, 1962). Such a narrative from the officer who, in 1940, embodied resistance against the occupier was largely unexpected. To the president of the German parliament, this speech "not only put an end to the chapter from 1940 to 1945. More than that, a debt two centuries old was erased" (Gerstenmaier, 1964, p.2).

A couple of months later, on January 22, 1963, Charles de Gaulle and Konrad Adenauer signed the Élysée Treaty. This fundamental step ensured a lasting Franco-German rapprochement, by creating a twofold link between the countries: a requirement for regular official consultation and the promotion of "people-to-people" interaction. The institutional mechanisms established by the Élysée Treaty, and added to in 1988, created a structure of constant negotiation through half-yearly meetings of Heads of State, consultations of foreign and technical ministers, as well as joint councils in all fields. Furthermore, the Franco-German Youth Office created by the Treaty was conducive to revitalizing youth exchanges, conferences, and reciprocal language teaching. In 1964 alone, the Youth Office helped to organize meetings between 180,000 young people from both countries at 6,500 gatherings, seminars, and study trips – a process that gradually affected all levels of society (Figure 13.1). The existence of a jointly operated TV network – ARTE – and the creation of a Franco-German Parliamentary Assembly in 2019 are two other examples of this structural approach to reconciliation (Rosoux, 2008).

From outside. The Franco-German rapprochement was actively supported by official and private outsiders, especially in the United States. As it was critical for the United States to establish peaceful and prosperous Atlantic relations, American representatives initiated the Federal Republic's admission into NATO. In the private sector, the Moral Re-Armament Movement (MRA), founded by American Lutheran Pastor Frank Buchman, arranged conferences in Caux, Switzerland, which have, over the years, brought together thousands of French and German participants (government ministers, Members of Parliament, trade unionists, industrialists, clergy, media, and top educators).

To sum up, an opposite narrative based on reconciliation was conveyed both by efficient vectors of transmission (from churches to local organizations)

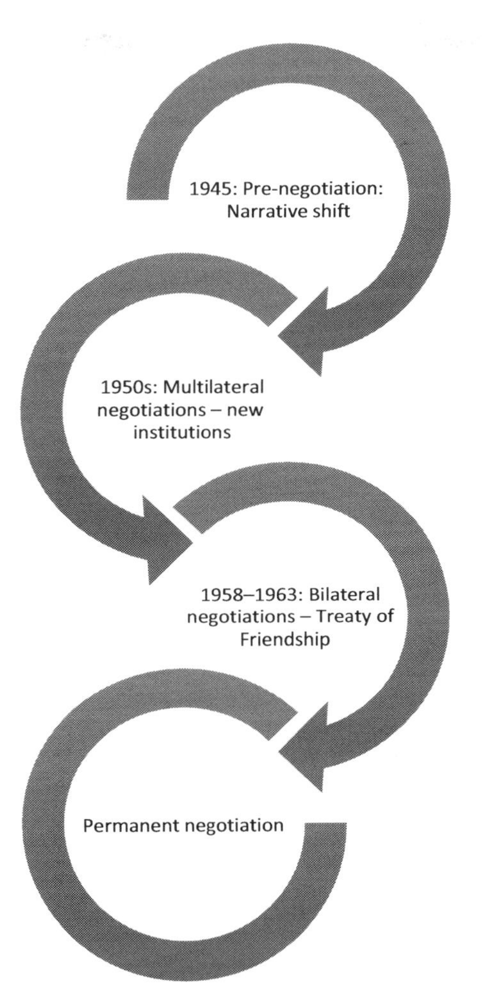

FIGURE 13.1 Franco-German process

and by key nodal actors and connectors who were credible on both sides of the Rhine (from the Europeanists to the leaders). One common feature can be found between pioneers, leaders, and external voices calling for reconciliation: they adopted a pragmatic approach that favoured negotiation processes at all levels (local, national, international) and permeated all societal institutions (the media, education, religion, culture) very effectively. The view of Germany which was most common in France in 1944 – once summarized as "no enemy but Germany" – had changed by 1960 to "no friend but Germany" (Grosser, 1967, p.6). Opinion polls confirm this dramatic change. In 1961, to give only one example, 57% of French nationals questioned in a poll considered that they could trust Germany in case of war, and 76% of the Germans polled expressed their confidence in the French. In 1955, these figures were only 38% and 37%, respectively (Puchala, 1970). Since then, all surveys have confirmed the high degree of mutual confidence across age groups.

Narrative: A shared destiny

To fight preconceived ideas about "the other," Charles de Gaulle repeatedly stressed an alternative meaning to be given to the past: "[T]he Germans were not really our enemies until 1870. It has only been three wars and three quarters of a century, [while] the Germans and the Gauls have known so many wars and so many centuries" (quoted by Peyrefitte, 1994, p.153). Nearly 25 years later, François Mitterrand strengthened this view by recalling that "the cruellest misfortunes, of barbarous dictatorships" could not deny the "co-ancestry" of France and Germany (January 20, 1983). In the view of the former French President, the rifts and ruptures could not weaken the "community of destiny" which has linked the two countries since the time of their common origins in the Frankish Kingdom (October 27, 1986).

Accordingly, joint commemorations were organized to pay tribute to the soldiers who fought in the opposite camps, but who were then brought together in a shared narrative. In 2004, German Chancellor Gerhard Schröder emphasized this idea by paying tribute to all soldiers who fell in the Second World War: "Through their deaths, all soldiers on all fronts were united – in the grief of their parents and wives, of their brothers and sisters and friends. We pay respect to the grief that oppresses them all." This view was particularly understandable from a man who never met his father, killed during the war: "It is only four years ago that my family found the grave of my father, a soldier who died in Romania. I have never had the chance to get to know him." Since then, all French and German leaders have confirmed that the hardship faced by soldiers and families on both sides of the Rhine was equally demanding. Nonetheless, the reconciliation narrative sets out a shared destiny, which links the two peoples not only in terms of collective martyrdom, but also in terms of collective victory. Moving beyond all the mistakes and horrors of the past, the two nations were eventually able to commemorate a common "liberation" from barbarism. In other words, the two peoples were not only brought together by grief and sacrifices, but were ultimately liberated – together – from "injustice" and "servitude."

Common victory against barbarism. This new interpretation was made possible, thanks to a differentiation between Germans and the Nazis. Thus, former French Foreign Minister Roland Dumas, whose father was a Resistance fighter and was killed in 1944, explained: "I don't confuse Nazism and the German people. That is to say that I hate fanaticism, fascism and violence, but I do respect peoples and I particularly respect the German people and their genius" (quoted by Rosoux, 2001, p.65).[2] More than two decades later, former French President François Hollande repeated the same argument when he asserted that the dignity of the "Germany of today" was to be able to face the "Nazi barbarism of

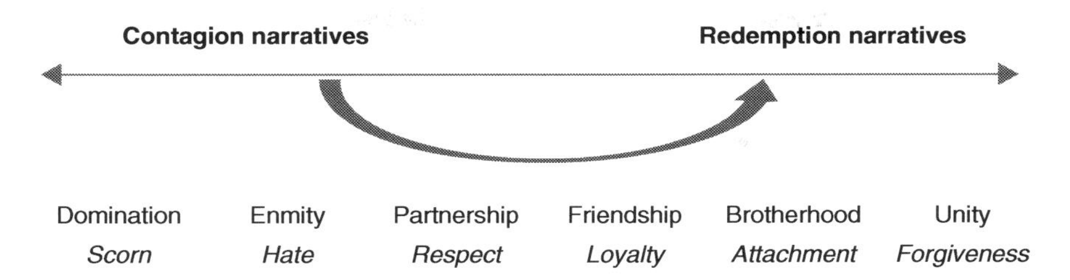

FIGURE 13.2 Narrative shift in the case of France and Germany

yesterday" (Oradour, September 4, 2013). These references are rooted in the aftermath of World War II. In as early as 1945, Joseph Rovan distinguished between Nazi Germany and *another* Germany, to be re-educated – the "Germany which we deserve" (Rovan, 1945). Likewise, when Charles de Gaulle referred, in 1958, to Germany's criminal and tyrannical past, he did so in order to draw attention to the personal heroism of German Chancellor Konrad Adenauer, who represented "a new Germany," "the Germany of today."[3]

In 1985, German President Richard von Weizsäcker expressed profound contrition for the transgressions of the Nazi past. His personal position, however, was quite different from that of Adenauer, since he joined the army in 1938 and took part in the invasion of Poland with his older brother on September 1, 1939. The next day his brother was killed just a few hundred yards from him, and he buried his brother himself. After the war, his father Ernst von Weizsäcker was tried as a war criminal and sentenced to seven years' imprisonment by the Allies, but was released in a general amnesty in 1950. This specific experience of the war made Richard von Weizsäcker's speeches particularly significant. On the 40th anniversary of the German surrender in World War II, he gave a much-celebrated statement in the Bundestag and insisted on the meaning of this defeat. Even if 8 May cannot be considered as a day of celebration for Germans, he explained, it was a "day of liberation. It liberated all of us from the inhumanity and tyranny of the National-Socialist regime."

Brothers and spouses. Nine years later, Jacques Chirac welcomed Gerhard Schröder to Caen, Normandy "as a friend" and even "as a brother" (June 6, 2004). In reply, the German Chancellor repeated one of the key arguments of the reconciliation narrative: "It is not the former Germany of these dark years that I represent today." Since then, French and Germans have alternatively been portrayed as spouses *and* brothers. In 2008, for instance, French foreign minister Bernard Kouchner used both metaphors in the same speech. He first remained faithful to his predecessors by telling the story of the "brothers beyond wars, hatred and mourning," and then finished his statement by a warning to "those who frequently predict the end of the Franco-German partnership: the marriage is a strong one!" (Berlin, April 24, 2008). The brotherhood metaphor emphasizes the destiny of nations who did not choose to be brothers, who fought against one another, and who eventually overcame their fratricidal combats (Figure 13.2).

The notion of a marriage, however, emphasizes a partnership entered into by choice. Ultimately, both analogies reflect a form of closeness – or interdependence – that French and Germans could no longer avoid. As Bernard Kouchner asserted, "[w]hen I speak about France and Germany, I say 'We' [...] When one knows history, this 'we' is immense" (April 24, 2008).

Counternarrative: The right to resentment

The reconciliation narrative can easily be romanticized. The brotherhood metaphor, for instance, has sometimes been used to describe the occasional fraternization between soldiers on the front lines. Thus, several novels and movies have told of the Christmas truce of 1914 and turned this into a fairy tale. The success of this narrative says more about the hopes and illusions shared by the populations on both sides of the Rhine than about the reality of the trenches during World War I.

Another way to romanticize a past of conflict is to associate the notions of reconciliation and forgiveness. While the concept of forgiveness was neither used by the founding fathers of Europe, nor by de Gaulle and Adenauer, some French leaders have used it to describe the process of rapprochement. Former President of the European Commission Jacques Delors believed that the notions of "promise" and "forgiveness" underpin the European integration process (Luxembourg, May 9, 2000). French President Emmanuel Macron also mentioned forgiveness when he commemorated the massacre at Oradour, where 642 men, women, and children were killed in June 1944. To him, the "scandal of Oradour" "demonstrates that we can – despite the horror, despite the barbarism, despite the wrongdoings, those of others but also our own – stand up together, able to be united and also able to forgive" (Oradour, June 10, 2017). However, the irreversibility of the crimes committed in Oradour explains why families with links to the village are highly unwilling to forgive.

This example reminds us of the limitations of the reconciliation narrative. When post-war stories are too easily based on forgiveness and family metaphors, they resonate only very little, if at all, with the vivid experience of tortured survivors or with relatives of massacred civilians. The trajectory of the Holocaust survivor Jean Améry is particularly emblematic in this regard (see Brudholm, 2008). Améry was born in Austria as Hans Maier in 1912. With the rise of the Nazi regime, Maier's Jewish ancestry became a potential liability. He then fled to Belgium where he joined the Resistance. He was soon caught, tortured by the Gestapo, and sent to a number of concentration and extermination camps including Auschwitz. Upon liberation, Maier returned to Brussels, and in 1955 he began publishing under the French pseudonym Jean Améry. In his book *Jenseits von Schuld und Sühne* (*Beyond Guilt and Atonement*), published in 1965, Améry not only refused to forgive but explicitly denounced forgiving "induced by social pressure" as immoral, and he discordantly scorned those who were "trembling with the vague pathos of forgiveness and reconciliation" (Améry,

1995, pp.65,72). Améry's story ends on a bitter note, since he took his own life in 1978. As he puts it, "the world which forgives and forgets" has sentenced him to loneliness. His words reflect the point of view of a person who has almost resigned himself to a sense of inescapable abandonment and mistrust: "Every day anew I lose my trust in the world." His attitude was not, however, unique. At about the same time, the French philosopher Vladimir Jankelevitch asserted that forgiveness "died" in the Nazi extermination camps (Jankelevitch, 1986, p.552). Three decades later, German theologian Hans Jonas made the same point, repeating that if the murderers wished for forgiveness they should go and ask the children who were burned alive (Jonas, 1994). If the survivor had a moral task to consider, it was the unending preservation of a resentful and unreconciled memory of those who were murdered (Jankelevitch, 1986, pp.565–572). This posture shows that even if the reconciliation narrative may seem deep to the younger generations, it remains shallow, artificial, or even indecent for those whose life has been irrevocably damaged. In such circumstances, the reconciliation narrative – regardless of its impact on negotiations – lacks existential depth and therefore meaning.

South Africa: Emphasis on a new narrative

The case of South Africa offers a different perspective on how narratives relate to negotiation processes. Three major differences should be highlighted. First, rather than selecting *another* story from the repertoire of available narratives, South African authorities tried to develop a *new* coherent narrative encompassing both the polarizing atrocities of the past and the hopes for future peaceful coexistence of equal citizens (Dwyer, 1999, p.91). Second, unlike in the case of France and Germany, the rapprochement between South African parties is not based on a structural approach to reconciliation, but on a spiritual one. The aim is not to create new institutional structures to address the *interests* and issues at stake, but to transform *relationships*, thanks to the healing power of forgiveness. Third, the South African transition resulted from a negotiation rather than a military defeat (as in Germany), which had huge consequences in terms of the balance of power.

Context: Radical asymmetry

For more than four decades, apartheid institutionalized racial segregation. This system of social stratification differentiated between white citizens on the one hand, and Asians, Coloureds and black Africans, on the other. This complete asymmetry was officially justified by a deep narrative of contamination that generated hatred, contempt, and fear. Unlike in the case of France and Germany, where hatred was mixed with cultural admiration anchored in secular exchanges between two interacting societies, the South African case can be summarized by signs put up in public areas: "Whites only." Yet, this constant discrimination provoked growing opposition within and outside South Africa.

International campaigns for the boycott of South African goods rapidly led to an increasing number of sanctions against the apartheid regime. The economic impact left even white South Africans dissatisfied with the government, and the often violent rivalries between the nation's black organizations intensified throughout the 1980s. In these tense circumstances, the two major political players, the outlawed anti-apartheid African National Congress (ANC) and the governing National Party (NP), perceived themselves to be in a mutually hurting stalemate. Neither could find a way out without the support of the other party (Zartman, 2000; Pruitt, 2008, p.40). Accordingly, a long negotiation process began, with secret talks from 1986 to 1990, which then led to multilateral negotiations between the apartheid government and 18 other organizations (political organizations, trade unions, and churches) to determine the rules for a transitional government.

The fact that the South African transition resulted from a negotiation rather than a military defeat had huge consequences in terms of balance of power. While the relationships between the National Party in power and the ANC had been totally asymmetrical for decades, ripeness/readiness (Pruitt, 2008) made them particularly aware of their interdependence and led them to the negotiation table. Interestingly, the dynamics are opposite in the Franco-German case. While the relationships between France and Germany had been symmetrical for decades (this was precisely one of the reasons for the almost obsessive rivalry between Paris and Berlin), they became completely asymmetrical after the crushing defeat of Germany.

Process: Spiritual approach to reconciliation

If we turn to the links between narrative and negotiation, the contrast between the two cases is also striking. In the Franco-German case, the narrative shift (coming from below, from above, and from outside) precipitated the negotiation process. In South Africa, the pre-negotiation phase consisted in back-room meetings, characterized by reconciliatory intent, but without any explicit focus on narrative shift. As Nelson Mandela explained, "the quest for reconciliation was the spur that gave life to our difficult negotiation process" (Cape Town, February 25, 1999). Yet, a new narrative emerged only later in the process, starting from above and rapidly confirmed by local and external voices. Far from being the origin of the rapprochement, the narrative of joint agency is, rather, one of its outcomes.

From above. The process led to the establishment of a Truth and Reconciliation Commission (TRC, 1996–1998) based on the philosophy of "ubuntu" (Boraine et al., 1994). Ubuntu, a Bantu word that translates roughly as "human kindness," has evolved into the philosophy that a universal shared bond connects all humanity. The traditional notion of ubuntu provided a zone of potential agreement (ZOPA) that made devising a compromise solution, somewhere between full justice and blanket amnesty, possible. To obtain

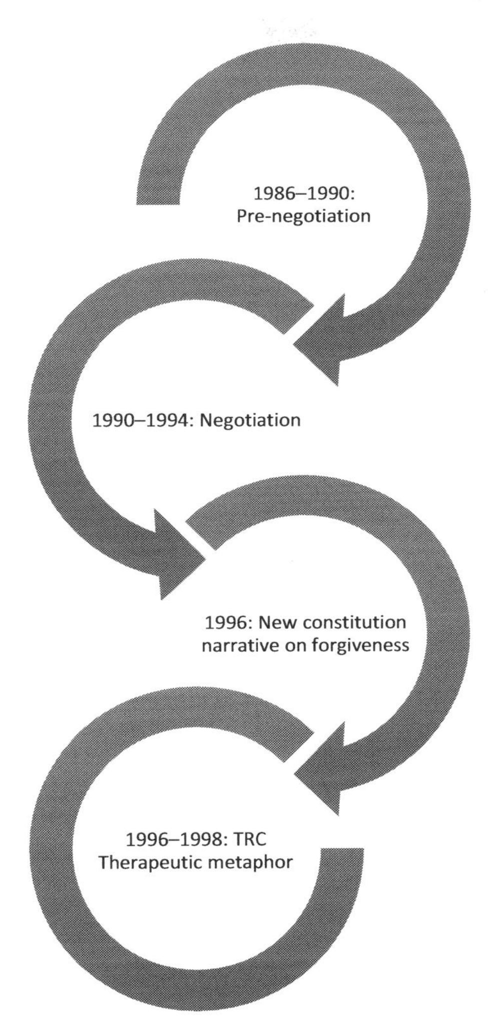

FIGURE 13.3 South African process

amnesty, an offender had to apply to the Commission, attend its hearings, and meet its requirements, including full disclosure. The purpose was not to punish offenders, but to reintegrate them into the community (Figure 13.3). It was to uncover the truth and to repair damaged communal bonds. The preamble to the new South African Constitution rejected retribution and called for past injustices to be addressed "on the basis that there is a need for understanding but not for vengeance, a need for reparation but not for retaliation."

Nevertheless, it would be naive to be too optimistic regarding this objective of restorative justice. Memory work in post-1994 South Africa was above all shaped by political constraints. Amnesty for human rights offenders was decided by a political deal between the outgoing political elite (the National Party) and the African National Congress (ANC). In other words, the TRC was a compromise solution forced on the country by the fact that those who had power were not going to surrender it without guarantees that they would not be prosecuted after stepping down.

From below. Human rights organizations played a certain role once the political settlement was struck between the two main political parties. They did a great deal of lobbying between the passing of the interim constitution and the National Unity and Reconciliation Act in 1995. Consequently, they prevented a blanket amnesty and were able to shape the form that the amnesty would eventually take. Groups such as the citizenship rights group Justice in Transition, headed by Alex Boraine, and the Centre for the Study of Violence and Reconciliation played a significant role in framing the terms of the Commission. Their impact on the negotiations was limited but still decisive. Moreover, a wide range of reconciliation initiatives, launched by local NGOs as well as church-based groups, included processes of restorative justice dialogue, local community healing meetings, and memorialization projects. External actors also played a decisive role in stigmatizing the apartheid regime. Nevertheless, the replacement of a narrative of contamination by one of redemption was not at all imposed from outside.

As in the Franco-German case, the rapprochement was advocated by key nodal actors. After 27 years in prison, Nelson Mandela asked the population to undergo a transformation that he has undergone himself – that is, to overcome resentment towards the former enemy. According to him, "reconciliation is a spiritual process, which requires more than just a legal framework. It has to happen in the hearts and minds of people" (Mthatha, September 18, 1994). Similarly, the personal role of Archbishop Desmond Tutu was decisive in terms of both credibility and mobilization. Their respective calls for a peaceful transition activated local networks in the whole country.

The establishment of the TRC literally shaped the post-apartheid master narrative. Aside from its frequently described shortcomings, it had at least one merit: it opened the floor to victims of each side and gave them a chance to "tell their story." The hope was that the process of talking would somehow alleviate the sufferings endured in silence for so long (Cobban, 2007). The television broadcasting, and more largely the wide dissemination of victims' testimonies, wiped out the possibility of denial and rendered some lies about the past impossible to repeat (Garton, 1997; Ignatieff, 2001). In 2003, the TRC issued its final report and recommended that reparations be paid to apartheid victims, urging businesses to contribute along with the government. To the commissioners, these reparations constituted "a matter of national urgency and honor," and the only way to give the victims of apartheid "closure with dignity" (Thompson, 2003). The South African government made a modest one-time payment to 21,000 individuals who were formally registered as victims by the Commission,[4] but it refused to release the remaining money reserved for reparations. Criticisms of the government's apparent reluctance to provide reparations grew (Colvin, 2006, p.177) and numerous voices denounced the contrast between the immediate granting of amnesty to perpetrators and the failure to compensate victims. For them, the equilibrium of the original agreement had been upset (Backer, 2010).

Narrative: A rainbow nation

The negotiations that made the transition to democracy possible were explicitly based on the need to acknowledge "grey zones" that occurred in the past and to undertake a common "work of memory" intended to "heal" the nation. This healing metaphor is based on the assumption that revealing is healing. Official statements insisted heavily on the wounds of all protagonists ("ANC wounds," "wounds of our people," "national healing," "wounds of the past"). In brief, the "grammar of suffering" became the template to script all stories, from victims to perpetrators (Moon, 2008, p.167).

From this psychological perspective, the process of reconciliation is understood as a "cathartic process" and a "narrative incorporation" of conflictual memories (Dwyer, 1990). To merge victims' personal stories into some sort of coherent narrative, South African authorities did not promote the shift from enmity to brotherhood (as in the Franco-German case), but the even more demanding transition from domination to unity. To Archbishop Desmond Tutu, this maximalist perspective required not only new common institutions, but also – and above all – the transformation of relationships based on forgiveness (Tutu, 2000). In his view, this attitude does not pretend

> that things are other than they really are – forgiveness can be confrontational telling it as it is, looking the beast in the eye. Forgiveness is letting go of your right to retaliation. It is like opening a window to let the fresh air rush into a dark closed room.

"To forgive," he continues, "is not being altruistic; it is the best form of self-interest" (Tutu, 2003). This "confessional narrative" (Moon, 2008, p.92) was presented as a key condition for building "a different and better society for all" (seventh volume of the TRC report), a *new* South Africa – the parallel with

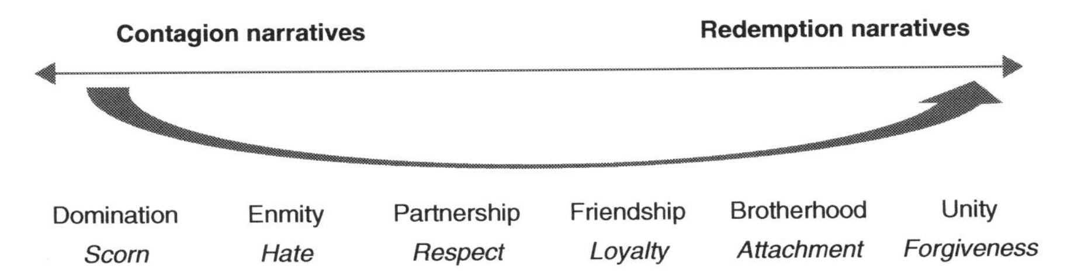

FIGURE 13.4 Narrative shift in the South African case

the *new* Germany is striking, a "rainbow nation at peace with itself" (Mandela, Pretoria, May 10, 1994).

Common victory over political oppression. In this line of argument, the TRC appears as a ritual to examine the past and to place it on record (Ross, 1997, p.10). The narrative emphasized throughout the process was based on the condemnation of all human rights violations, whether they emanated from the State or from those who fought for liberation.

In considering all sides' crimes, the TRC did not adopt a "moral equivalence position" towards actions taken to uphold an unjust system and ones taken to destroy that system (Cherry, 2000), but it described post-apartheid transition as a common victory over oppression. As Nelson Mandela asserted, the fundamental objective of this narrative shift is to turn "one of the world's most notorious symbols of racist oppression into a world-wide icon of the universality of human rights" (Mandela, Robben Island, September 24, 1997).

To achieve this goal, Mandela promoted "a common understanding of our history," which was fundamentally future-oriented (Cape Town, February 25, 1999). Even if the TRC focused on past abuses, its goal was not to dwell on the past, but to address it in order to move forward (Figure 13.4). This "narrative of becoming" abolished racial classifications and highlighted victims and perpetrators who were fundamentally all in need of healing (Moon, 2008, pp.87,102).

Counternarrative: The right to justice

At the end of the day, the TRC faced many criticisms and resulted in controversies and disputes. The fundamental objection was that it had somehow sacrificed the rights of victims and survivors and their legitimate need for justice. To cite an example, Churchill Mxenge, the brother of an assassinated activist, Griffiths Mxenge, objected: "Unless justice is done it's difficult for any person to think of forgiving" (Rosenberg, 1996, p.88). This statement recalls once again that the national process of making amends rarely coincides with individual processes.

From a philosophical perspective, the political use of forgiveness raises the sensitive question of double delegation. Who can ask for forgiveness and who can grant it? Can families of victims forgive on behalf of the dead? The reaction of Joyce Mtimkulu towards those who had applied to the TRC for amnesty for their killing of her son is emblematic. Siphiwo was 21, and the father of two children, when he was arrested, poisoned, and detained for six months in 1981. The rat poison did not kill him, but confined him to a wheelchair. The security police arrested him again. After being interrogated, he was shot, his body was burnt and his remains thrown into the Fish River. After years of uncertainty and anguish about the fate of her son, Joyce Mtimkulu felt outraged by the application for amnesty of those who tortured and secretly killed her son: "They are not asking forgiveness from us, the people who have lost their loved ones. They are asking forgiveness from the government. They did not do nothing to the government. What they did, they did to us" (quoted by Biggar, 2003, p.316). These words are interesting in at least three regards. First, they show that forgiveness is not necessarily a virtue, especially if it affects the dignity and self-respect of victims (Chapman, 2008, p.67). They also indicate that the healing of wounds remains an intimate process that cannot be handled by an institutional structure. Finally, they reveal a high degree of disillusionment and anger that characterized a large population in the townships.

Beyond this individual example, the deep frustration of victims who have been waiting in vain for some form of reparation, and the bitterness of a white minority that became increasingly defensive, remind us that the country is still deeply divided by the legacy of apartheid. Admittedly, the narrative shift undeniably contributed to the non-reoccurrence of violence and to more constructive negotiation processes at all levels. Nonetheless, it did not radically modify the life stories of a whole population. As is underlined in the final report of the TRC, "[l]anguage, discourse and rhetoric does things: it constructs social categories, it gives orders, it persuades us, it justifies, explains, gives reasons, excuses."[5] However, a change of narrative alone is not enough to bring closure. Important as it is, it is not sufficient to compensate for sustained levels of unemployment and poverty for so many people.

Conclusion: The tyranny of harmony

In post-conflict settings, the succession of generations does not systematically involve the creation of new interpretations of the past. Master narratives that simplify the past, stigmatize the other, and gratify one's own group are persistent. Yet, both case studies demonstrate that leaders can adopt new postures and renounce narratives of contamination. By relentlessly stressing that they were "all in the same boat," French, German, and South African authorities have constantly accentuated the interdependence that binds their fellow citizens. In terms of sequencing, two distinct dynamics took place. In the Franco-German case, a dramatic change of narratives favoured integrative negotiation processes, both multilateral and bilateral. In the case of South Africa, long secret "talks before the talks" helped to shape a whole new narrative that completely broke with apartheid.

In both cases, the focus on reconciliation offered an uncomplicated story line to replace the former premises (based respectively on hereditary enmity and white supremacy). Despite a radical change of plots (from "we hate them" to "we are brothers," and from "we dominate them" to "we are equal"), reconciliation appeared as a familiar theme to the general public. It played an important role in breaking the deadlock and initiating a virtuous circle in terms of negotiations. However, counternarratives coming from below show that some protagonists pay a higher price than others for reconciliation. In both cases, some resisting voices remind us that the issue cannot be reduced to the iconic pictures of handshakes between former adversaries. Narrative shifts matter, but they do not constitute a magical solution to transform enemies into "friends" (Kupchan, 2010).

At the end of this analysis, three main lessons should be emphasized. First, if master narratives differ too much from the experience lived and/or transmitted by particular groups, they effectively exclude them. This is not only a moral issue, but also a political and very pragmatic one. Without the support of the population, modifications made to official memory are sterile and in vain. In this regard, the attitude adopted towards hatred is symptomatic. The eagerness to renounce hate-based narratives is particularly appropriate in terms of conflict transformation. Nevertheless, this change in direction should not systematically lead to the negation of victims' emotions. To most survivors, hatred and resentment are not only understandable, but also necessary for self-respect and justice (Murphy, 2003, p.19; Hamber and Wilson, 2002, p.47). It is therefore critical not to accentuate a binary distinction between "pathological emotions" and desired feelings (Neu, 2008, p.33). Although reconciliation processes increase social capital and integrative negotiation, they can decrease individual well-being – at least for some victims (Cilliers et al., 2016). If the experience narrated by these victims is simply and purely ignored, their anger – and in some cases despair – will likely increase. Research carried out to date shows that these strong emotions are transmitted from one generation to the next, which means that victims' drive for truth and justice does not evaporate with the mere passage of time (Hamber, 2002, p.76; Rosoux, 2020).

Second, contrary to popular belief, the best outcome of negotiation is not a "shared narrative." A view of reconciliation as a gradual incorporation of narratives does not imply that the ultimate goal should be to share a consensual reading of the past. In the aftermath of mass atrocities, no single narrative, however unifying it might seem to be, can address the identity needs of the parties in an uncontested way. Some consensus may be reached on "forensic facts" established by historians and/or judges. This step is decisive for preventing denial and revisionism. It also allows the transition from contradictory to divergent narratives, which is already remarkable. Expecting more than that after mass crimes is unrealistic and even undesirable. Both case studies argue in favour of reconciliation as a process of taming differences, rather than eliminating them (Gardner Feldman, 2002, p.337). Moreover, the existence of a plurality of narratives does not systematically jeopardize negotiations. The question is not whether several narratives exist, but whether they are compatible and resonate with people's lived experience.

Third, a narrative shift may be a necessary pre-condition for forward-looking outcome processes, but it is not a sufficient one. In the absence of decent reparation measures, for instance, narratives of forgiveness cannot provide the miraculous "stickiness" to act as "political glue" able to keep former adversaries together (see the introduction to this book). Since reconciliation is an open-ended process characterized by slowdowns and setbacks, the persistence of deep structural divisions inevitably provokes backtracking and even sometimes fatal U-turns (Rosoux and Anstey, 2017). In this respect, narratives can constitute crucial points of departure, but not definitive points of closure.

Notes

1 ["Nous avons vu ce que les hommes ne 'doivent' pas voir; ce n'est pas traduisible par le langage. Haine et pardon n'y répondent pas davantage »] (Antelme, 2005, p.19).
2 During the war, German opponents of Hitler emphasized the same distinction. To give only one example, Friedrich Reck-Malleczewen (who was later arrested and died at the Dachau concentration camp) reacted to the German invasion of Poland in a few words: "Thus, the Nazis (since I refuse to say 'the Germans' in this respect), the Nazis are the victors" (Reck-Malleczewen, 2017, p.161).
3 When Adolf Hitler came to power in 1933, Adenauer was dismissed from all the posts he held. After intermittent persecution, he was held prisoner by the Gestapo for several months as an enemy of the regime, after the failed assassination attempt on Hitler.
4 Each victim registered by the TRC received a payment of R30,000 ($6,417). This was about a quarter of what the TRC had recommended.
5 *Final report* of the South African Truth and Reconciliation Commission, vol.4, para124, p.294. The seven volumes of the Report were presented to President Nelson Mandela on October 29, 1998 – www.justice.gov.za/trc/report/.

References

Ackermann, A. (1994) 'Reconciliation as a Peace-Building Process in Post-War Europe: The Franco-German Case', *Peace and Change*, vol.19, no.3, pp.229–250.

Améry, J. (1995) *Par-delà le crime et le châtiment. Essai pour surmonter le mal.* Paris, France: Actes Sud.

Anderson, B. (1983) *Imagined Communities: Reflections on the Origin and Spread of Nationalism.* Revised Ed. New York, NY: Verso.

Antelme, R. (2005) *Vengeance.* Paris, France: Farrago.

Backer, D. (2010) 'Watching a Bargain Unravel? A Panel Study of Victims' Attitudes about Transitional Justice in Cape Town, South Africa', *The International Journal of Transitional Justice*, vol. 4, pp.443–456.

Bernanos, G. (2014) *Les grand cimetières sous la lune.* Paris, France: Points.

Biggar, N. (Ed.). (2003) *Burying the Past. Making Peace and Doing Justice after Civil Conflicts.* Washington, DC: Georgetown University Press.

Boraine, A., Levy, J., and, Scheffer, R. (Eds.). (1994) *Dealing with the Past: Truth and Reconciliation Commission in South Africa.* Cape Town, South Africa: Institute for Democracy in South Africa.

Brudholm, T. (2008) *Resentment's Virtue: Jean Améry and the Refusal to Forgive.* Philadelphia, PA: Temple University Press.

Bucaille, L. (2019) *Making Peace with Your Enemy. Algerian, French, and South African Ex-Combatants.* Philadelphia, PA: University of Pennsylvania Press.

Chapman, A. (2008) 'Perspectives on the Role of Forgiveness in the Human Rights Violations Hearings', In A. Chapman, and H. van der Merwe (Eds.), *Truth and Reconciliation in South Africa. Did the TRC Deliver?* (pp.66–89). Philadelphia, PA: University of Pennsylvania Press.

Cherry, J. (2000) "Just War' and 'Just Means': Was the TRC wrong about the ANC?', *Transformation*, vol.42, pp.9–28.

Cilliers, J., Dube, O., and, Siddiqi, B. (2016) Reconciling after Civil Conflict Increases Social Capital but Decreases Individual Well-Being, *Science*, vol.352, no.6287, pp.787–794.

Cobban, H. (2007) *Amnesty after Atrocity? Healing Nations after Genocide and War Crimes.* Boulder, CO: Paradigm Publishers.

Cobb, S. (2013) *Speaking of Violence. The Politics and Poetics of Narrative in Conflict Resolution.* Oxford: Oxford University Press.

Colvin, C.J. (2006) 'Overview of the Reparations Program in South Africa', In, P. de Greiff (Ed.), *The Handbook of Reparations* (pp.176–214). Oxford: Oxford University Press.

Dalsheim, J. (2014) *Producing Spoilers: Peacemaking and the Production of Enmity in a Secular Age.* Oxford: Oxford University Press.

Dwyer, S. (1999) 'Reconciliation for Realists', *Ethics and International Affairs*, vol.13, no.1, pp.81–98.

Forsberg, T. (2003) 'The Philosophy and Practice of Dealing with the Past', In N. Biggar (Ed.). *Burying the Past. Making Peace and Doing Justice after Civil Conflicts* (pp.65–84). Washington, DC: Georgetown University Press.

Gardner Feldman, L. (2002). 'The principle and practice of 'reconciliation' in German foreign policy: Relations with France, Israel, Poland and the Czech Republic', *International Affairs*, vol.75, No2, pp. 333–356.

Gardner-Feldman, L. (2012) *Germany's Foreign Policy of Reconciliation. From Enmity to Amity.* Lanham, MD: Rowman & Littlefield.

Garton, A.T. (1997, July 17) 'True Confessions', *The New York Review of Books.*

Grosser, A. (1967) *French Foreign Policy under de Gaulle.* Boston, MA: Little Brown.

Gerstenmaier, E. (1964) 'L'influence de la France sur le sentiment national en Allemagne', *Articles et documents*, vol.1606, no.2.

Hamber, B. (2002) 'Ere Their Story Die': Truth, Justice and Reconciliation in South Africa', *Race and Class*, vol.44, no.1, pp.61–79.

Hamber, B., and, Wilson, R. (2002) 'Symbolic Closure through Memory, Reparation and Revenge in Post-Conflict Societies', *Journal of Human Rights*, vol.1, no.1, pp.35–53.

Harper, C. (2006) 'Mediator as Peacemaker: The Case for Activist Transformative-Narrative Mediation', *Journal of Dispute Resolution*, vol.2, pp.595–611.

Hobsbawm, E., and, Ranger, T. (1992) *The Invention of Tradition.* Cambridge: Cambridge University Press.

Ignatieff, M. (2001, October 13) *Something Happened*, The Guardian.

Jankelevitch, V. (1986) *L'imprescriptible.* Paris, France: Seuil.

Jonas, H. (1994) *Le concept de dieu après Auschwitz.* Paris, France: Rivage.

Krondorfer, B. (Ed.) (2018) *Reconciliation in Global Context.* New York, NY: State University of New York Press.

Kupchan, C. (2010) *How Enemies Become Friends: The Sources of Stable Peace.* Princeton, NJ: Princeton University Press.

Maddison, S. (2016) *Conflict Transformation and Reconciliation: Multi-level Challenges in Deeply Divided Societies.* New York, NY: Routledge.

Moon, C. (2008) *Narrating Political Reconciliation: South Africa's Truth and Reconciliation Commission.* Lanham, MD: Lexington Books.

Murphy, J.C. (2003) *Getting Even: Forgiveness and its Limits.* Oxford: Oxford University Press.

Neu, J. (2008, Summer/Fall) 'Rehabilitating Resentment and Choosing What We Feel', *Criminal Justice Ethics*, vol.27, no.2, pp.31–37.

Peyrefitte, A. (1994) *C'était de Gaulle.* Paris, France: Fayard.

Pruitt, D. (2008) 'Back-channel Communication in the Settlement of Conflict', *International Negotiation*, vol.13, pp.37–54.

Puchala, D. (1970) 'Integration and Disintegration in Franco-German Relations, 1954–1965', *International Organization*, vol.24, no.2, pp.183–208.
Reck-Malleczewen, F. (2017) *La haine et la honte. Journal d'un aristocrate allemand 1936–1944.* Paris, France: Perrin.
Rosenberg, T. (1996, November 18) *Recovering from Apartheid*, New Yorker.
Rosoux, V. (2001) *Les usages d ela mémoire dans les relations internationales.* Brussels, Belgium: Bruylant.
Rosoux, V. (2008) 'Reconciliation as a Peace-Building Process: Scope and Limits', In J. Bercovitch, V. Kremenyuk, and I.W. Zartman (Eds.), *The Sage Handbook of Conflict Resolution* (pp.543–560). London: Sage.
Rosoux, V., and, Anstey, M. (Eds.) (2017) *Negotiating Reconciliation in Peacemaking.* Cham: Springer.
Rosoux, V. (2020) 'Negotiating on Behalf of Previous Generations: Justice in Post-Conflict Contexts,' *International Negotiation*, vol.25, pp.93–108.
Ross, F. (1997) 'Blood Feuds and Childbirth: The TRC as Ritual.' *Track Two*, vol.6, no.3&4. https://journals.co.za/docserver/fulltext/track2/6/3-4/track2_v6_n3_a4.pdf?expires=1592919579&id=id&accname=guest&checksum=6611F97E2C2488C2D8CF2A31D1CFE0A0.
Rovan, J. (1945) 'L'Allemagne de nos mérites,' *Esprit*, vol.115, pp.529–540.
Sangar, E. (2020) *Diffusion in Franco-German Relations. A Different Perspective on a History of Cooperation and Conflict.* Cham: Palgrave Macmillan.
Thompson, G. (2003, March 22) *South African Commission Ends Its Work*, New York Times.
Tutu, D. (2000) *No Future Without Forgiveness.* London: New Ed.
Tutu, D. (2003) 'Speech: No Future Without Forgiveness,' *Archbishop Desmond Tutu Collection Textual.* 15, https://digitalcommons.unf.edu/cgi/viewcontent.cgi?article=1014&context=archbishoptutupapers.
von Kageneck, A. (2004) *Examen de conscience.* Paris, France: Perrin.
Wertsch, J., and, Billinsley, D. (2011) 'The Role of Narratives in Commemoration: Remembering as Mediated Action', In H. Anheier and, R.I. Yudhishthir (Eds.), *Heritage, Memory and Identity* (pp.25–38). New York, NY: Sage.
Zartman, I.W. (2000) 'Ripeness: The Hurting Stalemate and Beyond', In, P. Stern and D. Druckman (Eds.), *International Conflict Resolution after the Cold War* (pp.225–250). Washington, DC: National Academy Press.
Zartman, I.W., and, Kremenyuk, V. (Eds.). (2005) *Peace versus Justice: Negotiating Forward- and Backward-Looking Outcomes.* Lanham, MD: Rowman & Littlefield Publishers.
Zerubavel, E. (2003) *Time Maps: Collective Memory and the Social Shape of the Past.* Chicago, IL: University of Chicago Press.

14

DISCORDANT NARRATIVES

India and the US in the Indo-Pacific

Samir Saran and Akhil Deo[1]

Introduction: The first Indo-Pacific power

The "Indo-Pacific" as a strategic construct is increasingly gaining currency as a means of conceptualizing the interdependence of states, markets, and communities in the Indian and Pacific Oceans. As a geographical expansion of the "Asia-Pacific," the construct ostensibly captures an organic phenomenon: the movement of people, capital, trade, energy, and information flows across the two oceans. It is also, in part, a recognition of India's rise and expanding integration with Asia and Africa. Geopolitically, the Indo-Pacific has emerged as a theatre of engagement for a coalition of democracies to respond to China's Belt and Road Initiative (BRI), and by extension, Beijing's propositions for regional and world order.

Our study of the various geo-strategic narratives shaping the region begins with China because it was the first nation to have defined and then developed the Indo-Pacific while refraining from labelling it as such. As one half of its multi-continental ambition under the BRI, the maritime silk route connects China to three continents. Official documents describe three central "routes": (PRC, 2015) The first extends from China, across the Indian Ocean and onwards to the Mediterranean Sea, connecting China with Europe, the Gulf, and East Africa. The second integrates China's prosperous coastal provinces with the South East and South Asian littorals. And the third connects China to Europe via the Arctic, through the "Polar" Silk Road. It is apparent that much of China's planned theatre of operations encompasses the region that the US and India refer to as the Indo-Pacific.

Even as it added substance to the BRI designs, China was quick to realize that the rise of post-colonial Asia also required a new vocabulary. The new narratives had to project and propel Asia's communities and markets towards Europe and

DOI: 10.4324/9781003203209-17

Africa, gradually eroding the political boundaries established after WWII. At another level, these constructs would also need to position China at the centre of these political, economic, and security arrangements. In the conversations that have flowed thereafter, China has had animated discussions on both existing concepts such as Eurasia and newer processes like the Indo-Pacific.

Despite being the first indigenous Indo-Pacific power, China explicitly rejects this formulation, describing it as an "attention-grabbing idea that will dissipate like foam" (Birtles, 2019). In its July 2019 Defense White Paper, China continued to use Asia-Pacific to describe the region (Xinhua, 2019). Beijing's deep disdain for this new construct is best understood by examining the discourse that underpins its outlook and behaviour towards this region. Two interrelated narratives stand out: the pursuit of a "China Dream"; and efforts to build a sinicized international order, or what General Secretary Xi Jinping calls, a "community of common destiny." In their introductory paper, Hampson and Narlikar provide a useful typology of narratives, two of which are particularly suited to how China interacts with the world. First, the narratives of redemption—with the Xi administration framing its policies as being essential to overcoming its "century of humiliation" and to become a "global leader in terms of influence" by 2049. Second, are "deep" narratives—those that are crucial to the identity of social groups or national states and do not lend themselves easily to negotiation and compromise. As this paper will seek to bring to the fore, these narratives indeed define China's rise and growing influence, and make it less willing to negotiate equitable terms with other nations and limit the scope of concessions it is willing to make.

The return of history

At the WEF 2017 in Davos, General Secretary Xi emerged as an unlikely champion of globalization—juxtaposing himself against the then recently elected Donald Trump, who campaigned on a nationalist economic agenda (Parker, 2017). To the communist party, the financial crisis of 2008 and the populist surge of 2016 in the US were the moments of vindication—a testament to the resilience of China's development model and an implicit failing of democracy and capitalism. To Chinese leaders and scholars, Xi's claim to leadership at the WEF was an important moment in global politics (Tiezzi, 2018). It heralded a start of a period where China, having overcome its "century of humiliation" under an imperial West, was living up to its destiny with the Belt and Road Initiative heralding the return of the Middle Kingdom. Both the Eurasian route and the maritime route were launched amidst much cultural and mythical fanfare—extolling the virtues of past Chinese explorers, the cultural and social ties between China and the world, and China's economic leadership.

These narratives are a projection of a more significant political realignment in Beijing: what Xi calls the "great rejuvenation of the Chinese nation" or the "China Dream"—a process that will ostensibly culminate on the founding centenary of the People's Republic of China in 2049 (Saran and Deo, 2019). This thinly veiled narrative of Chinese exceptionalism has motivated a wide range of state endeavours in China, from addressing development challenges to emerging as a science and technology superpower (Saran and Deo, 2019). One such ambition is control over strategic trade routes, and consequently, the ability to set the terms of commerce and security. The ideal of becoming a naval power pre-dates the Xi administration, but has gained significant traction during his tenure (Xinhua, 2012). Xi has signalled that China intends to become a "maritime superpower" by mid-century—a process that is explicitly linked to geo-economic and maritime security efforts (McDevitt, 2016, p.9).

Complementing this "return to history" is China's strategic disregard for, and delegitimization of, the norms and institutions for sovereignty, trade, and security that have managed continental and maritime Asia. Consider as evidence, the following four developments over the past decade. First, China's militarization of the South China Sea (SCS) and refusal to adhere to the Hague Tribunals' ruling on the disputed region (Aneja, 2016). Second, Beijing's investments in the China-Pakistan Economic Corridor, an infrastructure project that passes through the contested territory of Pakistan-occupied Kashmir (Bhattacherjee, 2019). Third, the transfer of Sri Lanka's Hambantota port to China to offset debts (Ondaatjie and Sirimanne, 2019). Fourth, instigating a near regional conflict with India over Doklam (Wuthnow et al., 2018)—and most recently a bloody skirmish in Ladakh as well (Pubby and Anshuman, 2020).

There is a method to China's actions. The Chinese Communist Party (CCP) bears an enduring grudge against the Western order—and sees the Indo-Pacific construct as another extension of an old political order that once constrained its rise (see: Yamazaki, 2020; Lius, 2020). As discussed already, the extent to which Beijing has internalized its narrative of redemption makes it harder for China to "negotiate" or compromise with several other nations in its own periphery and around the world. With India and the ASEAN littorals, for instance, Beijing has repeatedly eschewed negotiations and adherence to international law in favour of territorial revisionism. This is despite the fact that India (see: Basu, 2020; Krishnan, 2020) and ASEAN member states (Zhou, 2020) have repeatedly demonstrated a preference to settle matters with China through established dialogue mechanisms.

It is, therefore, no surprise that Beijing rejects this new political map of maritime Asia that it views as antithetical to its rise. This is not new. China has always disregarded all political and economic arrangements of Asia's sub-regions that fail to adhere to its evolving whims. To China, West, South, or East Asia have always been 20th-century constructs ill-suited to a continent that is fast reintegrating and are remnants of a history that needs to be corrected. In their estimation, the Indo-Pacific has significant negative consequences to its ever-expanding network of infrastructure and influence across Eurasia, Africa, and maritime Asia and to its pan-continental ambition.

A community of common destiny underpinned by socialism with Chinese characteristics

Bear in mind that China's behaviour in the Indo-Pacific is shaped not by a regional strategy, but a global one. At the 19th Party Congress in 2017, General Secretary Xi announced that China intended to be a "global leader in terms of international influence" by the middle of the century. He engaged with this in much greater detail at the 2018 Central Foreign Affairs Work Conference (CFAWC), a forum intended to guide China's diplomatic establishment (Xinhua, 2018). Two key messages emanated from this forum. First, Xi called for China to "take an active part in leading the reform of the global governance system" (Xinhua, 2018) across its various political, economic, security, and developmental dimensions. Second, Xi explicitly added an ideological element to China's foreign policy—calling for "diplomacy of socialism with Chinese characteristics" (Xinhua, 2018). In the past, this phrase applied mostly to China's domestic ideological system, representing its unique brand of political authoritarianism and state managed capitalism. For the first time at the CFAWC, the CCP indicated that it would actively "externalize" or globalize its internal arrangements and value systems.

China behaves this way now because it continues to see a period of strategic opportunity for itself in the international system, although it is aware that escalating tensions with the US and other parts of the world will bring this to an end. It sees the US systematically undermining several multilateral agendas and institutions, including on climate change (Cohen, 2019), regional peace and security (*Europe*, 2020), and trade (Miles, 2019). Where Mao's China would have resisted fully participating in these processes and institutions due to their "Western control," Xi's China sees an opening in the West's retreat. China now seeks to recast global processes and institutions in a direction that protects and advances China's core national interests (*China's Approach*, 2020). The recent outbreak of a novel strain of the Coronavirus in Wuhan, China allowed the international community a glimpse into this behaviour. So normalized was China's influence over the World Health Organization's (WHO) and the International Civil Aviation Organizations' (ICAO) position on Taiwan that these institutions failed to include Taipei in their response to an international health crisis (Wert, 2020; *Taiwan,* 2020). The ICAO even went so far as to ape China's domestic censorship behaviour, questionably blocking voices on Twitter critical of its Taiwan policy (Ebrahimian, 2020).

Taken together, these tools guide China's efforts at achieving the "China Dream" and "building a community of common destiny"—amorphous and ever-evolving narratives intended to offer an alternative to the International Liberal Order (see: Tobin, 2018). That these narratives are "deep" and not prone to compromise is evident now from China's behaviour as much as from nations that engage with it. The European Union (EU), for instance, has come to accept that Beijing is now a "systemic rival" (Small, 2019); the Scott Morrison administration was willing to call for an independent enquiry into the cause and location of the COVID-19 outbreak despite the threat of economic coercion from China (Karp and Davidson, 2020); and the Indian government has decided to revise the "rules of engagement" at the Line of Actual control with China after a particularly gruesome military skirmish in Ladakh (Srinivasan, 2020). These measures and policy decisions reflect, to a large extent, the sentiment that engagement with China has proved counterproductive or ineffective.

This same instinct also shapes its behaviour in the Indo-Pacific. Although the term "community of common destiny" lacks a precise definition, several aspects of China's behaviour in the Indo-Pacific can be attributed to its proposition for this new era: a regionalism backed by the BRI where smaller states are subservient to China's economic and strategic preferences (Xinhua, 2017; PRC, 2013); Beijing's influence over international institutions and rule setting bodies (Ying, 2017); Chinese leadership in future technologies, including AI, 5G, and IoT across the Indo-Pacific (Yong, 2019); the expansion of its military and maritime interests (Jiayao, 2018); and a China-backed regional security order (PRC, 2014).

Trading old injustices for new inequities

Under General Secretary Xi, China's bid for global leadership has resulted in new balance of power arrangements in Eurasia and the Indo-Pacific; with sub-regional and middle powers either contesting, being coerced by, or supporting the "sinification" of Asia. In the process of ostensibly correcting old injustices, China has created a contradiction for itself by producing new inequities. The underlying narratives that shape China's behaviour have posed crucial questions for Asian actors and identities. "At issue," we wrote earlier, "is whether nation-states that exercised their hard-won right to self-determination and democracy will now be forced into a client-satellite relationship with Beijing as its economic dominance continues" (Saran, 2018). China's propositions will not be uncontested—and the interplay between competing visions of the region has catalyzed another important shift in the discourse of Asia's rise: from the Asia-Pacific to the Indo-Pacific.

Shift in the Western narrative: From the Asia-Pacific to the Indo-Pacific

As discursive instruments, regional constructs help states define the reason behind and the breadth of their political, economic, and strategic interactions. The narrative of and around the Asia-Pacific was born at a period when globalization was driven by favourable winds and new markets and business opportunities were the primary capitalist urge. It was also, as Hampson and Narlikar's framework would suggest, a narrative of "agency"; capturing the zeal and enthusiasm of markets in Asia to integrate with those in the Atlantic countries and the determination of the US to project itself as an Asian power. It was explicitly a positive-sum narrative. The locus of its sway was primarily the politics, markets, and communities in East and South East Asia. The economic rise of Japan and Korea, followed by Taiwan, the ASEAN and most importantly, China were significant constituents and consequences of the Asia-Pacific story.

The emergence of the Indo-Pacific is far removed from this reality of the 20th century. It is a narrative born amidst the dynamic interplay of cooperation with accelerating contest and competition. It captures the near-simultaneous rise of maritime Asia and the resurgence of old civilizational disputes. It also gives shape to realignments in the international balance of power and reveals the fault lines along which the battle for leadership of the 21st century is playing out. Responding to the political, economic, and maritime security risks posed by China's rise is arguably the raison d' être for the emergence of the Indo-Pacific. China's naval expansion, coupled with its "debt-trap diplomacy" through the BRI, has left other powers concerned about the emerging client-state architecture Beijing is creating in Asia. An escalation of long-running territorial disputes in the South China Sea and the Himalayas; rising instances of economic coercion in East and South East Asia; and targeted influence operations in New Zealand (NZ) and Australia all indicate that China's rise will compel states to adopt stronger security postures.

Even as the security challenges continue to multiply, the Indo-Pacific will take shape in a period of unravelling economic interdependence. The US and China—arguably the most critical drivers of globalization—are insulating their technology supply chains from vulnerability to each other. Prospects for successful negotiations on this front seem especially dim considering that the narratives of perverse dependence are increasingly becoming "deep," in that they are being entrenched across a wide range of commercial and national security choices (Gewirtz, 2020; U.S. Department of State, 2020; Saha and Feng, 2020). This phenomenon will lead to a fragmentation of well-integrated production lines and force Indo-Pacific states to make uncomfortable and sub-optimal decisions about their economic partnerships. The onset of the Fourth Industrial Revolution (4IR) has only complicated the challenge. Digital trade barriers are on the rise, threatening future prospects for integration. States in the region are uncertain about regulating and creating local value from the digital economy, leading to a proliferation of measures such as data localization, digital "taxes" and restrictions on e-commerce. It is no surprise that most major trade negotiations have seen discord and division, including the erstwhile Trans-Pacific Partnership, the Comprehensive and Progressive Agreement for Trans-Pacific Partnership (TPP minus America), or the Regional Comprehensive Economic Partnership.

Periphery to centre

These structural changes are not unexpected. They are indicators of Maritime Asia's importance to the world. The Asia-Pacific is better thought of as an extension of the Atlantic System; its networks of alliances, rules for international trade and commerce, and enforcement of international security. The Indo-Pacific on the other hand is likely to be the global economic and strategic centre of gravity for the international system in the 21st century. Numbers alone elevate its importance: Over two-thirds of the world's trade pass through these waters; the fastest growing militaries operate in this region, collectively accounting for a third of the world's defence expenditure; the region hosts 65 percent of the world's population and produces nearly 60 percent of the global GDP (U.S. Department of Defense, 2019). Given the region's economic and strategic potential, it is inevitable that the "destiny of the world will be deeply influenced by the course of developments in the Indo-Pacific region" as Prime Minister Modi suggested in 2018 (Government of India, 2019).

And so, it is unsurprising that the Indo-Pacific has attracted the attention of the world's powers. Popular discourse ordinarily surrounds the four countries that revived the Quadrilateral Initiative—the US, India, Australia, and Japan. However, these are far from the only powers motivated to stake claims in the region. The narratives shaping this region do not fit easily into the typologies offered by Hampson and Narlikar. The coming together of the Quadrilateral initiative, for instance, is likely motivated by a fear of losing agency over the governance of the Indo-Pacific—or the narrative of contamination as Hampson and Narlikar describe. This narrative also best describes the US' position – as we explore further in the next section – but not necessarily the positions of Japan or Australia, who are less concerned about their "global primacy" as much as they are about territorial integrity or the securitization of interdependence due to their engagement with Beijing.

This odd myriad of narratives also creates different pressures and priorities that other states respond to in their respective negotiating positions or strategies for the Indo-Pacific. For instance, the ASEAN, in a bid to balance their economic interdependence with China and security dependance on America, recently released an ostensibly "non-aligned" Indo-Pacific vision (ASEAN, 2019). France (Government of France, 2019) and the UK (Williamson, 2019) are also keen to shape this region and are leveraging their 20th-century assets in the Indo-Pacific to remain relevant in global debates. Brussels, meanwhile, is frustrated with China's systematic efforts to bridge Asia and Europe on its own terms and has announced an EU-Asia connectivity initiative of its own (European Commission, 2018). Even Russia is fast making its presence felt in the region, recently participating in a trilateral naval exercise with Iran and China in the West Indian Ocean, although it continues to ape China's official position of rejecting Indo-Pacific terminology (Zhakarov, 2020).

Shared interests, discordant visions? India and the US in a multipolar Indo-Pacific

Of these various initiatives, the India-US bilateral is perhaps most significant—and most capable of anchoring other visions that promote norms for good governance and international rules relating to free markets, open access to the global commons, and fair dispute resolution. A range of contributing factors make it so. India and the US will rank amongst the three largest global economies (alongside China) by mid-century (*The Long View*, 2017); both share a commitment to liberal values and market-based economics; both are likely to emerge as the most influential security providers in the region. The India-US bilateral has been closely associated with the recent evolution of the Indo-Pacific construct. Although the idea of the Indo-Pacific is over a decade old now, it is the explicit buy-in of India and the US that gave it political heft.

For a start, India was the first to reject China's propositions under the BRI. Boycotting the BRI Summit in May 2017, the Indian Ministry of External Affairs issued a brief statement outlining concerns about the sub-optimal norms and standards for China's connectivity initiative (Government of India, 2017). India's position quickly set off a similar chain of thinking across Asian democracies and in the US. The US' first official statements on the Indo-Pacific came in 2017 when then-Secretary of State Rex Tillerson set out to define "America's relationship with India for the next century" ahead of his state visit (*Defining Our Relationship*, 2017). Only subsequently was this vocabulary more formalized across US government policies and institutions, including the NSS 2017, the NDS 2018, and the officially renamed (Indo) Pacific Command.

The characterization indeed served both India and the US well—and has accelerated cooperation across a range of domains under the banner of "Major Defense Partners" (Saran and Verma, 2019). India, for instance, acceded to three of the four "foundational" defence logistic agreements, and both have agreed to expedite processes for the fourth (Saran and Verma, 2019). The US has provided the Strategic Trade Authorization designation to Delhi, paving the way for the supply of high-tech defence goods (Saran and Verma, 2019). Both states now actively participate in a range of military exercises and US defence sales to India have swelled from USD 220 million in 2005 to USD 18 billion in 2019 (Saran and Verma, 2019).

Despite this strong convergence of interests, events over the past three years have exposed many of the structural differences in their narratives, which threaten to undermine the utility of the Indo-Pacific construct. Three, in particular, stand out: a difference in their approach to China's role in the region; disagreement over the reconfiguration of Asia's mental maps; and currently incompatible visions for the region's growth and development amidst technological change.

Zero-sum vs inclusive

Perhaps the most immediate difference in narratives between the US and India is their approach to China. Beyond occasional acknowledgements of the need to cooperate with China, the US' Indo-Pacific strategy essentially views China as a long-term existential threat to US interests and the regional and global order. The 2017 NSS described the Indo-Pacific as being in a "geopolitical competition between free and repressive visions of world order" (United States of America, 2017, p.45). By defining its regional approach through the lens of zero-sum great power competition, the US has replicated several errors that it accuses China of—binary narratives, unilateral propositions, and coercive diplomacy. The strategy also neglects the agency of regional states entirely, apart from members of the Quadrilateral Initiative. Overall, it reflects broader insecurity that currently plagues American politics, even domestically, of managing or even averting decline.

India's perspective is quite different. As a self-described "leading power" (Prime Minister's Office, 2015) in the international order, India's Indo-Pacific vision rejects binary propositions—and attempts to create space for an independent choice. At the Shangri-La Dialogue, Prime Minister Modi stated that the Indo-Pacific should not be seen as a "club of members" (Government of India, 2019)—delinking the region from security initiatives like the Quad and explicitly recognizing the region's multipolar nature. Structurally, the Indo-Pacific is incapable of being defined wholly by an "American first" policy or China's proposition that creates perverse economic and strategic interdependencies. Critics may well argue that India's vision for the region reflects a tendency towards "strategic ambiguity." But like other states in the region, India acknowledges that while political confrontation is imminent, Beijing will be the largest investor in its economic growth. And while an American security presence is welcome, Delhi also understands that the Atlantic system can no longer drive growth and development in the region. A multipolar Indo-Pacific, by design then, must be one where the interests of the region shape state behaviour and not the other way around.

This is the first contradiction in the narratives underpinning the US-India relationship in the Indo-Pacific. In both cases, these narratives are "deep," in that they touch upon a fundamental interest that makes negotiating a compromise or arriving at a shared vision for the region more difficult. In the case of the US, it is that of a great power intent on "restoring" its primacy and its 20th-century order, while India is an emerging power keen (but often lacking in material resources) to shape a multipolar and multilateral order. Can China catalyze a new accommodation between the US and India? Chinese aggression in Ladakh and careless political expansionism may well incubate a new relationship between the two largest democracies—one where the US is willing to offer India much greater elbow room with its partnerships in the region (West Asia and Eurasia) and in which India becomes more comfortable supporting US propositions around trade, maritime issues, and defence matters. Is this the moment for that?

From Bollywood to Hollywood, or more?

These differences in motivations also contribute to the different mental maps that the US and India operate with. Admiral Harry Harris once described the US' Indo-Pacific interests as spanning the region from Hollywood to Bollywood, or from the US' West Coast to India's. India's, on the other hand, is substantially larger: extending across the West Indian Ocean, the Persian Gulf, and the littorals of East Africa (Ayres, 2019). The United States, it appears, is intent on pulling India's presence into regions where it is actively in conflict with China. New Delhi will no doubt actively resist this effort, bearing in mind both its material capabilities and its own security concerns in the Indian Ocean region. The US' indifference to the West Indian Ocean, meanwhile, undermines its effort to provide a comprehensive alternative to China in the region. Part of the problem is administrative: with legacy divisions between CENTCOM, AFRICOM, and INDOPACOM delaying broader institutional direction. The US does not want its evolving diplomatic and security interests with India to adversely affect its interests in Afghanistan and Pakistan. But the more substantial hindrance is the US' inability to think of Asia as anything but a shorthand for East and South East Asia. The US is certainly responding to these inconsistencies: the National Defense Authorization Act 2020 (*H.R.2500,* 2019/2020) now prescribes expanding US-India military cooperation to the "Western Indian Ocean" as well, although the process has yet to move through the US bureaucracy, let alone become an official part of the US Indo-Pacific Strategy (Lakshman, 2019).

Should the US be able to operationalize these efforts without friction between its various administrative institutions, another blind spot still awaits: the convergence of Eurasia and the Indo-Pacific. As we have argued earlier, these regions should not be considered isolated geographical constructs. There is a strong interdependence between the markets, communities, and states of both regions. China certainly does not see itself as an Indo-Pacific actor alone—instead, maritime Asia is only one part of its pan-continental ambition. India is increasingly beginning to see itself in much the same way. Among Prime Minister Modi's early foreign visits in 2015 was to the five Central Asian republics, where he argued that "Our hopes of an Asian Century will be realized when we see Asia as one…not as Central, South, West or East" (Government of India, 2015). India's expanding diplomatic presence also supports this thinking—be it in the Shanghai Cooperation Summit, the BIMSTEC, or its observer status at the ASEAN and East Asian Summits.

This is the second contradiction in the US and India's visions for the region. This contradiction is shaped by some "deep" narratives, but some are shallow as well, in that they are susceptible to influence and change. Divergence on the exact geographical dimensions of the Indo-Pacific are examples of shallow narratives—they are more a product of institutional arrangements than fundamental national interests. As we describe earlier, these differences will soon be reconciled once the US adopts a more expansive definition of the region. The real—and far more difficult to reconcile—differences lie in the partners they choose in these regions. With the US ignoring the reorientation of political geographies, India is unable to rely on its primary Indo-Pacific partner when it comes to Eurasian politics. The US' default position on Russia, in fact, only serves to consolidate Moscow's dependence on Beijing, preventing a stronger Indian entente with Russia. Meanwhile, continued reliance on Pakistan to manage Afghanistan and confrontational postures towards Iran also make India-US cooperation in West Asia unmanageable. Indeed, the US has often undermined India's efforts to partner with Iran (sanctioning India's purchase of oil, for instance) (*US Deadline Ends*, 2019) and Russia (sanctioning India's S-400 purchase) (Gady, 2020), holding its long-term interests hostage to American foreign policy priorities.

Shaping Globalization 2.0?

The disagreements between the US and India also extend to the future of growth and development in the region. The Indo-Pacific will mature as a construct amidst the 4IR, and attendant shifts in patterns of production, trade, and development. As we had argued in the previous section, a key structural characteristic of the Indo-Pacific is unravelling interdependence. This is driven both by the digitization of the global economy and a nationalist desire in the US and China to shape this new economic order. A key consideration for both as they claim leadership over emerging technologies will be addressing the concerns of emerging economies in the region, who will be unable to rely on low-cost manufacturing as a development ladder. China is responding to this concern by offering to build smart city infrastructure, create cloud computing centres, build undersea fibre optic cables, enhance internet penetration, invest in e-commerce and digital payments and cybersecurity infrastructure; all under the banner of the digital silk route (Cheney, 2019).

Proponents of an alternative Indo-Pacific order do not possess an answer for these challenges—including the US and India. Under President Trump's "America First" worldview, the "re-industrialization" of the US is a key priority, which is bound to create concern in emerging markets as digitization accelerates this process. So is undermining the global competitiveness of China's technology companies. Neither the US' withdrawal from the TPP nor its diplomatic offensive against Chinese technology platforms (Pandey, 2020) has inspired confidence amongst Indo-Pacific states. Although the Biden administration is likely to be less blunt about putting America first, its promise of a "foreign policy for the middle class" suggests a cautious approach to globalization (White House, 2021; U.S. Department of State, 2021). While new initiatives are now on the table, such as the Blue Dot Network (U.S. International Development Finance Corporation, 2019), they continue to focus excessively on infrastructure development, without paying due attention to convergences on digital policy in the Indo-Pacific. While many of America's traditional partners, including Japan, Australia, S. Korea, and Vietnam have restricted Huawei's presence in their 5G network, it is unrealistic to imagine a world completely cut off from Chinese technology.

This is the third divergence. The US believes that it can exert on the rapidly digitizing economies of the Indo-Pacific the same kind of pressure it could on the Asia-Pacific economic order. India, on the other hand, sees in the digitization of the Indo-Pacific an opportunity to correct the inequities of past periods of industrialization and globalization.

Differences on the future of digital globalization in the Indo-Pacific are also best understood as products of "deep narratives." A series of policy choices by India, including FDI restrictions in e-commerce and data localization rules, has irked the US trade establishment (Ayres, 2020). These efforts reflect a growing realization in India that it must chart its own "third way" in the global digital economy—interdependent with both American and Chinese technology systems, but designed to service India's development needs and to protect the rights and security of its citizens. The US, on the other hand, has already taken issue with India's efforts to localize data and to tax digital services (Ranipeta, 2020). These divergences are a product of the structural nature of both markets, the nature of the commercial actors who inhabit them, and larger national security considerations.

Delhi has not buckled to either US or Chinese pressure, attempting to retain space for its own industrial growth amidst technological transformations. For instance, Delhi was unwilling to accept the language on cross border data flows at the G20 summit in Osaka (Roy, 2019). Similarly, India is also the only hold-out on Huawei, with the other three members of the Quad banning China's telecom giant from their 5G networks (Pant and Tirkey, 2020).

Once again, however, some of these calculations seem bound to change in the aftermath of the face-off in Ladakh. Delhi has already prevented its public telecommunication companies from purchasing Chinese products, and seems likely to bar its private sector from doing so as well (*Government Asks BSNL,* 2020). There is also an emerging trend of large US technology platforms investing in their Indian counterparts, as the Facebook–Jio deal demonstrates (Singh, 2020). Can the push factor of Chinese aggression and the pull factor of alternative reliable pools of capital and technology from the US create opportunities for joint digital proposition in the Indo-Pacific? Once again, much depends on whether DC and Delhi can reconcile their different market cultures and structures.

Conclusion—Pax Sinica, "Westlessness" or a post-Western Indo-Pacific?

These three differences in narratives between India and the US, on China, on the region, and its future, are not irreconcilable but do pose a policy side risk to the long-term relationship in the region. As we described earlier, nearly all three are a product of existential interests—be it perspectives on the global balance of power, the matrix of relationships in the Indo-Pacific, or the future of growth and development in the region.

They suggest that neither country has yet fleshed out a broader mandate for joint engagement in the region beyond securing their narrow interests viz. China. Whether it is the reorganization of political geographies, the digitalization of our societies, or the declining faith in democratic capitalism, Beijing is either driving or benefiting from change. Beijing has successfully incorporated into its narratives the idea of a virtuous cycle of trade, investment, and economic growth through the BRI and has effectively exploited the grievances that states held against a western-led world order. Most countries that partner with Beijing are aware of the contradictions in China's narrative, but either see it as a hedge against Western excesses (such as Iran or Russia) or are dependent on its economic largesse. That China continues to expand its geopolitical influence despite a distributed and organic pushback from smaller states is a testament to the appeal and resilience of the "China model."

Part of China's success is also attributable to "Westlessness" (the informal theme of the Munich Security Conference 2020) (*Westlessness*, 2020). It is an international order where Western societies are struck by a deep unease about their identity and role in the world. It is also, consequently, an order less influenced by the West and its ideas. Washington DC's response to these developments has been to restore "American leadership" over global affairs—a thinking, we argued in 2018, that was "born amidst the lengthening shadow of China's rise, digital transformation of industrialization and the global economy, and America's increasing self-doubt over the continued dominance of its global position and the resilience of the world order it has shaped" (Saran, 2019). This narrative of containment that shapes US behaviour in the Indo-Pacific—and a belief that "restoring" American primacy is the solution to the region's challenges—does not lend well to its ability to forge coalitions and partnerships in a rapidly changing world. If recent events in Europe are any indicator, it is questionable whether the US is capable of compelling even its closest partner to conform to its policies on China. It is misguided to believe that Asia will turn out any differently.

In failing to look past a liberal order under a "restored" American leadership, DC may well fail to realize that a rules-based order need not be western-led at all—as India's foreign minister once pointed out (Saran, 2018). India sees the Indo-Pacific for what it is: a multipolar region being shaped by the agency of many. India's identity as an Asian and post-colonial democracy also make it more suitable to anchoring a liberal world order "in a part of the world where American leadership is no longer as welcome, and where China's offering is not universally accepted" (Tharoor and Saran, 2019). India has undoubtedly prepared such a narrative. When asked at the 2019 Raisina Dialogue about the features that define "brand India," the EAM's first reply was "non-disruptionist" (ORF, 2020)—a claim that is borne out by its willingness to provide public goods in the region and settling disputes peacefully (India lost and acquiesced to Bangladesh in a territorial dispute) (Habib, 2014). In his 2018 speech at Shangri-La, PM Modi presented a formulation for the Indo-Pacific driven primarily by the development interests of communities and states in the region. It is not, he claimed, a "grouping that seeks to dominate" or "directed against any country" (Government of India, 2019).

That said, while India may have more realistic assessments of and normative prescriptions for the Indio-Pacific, it is hobbled by several shortcomings. The most immediate challenge is state capacity and economic resources. Several of India's own infrastructure initiatives are routinely delayed for technical and operational reasons, its own military-industrial capabilities are in dire need of reform and upgrade, and its ability to devote resources to multiple geographies, institutions and issues might also spread its foreign services too thin. That India does not publish periodic and official strategy papers also inhibits its ability to align the multiple government, business and civil society actors that support its foreign policy objectives. Delhi's vacillations on the digital policy front are also cause for concern. Despite having rejected China's propositions under the Belt and Road Initiative, for instance, it has de facto surrendered to its technology ambitions, with China's hardware, software, and finance dominating India's technology sector.

Some of these challenges will fade away organically as India's path to a USD 10 trillion economy over the next decade creates new economic and strategic interdependencies in the Indo-Pacific. Much more will depend on multilateral efforts—efforts, which are increasingly being scuttled by a zero-sum US-China competition in the region.

Like others in the region, India is unlikely to support outcomes that privilege the role of any single actor in the Indo-Pacific. It remains to be seen whether the US is willing or able to create a new template for its partnership with India, one that is not based on its post-WWII framework. Currently, the narratives underpinning both the US and India's visions for the region suggest that this is not the case. A sustained long-term divergence on core issues will likely lead to fragmented regionalization in the Indo-Pacific, given that India's economic capacities are expected to rival the US' by the middle of the century. It will also strengthen China's hand, given its co-ordinated "all of the government" approach to global power.

Ideally, both the US and India would share a narrative that sees each other as co-sponsors and co-guarantors of a 21st-century liberal order. This is, however, easier said than done. The US for its part will have to re-examine what its exceptionalism implies in the 21st century. Can the template used for alliances and partnerships with the EU and nations in East Asia work for India, a large nation with its own great power ambitions? If the answer is no, how willing is it to make compromises on issues like the digital economy, India's relationship with powers like Iran and Russia, and to accept a greater role for India in institutions of global governance even if there is some divergence on policy interests? Answering these questions will require fundamental reorientations in the US perspective of India and in the institutional framework for engagement. India, for its part, must be willing to shed its much-vaunted principle of "strategic autonomy." Delhi will also have to reconfigure its trade and economic priorities—recent measures that impose new tariffs on goods and other protectionist tendencies suggest that it is not yet willing or able to accept some of the compromises of a more global economy. These are deep rooted and fundamentally different narratives that shape their engagement with the world and with each other—and untangling them will require new narratives that create space and opportunity for greater policy convergence. While this is a tall order, it is an expectation that both countries will have to bear given their potential to define the 21st century.

Note

1 Samir Saran is President, Observer Research Foundation. Akhil Deo is Junior Fellow, Technology and Media Initiative, Observer Research Foundation.

References

Aneja, A. (2016, July 12) *China Rejects Hague Tribunal Ruling as 'Null and Void'*, The Hindu. www.thehindu.com/news/international/China-rejects-Hague-tribunal-ruling-as-"null-and-void"/article14486651.ece.

Association of South East Asian Nations (ASEAN). (2019, June 23) *ASEAN Outlook on the Indo-Pacific*, Statements and Communiques. https://asean.org/asean-outlook-indo-pacific/.

Ayres, A. (2019, January 22) *The U.S. Indo-Pacific Strategy Needs More Indian Ocean*, Council on Foreign Relations. www.cfr.org/expert-brief/us-indo-pacific-strategy-needs-more-indian-ocean.

Ayres, A. (2020, February 13) *A Field Guide to U.S.-India Trade Tensions*, Council on Foreign Relations. www.cfr.org/article/field-guide-us-india-trade-tensions.

Basu, N. (2020, May 28) *India Will Resolve Border Standoff with China 'Peacefully' Via Dialogue, Says MEA*, The Print. https://theprint.in/diplomacy/india-will-resolve-border-standoff-with-china-peacefully-via-dialogue-says-mea/431382/.

Bhattacherjee, K. (2019, September 10) *India Asks China, Pakistan to End Activities Related to CPEC in PoK*, The Hindu. www.thehindu.com/news/national/china-pakistan-economic-corridor-is-on-our-territory-india/article29382571.ece.

Birtles, B. (2019, March 8) *China Mocks Australia over 'Indo-Pacific' Concept It Says Will 'Dissipate'*, ABC News. www.abc.net.au/news/2018-03-08/china-mocks-australia-over-indo-pacific-concept/9529548.

Cheney, C. (2019, September 26) *China's Digital Silk Road: Strategic Technological Competition and Exporting Political Illiberalism*, Council on Foreign Relations. www.cfr.org/blog/chinas-digital-silk-road-strategic-technological-competition-and-exporting-political.

China's Approach to Global Governance (2020) Council on Foreign Relations. www.cfr.org/china-global-governance/.

Cohen, A. (2019, November 7) *U.S. Withdraws from Paris Accord, Ceding Leadership to China*, Forbes. www.forbes.com/sites/arielcohen/2019/11/07/us-withdraws-from-paris-accord-ceding-leadership-to-china/#49a8312473c1.

Defining Our Relationship with India for the Next Century: An Address by U.S. Secretary of State Rex Tillerson (2017, October 18), CSIS. www.csis.org/events/defining-our-relationship-india-next-century-address-us-secretary-state-rex-tillerson.

Ebrahimian, B.A. (2020, January 27) *UN Aviation Agency Blocks Critics of Taiwan Policy on Twitter*, Axios. www.axios.com/as-virus-spreads-un-agency-blocks-critics-taiwan-policy-on-twitter-e8a8bce6-f31a-4f41-89e0-77d919109887.html.

Europe, China and Russia Urge Preservation of Iran Nuclear Deal (2020, February 26), Deutche Welle. www.dw.com/en/europe-china-and-russia-urge-preservation-of-iran-nuclear-deal/a-52544410.

European Commission. (2018) *Connecting Europe and Asia—Building Blocks for an EU Strategy*.

Gady, F.S. (2020, January 10) *Senior US Official: No Blanket Waiver for India on S-400 Buy*, The Diplomat. https://thediplomat.com/2020/01/senior-us-official-no-blanket-waiver-for-india-on-s-400-buy/.

Gerwitz, J. (2020, June 1) *The Chinese Reassessment of Independence*, China Leadership Monitor. www.prcleader.org/gewirtz.

Government Asks BSNL, MTNL Not to Use Chinese Equipment for Network Upgrade: Report, (2020, June 18), NDTV. www.ndtv.com/business/government-asks-bsnl-mtnl-to-not-use-chinese-equipment-for-4g-upgrade-2248502.

Government of France. (2019, May) *France and Security in the Indo-Pacific*, Ministry of Defense. www.defense.gouv.fr/layout/set/print/content/download/532754/9176250/version/3/file/France+and+Security+in+the+Indo-Pacific+-+2019.pdf.

Government of India. (2015, July 7) *Address by Prime Minister at Nazarbayev University, Astana, Kazakhstan*, Ministry of External Affairs.

Government of India. (2017, May 13) *Official Spokesperson's response to a query on participation of India in OBOR/BRI Forum*, Ministry of External Affairs. https://mea.gov.in/media-briefings.htm?dtl/28463/Official+Spokespersons+response+to+a+query+on+participation+of+India+in+OBORBRI+Forum.

Government of India. (2019, June 1) *Prime Minister's Keynote Address at Shangri La Dialogue*. Ministry of External Affairs. https://mea.gov.in/Speeches-Statements.htm?dtl/29943/Prime+Ministers+Keynote+Address+at+Shangri+La+Dialogue+June+01+2018.

H.R.2500–National Defense Authorisation Act for Fiscal Year 2020, (2019–2020), 116th Congress. www.congress.gov/bill/116th-congress/house-bill/2500/text.

Habib, H. (2014, July 9) *Bangladesh Wins Maritime Dispute with India*, The Hindu. www.thehindu.com/news/national/bangladesh-wins-maritime-dispute-with-india/article6191797.ece.

Jiayao, L (Ed.). (2018, October 18) *China's Military Achievements Benefit National Interests, World Order*, China Military. http://english.chinamil.com.cn/view/2017-10/18/content_7791317.htm.

Karp, P., and, Davidson, H. (2020, April 29) *China Bristles at Australia's Call for Investigation into Coronavirus Origin*, The Guardian. www.theguardian.com/world/2020/apr/29/australia-defends-plan-to-investigate-china-over-covid-19-outbreak-as-row-deepens.

Krishnan, A. (2020, June 19) *China Lays Claim to Entire Galwan Valley*, The Hindu. www.thehindu.com/news/national/chinas-galwan-valley-claims-mark-shift-from-past/article31867941.ece.

Lakshman, S. (2019, July 10) *U.S. House Will Vote on Watered-Down Version of India Defence Cooperation Legislation*, The Hindu. www.thehindu.com/news/international/us-house-will-vote-on-watered-down-version-of-india-defence-cooperation-legislation/article28364247.ece.

Lius, F. (2020, January) 'The Recalibration of Chinese Assertiveness: China's Responses to the Indo-Pacific Challenge', *International Affairs*, vol.96, no.1, pp.9–28.

McDevitt, M. Rear Admiral. (2016, June) *Becoming a Great 'Maritime Power': A Chinese Dream*, CNA, pp.1–160. www.cna.org/CNA_files/PDF/IRM-2016-U-013646.pdf.

Miles, T. (2019, May 13) *China Says U.S. Policies Are Causing Existential Damage to the WTO*, Reuters. www.reuters.com/article/us-usa-trade-wto-china/china-says-u-s-policies-are-causing-existential-damage-to-the-wto-idUSKCN1SJ1QI.

Ondaatjie, A., and, Sirimanne, A. (2019, November 30) *Sri Lanka Leased Hambantota Port to China For 99 Yrs: Now It Wants It Back*, Business Standard. www.business-standard.com/article/international/sri-lanka-leased-hambantota-port-to-china-for-99-yrs-now-it-wants-it-back-119112900206_1.html.

ORF. (2020, January 15) *India Is a Prisoner of Its Past Image: S Jaishankar, Raisina Dialogue 2020*, YOUTUBE. https://youtu.be/KufSx9RW-q0.

Pandey, E. (2020, March 5) *U.S. Bans Could Make Huawei Stronger*, Axios. www.axios.com/huawei-cybersecurity-china-decoupling-5g-11034740-797b-4f00-a17e-7b3265d8bbcd.html.

Pant, H., and, Tirkey, A. (2020, February 6) *Is India Betting Big on Huawei?*, Foreign Policy. https://foreignpolicy.com/2020/02/06/is-india-betting-big-on-huawei/.

Parker, C. (2017, January 17) *China's Xi Jinping Defends Globalization from the Davos Stage*, World Economic Forum. www.weforum.org/agenda/2017/01/chinas-xi-jinping-defends-globalization-from-the-davos-stage/.

People's Republic of China (PRC). (2013, October 25) *Xi Jinping: Let the Sense of Community of Common Destiny Take Deep Root in Neighbouring Countries*, Ministry of Foreign Affairs. www.fmprc.gov.cn/mfa_eng/wjb_663304/wjbz_663308/activities_663312/t1093870.shtml.

People's Republic of China (PRC). (2014, May 21) *New Asian Security Concept for New Progress in Security Cooperation*, Ministry of Foreign Affairs. www.fmprc.gov.cn/mfa_eng/zxxx_662805/t1159951.shtml.

People's Republic of China (PRC). (2015, March 28) *Vision and Actions on Jointly Building Silk Road Economic Belt and 21st-Century Maritime Silk Road*, National Development and Reform Commission. http://en.ndrc.gov.cn/newsrelease/201503/ t20150330_669367.html.

Prime Minister's Office. (2015, February 7) *PM to Heads of Indian Missions*, Press Release, Indian Press Information Bureau. http://pib.nic.in/newsite/PrintRelease.aspx?relid=115241.

Pubby, M., and, Anshuman, K. (2020, June 22) *Colonel Babu Got Hit in The Head: A Detailed Account of the Brawl at Galwan with Chinese Soldiers*, Economic Times. https://economictimes.indiatimes.com/news/defence/indian-soldiers-put-up-a-strong-fight-pla-officer-killed/articleshow/76499852.cms.

Ranipeta, S. (2020, April 28) *From Data Localisation to Privacy, US Raises Concerns over India's Digital Laws*, The Newsminute. www.thenewsminute.com/article/data-localisation-privacy-us-raises-concerns-over-india-s-digital-laws-123529.

Roy, S. (2019, June 29) *G-20 Osaka Summit: India Refuses to Sign Declaration on Free Flow of Data across Borders*, Indian Express. https://indianexpress.com/article/india/g-20-osaka-summit-narendra-mod-india-declaration-on-free-flow-of-data-across-borders-shinzo-abe-5805846/.

Saha, S., and, Feng, A. (2020, April 1) *Global Supply Chains, Economic Decoupling, and U.S.-China Relations, Part 1: The View from the United States*, Jamestown Foundation. https://jamestown.org/program/global-supply-chains-economic-decoupling-and-u-s-china-relations-part-1-the-view-from-the-united-states/.

Saran, S. (2018, January 25) *World in Flux: India's Choices May Help Manage Disruptions*, Observer Research Foundation. www.orfonline.org/expert-speak/world-flux-india-choices-may-help-manage-disruptions/

Saran, S. (2018, February) *India Sees the Belt and Road Initiative for What It Is: Evidence of China's Unconcealed Ambition for Hegemony*, The Security Times. www.the-security-times.com/india-sees-the-belt-and-road-initiative-for-what-it-is-evidence-of-chinas-unconcealed-ambition-for-hegemony/.

Saran, S. (2019, June 25) *'In India We Trust' Would Be Good US Policy*, Observer Research Foundation. www.orfonline.org/expert-speak/india-we-trust-would-be-good-us-policy-52345/.

Saran, S., and, Deo, A. (2019) *Pax Sinica: Implications for the Indian Dawn*. New Delhi: Rupa Publications.

Saran, S., and, Verma, R. (2019, June 25) *Strategic Convergence: The United States and India as Major Defence Partners*, Observer Research Foundation. www.orfonline.org/research/strategic-convergence-the-united-states-and-india-as-major-defence-partners-52364/.

Singh, M. (2020, April 20) *Facebook Invests $5.7B in India's Reliance Jio Platforms*, Techcrunch. https://techcrunch.com/2020/04/21/facebook-reliance-jio/.

Small, A. (2019, March 12) *The Meaning of Systemic Rivalry: Europe and China beyond the Pandemic*, European Council on Foreign Relations. https://ecfr.eu/publication/the_meaning_of_systemic_rivalry_europe_and_china_beyond_the_pandemic/.

Srinivasan, C. (Ed.). (2020, June 21) *Army Changes Weapon Rules Along Line of Actual Control After Ladakh Clash*, NDTV. www.ndtv.com/india-news/india-china-face-off-ladakh-rules-of-engagement-along-lac-changed-days-after-20-indian-soldiers-killed-2249913.

Taiwan Yet to Receive COVID-19 Meeting Invitation, Reigniting Allegations WHO Kowtowing to China (2020, May 4), ABC News. www.ifn.news/posts/icao-excludes-taiwan-from-cooperation-amid-coronavirus-rejects-criticism.

Tharoor, S., and, Saran, S. (2019, December 20) *An Inclusive Ascent*, Open Magazine. https://openthemagazine.com/features/an-inclusive-ascent/.

The Long View: How Will the Global Economic Order Change By 2050, (2017, February), PwC. www.pwc.com/gx/en/world-2050/assets/pwc-the-world-in-2050-full-report-feb-2017.pdf.

Tiezzi, S. (2018, January 30) *What China's Davos Coverage Reveals About Its Global Ambitions*, The Diplomat. https://thediplomat.com/2018/01/what-chinas-davos-coverage-reveals-about-its-global-ambitions/.

Tobin, L. (2018, November) 'Xi's Vision for Transforming Global Governance: A Strategic Challenge for Washington and Its Allies', *Texas National Security Review*, vol.2, no.1, pp.155–166.

U.S. Department of Defense. (2019) *Indo-Pacific Strategy Report: Preparedness, Partnerships and Promoting a Networked Region*.

U.S. Department of State. (2020, June 24) *The Tide Is Turning Toward Trusted 5G Vendors*. www.state.gov/the-tide-is-turning-toward-trusted-5g-vendors/.

U.S. Department of State. (2021, March 3) *A Foreign Policy for the American People*. www.state.gov/a-foreign-policy-for-the-american-people/.

U.S. International Development Finance Corporation (2019, November 4) *The Launch of the Multi-Stakeholder Blue Dot Network*. www.dfc.gov/media/opic-press-releases/launch-multi-stakeholder-blue-dot-network.

United States of America. (2017) *National Security Strategy*, The White House.

US Deadline Ends, India Stops Purchasing Iranian Oil, (2019, May 24), Economic Times. https://economictimes.indiatimes.com/industry/energy/oil-gas/us-deadline-ends-india-stops-purchasing-iranian-oil/articleshow/69475495.cms?from=mdr.

Wert, J. (2020, January 28) *ICAO Excludes Taiwan from Cooperation Amid Coronavirus, Rejects Criticism*, International Flight Network. www.ifn.news/posts/icao-excludes-taiwan-from-cooperation-amid-coronavirus-rejects-criticism/.

Westlessness (2020, February 16), Munich Security Conference. https://securityconference.org/en/news/full/westlessness-the-munich-security-conference-2020/.

White House (2021, February 4) *Remarks by President Biden on America's Place in the World*. www.whitehouse.gov/briefing-room/speeches-remarks/2021/02/04/remarks-by-president-biden-on-americas-place-in-the-world/.

Williamson, G. (2019, February 11) *Defence in Global Britain*, RUSI. www.gov.uk/government/speeches/defence-in-global-britain.

Wuthnow, J., Limaye, S., and, Samaranayake, N. (2018, June 7) *Doklam, One Year Later: China's Long Game in the Himalayas*, War on the Rocks. https://warontherocks.com/2018/06/doklam-one-year-later-chinas-long-game-in-the-himalayas/.

Xinhua. (2012, November 17) *Full Text of Hu Jintao's Report at the 18th Party Congress*, XinhuaNet. http://news.xinhuanet.com/english/special/18cpcnc/2012-11/17/c_131981259.htm.

Xinhua. (2017, May 14) *Full Text of President Xi's Speech at Opening of Belt and Road Forum*, XinhuaNet. www.xinhuanet.com//english/2017-05/14/c_136282982.htm.

Xinhua. (2018, June 24). *Xi Urges Breaking New Ground in Major Country Diplomacy with Chinese Characteristics*, XinhuaNet. www.xinhuanet.com/english/2018-06/24/c_137276269.htm.

Xinhua. (2019, July 24) *Full Text: China's National Defense in the New Era*, XinhuaNet. www.xinhuanet.com/english/2019-07/24/c_138253389.htm.

Yamazaki, A. (2020, February 28) *The PRC's Cautious Stance on the U.S. Indo-Pacific Strategy*, Jamestown Foundation. https://jamestown.org/program/the-prcs-cautious-stance-on-the-u-s-indo-pacific-strategy/.

Ying, F. (2017, June 22) *China's Vision for the World: A Community of Shared Future*, The Diplomat. https://thediplomat.com/2017/06/chinas-vision-for-the-world-a-community-of-shared-future/.

Yong, H. (2019, April 24) *Construction of Digital Silk Road Lights Up BRI Cooperation*, People's Daily. http://en.people.cn/n3/2019/0424/c90000-9571418.html.

Zhakarov, A. (2020, February 6) *While Criticizing the Indo-Pacific, Russia Steps up Its Presence*, Observer Research Foundation. www.orfonline.org/expert-speak/while-criticizing-the-indo-pacific-russia-steps-up-its-presence-61102/.

Zhou, L. (2020, December 29) *ASEAN Members up the Ante on South China Sea Amid Code of Conduct Talks*, South China Morning Post. www.scmp.com/news/china/diplomacy/article/3043772/asean-members-ante-south-china-sea-amid-code-conduct-talks.

15

NARRATIVES IN REGIONAL ARMS CONTROL NEGOTIATIONS

The Iran agreement

Henner Fürtig

Introduction

Both the United States and Iran have been disproportionately affected by the global Covid-19 pandemic. In early 2020, news and pictures of plague victims shifted the worldwide attention away from the renewed escalation of the decades-old conflict between Iran and the United States. On January 3, 2020, the United States killed one of Iran's top generals, Qasem Soleimani, whereupon the Iranians promptly fired missiles at US bases in Iraq in retaliation. An open war between the United States and Iran seemed possible. Finally, rationality prevailed, but Tehran decided on January 5, 2020 that it would revoke parts of the Joint Comprehensive Plan of Action (JCPOA), commonly known as the Iran nuclear deal, rather than taking the bait and engaging in an outright war.

The Iranian leadership was sure that this announcement would generate a maximum of international attention. After all, the JCPOA has proven one of the most prominent, if not the single most prominent, international agreements of the 21st century. It brought Iran together with the most powerful countries in the international arena – the five permanent members of the UN Security Council plus Germany (P5+1) – in a process of extremely intensive negotiations over the course of more than 12 years, with the goal of permanently resolving the conflict over the Iranian nuclear programme. It was finally signed in Vienna on July 14, 2015 by representatives of the P5+1 and Iran.

However, US President Donald Trump unilaterally cancelled the nuclear deal on May 7, 2018. Though Iranian President Hassan Rouhani had initially ensured continued compliance with the agreement, he announced the suspension of certain parts of it in July 2019. But, as mentioned above, it was only after the killing of Qasem Soleimani that Iran suspended further – more essential – parts of the deal.

DOI: 10.4324/9781003203209-18

It is clear that the JCPOA – including the process of its drafting – has been of central importance for Iranian politics over the last two decades. For the purpose of generating the utmost support for the process at home and as much sympathy as possible abroad, the Iranian leadership had to find a convincing rationale for its positions either by using pre-existing arguments and "stories," adapting them if necessary, or by creating new ones. As Hampson and Narlikar state in their chapter, such stories or narratives are essential to explaining to a constituency "who we are, how we should behave, what is important, and how the world works." And, of course, the best narratives are simple in their construction, so as to be easily understood. From recognizing the towering importance of narratives for the legitimization of policies, it is only a small step to also agree with Hampson and Narlikar's working hypothesis that "coherent, deep narratives matter not only to the formation of intersubjective identities and broader transnational movements, but also to the actual processes and outcomes of complex international negotiations." Therefore, we seem to have good reason to examine narratives that framed the JCPOA negotiations.

Considering the long and extremely complex negotiations, the existence of more than one narrative, even conflicting ones, was to be expected. But what if one or more of the parties attached itself to multiple stories and narratives? Even if each party confined itself to only one, it would be necessary to analyze six (5+1) narratives on one side of the negotiating table, and an additional one (Iran) on the other. For the purposes of this article, it is most useful to concentrate on only one: the Iranian narrative.

The Iranian narrative

The driving narrative behind the Iranian negotiation strategy was not developed shortly before or during the nuclear talks but decades earlier – immediately following the Islamic Revolution in 1979. It was the undisputed leader of the revolution, Ayatollah Ruhollah Khomeini himself, who articulated and communicated the narrative.

According to Khomeini, the Iranian Revolution implied an obligation to reintroduce Islam as a revelation for the whole of humankind, not only for the Muslim world. This universalistic approach was at least as total as he believed the West's global schemes were. He firmly declared:

> The Iranian Revolution is not exclusively that of Iran, because Islam does not belong to any particular people. Islam is revealed for mankind and the Muslims, not for Iran [...]. An Islamic movement, therefore, cannot limit itself to any particular country, not even to the Islamic countries; it is the continuation of the revolution by the prophets.
>
> *Khomeini, 1979, p.11*

He thus outlined an essential task of the Islamic Iranian state's foreign policy – namely, *sudur-e enqelab* – "exporting the revolution," which became the defining motto of early Iranian foreign policy, directly set by Khomeini.

> We will export our revolution all over the world because it is an Islamic one. The struggle continues until the call "There is no god but God and Muhammad is his prophet" is heard everywhere. As long as people on this earth are oppressed, our struggle continues.
>
> *Khomeini, 1979, p.28*

Consequently, the leader of the Islamic Revolution made sure that the propagation of the revolutionary Islamic message became, in articles 11, 152, and 154, a constitutional mandate of the Islamic Republic of Iran and, thus, one of its basic, constitutive elements.

The simple narrative's persistence and power were further strengthened by its deep roots in Iranian society. When we apply Hampson and Narlikar's three categories of narrative (contamination, redemption, agency) here, it quickly becomes obvious that Khomeini's narrative was mainly about "redemption" from a "contaminated" past. Khomeini had arranged his story on a set of societal experiences and certainties that went back to the 1950s and 1960s. The export of the revolution could thus be incorporated into a much broader discourse on the misbehaviour of the West and its institutions in Iran. Jalal Al-e Ahmad, a very popular intellectual, had accused his compatriots of "Westtoxication" ("contamination") in the early 1960s, and Ali Shariati, an arguably even more popular sociologist, had constantly criticized the West, particularly the United States, for its "imperialist" and "colonial" treatment of Islamic countries in general and Iran in particular (Rezaei, 2019, p.14).

Obviously, a narrative that calls for the export of a revolution would massively challenge the established international order. Luckily for Khomeini, a more radical view on the international order was shared by many other Muslim thinkers in the late 1970s. For example, in his book *The Quranic Concept of War*, the Sunni Pakistani general S.K. Malik had claimed that the imperative of *jihad*, or holy war, was to be shared by the entire Muslim community regardless of formal boundaries and individual status; non-combatants would therefore also be included (Malik, 1979). The groundwork was laid; Muslims only need rise up.

However, contrary to all expectations held by the Iranian leadership, the addressees of the narrative remained passive. Aside from some expressions of sympathy from other Muslim countries and a few Shiite upheavals in the immediate neighbourhood, the export of the revolution failed.

Sub-narratives

The devastating consequences of the Iran–Iraq War of the 1980s and Iran's subsequent near-total international isolation added to the country's woes. In 1988, after eight years of war with its neighbour, the mere survival of the Islamic Republic of Iran (IRI) was at stake. Still, in 1988, it was Khomeini himself who found a solution, by using his last will and testament. In contrast to all of his previous statements on the matter, he now declared that the interests (*maslahat*) of the Islamic Republic as a nation-state should take priority over those of the

Islamic community (*umma*) and Islamic law. Thus, in his testament, Khomeini finalized his metamorphosis from cleric to statesman.

With this course correction and extension, Khomeini created a sub-narrative to the prevailing one, the former seeming – at a first glimpse – to contradict the latter. How could a community committed to a "permanent" revolution with a global claim be content with the pursuit of national interests alone? However, as Khomeini had learnt the hard way, the core narrative insufficiently depicted reality. Even the official name of Iran – "Islamic Republic of Iran" – combines two conflicting elements: the global Islamic community (*umma*) and the state, deriving from a Western concept (*res publica*). The core narrative lacked something which the sub-narrative provided. The latter is an essential, "deep" narrative, because it addressed and included the deep-rooted national identity of the Iranians. Even today, Khomeini's *fatwa* justifies the pursuit of national Iranian interests in international politics without abandoning the revolutionary tasks mentioned in the original narrative. Not only did the combination create flexibility, it also perfectly mirrors the dual nature of the Iranian political structure, whereby an "Islamic" pillar, consisting mainly of the supreme leader (*rahbar*), the Islamic Revolutionary Guard Corps (IRGC – Pasdaran) and the Islamic endowments (*bonyads*), takes precedence – according to the Constitution – over the "national" pillar, which is mainly composed of the government, the parliament, and the regular army and police, not to mention provincial and local administrations. It is striking that other systems based on a mass social revolution and a strong ideology with global ambitions, such as the Soviet/communist one, developed similar dual power structures. In the Soviet bloc, the Communist Party set policy, while the state institutions were essentially responsible for its implementation. No wonder, then, that Khomeini's idea to export the revolution in some way recalls Trotsky's "permanent" revolution (Rezaei, 2019, p.3).

Ironically, it was precisely the end of the East–West conflict and the collapse of the Soviet bloc that caused Khomeini's successor as supreme leader, Ayatollah Ali Khamenei, to extend and embellish Khomeini's original narrative. In his own sub-narrative Khamenei began to argue that Iran's interpretation of Islam(ism) had replaced communism as the most consequential antidote to Western imperialism. Lacking an (if only potential) counter-balancing factor in international relations, Iran saw itself in direct confrontation with the "Great Satan" – that is, the United States and its Western allies. In 1993 Khamenei propagated a new kind of bipolarity in international politics, whereby a revitalized and politicized Islam would replace (the apparently ineffective) communism as the alternative to the West. Consequently, since the early 1990s every foreigner who enters Iran via the international Mehrabad airport in Tehran has read – in English – the illuminated and larger-than-life banner: "In future Islam will destroy Satanic sovereignty of the West" (Sciolino, 2000, p.14). Nevertheless, this sub-narrative never gained the importance of its "national interests" counterpart and remained a "shallow" narrative.

However, the Iranian narrative cannot be understood without referring to its very strong victimization aspects. As Hampson and Narlikar explained in their chapter, a remarkable group of narratives surrounds "contamination": a society being poisoned (e.g., by the West, as in Jalal Al-e Ahmad's "Westtoxication") and thus exploited, marginalized, abused and betrayed, and then becoming disillusioned. The Iranian leadership constantly recalls the major disasters of the country's history, such as the invasions of the Arabs and the Mongols, the Russian–British partition of Iran in 1907, the Allied occupation of Iran in the Second World War, the Soviet-backed separatist intentions in Azerbaijan and Kurdistan in 1945–1946, the US-backed coup in 1953, and the Iraqi invasion of 1980. The stories grow in detail the closer they are to the present. Literally, entire libraries exist in Iran comprised of works only on the 1953 coup that brought the Shah back to the throne, or on the overwhelming pain and hardship caused by the war with Iraq.

The documents acknowledging the CIA's role in overthrowing the democratically elected Iranian Prime Minister Mohammed Mossadegh in 1953 were not released before 2013, and when former CIA chief George H. Bush was running for the presidency to succeed Ronald Reagan in the late 1980s, he once declared on the campaign trail, "I will never apologize for the United States. I don't care what the facts are" (Kaplan, 2014). Of course, such statements only help to vindicate the Iranians' "victim" narrative. However, the Iraq–Iran War proved far more formative for Iran's narrative creation. An IRGC handbook from 2003 reads, for example,

> The war is part of the reality of Iran's history whose place and influential role leave no doubt that for a minimum of the next several decades the results and consequences of the war will be clear in [...] the political, social, cultural, and military life of Iran.
>
> *Tabatabai and Samuel, 2017, p.162*

Because Iraq started the war, only to be supported shortly thereafter by almost all Arab countries and later the West, the Iranians became convinced that the invasion was the result of a Western "conspiracy" against the Islamic Revolution and the very existence of the IRI, Iraq's dictator Saddam Hussein being the West's puppet. The massive US military aid and political support for Iraq even after that country had used chemical weapons against civilians added to that firm conviction of both the leadership and the majority of the Iranian people.

On July 3, 1988 the US destroyer Vincennes shot down an Iranian civilian aircraft over the Persian Gulf. Two hundred and ninety passengers and crew members died. US Naval Command declared it an accident, but the Iranians could hardly believe it when they learned seven weeks later that the captain of USS Vincennes had received a medal for "exceptionally meritorious conduct in the performance of outstanding service" while in charge of the vessel (Jett, 2018, p.27). All in all, the country's experiences with war decisively influenced its narrative and general strategy, which centres on freeing itself of contamination and on the victim role. The war and Iran's aspirations towards self-sufficiency became the driving forces for the country – despite possessing the fourth-largest oil reserves and the second-largest gas reserves in the world and even continuously exporting electricity to countries such as Iraq and Afghanistan – to develop a nuclear programme. It was meant to be *the* tool to deliver greater autonomy.

During the Iran–Iraq War, when Iraq had initiated a tactic that Iran subsequently reciprocated called the "war of the cities," which consisted of firing missiles at the most populated areas of the enemy, Ali Khamenei and Hashemi Rafsanjani (at that time Iran's president and head of parliament, respectively) decided that Iran needed nuclear weapons. In 1985 they initiated Iran's nuclear weapons programme without even notifying Supreme Leader Khomeini. As part of the sharp criticism of many of the Shah's domestic and foreign policies, the supreme leader had immediately after the victorious revolution denounced nuclear technology as a waste of resources (Tabatabai and Samuel, 2017, p.160). The Shah's nuclear programme was thus put on ice until the beginning of the war with Iraq. But even then, Khomeini had declared nuclear weapons un-Islamic (Rezaei, 2019, p.5).

Presumably in 1986, the Atomic Energy Organization of Iran (AEOI) turned to the notorious black-market network of Pakistani scientist A.Q. Khan to purchase components and designs for advanced centrifuges. The covert programme came to the public's attention only in 2002, when Iranian exile opposition group the National Resistance Council (Mojahedin-e Chalq) revealed the existence of two secret nuclear plants, in Natanz and Arak (Izewicz, 2019, p.63). This revelation led the International Atomic Energy Agency (IAEA) to ask probing questions, which Iran refused to answer sufficiently: the nuclear crisis had begun.

Even though the evidence of an Iranian nuclear weapons programme became overwhelming following an IAEA summary published in November 2015 and in the face of documents presented by Israeli Prime Minister Netanyahu in April 2018 (Fitzpatrick, 2017, p.11), Tehran continued to do what it has done since 2002: deny it has developed or been developing nuclear arms. Here again, the dual nature of the Iranian political system has helped bolster this claim. In the framework of the nuclear arms programme, Rafsanjani and Khamenei acted as officials of the nation-state pillar. The crucial Islamic pillar, on the other side, always condemned the development, possession, and use of nuclear weapons in principle. Khomeini did so in the 1980s, and Khamenei followed that example when he switched from a state role to an Islamic role as Khomeini's successor. In 2005 he declared nuclear weapons "unlawful" (*haram*), and in his statement to the Non-Aligned Movement summit in 2012 he announced, "I insist that the Islamic Republic is not pursuing nuclear weapons, and will never give up its right to peacefully use nuclear energy. Our people's slogan is: 'Nuclear energy for all, nuclear weapons for no one'" (Tabatabai and Samuel, 2017, p.174).

Since the Islamic side always has the last word in the IRI, the Iranian leadership has never viewed a change in narrative as necessary. On the contrary, it has framed the nuclear crisis simply as a continuation of the war against the Islamic Republic, another attempt to destroy the regime. A series of assassinations and assassination attempts against scientists connected to the nuclear programme between 2009 and 2012 (Jett, 2018, p.27) and the launching of a computer virus (Stuxnet) – alleged by whistleblower Edward Snowden to have been created by US and Israeli experts – that caused the centrifuges in the Iranian nuclear sites to destroy themselves (Parsi, 2017, p.126) suited that narrative nicely. Iranian propaganda began to proclaim that the Islamic Republic performs best when it is forced to hold off a "hostile world," and that Iran has always risen like a phoenix from the ashes and become even stronger in the face of such challenges. This position and the fitting narrative were also represented by the Iranian chief negotiator in the nuclear talks between 2007 and 2013, Said Jalili, whose main aim was to get concessions from the P5+1 without moving an inch himself. If his negotiation partners refused to give in, Iran could at least demonstrate that it was negotiating, even while stalling the process (Tabatabai and Pease, 2019, p.35).

Further corrections

The (most likely rigged) presidential elections in 2009 and the subsequent massive protests organized by the Green Movement marked the most severe crisis faced by the Islamic Republic's political system. The incident also illustrated the ways in which Iranian society had transformed over the previous 30 years. A new generation of young Iranians had grown up and gradually distanced themselves from their revolutionary parents and grandparents. Even though many share with earlier generations their religious beliefs and national pride, younger Iranians are far better educated than their parents (nearly five million young people are currently studying at university) but lack proper opportunities to use that educational advantage. The real power is still in the hands of the revolutionary leaders over 70 years of age, while approximately 60 per cent of Iran's population is under 30 (Florensa, 2016, p.17). Thus, the young generation's sheer quantity entails a permanent threat to the aged leadership.

This development is certainly not unique: all great revolutions undergo different phases in their development, including a stage of saturation usually after 30 or 40 years. For example, Nikita Khrushchev's thaw 40 years after the October Revolution and Stalin's years of terror come to mind. Indeed, a very slow and gradual reformist transition began in Iran after 2009 that allowed the moderate candidate Hassan Rouhani to take over the presidency in 2013 and allow Iranian delegates to begin to negotiate with their P5+1 counterparts seriously and with an orientation towards results. Of course, Iran's readiness to make this shift in its negotiations style was also substantially influenced by the fatal consequences of the international sanctions regime, which had been in place since 2006 and was substantially intensified after 2011.

The sanctions brought the economy to near collapse, the population suffering greatly. Hassan Rouhani won the presidency in 2013 mainly based on a pledge to improve the shrinking economy by getting the sanctions lifted through renewed negotiations. Supreme Leader Khamenei also conceded (after being convinced by his advisers) that the tight international sanctions regime would strangle Iran sooner or later. But, how to sell a new course of action without compromising the narrative and looking like a loser? Khomeini's *fatwa* concerning the priority of Iran's national interests helped once again in this regard, but Khamenei felt it necessary to make his own mark vis-à-vis the shift.

As of September 2013, Khamenei introduced the notion of "heroic flexibility" into the debate. While addressing IRGC commanders, he praised "flexibility" as a very useful tool to keep or (re)gain the upper hand. Using examples from the very popular sport of wrestling, he argued that the more flexible wrestler will probably win the fight. However, one should never confuse flexibility with capitulation. The main aim is to subdue the opponent and not to surrender. Khamenei was afraid that in the prevailing economic crisis in his country, friends and foes alike might interpret his enthusiasm for flexibility as an acknowledgement of defeat. Therefore, he cleverly resorted to his clerical skills by using Shia theology and history to further legitimize flexibility in the negotiations: By adding "heroic" to "flexibility" it was easy for a religious expert to find convincing examples of such behaviour in Shia history. Khamenei himself had translated an Arabic book into Farsi in 1970 that described how the Shiite Imam Hassan had attempted to negotiate peace with Muawiyah I, the founder of the Sunni Umayyad dynasty, rather than resorting to confrontation. This act of "heroic flexibility" prevented senseless bloodshed and secured the survival of the Shiites (Parsi, 2017, pp.221–222). According to this interpretation, "heroic flexibility" should be preferred to "stubborn resistance." Now Iran felt forearmed and prepared for real negotiations.

The negotiations

Fortunately, the new Iranian approach landed on fertile ground in Washington. As early as 2009 – coincidentally the year of the Green uprisings in Iran – US President Barack Obama started a new reconciliation strategy towards the Islamic world, including Iran, that was meant to heal the wounds of the past and foster forgiveness on the part of Muslims for previous "imperialist" behaviour. On the occasion of the Iranian New Year (Nowruz) in March 2009, Obama sent a letter to Khamenei that surprised the addressee and the wider public not only because it was simultaneously posted on YouTube with Farsi subtitles, but also because of its respectful tone – Obama used the official name Islamic Republic of Iran instead of simply Iran – and its many proposals for improving bilateral relations. Unlike many of his predecessors, Obama did not imply there was a deep rift between the people and the leadership in Iran, which would have acknowledged an imminent regime change. For the suspicious Iranian clergy, this clarification was a prerequisite for any serious negotiations. The letter culminated with an official expression that the United States wanted Iran to "take its rightful place in the community of nations" (Parsi, 2017, p.71).

But Obama had to wait until Iran's presidential elections in 2013 that resulted in Hassan Rouhani replacing Mahmoud Ahmadinejad. Whereas Ahmadinejad had done what he could to nurture the image of Iranian stubbornness, the newly elected Rouhani had won the approval of Iranian voters with a programme of reason and farsightedness. Obama was willing to give him a chance. Consequently, he called Rouhani in September 2013. For the first time since 1979, a US president had spoken directly with his Iranian counterpart. This phone call indicated the mutual desire to reach a "zone of possible agreement" (ZOPA) and thus opened the final phase of the negotiations (Tabatabai and Pease, 2019, p.36).

However, Obama had to overcome significant resistance at home. Since the relations between the two countries were broken for decades, there was a lack of face-to-face negotiating experience on both sides. For many US politicians, the IRI and its regime were a sort of "mystery" or "puzzle" (Pollack, 2005). Thus, the field was mostly left to speculators and people pursuing personal or political agendas. Without firsthand knowledge and well-founded analysis, US politicians were often left with distorted stereotypes about Iranians' basic "irrationality and egoism," relying on oversimplified statements, such as, "Iranians hate negotiations" (Limbert, 2008, p.3). Why would one negotiate with people who are evil and irrational?

American opponents of negotiations and a nuclear deal often employed historical analogies and "failure narratives" to fortify their arguments. Very often, they compared the current Islamic Republic of Iran with Nazi Germany and equated Obama's support for the nuclear agreement to the 1938 Munich agreement and Prime Minister Chamberlain's appeasement policy towards the Nazis. Others drew parallels to the negotiations with North Korea on its nuclear programme during the Clinton years in the 1990s (Oppermann and Spencer, 2018, p.279).

Without a doubt, Obama's strong aspiration to sign a deal came with many risks. Although the Iranians had their own good – economic – reasons to get the sanctions lifted, they became increasingly sure that Obama was more in need of a success than they themselves, since his entire Middle East strategy would fail without a nuclear agreement. Iran expert Robin Wright spoke for many when he stated that a nuclear deal with Iran would be "the single most important foreign policy achievement by President Obama [...] and the most important nonproliferation achievement in probably five or six presidencies" (Jaafari, 2014, p.1). Aware of this assessment, the Iranians became further convinced that the greater onus was on the West to get an agreement, because it obviously wanted an Iran free of nuclear weapons more urgently than that Iran wanted the lifting of sanctions (Esfandiary, 2013, p.2). Therefore, it is quite obvious that the Iranian narrative strengthened the best alternative to a negotiated agreement (BATNA) of its leadership. In the case of a no-deal it would be much easier for the Iranians to blame the American side and get the sanctions softened. To make the argument even stronger: since a compromise with Iran (including the JCPOA) was a prerequisite for Obama's reconciliation approach towards the Islamic world, Iran could afford to stick with its narrative. By contrast, any hypothetical nuclear negotiations with the Trump administration would have weakened Iran's BATNA.

In addition, the US negotiators – at the outset of the talks at least – tended to underestimate the impact and liability of Iran's narrative. A quotation from 2014 perfectly captures Khamenei's perspective in this regard: "Reconciliation between Iran and America is possible, but [it is] not possible between the Islamic Republic and America" (Sadjadpour and Taleblu, 2015, p.3). Khamenei's advisers managed to convince him that the economic crisis was severe enough for the country to need a "breather." This could be sold easily to the public as another example of Khomeini's appreciation of the national interest and Khamenei's "heroic flexibility." The persistence of Iran's narrative was proven once again by the extent and rigour of Trump's renewed sanctions regime that was even sharper than in 2011; Tehran was not looking for another negotiated relief. For Khamenei, this would have entailed the much-feared conflation of flexibility with surrender.

Iranian negotiation strategy

Iran's revolutionary narrative with all its strong "contamination" and "redemption" aspects contributed significantly to the revolution's longevity and charisma. However, the narrative also belied a rather narrow view of a multifaceted world. For example, the Iranian leadership is guided by the conviction that the Western powers have long manipulated international law and the international system to take advantage of weaker countries. In this view, therefore, the international system is inherently unjust towards Iran. Summarizing the experiences of the Iraq–Iran War, Rafsanjani stated in October 1988, "[The war] taught us that international laws are only scraps of paper" (Cordesman and Seitz, 2009, p.420). The narrative of deep distrust and of the need for self-reliance was later strengthened by the sanctions imposed on Iran in response to its nuclear programme.

Since some of the sanctions were imposed by the UN Security Council, an institution that was already accused of having abandoned the Iranians during the war with Iraq, the Iranian leadership also included the Security Council on its list of states and institutions that treat weaker and "non-compliant" countries unfairly (Tabatabai and Samuel, 2017, p.172). Consequently, for the leadership in Tehran the signing of the JCPOA would also embarrass all those "dark powers" behind the "illegal" and "unfair" sanctions against Iran. It would enable the country to improve its defence capabilities in the face of its many adversaries. President Rouhani went even so far as to put the historical importance of the nuclear deal for Iran on par with that of the Iraq–Iran War and even the Islamic Revolution (Tabatabai and Samuel, 2017, p.165). All in all, resting on these convictions, the Iranian negotiators mainly preferred an abstract ideal of "justice" to codified legal commitments.

The Islamic Revolution of 1979 not only produced a specific narrative but also caused a fundamental shift in Iranian diplomacy. As a theocracy, the Islamic

Republic now increasingly used religious elements in its negotiating approach or based its negotiation strategy on religious rules and norms. Not surprisingly, the main negotiation methods Iran used as of 1979 were rooted in Twelver Shiism: "*taqiyyah,*" "*tanfih,*" and "*khodeh.*"

Taqiyyah, translated as "pretense" or "denial," means "to shield or guard oneself" against a more powerful opponent. The Shia necessity for *taqiyyah* is based on their position as an oft-maligned Islamic minority. The method of *taqiyyah* was thus designed as an instrument to protect the faithful and their lives while preserving the Shia claim to spiritual primacy and leadership of the *umma* (Landsberg and Solomon, 2010, p.14). Of course, it has also been used in the context of the narrative: For many experts of Islamic studies, Khamenei's 2005 *fatwa* against nuclear weapons is a clear example of *taqiyyah*. It was announced only three months after the election of Mahmoud Ahmadinejad in June 2005, when Iran was under international fire due to Ahmadinejad's Holocaust denial. Therefore, many observers argued that the *fatwa* was a tactic to safeguard Iran's interests (Landsberg and Solomon, 2010, p.20).

Tanfih can be defined as "reluctance" in the sense of "reasonably doing nothing." In a world of constant flux, people and powers are also in constant flux. Only those who do nothing can therefore maintain their position and circumvent the constant turmoil around them. All actors inevitably make mistakes and must then put a lot of effort into undoing them. The message here is that you must be able to wait to win. This is how the Iranians learned to wait and calmly prepare to reach their goal. By contrast, they claim, Western culture demands immediate results. From the Iranian perspective, the one who has more patience usually wins in the end (Landsberg and Solomon, 2010, p.15).

Khodeh is closely related to *taqiyyah* as a historical Shia tradition of deceiving enemies in order to benefit from them. The frequent use of half-truths instead of direct lies is a well-known *khodeh* tactic. A very good example of this is Khomeini's tactic of making promises, as he often did in his many interviews from exile in France. For example, he promised freedom of expression to all Iranians. He did not lie in the narrower sense, because he always accompanied his promises with the (implied) caveat that all expressions should be "in line with Islam" (Landsberg and Solomon, 2010, p.15).

Of course, it took a while for the West to become aware of this completely new negotiating background and to be able to adapt to it. A second handicap tended to be that Western, and particularly American, negotiators overestimated the independence and latitude of Iranian negotiators. US media and politicians had gotten used to blaming the "conservative forces" and especially Khamenei for Iranian misdeeds. Therefore, the Iranian negotiators skillfully played the role of the "good cop," who urgently needed to win something to "convince the reactionaries at home." They presented themselves as representatives of the rational, national element in the Iranian leadership and often referred to their Western education and even to their enthusiasm for local American sports teams to demonstrate their trustworthiness. But no Iranian negotiator has ever been a real decision maker – everyone was under the mandate of Supreme Leader Ali Khamenei.

However, this does not mean that individual Iranian negotiators were not brilliant diplomats. This especially applies to Foreign Minister Mohammad Javad Zarif, who was praised by his counterparts as "exceptionally bright" and for "playing a weak hand superbly" (Parsi, 2017, p.365). Zarif convinced the Western delegates that he did not prefer zero-sum solutions and advocated the importance of mutual understanding and reciprocity. He indicated during the negotiations that he – of course – would like to end the ongoing economic downward spiral in his country, but – much more importantly – he would like to prevent an open war with the United States (Tabatabai and Pease, 2019, p.35). One can only speculate as to what extent Zarif's strategy was a reflection of the specific Iranian negotiation style.

Most scholars agree that culture has a large impact on the (mis)understanding of tactics and behaviours of negotiation partners. Therefore, knowledge of the Iranian negotiation culture/style turned out to be essential. The Iranian negotiation style generates both challenges and opportunities. One challenge is gaining trust and confidence. In Iran, a culture of political mistrust predominates, not least because of the long autocratic tradition; trust must therefore first be gained. In addition, Iranians are fundamentally more relational than task-oriented. They focus more on the person on the other side of the negotiating table than on the institution he or she represents. One way to gain trust is to guarantee that the other person not be forced into a losing position. In other words, Iranian negotiators must feel assured that they will gain something in the course of the negotiations (Khajehpour, 2017, p.2).

Another challenge is the poor image of compromise. Compromise is seen as a sign of submission and weakness. Compromising brings shame to those who do it. By contrast, someone who forces others to compromise increases his/her level of honour and reputation. For example, when the Obama administration signalled its desire to start negotiations, the Iranians added new preconditions. Negotiating before victory shows weakness, and the Iranian government interpreted Obama's readiness for a dialogue as a sign of weakness. If they would have had Obama's trump cards, they probably would not have entered into the nuclear negotiations (Rhode, 2010, pp.13,15).

Western countries have an opportunity vis-à-vis negotiating with Iran in that Iranian culture extols justice and thus also exalts agreements that it perceives as just. In addition, Iranians have a deep appreciation for Western technologies and expertise. Of course, despite all the asymmetries in power, they want to be perceived and treated as equal partners. This aspiration somewhat contradicts one of the challenges mentioned above, since the negotiation process from the Iranian point of view is akin to an arduous struggle to gain power (Khajehpour, 2017, p.2).

In addition, the deeply rooted Iranian bazaar tradition entails that the Iranians will name a very high price initially, with the understanding that it will be rejected and that a subsequent counter-offer will be made. The point of the first offer is to calibrate the subsequent negotiations rather than to achieve an immediate result. By contrast, the P5+1, including the United States, at least at the beginning of the negotiations, were convinced that they should pay the price on the tag. In other words, they viewed the Iranian entry offer as a sign of unwillingness to talk and not as the opening of the forthcoming negotiations (Esfandiary, 2013, p.1).

This misunderstanding can serve as a bridge to the concluding remarks.

Conclusions

Any future negotiations between Iran and the West, particularly the United States, should begin with a careful definition of what could be considered "successful" and "productive" in these negotiations. The US side is committed to ensuring that the Islamic Republic never becomes a nuclear military power, and that it stops supporting terrorist movements, considers recognizing Israel, and complies with established human rights standards.

For the Iranian side, the ideal outcome would be that the United States return to the JCPOA, lift economic sanctions, end support for Iranian dissidents, remove the Islamic Republic from the list of state sponsors of terrorism, and end the "regime change" discussion (Limbert, 2008, p.14). During the last months of the Trump administration, these kinds of meetings, not to speak of negotiations, became increasingly unrealistic. President Trump applied a "maximum pressure" campaign of sanctions and his Secretary of State, Mike Pompeo, even renewed the "regime change" demand in a press conference: "At the end of the day, the Iranian people will get to make a choice about their leadership. If they make the decision quickly, that would be wonderful" (Fitzpatrick, 2017a, p.56). Neither Trump nor Pompeo brought the Iranian leadership to its knees; in fact, they achieved just the opposite: they poured water on Khamenei's mills and strengthened the hardliners (ICG, 2019, pp.10, 18), who retook the parliament in 2020 and secured the victory of their like-minded fellow Ebrahim Raisi in the presidential elections on June 18, 2021.

Between 2018 and 2020, Khamenei did not tire of repeating proclamations of steadfastness. It was much easier for him and the whole religious establishment, including the IRGC and the religious endowments, to survive and even prosper under the circumstances of "maximum pressure" than it was for the middle classes and the poor, who bore the brunt of the economic misery. Consequently, the latter rose up against their leadership in 2017–2018 and in late 2019, but did not fundamentally question the JCPOA. In this regard, the Iranian leadership can still rely on the support of almost the entire population in two arenas: first, in closing ranks against potential or real foreign threats – the result of hundreds of years of common experiences; second, in warding off any attempt to deny the Iranian people basic rights. The national nuclear programme has become a matter of pride. Iranians will therefore support their government not caving to pressure on issues regarded as fundamental to the country's sovereignty. Iran would never accept limits to its nuclear programme that are not required of other states (Fitzpatrick, 2017a, p.33).

This consensus continues to strengthen Iran's negotiation power. In addition, the four years of the Trump presidency significantly weakened reform-oriented or at least moderate Iranian negotiators. Their highly respected chief, Foreign Minister Zarif, is currently fighting a ruinous battle against the IRGC. Thus, even if – as has been repeatedly stated – all Iranian nuclear negotiators were ultimately dependent on Khamenei's decision, the P5+1 have never before been confronted by such a homogeneous block of hardliners as they are today.

However, this is not the only burden that President Biden has inherited from his predecessor Trump. Since Biden – as vice president – had been part of the Obama administration since 2009, the Iranian leadership is expecting no less than a resumption of Obama's Iran policy. And, indeed, Biden has made it clear from the beginning that he wants his government to recommit to the JCPOA. His main precondition is that Iran should come back into compliance with the deal before he allows the lifting of sanctions imposed by Trump. Yet, in the meantime, the Iranians have increased the stakes. They returned to the enrichment of uranium well beyond the 3.67 per cent limit imposed by the JCPOA, hitting 20 per cent, and have even enriched smaller quantities to 60 per cent – not far from the 90 per cent level required for weapons-grade uranium. Tehran has further breached the terms of the deal by exceeding stockpile limits and operating advanced centrifuges.

All in all, future negotiations have become more difficult for the P5+1 in general and the United States in particular, and Donald Trump was – even if unintentionally – one of the strongest inspirations for the revolutionary Iranian narrative.

References

Cordesman, A.H., and, Seitz, A.C. (2009) *Iranian Weapons of Mass Destruction: The Birth of a Regional Nuclear Arms Race?* Santa Barbara, CA: Praeger.

Esfandiary, D. (2013, February 21) *Understanding Iran's Negotiating Style*, Lobelog. www.lobelog.com/understanding-irans-negotiating style/

Fitzpatrick, M. (2017) 'Introduction', *Adelphi Series*, vol.57, no.466–467, pp.9–18.

Fitzpatrick, M. (2017a) 'Assessing the JCPOA', *Adelphi Series*, vol.57, no.466–467, pp.19–60.

Florensa, S. (2016) 'Internal Transformation and Changing Mentalities: Impact on the Iranian Regime', In, S. Blockmans, A. Ehteshami, and G. Bahgat (Eds.), *EU-Iran Nuclear Relations after the Nuclear Deal* (pp.14–19). Brussels, Belgium: CEPS.

International Crisis Group (ICG). (2019) 'On Thin Ice: The Iran Nuclear Deal at Three', Middle East Report No. 195.

Izewicz, P. (2019) 'The JCPOA Procurement Channel', *Adelphi Series*, vol.57, no.466–467, pp.61–88.

Jaafari, S. (2014, November 11) *The Persian Art of Declining What You Really Want and Offering What You'll Never Give Could Play a Role in US – Iran Nuclear Talks*, PRI. www.pri.org/stories/2014-11-05/persian-art-declining-what-you-really-want-and-offering-what-youll-never-give.

Jett, D.C. (2018) *The Iran Nuclear Deal: Bombs, Bureaucrats, and Billionaires.* Washington, DC: Palgrave Macmillan.

Kaplan, F. (2014, July 23) *America's Flight 17*, Slate. www.slate.com/articles/news_and_politics/war_stories/2014/07/the_vincennes_downing_of_iran_air_flight_655_the_united_states_tried_to.html.

Khajehpour, B. (2017, October 26) *Negotiating with Iranians? Build Rapport Right from the Onset*, Schranner. www.schranner.com/de/news/2017/10/26/negotiating-with-iranians-build-rapport-right-from-the-onset.

Khomeini, R. (1979) *Rahnemudha (Guidelines).* Tehran, Iran: Ministry of Islamic Guidance.

Landsberg, C.M., and, Solomon, H. (2010) 'How Do Iranian Diplomats Negotiate?' *American Foreign Policy Interests*, vol.32, no.1, pp.13–25.

Limbert, J.W. (2008) *Negotiating with the Islamic Republic of Iran: Raising the Chances for Success – Fifteen Points to Remember.* Washington DC: United States Institute of Peace (USIP).

Malik, S.K. (1979) *The Quranic Concept of War.* Lahore, Reprint in India: Adam Publishers and Distributors.

Oppermann, K., and, Spencer, A. (2018) 'Narrating Success and Failure: Congressional Debates on the 'Iranian Nuclear Deal', *European Journal of International Relations*, vol.24, no.2, pp.268–292.

Parsi, T. (2017) *Losing an Enemy: Obama, Iran, and the Triumph of Diplomacy.* New Haven, CT and London: Yale University Press.

Pollack, K.M. (2005) *The Persian Puzzle: The Conflict Between Iran and America.* New York, NY: Random House.

Rezaei, F. (2019) *Iran's Foreign Policy after the Nuclear Agreement: Politics of Normalizers and Traditionalists.* Washington, DC: Palgrave Macmillan.

Rhode, H. (2010) *The Sources of Iranian Negotiating Behavior.* Jerusalem, Israel: Jerusalem Center for Public Affairs.

Sajadpour, K., and, Taleblu, A.B. (2015, May) 'Iran in the Middle East: Leveraging Chaos', FRIDE Policy Brief No. 202, pp.1–18.

Sciolino, E. (2000) *Persian Mirrors: The Elusive Face of Iran.* New York, NY: Free Press.

Tabatabai, A.M. and, Samuel, A.T. (2017) 'What the Iran-Iraq War Tells Us about the Future of the Iran Nuclear Deal', *International Security*, vol.42, no.1, pp.152–185.

Tabatabai, A.M., and, Pease, C. (2019) 'The Iranian Nuclear Negotiations', In I.W. Zartman (Ed.), *How Negotiations End* (pp.27–45). Cambridge: Cambridge University Press.

16

THE RISE AND FALL OF ARMS CONTROL

How narratives impacted US-Russia post-Cold War arms control negotiations

Mikhail Troitskiy

Introduction

Since the end of World War II, relations between the United States and the Soviet Union and—subsequently—Russia have been one of the major factors defining the global security environment. Even after China took the position of number two in the world by the size of its defense spending, Russia remained militarily agile and determined to challenge US preponderance as the main security provider in several key regions including Europe and the Middle East. In such circumstances, arms control has always been a key activity giving Washington and Moscow a common cause, a reason to engage in negotiation, as well as a chance to mitigate arms races and reduce the risk of a deadly conflict. Understanding the motive forces behind US-Russian arms control arrangements may help not only to explain the dynamic of US-Russia relations over the last half-century, but also to identify prospective solutions to the existing challenge of ensuring international security in a multilateral setting—with participation of more than two technologically advanced states with foreign policy ambitions that may require the use of force.

Experts offer a variety of perspectives on the forces and factors that make arms control possible (Freedman and Michaels, 2019; Kuehn, 2020a). Some observers argue that technological advancement plays a key role in enabling cuts in the outdated weapon systems. Others emphasize the role of worldviews of national leaders who may opt for arms control as a means of signaling their intentions. Another group of scholars posit that arms control is secondary to the politics of inter-state relations and only becomes possible when the parties are sufficiently reassured about mutual intentions (Troitskiy, 2020). And yet one important factor that is often overlooked in those analyses is narrative.

DOI: 10.4324/9781003203209-19

This chapter explores the impact of narratives on the successes and failures of arms control from the second part of the 1980s until the 2020s. The whole period under investigation is split into four parts. During each of them, a distinct influential narrative either facilitated or hampered arms control negotiations between Washington and Moscow. Available documents often shed enough light on the actual mechanisms whereby prevailing narratives translated into policy decisions favoring or undermining negotiated arms control solutions. Indeed, one cannot claim that narratives always shaped arms control outcomes. However, their tangible impact is relatively easy to demonstrate. The overall post-Cold War dynamic in US-Russian arms control can be described as a gradual shift from redemption to contamination narratives, as they are defined in Chapter 1, with sporadic attempts to re-invoke the need to take bold action for the sake of common benefit and social progress.

Narratives in arms control: A definition and rationale(s)

For the purposes of this chapter, narrative is defined by two core features. First, in contrast to a statement of fact or logically sound analysis, narrative is uncritical. For a story to qualify as a narrative, it has in some way to fall short of what is broadly—if not universally—accepted as fact and/or what is commonly considered to be impartial analysis. This shortfall usually comes in the form of contravention to, omission, or "invention" of facts compounded by a logical inconsistency, such as a hasty generalization or a leap from correlation to causality. Most convincing—and therefore influential—are the narratives that do not directly mislead (i.e., contradict widely accepted statements of fact), but rather intentionally overlook or make up facts in limited numbers and/or rely on hasty generalizations to reach exciting conclusions. In a way, such narratives not so much distort the truth, but augment reality—in terms of facts and/or logic.

Second, those exciting conclusions usually make a narrative emotionally appealing, so that it attracts a constituency of believers despite—sometimes obvious—contradictions with facts or logical inconsistencies. The attractiveness of a narrative usually stems from a principle of justice or ethics.

Often—and in particular, in the international security and arms control domains—narratives take the form of a causal argument or even a full-fledged theory postulating a causal connection between certain phenomena or groups of phenomena. When it comes in the form of a narrative, such argument has significant logical gaps. For example, it can be based on insufficient evidence, employ contestable methodology to prove the causal link, or engage in an outright logical fallacy, such as hasty generalization. International security narratives often involve conspiracy thinking typically based on unverified and unexplained motives ascribed to actors: for example, "nation A has always been out to subvert and exploit nation B" or "rich in natural resources, nation X will always be targeted by other powerful players, particularly nation Y, that will invariably look to subjugate nation X." Quite often, narrative comes in the form of a valid concept or theory extended far beyond its narrow applicability domain.

In arms control and in general, I am interested in the nontrivial impacts of narratives on negotiation. Proving that a certain narrative has impacted a negotiation process in a nontrivial way requires that several conditions be met. First, the narrative must not pertain directly to the subject matter under negotiation. If it does, the case becomes too easy because the influence is direct, and it becomes hard to establish whether the narrative influenced the negotiation or negotiation shaped the narrative. Second, the narrative must be deep and broad enough to be capable of exerting undisputed substantive influence on identities or create strong enough biases that would affect negotiating parties' views and positions.

As discussed elsewhere in this volume, deep narratives tend to address the core needs of individuals and groups. In international politics these needs usually include security and identity. When security was the main item on the agenda of US-Russian relations, arms control usually worked. Out of the four main periods of US-Soviet and US-Russian arms control negotiations explored below in this chapter, the primacy of a cooperative security (redemption) narrative was characteristic of the late 1980s and 2009–2011. When an identity narrative—based largely on "contamination"—moved to the forefront of the public discourse for at least one party—as it was the case during the most part of the 1990s, late in the 2000s, and then after 2012—reducing the risk of conflict or limiting potential damage should a conflict break out largely became secondary to the goal of asserting identity.

Shallow narratives, as they are defined in this book, may have also impacted Soviet Union's, Russia's, and United States' arms control postures. However, it is difficult to assess whether and to what extent shallow narratives were shaping those postures rather than just explaining them *post hoc*. Even if there is reason to believe in the independent impact produced by shallow narratives, how much they swayed the actual policy is always difficult to gauge because they do not have enough influence to enable important decisions.

Why studying the impact of narratives on arms control is an important and potentially rewarding task? As mentioned earlier, arms control plays a significant role in international relations because it reduces the risks of and damage from potential conflict and saves money without compromising security of the parties involved and stability of the international order.

Yet, arms control is a challenging process because it is prone with risks of exploitation: forswearing or reducing the arsenal of any weapon—if it is not completely outdated and therefore useless—may increase the vulnerability of the party that engages in reductions, especially if it incorrectly assesses the resulting balance of forces or falls victim to outright cheating by its negotiation counterpart (Montgomery, 2006). Effective arms control requires credible mechanisms of signaling—providing the counterparts with reassurances of benign intentions and absence of plans to cheat or otherwise abuse their trust. Every means of signaling has its flaws and can be refuted on the grounds of pure rationality (Rosato, 2014).

Verbal commitment stands out among all the imperfect methods of signaling the intention to implement in good faith a deal that has been agreed upon. A mere promise to abide by the agreement and refrain from cheating on other parties may not be a strong enough means of reassurance, even if expressed publicly at the highest political level several times. One may argue that such talk is cheap, offers no guarantee against deception, and may legitimately be reneged upon by the following government. In such circumstances, narratives carry a better promise as widely accepted arguments in support of a certain perspective on relevant postures and ways of behavior. The fact that a whole nation or a sizeable chunk thereof, along with their political leaders, tend to believe in a certain "augmented reality" story may be taken as a sign of credible commitment by the nation and its leaders to the main tenets of such story.

Usually, an arms control-facilitating narrative has been one of (some) weapons becoming gratuitous in a situation short of imminent security threats and under perceived stability of intentions of the main players. Such narrative usually also posits that large arsenals of weapons generate a significant risk of their inadvertent destructive use while their reductions would bring an economic peace dividend. Indeed, every major power takes the existence of adversaries—at least potential—for granted, acknowledging that the kingdom of peace and friendship is yet a distant perspective. And yet if we know what our adversaries are up to, we feel secure and could afford forgoing some of our (redundant) military capability.

In sum, there are at least three possible avenues for a narrative to foster (or hinder) progress in arms control negotiations. *First*, as negotiating sides look for clarity in mutual intentions, one way to become reassured of the counterparts' non-adversarial intentions would be to hear a relevant narrative, usually based on redemption—for example, the touting of peaceful resolution of disputes, absence of aggressive claims vis-à-vis other nations, record of commitment to shared security and prosperity, etc. *Second*, to be successful, arms control efforts need to be facilitated by a narrative of collective agency, praising them as a prestigious, status-conferring, and economically expedient activity. Otherwise, even when the sides do not have acute concerns with each other's intentions, they may nevertheless refrain from disarmament if it does not hold out the promise of clear benefits to the main stakeholders. Moreover, an adverse (contamination) narrative—for example, one about the need to prevail in all thinkable conflicts against any potential adversary—can scuttle precarious arms control efforts, even if the credulity and popularity of an adverse narrative are relatively weak. *Third*, narratives can affect the negotiating sides' BATNAs—for example, by pointing to the past cases of great power overstretch because of arms races or, adversely, to the ongoing decline of one's negotiation counterpart that makes immediate deals with such actor unnecessary.

The importance of narratives for the cause of arms control was evident to the Soviet Communist Party Secretary General Mikhail Gorbachev as he was looking for ways to achieve a breakthrough in arms control negotiations between Moscow and Washington. In a December 30, 1985 meeting with the leadership of the Soviet foreign ministry and Soviet ambassadors to the main bilateral and multilateral negotiation forums he stated with "agitation":

> The Americans are being arrogant and impudent [...] They do not want to implement the agreements reached in Geneva (at the summit between Gorbachev and US President Ronald Reagan in November that year—*author*). We should force them to pursue peaceful settlement of disputes. There is simply no other way. We should excite the people of the world and Europe by proposals that could bring these people together and ultimately force the US government to make an agreement with us [...] The only way to influence the Americans—is to subject them to the pressure from [their] society. Our initiatives should be conducive to that. Even if we do not reach an agreement, we will still push them in the right direction.
>
> *Grinevsky, 2004, p.74*

In his memoirs, Soviet envoy to the Stockholm negotiations on confidence building measures in the 1980s, Oleg Grinevsky, described a paradoxical case of an over-facilitation of arms control negotiation under the excessive influence of a narrative. He complained about the ease and neglect with which Soviet arms control negotiators were pushed by the country's political leadership—the members of which were apparently carried away by the narratives they cherished—to abandon their elaborate positions and agree to the conditions set by their Western counterparts. Contrasting top Soviet foreign policy advisors to those of US President Reagan, Grinevsky points out that the US establishment was always very well versed in the details, including technical characteristics of the weapons systems under negotiation. They were surrounding Reagan with the "walls of realistic and rigid positions developed on the basis of national interests and the doctrine of nuclear deterrence." According to Grinevsky, it allowed Reagan to come up and play with his "pipe dreams of a nuclear-free world." In contrast, Gorbachev's top aides, Alexander Yakovlev and Anatoly Chernyaev, "knew nothing and—most importantly—did not want to learn anything." They were "squeamish" about "concrete details" and in their memos to Gorbachev they blasted the expert views and positions prepared by the foreign and defense ministries. Instead, they were looking to "overwhelm Reagan by the boldness, or even riskiness, of their approach to the main challenges of world politics" (Grinevsky, 2004, p.82).

More recently, a top US arms control policymaker, Assistant Secretary of State Christopher Ford, in a February 2020 speech argued that the whole business of arms control in fact hinged on a narrative. At the same time, Ford suggested that such narrative was deeply flawed because it was designed to create a rationale for overriding the security concerns that would be natural for any nation and instrumental for its survival. In Ford's view, that era was one of rosy pictures of the future and unfounded expectations that were relatively soon dashed by the reality of inter-state competition (Ford, 2020).

The above examples demonstrate that enthusiasts and skeptics of arms control alike emphasize the need for a supporting narrative in arms control negotiations. Adverse narratives can hamper—"contaminate"—arms control agreements, although it is usually difficult—if not impossible—accurately to measure the impact of narratives on negotiations and deals reached therein.

From redemption to contamination: The fits and starts of US-Russian post-Cold War arms control negotiations

Given the halted nature of frequently stalemated arms control negotiations over the last quarter-century, it would be easy to discount enthusiasm for arms control as a unique phenomenon that only emerged and stayed alive for a brief period as the Cold War was ending in the late 80s and early 90s. If that were the case, there would not be enough data and variation systematically to study the impact of narratives on the arms control process, and the corresponding research question would hardly make any sense.

Indeed, arms control in Russia-West and especially in US-Russia relations nearly ground to a halt in the second half of the 1990s as the two sides were increasingly finding themselves at odds over manifold security challenges—from the Balkans to post-Soviet Eurasia. Although over the 1990s, NATO and Russia managed to adapt to the post-Cold War realities the Treaty on Conventional Forces in Europe that was initially signed in 1990, the treaty never entered into force because of an acute controversy over Russia's military presence in Georgia and Moldova in the 2000s. US-Russian bilateral ABM and START II treaties collapsed over Washington's determination to pursue ballistic missile defenses since the late 1990s. START I—the last leftover, along with the INF Treaty, from the arms control heyday—was set to expire at the end of 2009. Such downward dynamic, punctured by the Russia-Georgia war over South Ossetia in August 2008, gave all possible reasons to be pessimistic about the future of any measures agreed upon by two or more countries to reduce their weapons arsenals for the sake of controlling the risks of a devastating conflict.

However, against all odds, the arms control of the early 1990s surprisingly rebounded in 2009–2011. During that period, Moscow and Washington proved capable of negotiating, signing, and ratifying the New START treaty, came close to resolving their decades-long dispute on ballistic missile defense, and even briefly discussed further reductions in the US and Russian nuclear arsenals—before descending into another "dark age" for arms control beginning around 2012–2013. Over the years that followed, Russia and the United States ended the INF Treaty, barely extended the New START, and buried any hope of resuming conventional arms control in Europe. Toward the end of 2020, the United States announced its intention to terminate the Open Skies Treaty, effectively dismantling the last major agreement in the field of disarmament and confidence-building. While Washington and—to a lesser extent—Moscow expressed interest in a trilateral (Russia, the US, and China) or even multilateral (all or most of the nuclear-armed states) format of further arms control negotiations, as of late 2021, it was far from clear whether Beijing, Paris, or London could be amenable to even discussing the size and purpose of their nuclear arsenals. What kind of narratives set the stage for arms control talks and agreements throughout that period, and what are the reasons to believe in their material impact on the outcomes?

Competing narratives

Since the second part of the 1980s, succeeding narratives focused mostly on the various aspects of collective security and individual identity of the main players involved in arms control negotiations. While collective security (redemption) narratives were conducive to positive arms control outcomes, narratives of identity—usually the identity that actors look to assert and have others recognize—"contaminated" the arms control discourse and hampered arms control by disincentivizing its participants or weakening the rationale for reducing the risks and potential damages of an armed confrontation.

Perestroika, "new political thinking," and the peace dividend of the late 1980s

The times of Mikhail Gorbachev's "new political thinking" in Soviet Union's foreign policy proved to be the most favorable period for arms control negotiations, even if their achievements did not become fully visible until the first part of the 1990s—following the dissolution of the USSR. Redemption narratives of shared threats to survival, the need to stop arms races and avoid the worst of excesses of confrontation surged on the political agenda in the Soviet Union and eventually resonated with parts of the US policy community.

An unparalleled account of the motives that were driving Gorbachev and his close associates in the Soviet Communist Party and other segments of bureaucracy was provided by Oleg Grinevsky. A Soviet and subsequently Russian envoy to the main arms control negotiation forums and one of the key Soviet bureaucrat players in arms control policymaking, Grinevsky published a surprisingly candid book of memoirs. Key turning points in his accounts are corroborated by other participants—both Soviet/Russian and American.

Initial signs of a revolutionary change in the Soviet national security discourse toward redemption appeared as early as several months after the ascent of Mikhail Gorbachev to the post of the Communist Party secretary general. As discussions in the top Soviet bureaucracy were unfolding in July 1985 about the fate of intermediate-range missiles in Europe, the deputy chair of the Soviet Communist Party Central Committee's Defense Department Vitaly Kataev argued in a conversation with the deputy chief of the Soviet General Staff General Valentin Varennikov that

> time has come when the accumulated stocks of nuclear weapons [...] are no longer a means of deterrence, but a source of high nuclear danger, primarily, for the USSR, not so much for the Americans. [...] We used to think: the more missiles, the better. But now we have reconsidered. We've had the guts to tell our leadership: it's not about Reagan with his "zero option." We have to deal with the danger, not Reagan.

Kataev was appointed by Gorbachev to coordinate the Group of Five—a high-level inter-agency commission shaping the Soviet position in the Helsinki arms control negotiation forum (Grinevsky, 2004, p.61).

The risks of stockpiling nuclear weapons were recognized by the Soviet leadership simultaneously with the need for a peace dividend, given the worsening state of the Soviet economy because of the drop in oil prices after 1985. In early October 1986, Gorbachev told his top aides and the leadership of the Soviet armed forces, KGB, foreign ministry, and the Communist Party that the purpose of the ambitious Soviet-American arms control agenda that he was urging them to develop was primarily to "thwart a new round of arms race." According to Grinevsky, Gorbachev said,

> If we do not offer specific concessions [to the West], we are going to lose big. We shall be dragged into a back-breaking race, and we shall lose it because we are now stretched to the limits of our [economic] capacity.
>
> *Grinevsky, 2004, p.112*

In another meeting with advisors in late December 1986, Gorbachev acknowledged that the arms race with the United States had "bled dry and deformed the [Soviet] economy and finances and nearly caused poverty among people." He fumed about the Soviet military expenditure which "exceeds not only our economic capacity, but also the real threat to [Soviet] security and reasonable sufficiency." "Therefore," he told his foreign policy aides, "We need disarmament—not just cheap talk or propaganda, but real moves" (Grinevsky, 2004, p.124).

At the highest point in Soviet-US arms control negotiations, several days after the INF Treaty was signed in Washington in December 1987, Gorbachev assessed the impact of his ideas and narratives on Soviet foreign policy and relations with the United States. He told the top Soviet decision-making body—the Communist Party Politburo—that Moscow had been

> acting in accordance with the spirit of new political thinking for over two years. The ideas that we proclaimed and wanted to introduce into the practice of international relations had to be tested in real life; it was obvious that we needed practical results. The world was expecting and demanding that. Its trust in our new foreign policy depended on that [...]. And the

> decisive aspect [of that test] was the challenge of the Intermediate Nuclear Forces Treaty that has just been resolved.
>
> *Grinevsky, 2004, p.147*

Signed in December 1987, the INF Treaty became the first tangible result of the period of close engagement on arms control between Moscow and Washington.

Assessing the extent to which narratives impacted the Soviet position on arms control in the late 1980s—early 1990s is relatively easy. Anatoly Adamishin, a known Soviet and Russian diplomat and an active participant in the Soviet foreign policy process during perestroika, testified to Gorbachev's "idealism" that included the classical redemption narratives of "prioritizing universal humanitarian values, social justice, the making of a democratic world order." Those idealistic narratives "did not impede Gorbachev's pragmatic foreign policy. On the contrary, [they were] helpful because [they] fostered thinking about the future and prepared the ground for 'breakthrough ideas.'"

Mikhail Gorbachev's doctrine of "new political thinking" and the narratives of the shared imperative of survival between the East and the West as well as of the peace dividend required for the USSR to remain stable brought a number of deliverables aside from the INF Treaty. These were chronologically first and foremost the multilateral Treaty on Conventional Forces in Europe signed in November 1990 as well as bilateral US-Russian START I (July 1991) and START II (January 1993) treaties. START II was signed by Russian President Boris Yeltsin and US President George H.W. Bush, but the momentum for strategic arms control negotiations between the two nuclear superpowers goes back to the indispensable ice-melting and heavy-lifting done by Gorbachev and his US counterpart President Ronald Reagan.

That momentum of redemption carried well into the future. Adamishin opined that Gorbachev's idealistic narratives had a significant staying power, helping to manage differences between Russia and the West down the road—as late as 2014 when the crisis around Ukraine could have been "far more acute" if there had been no "positive experience accumulated during perestroika of overcoming difficult situations" (Adamishin, 2015). At least, throughout the 1990s and even in the first years of the new century Russia and the United States were under a certain influence of the collective security narrative. However, it was dissipating rather quickly and crowded out by adverse identity-based narratives.

Narratives adrift: From the former Yugoslavia to the US-Russian "reset"

From the second half of the 1990s until 2009 no clear-cut shared influential narrative worked in favor of arms control. At best, only one side's approach to arms control would for a certain period be conducive to preventing arms races and reducing the risk of an open conflict.

In the last decade of the 20th century the United States and some of its allies—the collective West—came to believe in the augmented reality of the "end of history." The international security dimension of that narrative postulated that an armed conflict between Russia and the United States or NATO has become completely unthinkable under advancing globalization. As a result, the time has come, that narrative suggested, to dispose of the weapons that were designed for a potential great power war.

For example, a group of 61 high-ranking retired generals and admirals from the United States, Russia, NATO countries, and several other states across the globe mentioned in their high-profile statement:

> The end of the Cold War created conditions favorable to nuclear disarmament. Termination of military confrontation between the Soviet Union and the United States made it possible to reduce strategic and tactical nuclear weapons, and to eliminate intermediate range missiles. It was a significant milestone on the path to nuclear disarmament when Belarus, Kazakhstan, and Ukraine relinquished their nuclear weapons.
>
> *Joint Statement, 1996*

Two retired top US military commanders concurred in their December 1996 "Joint Statement on Reduction of Nuclear Weapons Arsenals: Declining Utility, Continuing Risks." They emphasized the advent of a new era in international politics after the end of the Cold War and expressed conviction in the waning need for nuclear weapons in these circumstances:

> With the end of the Cold War, these weapons are of sharply reduced utility, and there is now much to be gained by substantially reducing their numbers and lowering their alert status, meanwhile exploring the feasibility of their ultimate complete elimination. The roles of nuclear weapons for purposes of security have been sharply narrowed in terms of the security of the United States [...] We believe the nations that possess these weapons should take the necessary steps to align their nuclear weapons policies and programs to match the diminished role and utility of these weapons, and the continuing risks they involve, joining in reducing their nuclear arsenals step by step to the lowest verifiable levels consistent with stable security, as rapidly as world conditions permit. Taking the lead, US and Russian reductions can open the door for the negotiation of multilateral reductions capping all arsenals at very low levels.
>
> *Statement on Nuclear Weapons, 1996*

Another facet of the pro-arms control narrative of the 1990s included the discussion of the need to overcome mutual nuclear deterrence in US-Russia relations. In the immediate aftermath of the Cold War, a number of influential authors were arguing that such deterrence had become obsolete and needed to be done away with if the world in general and the two nuclear superpowers in particular were to develop and rely on a "logic of peace" in international relations. In 1998, one of the active participants in US-Soviet arms control negotiations in the 1980s, US Ambassador James Goodby, wrote: "Until nuclear deterrence is no longer a determinant of many aspects of the US-Russian relationship, there will be a threshold in the relationship that neither side will ever cross" (Goodby, 1998, p.142).

Echoing Goodby, the influential Russian analyst Dmitri Trenin in his book titled *Unconditional Peace: The 21st Century Euro-Atlantic as a Security Community* described expectations of a democratic peace in the Euro-Atlantic area that could have rendered arms control largely irrelevant after the end of the Cold War, given the confirmed absence of adversarial intentions on the part of the West and Russia. Trenin stressed the importance of a shared "historical, political, and moral narrative" that would underlie the "notion of a community that is based on more than just [common, collective] security." From his perspective, the term "community" describes an

> essentially new type of relations among states. It is distinct from both traditional blocs and various models of collective security. Community prioritizes cooperative, shared security, but the meaning of community goes beyond security. It is based on values, mutual trust and an historical, moral, and political narrative shared by all members.
>
> *Trenin, 2013, p.21*

From Trenin's perspective, many prerequisites for a "community of states and an accompanying narrative" were in place at the end of the Cold War. These included

> [t]he Soviet consent to the tearing down of the Berlin Wall and German re-unification, Moscow's tolerance vis-à-vis the "velvet" revolutions in the Warsaw Pact, the pullout of the Soviet troops from Eastern Europe, the overthrowal of the communist regime in the USSR followed logically by the dismantlement of the Soviet Union, the emergence in its place of the Russian Federation with its democratic constitution [as well as the disappearance of] an urgent military threat.
>
> *Trenin, 2013, p.139*

Among other implications, such cooperative security narrative encouraged European Union to deepen its integration and helped both the EU and NATO to find rationales for respective enlargements. However, after an initial period of high expectations of a new partnership with the West, Russia came to share the optimistic cooperative security narrative only in a relatively small part. As a German arms control expert recognized, the United States and Russia

> both had problems in their mutual interpretation of certain key norms. One of those norms is the so-called indivisibility of security, which means that "my security is your security and whatever I do should not be to your detriment and vice versa." Particularly on the European continent, both Russia and America interpreted this and other norms according to their own gusto.
>
> *Kuehn, 2020b*

However, a few years after the end of the Cold War, Moscow was no longer prepared to embrace the redemption narrative and began to resent the triumphalism of cooperative security—largely because the Russian public and many of the country's leaders did not see significant immediate benefits from joining the cooperative security community led by the West. In the meantime, the costs for Russia of joining such community were not to be underestimated—at the very least, they would have included abandoning the positive view of the Soviet foreign policy record, a sacrifice the Russian public and many leaders were not ready to make (Clunan, 2014). Instead, from the mid-1990s, Russia steadily drifted toward an identity of a great power that inherits to the Soviet "superpowerness" and the Soviet foreign policy and diplomatic tradition. An integral part of Russia's foreign policy narrative has since been the belief that Russia forswore its superpower status in return for the special status of an "autonomous" great power not aligned with any bigger nation or bloc, yet demanding respect for its declared interests regardless of the unfavorable balance of forces.

The identity and narrative of a great power keen to protect its sovereignty—understood as the right to make decisions with little regard for the views of other great powers—implied limited interest in arms control as a means of promoting global security or ensure common survival. In Moscow, such motives were widely considered manipulative and designed to finish the business of disarming Russia for the one-sided benefit of its triumphant former Cold War rivals. Having lost the Gorbachevian penchant for arms control, over the 1990s Moscow retained interest in a number of arms control areas that it considered important because of specific security concerns.

In such circumstances, arms control slowed down significantly after its initial successes of the early 1990s, but still remained afloat: by 1999, Russia and NATO countries managed to finalize and put their signatures to the Adapted CFE Treaty. That happened several months after the highly controversial NATO aerial operation against Yugoslavia. Washington and Moscow also discussed opportunities for further reductions in strategic nuclear arms. Despite the contradictions that were piling up between the two sides, US and Russian presidents met in 1997 to look for an agreement on the distinction between permissible (nonstrategic, theater) and prohibited (strategic) missile defense systems. Such agreement could have removed hurdles to the ratification of START II by Russia and opened the way for negotiations on a new strategic arms reduction treaty. In the same year, Russia and NATO also signed a Founding Act on Mutual Relations—a high-profile declaration of commitment to avoid confrontation or an arms race. Those partial successes of arms control in the 1990s were not driven by any narrative, while the perception of Russia's opinion being unfairly ignored at key junctures in foreign policy decision making by the West did nothing to help the advocates of arms control.

To make matters worse, Russia' steep economic decline in the 1990s gave rise to a new contamination-type narrative of Russia's strategic irrelevance as a competitor of the West. That narrative initially enabled arms control negotiations in 2001–2002, but eventually dealt a major blow to the risk reduction and damage control business as Moscow developed an acute feeling of being exploited and decided to focus on status as an essential currency of international politics.

As Dmitri Trenin noted,

> [t]he ways and means of Russia's transformation raised concerns in the West. Expectations of a quick democratic transit were dashed. The rise of nationalist sentiment and a partial resurrection of communism in Russia after 1993 became a source of major concern [...] Russia's 1998 default on the public debt was perceived as the ultimate sign of the failure of Russia's engagement into the Western orbit. Russia came to be seen not so much as a partner, but a problem country—both because of its internal weakness and its lingering proclivity for grandstanding.
>
> *Trenin, 2013, p.140*

Early in the new century Russia made another attempt to assert its role in world politics as an "independent great power"—a major pillar of the global order that can make a decisive contribution to addressing challenges to that order, but requires unquestioned respect to what it calls its national interests. Such expectations generated a certain momentum in arms control around 2001–2002 (the signing of the US-Russian Strategic Offensive Reductions Treaty and a new progressive joint declaration on mutual relations between NATO and Russia in 2002), but then foundered on contradictions between the sides over managing their relations with Georgia, Ukraine, and other countries in post-Soviet Eurasia (Istomin, 2017).

No narrative emerged to back up the short-lived arms control deliverables at the beginning of the 21st century. To make matters worse for the Russian great power and status emancipation narrative, "[w]ith the September 11, 2001, attacks, Washington's immediate concern shifted away from Russia to the War on Terror and, later, toward China. Russia dropped out of the focus. Cooperation was not a direct priority of the White House anymore" (Kuehn, 2020b). The US narrative of America's dominance in global affairs (United States of America, 2002) was clearly incompatible with the Russian emancipation narrative because Russia was not considered a serious challenge to the US effort to upgrade its missile and advance democracy worldwide. Moscow, considered as distinct jabs at Russia the pullout from the ABM Treaty of 1972 by Washington, continued enlargement of NATO, and US support for the newly elected leaders in Georgia and Ukraine. Russia pledged a campaign of resistance that simultaneously made any attempt at bridging the gaps between narratives a fool's errand.

As favorable redemption narratives were giving way to identity- and status-based contamination narratives, arms control seemed to be doomed—before it surprisingly resurged briefly on the US-Russian agenda between 2009 and 2011. One of the immediate casualties of the erosion of the supporting narrative in the 2000s was the agreement on conventional forces in Europe. A negative feedback loop was thereby created: the absence of a supporting narrative hampered arms control which resulted in the demise of key agreements which, in turn, fully released Russia from its wavering commitment to the European security order, which, in its own turn, severely narrowed down potential options for a new unifying narrative of redemption. As the former US diplomat Philip Remler observed with the benefit of hindsight in 2019,

> [s]ince Russia's main goals for the Adapted CFE Treaty, including Baltic treaty accession, could no longer be met—nor could the CFE or Adapted CFE guarantee Russian security by stopping the enlargement of NATO—its interest in conventional arms control waned [...] Hard security and arms control were the main reasons Moscow accepted the international order laid out in the Helsinki Act, Charter of Paris, and OSCE. As arms control faded, so did Russia's reasons for committing to the order.
>
> *Remler, 2019*

The swan song: US-Russian "reset" and beyond

Arms control scored at least one success late in the 2000s. It was an unexpected development given the downward dynamic of the previous decade. The extent of direct impact of narratives on that most recent productive phase of arms control negotiations is difficult to assess at the time of this writing. Available documentary sources (McFaul, 2014; Burns, 2019) point to a significant role played in the unfreezing of arms control by the worldviews of the newly elected presidents of the United States and Russia—respectively, Barack Obama and Dmitry Medvedev. Each of the two leaders had his own personal convictions that shaped his political agenda—at least early into their presidencies. While Obama seemed to have been driven by the vision of a nuclear-free world, Medvedev was looking to set Russia on a new course of cooperation with America. In his April 2009 speech in Prague, Obama committed to pursuing ratification of the Comprehensive Test Ban Treaty and promoting the Fissile Materials Cutoff Treaty (*President Barack Obama*, 2009). Several days before Obama's Prague speech, Russian President Medvedev signed up in London to a joint US-Russian declaration, which committed Moscow and Washington to "achieving a nuclear-free world, while recognizing that this long-term goal will require a new emphasis on arms control and conflict resolution measures, and their full implementation by all concerned nations." The London declaration opened with language typical of the heyday of US-Soviet arms control:

> Reaffirming that the era when our countries viewed each other as enemies is long over, and recognizing our many common interests, we today established a substantive agenda for Russia and the United States to be developed over the coming months and years.
>
> *Joint Statement, 2009*

Medvedev, however, was not as much driven in the cooperative arms control effort with Obama by the narrative of a nuclear-free world: the spirit of the partnership in ending the Cold War was never to be restored. Redemption narratives of common survival, reasonable sufficiency of weapons arsenals, and peace dividend remained a far cry for Russia as well as—frankly speaking—the United States. Instead, as Medvedev's remarks at the New START Treaty signing ceremony indicated, the new Russian president was motivated mainly by the prospect of a new pragmatic partnership between the two countries that could help Russia overcome the consequences of the 2008–2009 economic crisis and achieve the goals of "modernization" set by Medvedev (*Remarks by President Obama and President Medvedev*, 2010). Hence, there was no new cogent pro-arms control narrative during the short-lived "reset" in US-Russia relations. However, the "reset" documents, such as the London declaration, pointed to the significant staying power of the initial post-Cold War arms control momentum that came back as soon as major hurdles were removed (Adamishin, 2015).

Whatever remained of the post-Cold War shared survival and security narrative deteriorated rapidly after 2012. While the second Obama administration upon taking office in January 2013 tried to advance arms control negotiations beyond the New START, Moscow remained lukewarm, expressing utter dissatisfaction with the lack of progress in negotiations on a joint ballistic missile defense system. Russia conditioned further nuclear cuts on development of such system or suspension of the US plans to upgrade its national missile defense capabilities to the level of strategic missile interception.

But even those seemingly insurmountable "technical" contradictions between the sides were dwarfed as obstacles to arms control by the narrative of resurgent great power politics that started to get traction among policymakers globally in the first half of 2010s. The two key trends that the advocates of the new great power narrative liked to point out were China's new assertiveness under Chairman Xi Jinping and Russia's Ukraine gambit from 2014 (Mearsheimer, 2018; Cooley and Nexon, 2020; Sciutto, 2020). That narrative originated from the main discontents of *Pax Americana,* such as Russia, Turkey, Iran, and—to a growing extent as time went by—China which commonly refrained from voicing revisionist aspirations (Nau and Ollapally, 2012).

Despite vocal criticism for failure to capture the enduring factors of our US global preponderance (Nye, 2015), the narrative of great power politics had to be contended with by the second Obama administration and was enthusiastically embraced by the Trump administration (United States of America, 2017; Economist, 2018). As opposed to the narrated redemption imperative of shared survival, the great power contamination narrative, in its various reincarnations throughout history, has implicitly or explicitly included the notion of a constant and significant security risk that requires hedging. Hedging is a strategy that is aimed at preventing destructive scenarios the most dangerous among which is to find oneself defenseless against an existential—if not very likely—threat. According to a Russian nuclear strategy expert,

> [t]his might sound like a paradox, but both [nuclear] superpowers (the United States and Russia—*author*) are escalating the strategic nuclear risks by solving situational problems caused by the lack of political trust. One problem deals with the imaginary lack of low-intensity deterrence against Russia's aggressive behaviour, while the other continues to safeguard the risks of a no-less-imaginary NATO intrusion amid the continuing weakening of conventional forces.
>
> *Bogdanov, 2020*

Given the significant risks of exploitation, arms control is usually not considered a viable hedging strategy. When survival is at stake, the peace dividend loses its value as a policy goal, while the danger of being exploited by the negotiation counterpart remains significant and potentially destructive (Montgomery, 2006). No binding, conclusive, and consequential arms control deals have been implemented in situations of utter uncertainty (Troitskiy, 2020). Therefore, a credible and widely shared narrative of a "new era of great power politics" appears incompatible with breakthroughs in arms control, especially when the bar has been set high enough by recent achievements, such as the New START of 2010. The best that can be expected in such circumstances is an occasional idea for an ambitious yet hardly realistic multilateral arms control initiative—akin to the Trump administration's demand for involving China in US-Russian bilateral nuclear arms control. Otherwise, under multipolar great power politics—whether real or imaginary on the basis of a narrative—the sides are much more inclined to tout their capabilities, sovereignty, and resolve to prevail in disputes under any circumstances rather than to commit to self-constraints in military doctrines, such as no first use of nuclear weapons.

Overall, as an identity-based narrative, great power politics makes agreements—results of collective action in pursuit of a stronger security for all—very problematic. Indeed, such prerequisites for collective action as communities of shared ideas and values described by Trenin become anathema to the policymakers who come under the influence of such contamination narrative. In February 2020, the top US State Department official in charge of arms control in the Trump administration, Christopher Ford, likened arms control to "performative politics" and opined that

> [c]ommitment to an ideal of arms control is one of the indicia of membership in a progressive global community that demands performative acts of solidarity and is thus preoccupied by the boundary-maintenance chore of creating symbolic distance from those with incorrect attitudes—attitudes such as the idea that geopolitics has something to do with power and with competition.

Ford recognized the role of narratives in enabling arms control and disarmament and confessed that he "want[ed] to replace them with a discourse much more likely to be relevant to current conditions, more likely to improve real-world outcomes, and much less desperately maladaptive in the contemporary geopolitical environment of great power competition." According to him, great power politics have never left the stage, but was mistakenly placed on the backburner as a motive driving Western policymakers. Now that its comeback is widely accepted, the West needs to deal with some "notably bad habits" that for Christopher Ford certainly included "misguided and increasingly dangerous post-Cold War arms control mindset" (Ford, 2020). As a leading US arms control expert explained, "Trump's rejection of the Iran nuclear deal—which also matches [US Assistant Secretary Christopher] Ford's good agreements description—was completely based on identity politics rather than security interests" (Squassoni, 2020).

Moscow did not need much convincing to endorse the great power narrative, with its highly negative implications for nuclear arms control. "Nuclear weapons, to Russia, are the ultimate security guarantee," Dmitri Trenin explained. "Now the United States has affirmed their growing utility [...] In the Russian mind, [a nuclear-free world] is firmly associated with the failed visionary Mikhail Gorbachev, who back in 1986 produced a plan of eliminating nuclear weapons by 2000" (Trenin, 2019, p.15).

Conclusion: Recognizing the benefits of arms control

Narratives have never been sufficient factors of success in arms control negotiations. Those negotiations were often thwarted by many short-term trends or even random events. But available evidence suggests that narratives have been necessary conditions that set the stage for arms control breakthroughs. Sometimes they created incentives for risk reduction by emphasizing the havoc that could be brought upon the warring parties should they use particular weapons system in a mutual conflict. At other times, they contributed to slowing down or avoiding arms races by emphasizing the benefit of risk reduction for social progress and economic development. Narratives have also served as means of credible signaling about the readiness of a party to engage in substantive arms control efforts instead of looking for opportunities to exploit the counterpart's trust.

The defining feature of narratives—overstatement of particular trends, events, or factors—is instrumental in tilting policymakers toward agreements, the full consequences of which may be incalculable at the time of signing. A strong favorable narrative is capable of overriding a plethora of technical challenges or arguments against an agreement on arms reductions or confidence-building measures. A vivid example of such dynamic was provided by the common survival narrative reinforced—primarily from the perspective of the Soviet leadership—by the need to trim down military expenditures in the face of the crumbling Soviet economy in the second half of the 1980s. Russian President Medvedev's declared goal of "modernization" of the country was the pivot of another narrative driving Russia and the United States together for a brief period during Medvedev's presidential term.

In a similar vein, narratives can effectively block arms control by stressing—even without overstating—its downsides. They can demotivate policymakers by pointing to the lack of a successful experience. They can also explain how and why a particular promising technology may give an edge to its owner and should therefore not be constrained by an agreement. The bar for spoiling is usually lower than for enabling because, as a delicate form of collective action, arms control is vulnerable to a broad variety of party-breakers—from the assertion of the legacy of "unbreakable resolve" to prevail in conflicts to the allegedly irreversible track record of mutual distrust between the parties. The impact of narratives on risk reduction was summed up by the old Soviet-time song: "The day when the havoc of the old war is forgotten, a new war is born."

Indeed, the sobering stories of the old-day destructive conflict have been continuously fading away in both Western and Russian narratives. Led by the United States, the West increasingly discounted Russia in the 2000s as a weakening actor whose aspirations could be disregarded if disliked by the leaders of the global community. In its turn, toward the 2010s, Russia's policymaking began to pivot around the country's declared resolve to prevail in a major conflict—largely regardless of the cost—coupled with the lack of certainty about the boundaries of Russia's national interest. Those twin trends crowded out redemption narratives of conflict avoidance and left both the sides with virtually no narrated rationale for productive arms control efforts.

References

Adamishin, A. (2015, June 1) *Idealizm vysokoi proby* [High-Fineness Idealism], Russian International Affairs Council. https://russiancouncil.ru/analytics-and-comments/comments/idealizm-vysokoy-proby/.

Bogdanov, K. (2020, March 10) *Not-So-Nuclear War*, Russian International Affairs Council. https://russiancouncil.ru/en/analytics-and-comments/analytics/not-so-nuclear-war/.

Burns, W. (2019) *The Back Channel: A Memoir of American Diplomacy and the Case for Its Renewal*. New York, NY: Random House.

Clunan, A.L. (2014) 'Historical Aspirations and the Domestic Politics of Russia's Pursuit of International Status', *Communist and Post-Communist Studies*, vol.47, pp.281–290.

Cooley, A., and, Nexon, D. (2020) *Exit from Hegemony: The Unraveling of the American Global Order*. New York, NY: Oxford University Press.

Ford, C. (2020, February 11) *The Politics of Arms Control: Getting Beyond Post-Cold War Pathologies and Finding Security in a Competitive Environment*, Remarks at the International Institute for Strategic Studies, London. www.state.gov/the-psychopolitics-of-arms-control/.

Freedman, L., and, Michaels, J. (2019) *The Evolution of Nuclear Strategy*. London: Palgrave Macmillan.

Goodby, J. (1998) *Europe Undivided: The New Logic of Peace in U.S.-Russian Relations*. Washington, DC: United States Institute of Peace Press.

Grinevsky, O. (2004) *Perelom: ot Brezhneva k Gorbachevu* [The Turning Point: From Brezhnev to Gorbachev]. Moscow, Russia: OLMA Press.

Economist (2018, November 8) *Mind-Boggling: China Is Struggling to Explain Xi Jinping Thought*, The Economist. www.economist.com/china/2018/11/08/china-is-struggling-to-explain-xi-jinping-thought.

Istomin, I. (2017) 'Negotiations under Disagreement: Limitations and Achievements of Russian-Western Talks on NATO Enlargement', In, F.O. Hampson and M. Troitskiy (Eds.), *Tug of War: Negotiating Security in Eurasia* (pp.35–52). Toronto, ON: CIGI Press.

Joint Statement by President Barack Obama and President Dmitry A. Medvedev of Russia, (2009, April 1), Authenticated U.S. Government Information. www.govinfo.gov/content/pkg/PPP-2009-book1/pdf/PPP-2009-book1-doc-pg394.pdf.

Joint Statement on Reduction of Nuclear Weapons Arsenals: Declining Utility, Continuing Risks, (1996, December 4), *The Acronym Institute for Disarmament Diplomacy*, no.10. www.acronym.org.uk/old/archive/10pro0.htm.

Kuehn, U. (2020a) *The Rise and Fall of Cooperative Arms Control in Europe*. Baden-Baden: Nomos Verlag. doi: 10.5771/9783748903239.

Kuehn, U (2020b, March 5) *Why Arms Control Is (Almost) Dead*, Carnegie Europe. https://carnegieeurope.eu/strategiceurope/81209.

McFaul, M. (2014) *From Cold to Hot Peace. An American Ambassador in Putin's Russia*. New York, NY: Houghton Mifflin Harcourt.

Mearsheimer, J.J. (2018) *The Great Delusion: Liberal Dreams and International Realities*. New Haven, CT: Yale University Press.

Montgomery, E.B. (2006) 'Breaking out of the Security Dilemma: Realism, Reassurance and the Problem of Uncertainty', *International Security*, vol. 31, no.2, pp.151–185. doi: 10.11 62/isec.2006.31.2.151.

Nau, H., and, Ollapally, D. (Eds). (2012) *Worldviews of Aspiring Powers: Domestic Foreign Policy Debates in China, India, Iran, Japan and Russia*. Oxford: Oxford University Press.

Nye, J. (2015) *Is the American Century Over?* Cambridge: Polity Press.

President Barack Obama Remarks in Prague, (2009, April 5), White House. https://obamawhitehouse.archives.gov/the-press-office/remarks-president-barack-obama-prague-delivered.

Remarks by President Obama and President Medvedev of Russia at New START Treaty Signing Ceremony and Press Conference, (2010, April 8), White House. https://obamawhitehouse.archives.gov/the-press-office/remarks-president-obama-and-president-medvedev-russia-new-start-treaty-signing-cere.

Remler, P. (2019, March 1) *Russia and Cooperative Security in Europe: Times Change, Tactics Remain*, Carnegie Endowment for International Peace. https://carnegieendowment.org/2019/08/01/russia-and-cooperative-security-in-europe-times-change-tactics-remain-pub-79611.

Rosato, S. (2014) 'The Inscrutable Intentions of Great Powers,' *International Security*, vol.39, no.3, pp.48–69. doi: 10.1162/ISEC_a_0 0190.

Sciutto, J. (2020) *The Shadow War: Inside Russia's and China's Secret Operations to Defeat America*. New York, NY: HarperCollins Publishers.

Squassoni, S. (2020, March 2) *Trump Appointee Wants 'Arms Control for Adults, Experts Couldn't Agree More'*, Bulletin of the Atomic Scientists. https://thebulletin.org/2020/03/a-top-us-officials-straw-man-critique-of-arms-control-experts-explained/

Statement on Nuclear Weapons by International Generals and Admirals (statement by 61 retired Generals and Admirals), (1996, December 5). *The Acronym Institute for Disarmament Diplomacy*, no.10. www.acronym.org.uk/old/archive/10pro0.htm.

Trenin, D. (2013) *Mir bezuslovnyi: Evro-Atlantika XXI veka kak soobschestvo bezopasnosti* [Unconditional Peace: The 21st Century Euro-Atlantic as a Security Community]. Moscow, Russia: ROSSPEN.

Trenin, D. (2019) 'Russian Views of US Nuclear Modernization', *Bulletin of the Atomic Scientists*, vol.75, no.1, pp.14–18. doi: 10.1080/00963402.2019.1555991.

Troitskiy, M. (2020) 'Why US-Russian Arms Control Can Succeed Even in a Climate of Confrontation', *Bulletin of the Atomic Scientists*, vol.76, no.2, pp.91–96. doi: 10.1080/00963402.2020.1728978.

United States of America. (2002, September 17) *National Security Strategy*, White House.

United States of America. (2017, December) *National Security Strategy*, White House.

PART IV

Conclusion

17

NARRATIVES AND NEGOTIATIONS

Lessons for theory and practice

Fen Osler Hampson and Amrita Narlikar

Introduction

We embarked on this book project to explore the "stories" that actors develop to advance their respective values and interests during negotiations, sometimes in ways that might not be utility maximizing in a conventional sense. Through comparative case studies that cover a range of issue areas and regions, this volume demonstrates that political narratives matter not only for the formation of intersubjective identities and social networks (as has been argued by international relations scholars), but also for the processes and outcome of complex international negotiations. Using certain narratives, key actors are able to successfully mobilize vast social, economic, and political constituencies either in support of, or against, a negotiated agreement. Our contributors offer us examples of such successes in international negotiations, and also point to deadlocks or negotiation failures resulting from the emergence of competing narratives that are better able to garner public and political support. The case studies further explore reasons as to why some narratives are more successful than others in gaining acceptance. In this concluding chapter, we bring together the main lessons of this collection for the theory and practice of international negotiation.

Narratives and theories of negotiation

Narratives, as this book illustrates, are an important – and often overlooked – variable that affects negotiation outcomes. Factoring narratives into standard theories of negotiation enhances the explanatory power of the latter.[1] In this section, we highlight some useful refinements that this volume offers to key concepts, and suggestions for sharpening the existing tools that negotiation analysts normally work with.

DOI: 10.4324/9781003203209-21

Narratives and pre-negotiation

Negotiation analysis tells us that before the bargaining actually begins, the pre-negotiation phase is critical for two purposes: "defining the problem and developing a commitment to negotiation" (Zartman, 1989; Stein, 1989). Both purposes can be difficult to fulfil, especially when there are high levels of distrust among the parties, conflict is deeply entrenched, and domestic audience costs are high.

Narratives can play a crucial role in this key phase. But as we emphasize here, not all narratives are the same. There are different kinds of narratives and whereas some narratives have saliency because they "speak" to the existential needs, aspirations, or fears of different groups, others do not because they lack existential import. Accordingly, deep narratives of redemption are often necessary to convince domestic constituencies of the value of cooperation and engagement. Sophie Haspeslagh and I. William Zartman illustrate this in the context of the peace process in Colombia. President Uribe, they argue, had framed the conflict as a war on terrorists; this narrative rendered negotiation impossible. This changed under President Santos through a new narrative that recognized the armed conflict and also recognized the "other." The new narrative, moreover, was one of redemption, which FARC shared: the end of bloodshed, building a fairer society, and developing a vision of a peaceful, prosperous, and "of course, happier" Colombia.

However, even though some messages are laden with hope, they will also not suffice if they are seen as being too shallow by electorates and fail to address their fundamental needs and concerns. This theme recurs in several of the chapters. Valérie Rosoux's analysis illustrates this powerfully with reference to post-conflict societies:

> if master narratives differ too much from the experience lived and/or transmitted by particular groups, they effectively exclude them. This is not only a moral issue, but also a political and very pragmatic one. Without the support of the population, modifications made to official memory are sterile and in vain.

Haspeslagh and Zartman similarly explain the rejection of the referendum in Colombia in 2016 "as a failure of the narrative shift to having an impact beyond the conflict parties themselves." In other words, although the narrative shift helped in the pre-negotiation and early phase of the negotiations, its failure to resonate with the public at large undermined its sustainability.

This volume shows that to bring opposing parties to the negotiating table in the first instance, and then to keep them talking thus requires a transformation in narratives. This can be achieved by framing the future in terms of redemption and agency for both sides; to resonate with people and to sustain their support, deep narratives that tap into shared identities are also usually necessary. In the aftermath of violent conflict though, the use of deep narratives that draw on collective memories may turn out to be a double-edged sword. For such situations, Rosoux's chapter offers an important caveat, and also a potential solution:

> In the aftermath of mass atrocities, no single narrative, however unifying it might seem to be, can address the identity needs of the parties in an uncontested way. Some consensus may be reached on "forensic facts" established by historians and/or judges. This step is decisive for preventing denial and revisionism. It also allows the transition from contradictory to divergent narratives, which is already remarkable. Expecting more than that after mass crimes is unrealistic and even undesirable.

Narratives and BATNAs

The best alternative to a negotiated agreement (BATNA) is a key concept in negotiation analysis (Fisher and Ury, 1981). It is an important measure of bargaining power; the willingness to walk away from a negotiation (and accept a no-deal outcome) depends on the alternatives available. Our study adds two important theoretical refinements to this concept.

First, narratives can alter perceptions of one's own BATNA and also that of the other parties, "irrespective of objective structural conditions" (Swedlund, this volume). Mikhail Troitskiy illustrates this in his chapter on arms control negotiations. Contamination narratives about costly arms races worsen BATNA perceptions and encourage parties to move toward agreement; in contrast, narratives about the other adversary's decline and growing military weakness may lead to a shift in BATNA perceptions and encourage a preference to wait until the strategic balance has shifted in one's favor.

Second, deep narratives, with messages of redemption and agency in getting parties to the negotiating table, may also sometimes have the opposite effect: They lead to overconfidence in one's own BATNA, which can hamper breakthroughs, exacerbate deadlocks, and indeed deter parties from entering into a negotiation all. Akhil Deo and Samir Saran illustrate this clearly in their chapter on how deeply held narratives of redemption in the US and India are preventing both sides from acting even though their interests are closely aligned. Dan Ciuriak et al. came up with similar findings in their chapter on the technology nexus between Artificial Intelligence and Big Data, and the differences in outlook between key players in the digital space. They write: "In a sense, narratives lead to what in game theory is called a self-confirming equilibrium with beliefs: the narratives themselves help to form expectations that the negotiations would necessarily fall apart due to the 'unbridgeable gap' of the initial positions." Obverse narratives can therefore serve as a major barrier to negotiation by eliminating any prospect that the parties will entertain the pre-negotiation possibility of committing themselves to a negotiation process that would secure a cooperative outcome.

Narratives and networks

Narratives play an important role in the building, preservation, and mobilization of coalitions, networks, and social movements. These groups, which coalesce around a common narrative that shapes their identity, are, in turn, essential to the dissemination of narratives. The success with which some actors are able to mobilize coalitions and social movements to promote a particular narrative (over rival or competing narratives) also has a significant effect on negotiation outcomes. Indeed, as mentioned above, to be effective narratives must resonate with relevant constituencies and have widespread appeal; effective narrative-building is not just a technocratic exercise but a political one (also see: Narlikar, 2020).

Fen Osler Hampson and Paul Twomey show in their chapter on internet governance that the successful campaign by western countries for an open and multistakeholder internet (against the model advocated by authoritarian regimes) in WSIS negotiations on internet governance owed a great deal to narratives promulgated by civil society actors and the epistemic community of internet technologists. China and Russia, in contrast, lacked the "broad-based reach of technologists and civil society activists to support their own narrative" to win over key undecided states in the developing world to their camp. Rodger Payne investigates the similarities in the narratives that the US advanced in the two Iraq wars to negotiate the formation of supportive international coalitions in the war effort. He suggests that one explanation for the variation in US success in the two military campaigns lay in the saliency of the two political narratives that accompanied US coalition-building efforts: a successful narrative around preserving state sovereignty and a "rule-based" international order that was central to the narrative in the first Gulf War, was missing in the second, which was centered on toppling Saddam Hussein's regime and dubious intelligence reports about Iraq's weapons of mass destruction (WMD) capabilities.

Narratives and resolving formulae

Street Talk (offering inducements in a negotiation) and Happy Talk (negotiations which focus on how to build a better future for the parties and their constituents) can form vital components of resolving formulae (Hampson and Zartman, 2012). Several chapters, such as Meredith Lilly's discussion of successive negotiations in North America on free trade, confirm that successful narratives are often of redemption and agency (in keeping with Happy Talk). Their messages of hope and a better future work in tandem with deep narratives that appeal to multiple stakeholders, and quickly move outside the technocratic bubble in which they have originated (in keeping with Street Talk; on the problems with technocratic bubbles, and the importance of using coalitions, networks, and transnational social movements; also see: Narlikar, 2020).

That said, contamination narratives may not always be doomed to failure. Brendan Vickers, in his chapter on Brexit narratives, reminds us that Harold

Wilson successfully persuaded the British electorate to remain in the European Economic Community in 1975 via a contamination narrative that resembled the "Project Fear" narrative of the Remain campaign in the more recent Brexit negotiations between the UK and Europe. A crucial difference, however, lies in the context of the two negotiations. Vickers writes:

> Wilson's warnings about the dangers if Britain left the common market were not abstract forecasts but resonated with an entire generation's collective memory and lived experience of economic crisis, food rationing, and war. The EEC referendum was held just thirty years after the end of the Second World War (1939–1945). In the case of the Brexit referendum, there was no such comparable experience.

By tapping into tradition, myth, and folklore, and combining it with an upbeat narrative of "Take Back Control" of Britain's future (and "Get Brexit Done"), the Leave campaign, in effect, used Street Talk and Happy Talk to win the referendum.

Context also matters. Oliver Stuenkel's chapter shows how in the context of 5G negotiations, neither the contamination narrative of the US nor the redemption narrative of China have been successful in winning over Brazil's support because they are too shallow and fail to tap into Brazil's own sovereignty narrative about national identity; accordingly, Brazil has chosen a "wait-and-see" approach thus far. In such cases, a mix of contamination, redemption, and agency may be needed; as illustrated in Thomas Bagger's chapter, it shows Germany's successful twin narratives of "never again" and "never alone" in the aftermath of the World War II contained elements of both redemption and contamination types.

The temptation to recycle successful narratives, that is, narratives that have formed a key part of a resolving formula, is high, sometimes with good reason (if it ain't broke, why fix it?). But overuse and misapplication of winning narratives can be counter-productive, damaging the credibility of the original narrative and making breakthroughs harder to achieve (see Bagger, this volume; also see: Narlikar, 2020). A shared meta-narrative can serve as a unifying – even if differently interpreted – factor to bring together divergent positions. But it can also be a false friend; when micro-narratives collide, the macro-narrative "can wilt in the heat of the moment and cede full place to the micro-narrative" (Zartman, this volume; also see: Fürtig's chapter in this volume, which reveals contradictions within national narratives in the JCPOA negotiations). If narratives are to help develop resolving formulae, they must appeal not just to the shared experiences of the key protagonists, but also their different constituencies.

The central contribution of this book has been to focus on narratives either as an explanatory variable, or as an intervening variable that filters other higher-order causal factors. But narratives are themselves shaped by negotiation. This reflexivity can make narratives a very pliable and responsive policy tool, but also one that can be easily appropriated and misappropriated (chapters by Strasheim, and Stuenkel in this volume; also see: Narlikar, 2020). This reflexivity complicates the process of studying narratives. Bringing an explicit temporal dimension to the research design, clear specification of the causal hypotheses, and consideration of alternative/additional explanations can help mitigate against the problem of endogeneity. We recognize that the qualitative research design of this project cannot eliminate this problem and believe that the limitations are outweighed by the richness and depth of the case studies, and the insights they generate from a comparative perspective. This book has utilized a cross-section of case studies – covering a wide range of issue areas and regions – to show how a better understanding of how narratives work can enrich academic analysis of negotiations. Quantitative large-N studies would be an important complement to this research.

Narratives in the practice of negotiations

As the previous pages have shown, narratives can critically influence the decision by parties to pre-negotiate (or not). They also shape how parties perceive and use their BATNAs, influence the win-set in two-level games to thereby allow for the creation of a resolving formula, and help build and sustain the coalitions, social movements, and networks that are necessary to developing and sustaining negotiated solutions. But narratives are interesting not only for their theoretical value. Rather, their incorporation into the *practice* of negotiation can have major consequences for the lives and livelihood for those affected by the outcome of negotiations. This has been dramatically illustrated amid the politics of the COVID-19 pandemic and global summitry. In the run-up to the June 2021 G7 Summit, which was hosted by the UK in Cornwall, Western countries negotiated new commitments to try and prevent future pandemics and provide vaccines to developing countries as well as a new infrastructure plan to compete with China's Belt and Road Initiative. The Carbis Bay Declaration on health committed G7 countries to use "all their resources to prevent a global pandemic from happening again" and included concrete measures to reduce the time taken to develop and license new vaccines, strengthen global surveillance networks and genomic sequencing capacities, and "support for reforming and strengthening the World Health Organization" (G7 UK, 2021). G7 countries also pledged that together they would make 1 billion doses of vaccine available to the world's poorer countries. The initiative was a clearly directed change from the former President Donald Trump's "America First" narrative and go-it-alone approach to the global pandemic. The new Biden administration and its G7 partners clearly sought to use the meeting and the announcement to advance a new narrative that would see the world's leading democracies work more closely together to combat the pandemic and strengthen the global health care infrastructure to deal with future global health crises (Specia and Shear, 2021).

At the same time, the meeting's focus on pledging new monies to help poorer countries build better infrastructure to counter with what some refer to as "China's debt diplomacy" though its Belt and Road initiative was also an attempt to promote a new "Build Back Better World" narrative that, in the words of the G7 communique, is "values-driven, high standard and transparent" (White House, 2021b). The norms and principles underlying this new narrative of cooperation among the world democracies were also spelled out in *The New Atlantic Charter*, which was signed by President Biden and British Prime Minister Boris Johnson, where the two leaders of the world's two oldest democracies reaffirmed "their commitment to work together to realize our vision for a more peaceful and prosperous future...and [work] closely with all partners who share our democratic values and to [counter] the efforts of those who seek to undermine our alliances and institutions" (White House, 2021a).

Importantly, however, Biden's pro-multilateralism foreign policy narrative has worked hand-in-hand with a domestic narrative that has prioritized the concerns of the American electorate. For instance, when asked about exporting much-needed vaccine doses to its Northern neighbor and ally, Canada, the White House spokesperson, Jen Psaki, is reported to have replied that the US could discuss sharing supply after the 300 million-plus eligible Americans had been vaccinated (Tasker, 2021; also see: Bloomberg, 2021 on export restrictions on vaccine supplies). Secretary of State, Antony Blinken's speech, "A Foreign Policy for the American People" (Blinken, 2021) encapsulates the new administration's narrative that seems to be building an innovative mix of national and global appeal. While much depends on how the narrative will be further developed and implemented, its promise lies in its qualities of depth (at the national level), cultivation of a credible BATNA (via an alliance for democracy), and redemption and agency that work for both national and global levels (and thereby harness two-level games effectively).

Narratives are a powerful force of political agency, and thereby also of bargaining and negotiation. Their importance is likely to only increase amid the chatter of social media and digital networks. Given their real-world relevance, we advance some guidelines below on how practitioners might build and harness narratives to negotiate more effectively.

1. Narratives themselves are a product of negotiation. Working with epistemic communities and ensuring that narratives are substantiated by "facts" is important for narratives to have credibility, legitimacy and traction, but engaging with diverse stakeholders is just as important. Even a perfect narrative, built in a hermetically sealed technocratic bubble, is unlikely to be effective unless it resonates with the core identities of its intended constituents.
2. "Master" narratives or "meta-narratives" must be connected with the real-life experiences of individuals and their daily concerns. This is especially important when dealing with one's own domestic constituencies, but can

also be useful to keep in mind with negotiation partners to harness two-level games to achieve win-win sets. Using deep narratives that appeal to the collective experiences of the populace is essential to crafting an effective negotiating strategy and garnering public support for negotiated agreements.
3. Coalitions, networks, and transnational social movements are conveyors of influence in negotiations.
4. Deep narratives of redemption and agency are usually more likely to deliver successful outcomes in negotiation, rather than contamination narratives that focus on threats, stir fears, and which generally tend to undermine the prospects for cooperation.
5. But narratives of contamination are not automatically doomed to failure; context matters and needs to be taken into account when choosing redemption, contamination, or agency – or a mix of two or all of these narrative types – simultaneously or in different phases of the negotiation.
6. Narratives shape negotiations, but have to be updated to reflect changing conditions and circumstances; they are "living" identities that require nurturing and care: to be effective, they need to be frequently updated, depending on the outcomes they produce; as winning narratives tend to be emulated and appropriated by others (including competitors) and can lose their effectiveness with increasing overuse and misuse, such updates are all the more essential.

Narratives are essential elements of negotiations. They can be manipulated to undermine negotiations and thwart the prospects for international cooperation. But new narratives that are forward-looking and point to a better future can also empower leaders, galvanize their constituents, amplify supportive social networks and coalitions, and help secure successful negotiated outcomes.

Note

1 Getting the narrative "right" however is only a necessary, not sufficient condition for reaching agreement (see chapters by Lilly, Haspeslagh and Zartman, Rosoux, and, Troitskiy). Other key ingredients that authors touch upon include gender, "ripeness," and indeed material prerequisites, such as adequate reparations.

References

Blinken, A.J. (2021, March 23) *A Foreign Policy for the American People*, U.S. Department of State. www.state.gov/a-foreign-policy-for-the-american-people/.

Bloomberg. (2021, March 24) *Biden Uses Trump's 'America First' Vaccine Plan to Corner Market.* www.bloomberg.com/news/articles/2021-03-24/biden-uses-trump-s-america-first-vaccine-plan-to-corner-market.

Fisher, R., and, Ury, W. (1981) *Getting to Yes: Negotiating Agreement Without Giving In.* New York, NY: Penguin Books.

G7 UK. (2021, June 11) *G7 Leaders to Agree Landmark Global Health Declaration,* G7 UK 2021. www.g7uk.org/g7-leaders-to-agree-landmark-global-health-declaration/.
Hampson, F.O., and, Zartman, I.W. (2012) *The Global Power of Talk: Negotiating America's Interests.* Boulder, CO: Paradigm.
Narlikar, A. (2020) *Poverty Narratives and Power Paradoxes in International Trade Negotiations and Beyond.* New York, NY: Cambridge University Press.
Specia, M., and, Shear, M.D. (2021, June 15) *Leaders Gathered for the G7 Outline a Plan to Offset the toll of Future Pandemics,* The New York Times.
Stein, J.G. (Ed.). (1989) *Getting to the Table: The Processes of International Prenegotiation.* Baltimore, MD: The Johns Hopkins University Press.
Tasker, J.P. (2021, March 1) *Biden Spokesperson Rules Out Helping Canada, Mexico with Vaccine Supply Before All Americans Are Inoculated,* CBC. www.cbc.ca/news/politics/biden-vaccine-help-canada-mexico-1.5932176.
White House. (2021a, June 10) *The New Atlantic Charter,* The White House. www.whitehouse.gov/briefing-room/statements-releases/2021/06/10/the-new-atlantic-charter/.
White House. (2021b, June 11) *Build Back Better World (B3W) Partnership,* The White House. www.whitehouse.gov/briefing-room/statements-releases/2021/06/12/fact-sheet-president-biden-and-g7-leaders-launch-build-back-better-world-b3w-partnership/.
Zartman, I.W. (1989) 'Prenegotiation: Phases and Functions', In J.G. Stein (Ed), *Getting to the Table: The Processes of International Prenegotiation* (pp.1–17). Baltimore, MD: The Johns Hopkins University Press.

INDEX